Praise for *Shadowlands*

"Anthony McCann's *Shadowlands* is an extraordinary book. The story it tells is compulsively fascinating, and an excellent microcosm by which we might better understand our difficult national history and distressing political moment. But *Shadowlands* is much more than a compelling, timely tale. By combining journalism, historical research, and profound intellectual reflection, McCann has created an epic exploration of freedom, care, sovereignty, violence, race, nationalism, punishment, social media, nature, and justice. His magnificent prose, ever-questing intellect, wry humor, and uncommon empathy for human and nonhuman forms of life alike make *Shadowlands* a truly rare and stunning achievement." —Maggie Nelson, author of National Book Critics Circle Award winner *The Argonauts*

"With empathy, poetry, and a keen, clear-eyed sense of the weirdness of it all, Anthony McCann goes far beyond the cartoon version of the Malheur occupation that we all watched on the news, peeling through the layers of the past to reveal the many battling ghosts and fictions that together create the thing we call America. If you want to understand the tortured longings that have brought us to this perilous juncture, I can't think of a better primer. *Shadowlands* is an extraordinary achievement, a powerful reckoning with history and all the Big American Words—*freedom, democracy, sovereignty*— that echo through the silence and violence of the American West." —Ben Ehrenreich, author of *The Way to the Spring*

"A vivid and exciting account of a telling historic event." —Arlie Hochschild, author of National Book Award finalist *Strangers in Their Own Land*

"As cable-news programmers and even congressmen find their profit in driving ordinary Americans and right-wing paramilitaries ever closer to civil war, Anthony McCann's provocative, empathetic, and patriotic *Shadowlands* is our alarm bell in the night." —Woody Holton, author of National Book Award finalist *Unruly Americans and the Origins of the Constitution*

"*Shadowlands* is an extraordinarily thoughtful exploration of division in this country that treats the Malheur standoff for what it was: a reckoning over what kind of country we should, or shouldn't, be living in. It's a testament to Anthony McCann, and to his reporting, that you might not always find yourself standing where you thought you would." —Nick Reding, author of *Methland: The Death and Life of a Small American Town*

"What makes *Shadowlands* exceptional is not only the way it provides a critically informed look at the Oregon standoff and its aftermath, but how it offers a full articulation of the overlapping notions that have gone into generating a variety of western identities. McCann gives these notions their just due, considers them with compassion and care, but doesn't hesitate to reveal all the unexamined contradictions spidering through them. Shadowlands offers a clear exegesis of the accumulated history that has gone into forming the American West and, by extension, America itself. And by doing so, it begins to pry open a whole lot of words too often left unquestioned (or questioned only sloppily) and on which America is based: freedom, property, land, law." —Brian Evenson, author of *A Collapse of Horses* and *The Wavering Knife*

"Anthony McCann knows the western past has not vanished; it has just gotten weirder. *Shadowlands* takes us down a Western rabbit hole where a delusional settler story staged for the internet on sacred Native ground illuminates the United States we now inhabit. This is a classic American story." —Richard White, Pulitzer Prize finalist for *Railroaded*

Shadowlands

SHADOWLANDS

Fear and Freedom
at the Oregon Standoff

A Western Tale of America
in Crisis

ANTHONY McCANN

BLOOMSBURY PUBLISHING
NEW YORK · LONDON · OXFORD · NEW DELHI · SYDNEY

BLOOMSBURY PUBLISHING
Bloomsbury Publishing Inc.
1385 Broadway, New York, NY 10018, USA

BLOOMSBURY, BLOOMSBURY PUBLISHING, and the Diana logo are trademarks of
Bloomsbury Publishing Plc

First published in the United States 2019
Copyright © Anthony McCann, 2019

Bloomsbury Publishing Plc does not have any control over, or responsibility for,
any third-party websites referred to or in this book. All internet addresses given in
this book were correct at the time of going to press. The author and publisher regret
any inconvenience caused if addresses have changed or sites have ceased to exist,
but can accept no responsibility for any such changes.

ISBN: HB: 978-1-63557-120-2; eBook: 978-1-63557-121-9

LIBRARY OF CONGRESS CATALOGING-IN-PUBLICATION DATA IS AVAILABLE

2 4 6 8 10 9 7 5 3 1

Typeset by Westchester Publishing Services
Printed and bound in the U.S.A. by Berryville Graphics Inc., Berryville, Virginia

To find out more about our authors and books visit www.bloomsbury.com
and sign up for our newsletters.

Bloomsbury books may be purchased for business or promotional use.
For information on bulk purchases please contact Macmillan Corporate and
Premium Sales Department at specialmarkets@macmillan.com.

to my mother, Karen McCann
for the world shapes, for the shapes of the earth
for teaching me to see

America never was; and it is only if it is utopia . . .

—OCTAVIO PAZ

Contents

Part III: Afterworlds

Prologue

The Boisterous Sea

THIS BOOK TELLS A STORY ABOUT American democracy in the midst of one of its many difficult historical moments. It's also a book about common Americans, out in the shadowlands of the republic, demanding, in their different ways—some twisted, some inspired—that the Beautiful Democratic Words of their nation come true on their terms. It's about unpowerful people insisting that they have power, and that the American public square be a true and meaningful "boisterous sea of liberty"—to borrow the words of one of the nation's more optimistic, and troubling, founders. In its pages you will encounter a wide cast of characters: western ranchers, right-wing militia members, armed religious mystics, environmentalists, Native American tribal leaders, defense lawyers, Black Lives Matter protesters, rural political leaders, and others. All these people will be seen contending, in their own ways, with what it means to be American today. Many of them will be seen actively demanding, or taking, a direct share of the elusive popular sovereignty that the idea of our republic has always seemed to promise—and withhold.

The book traces the dramatic 2016 occupation of Oregon's Malheur National Wildlife Refuge by a group of well-armed and divinely inspired right-wing protesters. It follows this drama, through moments farcical and tragic, from its beginnings in late 2015 in the high desert of remote southeastern Oregon to the dramatic trials of the occupiers in federal court in downtown Portland in late 2016 and early 2017. It ends with the aftermath of those trials. Along the way, the nation also undergoes the long trauma of the 2016 presidential election and its ongoing aftermath—an election that found many Americans asking themselves, and each other, what exactly their country was; what, and who, its great power was for; and where, if anywhere, the nation was headed. This book will not answer those questions, but it will tell the story of different ordinary Americans who have taken up these questions and in doing so found moments of possibility, autonomy, and even, in some cases, religious exhilaration in the American public arena.

This is not a simple, edifying tale about finding hope in American democracy; much of what happens here will be disturbing. This book tells a story of Americans reckoning with America and with themselves in a time of many great reckonings—it gets messy and ugly at moments. Some of the ideas and acts of the denizens of these pages, especially of some of the occupiers and their supporters, will seem contradictory, naive, half-baked, dangerous, or even hateful at times, sometimes because they patently are. Still, the book is the tale of a country where the possibility of a truly dynamic popular democracy has not wholly died a quiet death at the hands of corporate money and power, nor been subsumed in the arena-worship of a post-Nixonian, proto-fascist demagogue. It's a story where a vision of civic life remains at the core of human purpose and being. As such, it's a story of people who—in very different and at times conflicting idioms—continue to believe (perhaps delusionally) that the dream of America as a great incubator of liberty might still, in some sense, finally come true. While some of the people who appear in its pages might do otherwise, this book does not stake a claim for the United States as some kind of "indispensable" country or "last best hope," as our leaders regularly like to effuse. The book does, however, regularly, in fleeting glances, note moments when America, as a place and as an idea, still seems plausible, potentially renewable, and maybe even useful.

Desert Training

Before 2016, I had no desire to write a prose book about America. I didn't particularly believe in it. I had no interest in its providential vanity, its outsize faith in its singular mission. Back then, what I wanted was to write a book about the desert. But the desert changed all that.

It wasn't really the desert that did it. Not alone, anyway. Really, it began with the Marines, as the world I thought I was looking at changed right in front of my eyes. I was sitting on a big lump of basalt, on a rise in the open desert north of my new home. I'd just begun moving my life to the Mojave. I was doing so eagerly; I was finished with Los Angeles, with the daily folly, the constant roar of traffic, the helicopters of the police and the superrich thrumming overhead, while our alienated social life overheated on the platforms of the internet. Besides, I could hardly afford it there anymore anyway; fewer and fewer could.

That day in the Mojave, sitting on my rock, I was gazing at a mountain to the north, a big, striated slab of desert range, red and dark. Beyond it was more mountain, range after range, folded and craggly, turning bluer and bluer, under the wild blue sky. I knew that the mountain I was gazing at, Hidalgo, was on the desert training center of the U.S. Marines—I knew I couldn't just walk there even though there were no fences between me and it, no physical boundaries. I knew if I tried, I'd end up detained, but the mountain didn't know anything about that, and I liked that about mountains.

I liked that about the desert too. It's a portal to a different world, one characterized by a more intimate relationship with the remote, as Edward Abbey put it. You can often see fifty miles or more in all directions, sometimes while looking at landscapes not massively altered from the way they looked one hundred years ago, two hundred years ago, five hundred years ago. Thousands and thousands of years even. If you spend enough time out there, something in you changes—something to do with time. The imaginariness of human societies and institutions becomes palpable as they all vanish. It's a sweet and cool feeling, like a slow cloud shadow passing over land. It relieves you, peeling you, I think, momently, momentarily, of your soul. Maybe not—maybe souls, whatever they are, aren't so easily peeled. But relief is certainly what it is. When you are tired of specific human worlds, or of the American versions of them, as I was, it is a very nice feeling. It's the pleasure of being already gone. And I was really gone that day, out there, adrift in it. But then the world right in front of me began to explode.

I mean that it really was exploding. There were big puffs of white smoke, turning into great plumes. Flashes of bright light accompanied each new eruption. This was happening all along the upper rim of the alluvial fan that spread down from Hidalgo into the big desert basin where I sat. What I had long taken for a toothy ridgeline of pale rock had begun to boom and send up smoke. Because these weren't rocks—this, my screen told me, as I pulled it from my pocket, was another imaginary world.

An imaginary city: a fake one, made for invading and occupying. And that's what was happening right now. The Marines were on the move. The place was a training ground, built and rebuilt, my phone quickly informed me, out of shipping containers and other modular materials—all to resemble a small Middle Eastern city. The pictures of the place I pulled up all looked like full 3-D expressions of the streets and interiors of first-person shooter video games. Today the Marines were practicing capturing it, or securing it, or fighting door-to-door urban skirmishes in it—storming with live weaponry through an imaginary town in the middle of the desert.

That day there'd be no more wanderings in imagination back to the Pleistocene, or to some future epoch in the dreamtime of the earth. I was back in what geologists themselves were considering calling the Anthropocene— a new epoch, *ours*, the one in which humans had begun to substantively alter the composition of the earth, both the atmosphere and the interior of the living crust of the planet. I was no longer lost in the desert, I was back in the USA.

*   *   *

I didn't really want to be there, but I was. That's what the desert and the Marines reminded me that day. I was not a desert nomad—or a lizard, or a rock—and I wasn't a Marine. I was a civilian, a resident of the troubled place between the two, between the earth and the absolute sovereign power of the state that its military represents. But where was that place? I supposed it was everywhere in a sense, all around me, but it was also hard to find, and not just because I was out in the big empty of the Mojave. Our public life had grown so strange in recent years; arguably, people were more engaged than ever, thanks to social media. But was that our new public square? Or was that something else? Weren't all those sites privately owned platforms designed explicitly to monetize social existence in order to turn it into private wealth? Didn't they do so by amping up social feelings, ugly ones as much as (or more than) constructive ones? Wasn't it all done just to keep people glued to their screens? That hadn't felt entirely like democracy or public life to me. Platform World had merged troublingly with everyday life in recent years, and that had a lot to do with why I was out here in the desert sitting on this rock in the first place. Now the Marines and the desert gave me my discomfiting reminder. I lived in a nation, a society, and an economy sustained, in different ways, by both sovereign power and the diminishing bounty of the planet. But what was that society, what was that economy, what was that nation really for? Who was it for? And where was the public life where such questions could become real conversations? These were the questions that came for me that day on my rock. I didn't want them, I'd been avoiding them, but there they were. In different ways, they'd be coming for all of us in 2016.

A Voice in the Desert

It was on another day, back in 2014, sitting on that same exact rock, that I got my first inkling of the story that this book tells. I wasn't time-traveling in desert space, I was scrolling through the news on my phone. There it was, on my screen, beamed to me via satellite and the cell phone towers, which out here are disguised as Old West ghost-town kitsch: the fake windmills and water towers of abandoned ranches. The story that was being beamed to me was actually about a real desert rancher, still living the life these fake towers quoted. An old Mormon cowboy, a fanatic evidently, somewhere on the other side of this same desert was having a showdown with the federal government over the management of his public lands' grazing allotments. In the course of all this, he'd stopped recognizing the federal right to own public land at all. The feds had no sovereignty there, he said. He wasn't saying the land was his, exactly, but he was saying it wasn't theirs. It belonged, he said, to something called *We the People*. "I don't recognize the United States government as even existing," Cliven Bundy had told a reporter in a radio interview. Dozens of other reporters were now flocking to his ranch, to see what other such verbal curios they might collect. There would be plenty more.

Well, well, I thought. The desert had gotten to this weirdo. Sure, much of what he was warbling on about was just extreme Tea Party–ism on some level, but on another, these were the words of a person who'd lived his whole life in the desert, and it showed. He called himself an American Patriot, but he was one who had evidently seen himself clear through to the near absence of his nation. His doubt, however incoherent and rambling his expressions, had reached the philosophical, the ontological. In what senses does a nation have *being* anyway? It was a big question.

Somehow Bundy was finding support for all his notions in the Constitution, which he claimed had been created through the inspiration of God. It was confusing, since that was the document that founded the power whose very being he doubted. Still, he carried a copy in his pocket seemingly everywhere he went. His favored constitutionalist rhetoric also peppered the speech of the militant-looking dudes who'd assembled at his ranch. This impromptu Facebook army had materialized nearly instantly to support him in his resistance to the Bureau of Land Management's efforts to round up his cattle. A court order had declared Bundy's cows forfeited to the nation in lieu of his long-overdue federal grazing fees, which, of course, he hadn't paid, since this entity, to his mind, had no rightful authority or even existence.

All this was very entertaining, and for a moment, America was very interested. The liberal comedy news-spoof programs had an especially good time with Cliven. Here he was going on about the United States not existing while posing for news cameras up on a desert hill, on horseback, flying Old Glory. What the hell was he talking about? Wasn't that the flag *of* the federal government? On the other side of the spectrum, the right wing loved him— he was standing up for property rights, or that's how his grazing rights were understood. More importantly, he was standing up against the government, now headed by Barack Obama, our first African American president, whom the right vilified as a tyrant-in-waiting. It was clear, they said—just look at the abomination of the Affordable Care Act, with its evil insurance *mandate*. Commentators like Sean Hannity eagerly—if incoherently—linked Bundy's stand to the supposed tyranny of Obamacare. This meant Cliven was being interviewed nearly every day and soon that did him in. In his rambling discourses on freedom, his favorite subject, he eventually came to link what he saw as his struggle for liberty to the struggle for freedom of those Americans (oppressed, to Cliven's mind, by federal government assistance) that he still referred to collectively as "the Negro." It went downhill from there. Now everyone ran from Cliven, and he eventually disappeared from the news. I forgot about him too. But I remembered the man's last name when a year and a half later word reached me down in the Mojave that his son Ammon, along with a ragtag band of hastily gathered followers, had taken over a federal wildlife refuge in remote southeastern Oregon, at the farthest northern reaches of the Great Basin Desert. The group would eventually announce plans for holding the place until the federal government relinquished its ownership—and its sovereignty—over *all* the public land of the West. The date was January 2, 2016. One of the wilder, more unsettling political years in the recent history of the republic had begun.

"The Freest Place on Earth"

According to one recent reputable estimate, 20 percent of the marketable assets *of the world* are held in American real estate. The U.S. dollar remains the world currency. That currency is backed up by the huge debt of the United States and by a creature of that debt: the U.S. military, the most powerful military the planet has ever known. These things together tell us a story about the centrality of America to the global order and to the global economy, a centrality that became uncomfortably visible to Americans in the first decade of the new century, and complicated terribly the big question underlying the squabbles of our political moment: If America mattered so much, why did so many people, on the right and the left, feel that they mattered little or not at all?

The economic crisis of 2008 had added a new urgency to the question of American purpose and of the worth and meaning of individual American lives. As the legislative and executive branches huddled with the princes of the global financial sector to craft bailout plans, Americans on both the right and the left saw definitive proof that they did not seem to be the answer to any of the questions about what America was for, nor about who mattered in the national community and economy. It was impossible not to see that Americans increasingly existed as vehicles for financial products—made of bundled, securitized debt—that helped a tiny, superrich global financial elite surpass ever more boundaries in the growth of their incomprehensibly vast wealth and power. In the wake of the financial meltdown, this class quickly negotiated itself out of ruin and right back into oligarchic splendor, leaving the rest to pick up the pieces—or that's how it looked to many on both sides of the famous partisan divide. On the left, people bemoaned the loss of public goods and decent working-class jobs that had accompanied the redistribution of wealth upward in recent decades, a situation made worse by the crisis. On the right, members of the new Tea Party movement mobilized imagery of the American Revolution in support of the contention that taking tax money from struggling Americans and giving it to irresponsible bankers here and abroad was not what America was for.

The Tea Party, and the leftist anti–corporate power movement that followed it in 2011, Occupy Wall Street, brought fully into view another major change in American life. Social media platforms had transformed political life on every scale. Via Facebook and Twitter, political movements could accomplish logistical feats in weeks, days, and hours that had previously taken months, years, and decades. Thanks to the new platforms, atomized individuals, previously alienated from the political process, could find intense communities of civic purpose and meaning seemingly instantly. In 2015, the Black Lives Matter movement leapt from the internet into the streets and named what was at stake: that the nation and economy of America as it existed was also an economy of mattering. The maelstrom of controversy that followed Black Lives Matter's seemingly uncontroversial eponymous assertion only confirmed that mattering was at the heart of the matter. Now, at the beginning of 2016, Ammon Bundy and his friends, openly inspired by the strategies, if not the content, of all these earlier platform-based movements, had taken internet-organized popular politics one momentous step further. To many this extra step was a terribly frightening one. The version of *We the People* they had discovered in one another now stepped, *armed*, from Facebook to claim sovereignty over actual American land. The occupied refuge, they said, because of their presence, was now free. "The Freest Place on Earth," some of them said. And what, in American terms, could matter more than that?

Bad Luck National Wildlife Refuge

I got out my maps, and I looked it up. The Bundy Rebels were really out there, in a place in the far Oregon high desert, a place called Malheur. Wasn't that *misfortune* or *catastrophe* in French? Indeed it was. These maniacs had taken over a thing that might be called, if you translated it, the Bad Luck National Wildlife Refuge. And the story wouldn't really get less allegorical from there on out. Divine Providence, they said, was what had brought them there. "We the People," they said, a lot.

It all sounded thoroughly messianic: Ammon Bundy had urged his followers to join him and participate in the wonderful thing the Lord was about to accomplish. These rebels were promising to restore the Constitution as suited the demands of God himself and put America back on the right track as the world homeland of Liberty and the culmination of human history. Unsurprisingly that wasn't going to be so easy. The first step, they said, was to give *the Land* back to *the People*. To give *the Land* back to *the Rightful Owners*, some of them added. But who were "the rightful owners"? What about the Northern Paiute to whom this land had traditionally belonged? Sure enough, the local band of Paiute quickly entered into the fray, with some choice words about rightful ownership and some other ideas about who We the People might be.

That fall, I'd been studying the history of the Northern Paiute already on my own, reading specifically about the prophecies of the seer of the famous Ghost Dance religion, a nineteenth-century Nevada Paiute man named Wovoka, who'd had a very different vision of life and nation on the American continent. Like Ammon Bundy's, his visions had been messianic ones, but with the earth and with the dead, not the Constitution or the United States, in the role of restored redeemer. Along with Wovoka, I had been studying messianism generally, its theological and political elements. My reading had confirmed that what characterized messianic understandings of history and time more than anything was *return*: the return of the past, in a great time of reckoning, the Latter Days, as Ammon Bundy's faith understood them. America sure had been having a lot of recapitulation and reckoning recently: heated battles over Civil War statues, sports-team mascots, and whose lives really mattered in the national dispensation. It seemed all the unresolved past was returning for us—as intense political feeling—on our streets, in our institutions, and in the strange new No Place of the interweb.

As if to confirm my suspicions about the Last Days flavor of this American circus, in the second week of the occupation, the armed Bundyites on the Bad Luck National Wildlife Refuge received a mysterious visitor from out of the past. An unknown man arrived dressed in the full eighteenth-century garb of the first American messiah, George Washington. This specter had mingled among the occupiers, staying in character, blessing their endeavor, before vanishing back into the sagebrush desert or Facebook or wherever he'd emerged from. Images of his visit circulated quickly across the American screenworld, now transfixed by the spectacle of Malheur. No doubt about it: this was one whacked-out American story. At the same time, I'd grown certain that it was gathering up something serious about my time and my place, something I needed to understand. Eventually I, too, would have to make my way to Malheur.

PART I

Sovereign Feelings

CHAPTER ONE

My Dear Friends

"MY DEAR FRIENDS," AMMON BUNDY BEGAN—and begins again and again every time someone hits play, from 2016 all the way till the end of the internet. It was the first day of a year that was to scramble an already agitated nation. Along the invisible pathways of the collective mind, the virtual tabernacle of the World Wide Web, Ammon Bundy—cowboy prophet and Facebook hero of Liberty—was calling his people to the desert. Soon his friends in what they called the Patriot movement were all hitting play, activating his familiar face, and sitting back in the glow of their screens, as Ammon filled their hearts with urgent feeling.

It was time, Ammon was saying, for what he called "a hard stand." There had been some confusion about what he'd meant in previous communiqués, he'd received some pushback, and he'd sat down now on the eve of calamity in front of the camera to try to clear things up. He's at his desk in a cowboy hat—he wouldn't appear in public much again without one until his arrest, weeks later, on a mountain road, in the snow and pines of Oregon's Hard Luck National Forest. He's wearing a checkered western shirt and sporting what was for him a new, neatly trimmed growth of beard, further softening his visage. But even with a beard, Ammon Bundy couldn't help seeming what he was: a Latter-day Saint, clean-cut to the core. The strongest word I or anyone I know has yet heard him use is "creep." Or "hell." (Or, once, with evident discomfort *and* while making it clear he was quoting someone else, "horseshit.") Before being summoned to the desert of Oregon by his God, that fall he'd been enjoying making apple pies for his Idaho neighbors, using apples from his new orchard and delivering the pies himself. But the quiet idyll of that autumn was already long over. This was to be his last video address to his online community before leading, the very next day, an armed takeover of Oregon's Malheur National Wildlife Refuge. A MacBook Air laptop is open on his desk, its icon doing its quiet, intrepid work to place all our American lives and dreams—even those of right-wing holy insurrection—under its sign. Pale winter light comes through the blinds of the window behind him.

* .* *

In the video, which he titled "Dear Friends," Ammon explains how it was God who had guided him to Oregon two months earlier, through news of the plight of two Harney County ranchers, a father and son, Dwight and Steven Hammond. Mandatory federal sentencing guidelines were about to send the Hammonds back to prison for arson charges stemming from fires on public land—charges for which they'd already served time. Others, including his own father, had been urging him to look into the story. Like the Hammonds, Ammon's father, Cliven, was also a rancher; the Bundy family had achieved a national profile for the dramatic culmination of their twenty-odd-year struggle with federal authorities over their grazing rights on Mojave Desert lands in southern Nevada. That conflict had come to a head in April 2014, in a remarkable event: an armed standoff with federal agents that had resulted, shockingly, in a seeming victory for the Bundy clan. This standoff, and the family's ongoing struggle with the aftermath of their life-changing actions, had felt like enough to Ammon, who had recently moved far from southern Nevada, to a new home with his wife and six children in the sagebrush of southern Idaho, at the far northern end of Mormon country, on the outskirts of Boise. He himself was not even a rancher anymore, had not been for years. He ran a trucking-fleet maintenance business, still headquartered in Arizona.

As it turned out, even that move to Idaho would come to seem, to Ammon, a part of God's larger plan for himself, his friends, Harney County, and America. There had been something a little strange about the move, even at the time. He and his wife, Lisa, had felt a strong simultaneous urge to relocate. It had been a feeling that had descended as if from nowhere. They couldn't understand it entirely, but they'd followed it anyway, and headed out in the spring of 2015—traveling about the Intermountain West looking at houses. Nothing had been quite right, but then on the very last day of their trip, they'd come to this very last house, in a beautiful valley in Emmett, Idaho, and had known instantly that this was the place. It was one of many decisions Ammon would be guided to that year; that guidance, to Ammon's mind, had all been providential. How else to explain that he'd ended up moving to within three hours of remote Harney County, Oregon, where the whole Hammond story, which he had known nothing about at that time, had taken place? And now here he was, just a few months later, barely settled into this new home, asking his online community to join him in Oregon, to take a momentous stand, a stand so big, he said, that nothing less than the future of American freedom might be at stake.

*   *   *

After the move to Idaho, his next big revelation had come late one Monday evening in November 2015. On January 1, seated in front of his camera, he told the tale of that night to his online followers. Lying in bed in his family's new home, tired after a long day, he'd received a message on his phone, a link to yet another article about the Hammonds. In the past he'd shrugged off messages about the case. "I felt that our family was fighting hard enough," he explained. "We didn't need to go fight somebody else's battles." But this time something was different—an urge quickly took possession of him, a sudden impulse to learn all he could about this family. He searched the internet and read everything he could find about the case. Unable to sleep, he read on into the dawn. Come sunrise, his dark night of research was followed by a second urge, a desire he recognized as divinely inspired. This was an impulse to expression. "I felt this urge again, this desire to begin to write."

It wasn't easy at first—writing rarely is. "My emotion about the Hammonds," Ammon continued, "after I saw what was happening and found that what was happening to them was the *same* thing that happened to us. So, my emotions were clouding my thoughts." But then inspiration came to him, as it often seems to come, mysteriously and from somewhere *outside*. "I got on my knees, and I asked the Lord. And I said, 'Lord, if you want me to write something, then please help me clear my mind and show me what I should write.'"

And so, among the many other images to come, our story will start with this one: a bewildered and overtaken man—God-ridden, down on his knees, begging that unseen power to uncloud his mind so that he might write, so that he might simply sit down and begin.

God's Feelings

Ammon is devoutly religious, and his religion was also born in a mystical
writing performance. The Book of Mormon's original golden tablets, allegedly discovered in a hillside in the famous "Burned-Over District" of western
New York, were "translated" from an unknown ancient tongue, with divine
guidance and occult flair by the inspired founder and prophet of the Latter-day
Saints. Poorly educated but endlessly enthusiastic and possessed of a remarkable imagination, young Joseph Smith had dedicated much of his adolescence and young adulthood to a local craze: treasure hunting—which seems
to have consisted largely of robbing the mysterious Native American burial
mounds so common in the area. Unaware, in the beginning, of the liturgical potential of his first literary work, Smith had initially hoped that his
Book of Mormon would strike lucratively into the rich vein of the current
mania for theories linking the origins of Native Americans to the tales of the
Old Testament. His immediate hope seems to have been that the book's
success might save his parents' farm from foreclosure. The book wouldn't
arrive in time to save the Smith family farm, but it came to do so much
more, tapping into the current of powerful evangelical feelings then
convulsing the American frontier. In doing so, it would utterly transform
the life of its author and change the lives of millions, and, with them, the
history of the young American republic.

America loves to make fun of its Mormons. So many of the Mormon
clichés of Ammon's video were already well-worn tropes of American popular
religious experience even in the time of the prophet. But to laugh them off
then and now is to ignore how deftly these hackneyed but paradigmatic
elements of religious experience had found themselves reshuffled and newly
deployed in the hands of Smith, a singular font of rural American dynamism. Marginally schooled, Smith was a master communicator who intu-
ited something vast about the volatility and openness of his times, what they
asked for, and what was possible in them. He called that ever-evolving, often
cloudy, but occasionally crystal-clear understanding *God*. While Ammon's
inspirations and intimations may not have matched the grandeur of
Smith's—few did—his understanding of the whisperings and emotions
that visited him, and the way they condensed something about our time,
were very much in line with his prophet's. The two men's interpretations of
the divine guidance they felt differ really only when it comes to Ammon's
emphasis on feeling. Smith described the sensation of revelation as a "pure

intelligence" that would enter him: "It may give you sudden strokes of ideas, so that by noticing it, you may find it fulfilled the same day or soon; those things that were presented unto your mind by the spirit of God." To Ammon, on the other hand, this external intelligence seems to have presented itself first and—at times—primarily as intensity of emotion: urge, obsession, sympathy, outrage, and need. The more he had become emotionally involved in the tribulations of this one ranching family from the remote high desert of Oregon, the more Ammon had come to see himself as a conduit, a vehicle for the expression of God's feelings, God's feelings about America.

"I began to understand how the Lord felt about the Hammonds," he told his internet friends on the first day of 2016. "I began to understand how the Lord felt about Harney County and about this country. And I clearly understood that the Lord was not pleased with what was happening to the Hammonds, and that what was happening to them, if it was not corrected, would be a type and a shadow of what would happen to the rest of the people across this country."

* * *

Mostly it wasn't through writing that Ammon conveyed God's feelings directly into the lives of his followers. The intimacy of the Facebook or YouTube video is the true medium of the loose coterie of co-feeling that is the Bundy Revolution. In keeping with the formally anarchic tendencies of social media, the Patriot community has many members, many leaders, and ever-shifting priorities and tones, but for those attached to the Bundy cause, its single most important focal point and greatest source of inspirational feeling has remained Ammon himself: his life, his voice, his face.

Especially his face. There's an earnestness and openness of expression and care to Ammon's face that is uncommon among men of the American right wing. Throughout all his intimate Malheur video addresses, Ammon's bearded countenance pours out a live stream of concern into the camera and the hearts of his viewers. His expression remains virtually unchanging: *open*, always *open*. From beginning to end in his "Dear Friends" video, his eyes are wide; sometimes when he blinks, you can see the deliberate micromuscular effort to get his peepers fully opened again immediately. His blond eyebrows are sloped upward and inward, pointing at the crown of his head, hidden under his cowboy hat. This serves to push back his brow, thus enlarging his already fairly large and expressive mug, while his hands move in soft emphasis to the slow, clear cadences of his slight Nevada twang. All the while his head is held at a slight, sad puppy-dog tilt. There is no Limbaugh-like apoplexy, no snide Breitbart affect here. Ammon is a different figure of masculinity—a right-wing version of the sensitive man. His public face is a pure stream of real-time concern that he has consistently poured forth in every interview, every press conference, every appearance on the witness stand, delivering his payload of sincerity each and every time. Few, even among his worst enemies, have ever doubted that Ammon Bundy mostly means what he says, but the full power of Ammon's direct address comes from his ability to make it clear, again and again, just *how much* he *really* means it (and—maybe most importantly for the faithful—just how much, through him, his God *really cares*).

*   *   *

The urges that had gripped Ammon and set him to googling and writing were far from finished with him. Once God had cleared his mind and the writing had come, it led only to the development of stronger understandings and urges—further revelations of God's desires—and an irresistible impulse to travel, to know the land of Oregon firsthand, to go to that place where all would be revealed. "Once I got the letter written," he told his followers, "I felt this desire, this urge, to go to Burns and go to the Hammonds' Ranch."

Desires, urges, shadows, and types—our story begins with huge feelings, historical feelings. Types and shadows are key figures in Mormon doctrine, where history is revealed history, and human time is always unfolding toward its apotheosis; "the dispensation of the fulness of times," as Joseph Smith liked to put it, quoting from Ephesians.

Sometimes when I listen to Ammon telling the story of his first Oregon incursion, I see these doctrinal shadows and their precursors—the historical *types* that cast them—as windswept clouds, dragging their blots of shade alongside him over the golden buttes, as he drives on, sealed in his holy bubble of urge. There he goes, tiny now, snaking along the Malheur River, tracing the ill-fated route of more than one disastrous wagon train seeking a way around the Blue Mountains of the Oregon Trail. I follow him as he goes on, crossing over the Drinkwater Pass and the Stinkingwater Mountains, into the Harney Basin and the land called Malheur. Had Ammon noticed that this word *Malheur*, so prevalent in this immense swath of east Oregon, meant "misfortune" in French? Would this sign have mattered? He was receiving so many. Yet another one arrived as he approached the town of Burns. Just as he was headed into the outskirts, he received more divine direction—again, as an overwhelming feeling. Suddenly he knew he was *supposed to* change his route, not stop at the Hammonds' house in town; instead he was to drive south, over the great forehead of Wright's Point, the basalt butte that divides the town lands of Burns from the wide-open marshlands and sagebrush steppe at the heart of the Harney Basin. Cresting the point, he dropped now into that huge bowl of wind and distance to which he was about to bring so much human calamity.

CHAPTER TWO

Shadowlands

THE LANDSCAPE AMMON WAS MOVING through has an unsettling power. It arrives through your chest and it melts your heart, as another aficionado of the basin once described it to me. It sounds sentimental and overdramatic—because it is. There's a special, thrilling kind of loneliness to the place. To me it seems somehow inherent to the land. I know that land probably can't *be* lonely, not even for itself, but there's such a tone of vanishment to the Harney Basin, of things present and absent all at once. Folks say people come to Harney County to disappear—it's not hard to understand why.

I live in a crazy big landscape myself—but the Mojave Desert isn't lonely like this. The Mojave obviates loneliness—there the blue exhilaration of space shoots me past melancholy into geologic silence and soothing intimations of my absolute irrelevance. The Harney Basin, on the other hand, with its sagebrush and its golden meadows, looks like a place one could really dwell. But then if you get up on a rise and peer about, you'll note that for miles and miles there's hardly a human soul or lasting trace of one to be seen. It gives a rush of desolation that I experience as a kind of joy.

Every place has a tonality. In the land south of Burns, it's in the light and it's in the movement of clouds and their shadows. It's in how the whole land swoops so much, so that your eye is always tracing curves—over the sage, over the hills of golden grass and the buttes of red and black basalt. It's also in the wind, rising off the silence in whirls, lingering in the high stories of the sky, then descending, pouring through. If the wind isn't here yet, it's coming. There's a regular sway above the land's stillness, the transparent hand of the sky always passing, about to pass, having just passed by. This is a place that *whooshes* a hell of a lot and it makes everything seem like it's already gone.

*   *   *

Ammon Bundy was not here to disappear. Neither does he seem given to the landscape raptures of an aesthete or an environmentalist. Still, in a different register, the place was getting to him. As the son of a rancher, he saw something else entirely from what other eco-tourists and I see, something that made him giddy, and also a little envious. "It's beautiful cattle country!" he exclaims, speaking of the Harney Basin in an earlier video on the Hammond situation, made a few weeks after his first divinely guided visit to the family's ranch. On my screen, he falls into a quick burst of almost bitter-sounding laughter as he visits another landscape in his mind. "Much better . . ." he continues, shaking it off, regaining the powers of speech, "much easier than the ranch I came from."

It's an understandable reaction; Ammon Bundy is from the desert I now call home—the Mojave. The Blitzen Valley, at the southern end of the Harney Basin, where the Hammond Ranch sits, was nothing at all like the hard-scrabble land of his youth. Here, along the Donner und Blitzen River, are marshlands and thick meadows of high native grasses. Beyond these are the sage lands and the bunchgrass of the high desert steppe. What Ammon had seen as he headed south through the basin were different expressions of altitude and the presence and absence of water. Everywhere around him had been meander lines and borderlands—it's the same across much of Harney County. You go from the whispering pines into the wide-open silence of the sage—or from sun-crisped juniper into the fecund muck and fragrant plant life of riparian canyons and valleys. If you close your eyes and use your nose, you can feel the boundaries even more strongly.

But all the beauty—and the exuberant life of the wetter parts of the Harney Basin—have deceived many newcomers. There's a reason the place earned the name Malheur. If you turn away from the narrow wetlands on a hot summer or fall afternoon and dive into the brush, you can find out all about it. The pale, alkaline dust can quickly coat your boots and, soon enough, your arms and face. Mostly this is a very dry place. It gets ten inches or fewer of rain per year. The more time you spend trudging through it, the easier it gets to imagine just how hard the hard years have been.

They have been very hard. For all the lushness of the riparian strip that accompanies the Donner und Blitzen River as it travels north up the Blitzen Valley, this land is nearly true desert. Most folks in these parts call it *high desert*, and often that's just what it is. The Harney Basin is the northernmost basin of the endless-seeming array of basins and mountain ranges that make up the Great Basin Desert—the dry heart of the Intermountain West. The Great Basin encompasses much of Nevada, western Utah, southern Idaho, the remote reaches of eastern California, and the southeastern high desert of Oregon. No river running through it empties toward the sea: thus the name—it is literally a great basin, a big tub made up of many small ones. All the flows of water off its many peaks end up pooling and evaporating in alkaline flats, marshlands, and shallow, fluctuating bodies of water like the Harney Basin's Malheur Lake. Malheur takes in the flow, from the south, of the Donner und Blitzen River; from the north comes the Silvies River, draining the Blue Mountains of the Malheur National Forest. Its companion, Harney Lake, also takes in water off the Blues, through Silver Creek, farther west. These lakes can morph madly throughout a year, and even more so across a decade. Sometimes they seem to almost vanish, leaving behind a dusty bed of crinkly grasses and alien-looking reeds. Other times, they seem to swallow portions of the landscape entirely.

Kings of Cattle

The history of the Harney Basin after white conquest, like that of much of the region, has been a history of the collisions of American dreams with the rocky reality of the arid West. That history can be epic and it can be ugly. Before 2016, when Ammon added his name to the rolls, no single Anglo name had stood out in the tale of this remote land quite like the name Pete French.

French had also liked what he'd seen when he came over the gap from the arid Catlow Valley and gazed—in 1868—on the watered valley of the Blitzen for the first time. Wiry, with piercing eyes and an opulent mustache that in photos can seem far too large for his tiny head, French was possessed of uncommon energy, notable even in his era. In the southern lands of the basin, along the flanks of Steens Mountain, he'd establish—within a few years—one of the greatest cattle empires the West would ever know. His name is still heard often in that country—and much is coalesced in its two brightly stressed syllables. *Pete French* is contemporary shorthand for French's time, the era of the great cattle kings. It evokes both the overbearing, often corrupt, and sometimes brutal monopolistic drive of French and his fellow cow barons, while also conjuring feelings of nostalgia for the first epoch of cattle ranching in the county. While always relentless and sometimes openly ruthless in the pursuit of more territory for the massive P Ranch, French did as much as or more than anyone else for the development of a local style of ranching, which remains a source of great pride.

French's P Ranch devoted much attention to the production of hay for winter feed. Hay is the only crop that can be grown with any reliability in this cold climate, with its very late and very early frosts. All this made for a kind of ranching not practiced in the warmer parts of the West or down in Texas. To grow hay, French took to creating irrigated flood meadows—essentially turning the meadows into little shallow lakes every spring, when the dry land was drenched with the snowmelt that ran off the back and down the wild gorges of Steens, the long fault-block mountain that rises above the valley. Steens is more like a tilted horizon than a mountain. It grows upward at a regular angle for thirty miles through grassland and sage to the high alpine wonderland of its ridgeline—a great claw that catches copious snowfall each winter. The spring flow off the mountain, which French and his men redirected into their meadows, spurred hearty crops of native grasses, local varieties accustomed to growing in this dynamic, regularly flooding landscape. Ecologists now suspect that doing this, French and ranchers like him, without knowing it, may have partly restored elements of the landscape that had recently been lost because of other white incursions—those of the trappers, who had hunted beaver to near extinction across the Great Basin in the early nineteenth century. Now new beavers were in town, and with them, new floods—which was something appreciated by the huge populations of migrating birds that had been stopping for centuries in the Harney Basin to bulk up each spring in preparation for nesting and the rest of their migration north.

But if Harney County's story had been one solely of innovative ranchers living in creative synergy with the dynamic ecosystem of the region, none of us would have heard of the place—neither I nor you nor Ammon Bundy. After the cavalry and the encroachments of settlers had pushed local Paiute people to a reservation in the northern edges of the basin—and then taken that from them as well—battle lines began to appear among the newcomers. Now the contention was between the big-timers like French and small-time homesteaders. These latter interlopers were hoping against hope to make a life of farming in a dry, cold place where the last frost often came in July and the first as early as August. The landscape still bears the traces, like much of the West, of their broken dreams. Ruins of homesteader shacks in the sage now make lovely photographic images, drenched in western melancholy, but in their day they must have hosted their share of the shouts and tears of hunger and despair. Land-hungry cattle kings like French and his backer Hugh Glen, or Henry Miller and his partner Charles Lux, didn't make it any easier for their homesteading neighbors. These men could be brutal in squeezing out competition as they engorged their ranches. Miller and Lux, who controlled well over a million acres from Idaho and Oregon down to the San Joaquin Valley in California, had 200,000 acres at one point in the Harney Basin and the Harney Valley. Hugh Glen and Pete French's P Ranch grew to 140,000 acres at its zenith. (The P Ranch's starter herd of 1,200 cows would grow as large as 45,000—along with 3,000 horses and mules.) The drier the country, the more range the cattle need to fatten, and the cow barons had little tolerance for the foolhardy farming or small-scale cattle-rearing fantasies of pioneers. In the end, this would cost Pete French everything.

French's time was part of what historian Peter K. Simpson has called the heroic epoch in Harney County cattle rearing; that period, Simpson writes, can be seen to come to its close with French's violent death. By the 1890s the frontier era had famously mostly come to an end in America, and the small bonanza in the Harney Basin and the Blue Mountains to the north had reached a crisis point. Overgrazing and competition between roaming sheep-herders and small-time and enormous cattle operations was exploding into open violence as range after range was munched down to dirt and rock. Violence was just one result of the convergence of too many dreams upon a cold and arid land that could only ever sustain a few hard-won dreams at a time. But dreams don't die so easily in America, and the alkaline soils, the constant threats of frost or drought or flood, or the competing claims of a powerful rancher like French hadn't stopped a group of hard-luck, land-hungry settlers from grabbing land and squatting in plots along the meander lines of the always fluctuating Malheur and Harney Lakes. It was conflict with one especially hardheaded settler from this bunch that would cost French his life, in a violent incident that cast a quiet shadow across the history of the county and onto the lives of the Hammond family and the plot of the traveling Wild West show that Ammon Bundy was about to bring to town.

* * *

Ed Oliver was known to be stubborn, irascible even, and he had fought long and hard to get an easement through some of the pastureland of French's P Ranch, on the southern shore of Malheur Lake, where he had homesteaded. Oliver had won the right-of-way, to the deep irritation of French, who thought that Oliver was taking advantage by letting his cattle graze unduly on P Ranch lands. When the squatter moved his stock along the easement through the pastures of the P Ranch, there was nothing to stop his beasts from gobbling forage all the way, and so they did.

The conflict came to a head on December 26, 1890, when Oliver came down his easement path to find French and company putting in a new fence to further cut off his access. What happened next is not entirely clear, but there was a confrontation that became immediately physical and then mortal. One account claims that Oliver drove his horse directly into French's and that French had then proceeded to humiliate Oliver by beating him about the head and torso with his horsewhip. When an enraged Oliver pulled out his gun, the unarmed French rode quietly away, this story goes, only to be shot in the head. There are other versions, but they all end like this, with Oliver shooting an unarmed French from behind. What happened when the case went to trial gives you an idea of the nature of the conflict in the county: Oliver was acquitted by a jury of his peers. Self-defense, he'd said. His peers had agreed.

New Dispensations

In the years after French's death, the land power in Harney County and much of the Intermountain West had shifted slowly from the cattle kings to the federal government—to such a degree that more militant ranchers like the Bundys in the Mojave and the Hammonds in Oregon had come to despise the agencies and the regime of public lands as much as or more than their nineteenth-century ancestors had resented French and his ilk. This despite the fact that it was the existence of federal public lands that had arguably done more than anything to keep the livelihoods of smaller family ranches sustainable in the hard country of the West. Every region had its own version of the story; in Harney County, the lands of Pete French's ranching empire were at the center of it.

In 1916, the ranch's new owners reorganized for a second time and sold 46 pecent of their operation to an entity emblematic of the larger powers at work in the nation. The immediate interest of Louis Swift of Swift & Company, the great Chicago meatpacking concern, lay not only in the cattle raised on the lands of what was now called the Eastern Oregon Livestock Company, but in the large number of hogs rooting about through the marshes and meadows of the Blitzen Valley. These succulent, feral swine were the living legacies of all the failed homesteader dreams of the region. Louis Swift efficiently transmuted these to sausage and bacon, shipping them out on the railway line that had just reached the north end of the basin, but afterward neither Swift nor his partners ever seemed to figure out what exactly to do with their holdings, which included the whole southern half of the watershed of the region. There were ill-conceived development schemes involving irrigation projects; these, it was hoped, might sucker in some more would-be farmers, but they never panned out. In 1928, Swift bought out his partners' shares, but in the hard drought years of the Depression, with Swift & Company facing financial problems of its own, he sold out to the Malheur National Wildlife Refuge. With this acquisition, the federal sanctuary doubled its size and gained control of some of the most important bird and fish habitat in the region. The refuge, one of the first in the nation, had come into existence earlier in the twentieth century, when Teddy Roosevelt, the first true conservationist president, had designated it in an emergency effort to save the birds that migrated and nested throughout the zone. Many of these had become subject to wholesale slaughter by outsider commercial hunters. It was all for the millinery market. The early twentieth century, with its human mania for feathered hats, had been a very tough time to be a crane or an egret.

A new generation of small-to-midsize ranchers had prospered in the mid-twentieth century after the end of the cattle barons and the near-catastrophic overgrazing that had characterized the Depression era. Some of these ranchers were descendants of the small-fry homesteaders who'd tried to farm the bed of Malheur Lake in dry years—and whom Pete French had fought hard for many years to remove. They'd held on into the twentieth century and eventually lost their case—now with the new owner of the lands around the lake: the federal government's bird refuge. They'd lost, but really they'd won, because they'd received generous court-ordered cash settlements for the long-term hardship they'd endured waiting for the case to be resolved. Some had used the money to buy much better land and go into Pete French's old business. Descendants of these homesteaders are among the most prominent ranching families in the region today.

The mid-twentieth century had also seen the new federal wildlife refuge develop an at times uneasy but mostly smooth accommodation between itself and local cattlemen. The refuge manager for much of the time, John Scharff, had a ranching background, and he saw no inherent conflict between his mission of increased wild bird "production," in the lingo of the Fish and Wildlife Service, and grazing access. The refuge was run more or less like a farm for wild birds; ensuring grazing and haying access for the refuge's neighbors also stayed a priority. It was late in this era, perhaps the most tranquil one the still-young county has known, that the young Hammond family had arrived, in the early 1960s. Their newly purchased ranch was squeezed between the marshlands of the Fish and Wildlife Service's refuge and the Bureau of Land Management rangelands that sloped up Steens—and it came with grazing access to both. When the Hammonds had arrived in the basin, they'd not just bought a ranch; they'd also bought into a larger land-management dispensation, a world order that first slowly, and then with alarming speed, began to change.

Sagebrush Rebels

The Fish and Wildlife Service's refuge is a large federal landholder in the Harney Basin, but much larger in the county and throughout the West is the Bureau of Land Management. The story of the Bundys and the Hammonds is inseparable from the story of the BLM. The agency had come into existence through the crisis of the Dust Bowl years of the Depression. After the period of the cattle barons, federal management of the public lands had gradually become more direct. Really, in much of the West, there'd been hardly any management at all. What little had come in at first had been state or local— water boards and the like—establishing vest-able water rights for individual ranchers in the effort to head off range wars and the pernicious problem of overgrazing. But overgrazing had persisted. Sheep and cows were nibbling the West to dust, and by the era of the Great Depression something had had to be done. In 1934, with the passage of the Taylor Grazing Act, the federal government stepped in as a referee and guarantor, helping to stabilize the business—establishing marked-out exclusive grazing areas for ranchers who could demonstrate their long-standing use and/or water rights on a stretch of public land. Some ranchers welcomed this eagerly, others with suspicion, but overall it had worked for many. The BLM was established in the forties to oversee the lands newly delineated under the Taylor Grazing Act. At first its priorities had been the health of the grazing lands and the western ranching sector. Nobody could really see what else these arid lands could possibly be good for besides ranching.

Over the years, that had changed. All the branches of the military had established massive bases in the West after World War II. By the seventies, there were also new and urgent ecological concerns, and a new feeling for the landscape value of the American deserts. These were accompanied by increasing desires for outdoor recreation among the huge populations of the new cities of the West—itself creating a new booming economic sector that would soon dwarf western public-lands ranching. Pressures on federal agencies to adapt began to build, and soon ranchers were feeling the pressure too. It was the same throughout the West, and by the eighties and nineties tensions were high. Some now advocated the removal of cows from sensitive public lands like the Malheur National Wildlife Refuge; some even advocated the removal of cows from *all* public land. The principal prophets of this more radical approach happened to live in Harney County, on the refuge, right down the road from the Hammonds.

Throughout much of the 1970s and into the '80s, biologist Denzel Ferguson and his wife, Nancy, ran the Malheur Field Station, a small research center. What Nancy and Denzel Ferguson saw happening on the refuge with grazing and the shortsighted destruction of desert riparian habitat had led them to become leaders in the vanguard of an environmentalist push to end public-lands grazing entirely. Western public-lands ranchers provided a very small portion—arguably negligible—of the nation's beef. Why were they allowed to nearly monopolize and damage land better used for precious wildlife habitat and recreation opportunities for an immensely larger portion of the public? This didn't earn the couple any love in the local community, and the legends of the scuffles and hard words still reverberate around the county. The Fergusons gave as good as they got. Their famed book on the subject, *Sacred Cows at the Public Trough*, ends with these unambiguous words about public-lands ranchers and their cattle: "The public should boot every last one of them off the public lands. The nation no longer needs them."

Ranchers responded to the stresses and fears of the new era differently. Jack Southworth, who ranches at the northernmost point of the Great Basin, in Bear Valley up in the Malheur National Forest, about an hour north of Burns, responded to the challenges of the new dispensation and the scientific knowledge that accompanied it with determination to become a better caretaker of riparian habitat. He ruefully recalled his pride as a boy, when, using the family's new tractor, it fell on him to rip out the last willow along the Silvies River running through his family's land. Since taking over the ranch as an adult, he had been trying his best to undo the damage and restore those waterways; his work had been bearing fruit for some time. Even the beavers were back now in the wetlands on his ranch. As for the public lands, sharing the national forest with recreators, hunters, and wildlife just made sense to Jack—these lands were not only for him—though he remains steadfast in his conviction that there is an important place for cows in the forest and down on the ranges as well. Many ranchers have responded to the new era in this manner, but not everyone was of the same mind as Jack. Other ranchers, like the Hammonds, fought the new dispensation tooth and nail. The family was known to be anti-federal by disposition. Unsurprisingly, they had not responded well at all to new rules, restrictions, and fence lines keeping their cows out of pastures and waterways they'd come to think of, through their grazing permits and long-standing use, as more or less extensions of their ranch.

* * *

"History doesn't repeat itself, but it sure does rhyme," Jack Southworth told me once, citing the fertile apocrypha of Mark Twain. We were talking about Ed Oliver and Pete French, and also the Hammonds, and all the trouble Ammon brought to the county in January 2016. It was one incident in particular that was on our minds: an event from the bad days of the 1990s. On August 3, 1994, Dwight Hammond took direct action to stop construction of a new Fish and Wildlife barrier. The new fence was intended to impede his ability to move cattle across Fish and Wildlife land, as he had done for decades and for which he believed he had a long-standing legal right. Like Pete French with Ed Oliver, the Fish and Wildlife Service had grown weary of the Hammonds' incursions. Workers alleged that the

Hammonds had let their cattle linger for multiple days while moving them across the refuge, and that the hungry cows had trespassed into riparian habitat and trampled young willows refuge employees had only recently planted as part of their restoration efforts. This was just the sort of move French had accused Ed Oliver of a century before. Finally the tension spilled over into a full-on fence line showdown. A federal agent described in a sworn affidavit how Dwight Hammond pulled up his Caterpillar scraper and parked it on the federal boundary line in order to stop the Fish and Wildlife Service's efforts. He removed the battery and drained fuel lines so the big earthmover would have to be towed. When a tow truck finally arrived, according to the agent's description of events, Dwight leapt back into the driver's seat and brought down the scraper's bucket, barely missing smashing another agent who was on the scene.

Dwight was arrested. His case became a cause throughout eastern Oregon and the rangelands of the West; hundreds of ranchers and their supporters descended on Burns. Fish and Wildlife workers received regular threats, and soon the criminal case was negotiated into oblivion. The Hammonds came out as local and regional heroes or villains, depending on your perspective. The incident even brought Harney County a little bit of national attention when Dwight and Susie Hammond ended up at the center of an extended CNN report on what was being called the "Sagebrush Rebellion."

Ammon's father, Cliven, was also what people were calling in those days a "sagebrush rebel." This was shorthand for ranchers and other westerners who'd taken up direct action and stubborn refusal in their fight against new environmental restrictions to their generational use of public land—a use many had come to think of as proprietary. Across the West, closed roads had been opened, fences cut, federal employees threatened; there'd been a couple of agency office bombings (with no injuries). A few ranchers, like the Bundys, had refused all management of their grazing allotments. Others, like the Hammonds, had resisted federal management when they could, and been ornery in their dealings with federal employees. (Once, Dwight had allegedly threatened to tear off a land manager's head and shit down his neck.) This sort of thing had become somewhat common region-wide by the '90s. Since then, new conciliatory and collaborative modes of engagement had calmed things down considerably, at least in Harney County. Over the last decade, ranchers had been involved directly in the consensus-based crafting of conservation plans in the basin—alongside environmentalists and federal workers. Still, hardheaded sagebrush rebels like the Hammonds and Bundys had carried on with their informal resistance campaigns on their own.

Back in the Reagan and Clinton eras, the ranchers' struggle with federal bureaucracy and new conservation priorities had steeped itself in standard talk of the evils of big government. After the 2008 financial meltdown, this kind of language fit easily into the Tea Party movement, with its often-apocalyptic rhetoric about the allegedly imperial reign of Barack Obama. What was being fought here, if you listened to folks like the Hammonds and especially the Bundys, wasn't just a ranching struggle anymore. It wasn't just about cumbersome regulation and "government overreach." This was a bigger fight against federal tyranny—a battle for freedom itself. Ammon Bundy had grown up in a Latter-day Saint version of the sagebrush rebel milieu, and he was determined to save America and its Constitution. It was for this that the Spirit of God had guided him over the Stinkingwater Mountains and down over Wright's Point, into the shadowlands of Malheur. The next battle in the struggle for America was to begin with the Hammonds— with saving the Hammonds. But there was a problem. Steven Hammond didn't seem to want to be saved.

* * *

Steven Hammond is around Ammon Bundy's age, just a little bit older. He, too, had grown up in the Sagebrush Rebellion. He'd already gone to federal prison for it, and now he was headed back again. Two kinds of stories circulated about Steven and the rest of his family, sometimes from the same sources. These were the kindest, gentlest people you could ever know, folks said. They were also the meanest, when hate got into their hearts. The bad things Steven had supposedly said over the years, the things he'd supposedly done, didn't reconcile easily with the thoughtful, quiet, and considered man he could also be in public, where he seemed an awkward and gangly westerner with an aw-shucks manner and a big, melancholy smile. Everyone knew how generous he and his parents were to local causes of all sorts; everyone also knew that he and his father were fighters, with famously bad tempers.

While it was fighting over access to riparian grazing that had caused so much of the family's trouble with the refuge back in the '80s and '90s, the much bigger trouble the Hammonds were in now had come from later quarrels with the BLM. Western land disputes are often pitched at the intersections of the ideological and the elemental, and in this case the element had not been water but fire. The Hammonds, stubborn as they were, had proved reluctant over the years to surrender fire as a ranching tool. Traditionally, in healthy sagebrush communities, fire has been crucial in the regeneration of forage. Conflict over the use and management of fire—one of the biggest, most difficult issues facing Oregon and the entire West today—was now about to send the father and son back to prison on charges for which they'd already served out sentences.

No single book can exhaust the political, ecological, and historical complexities of the fire issue in the West; climate change is only making things even more fraught. The suppression of fire for more than a century in the region has led to a knot of dire conundrums with tremendous implications for habitat and resource use. Across eastern Oregon, among the many urgent concerns for ranchers and environmentalists alike is the rapid growth of juniper, which, in the absence of regular fire, has been turning sage and grasslands into monoculture, juniper forest, depriving ranchers of range and species of habitat. But just returning to setting fires has not been judged by range scientists to be the optimal solution anymore either, because of invasions of other non-native grasses, which tend to rush in to replace the sage and juniper in burned-out areas, resulting in less sustainable range for cattle and loss of crucial habitat for wildlife.

The Hammonds don't seem to have entirely agreed with these sorts of nuanced assessments, and continued to press for more burns. They were also charged with starting fires of their own on public land. One of these was the Krumbo Butte fire of August 2006. Lightning strikes had recently set off blazes in the crispy sagebrush and grasslands of the public land in the south end of the Harney Basin. Steven Hammond lit another fire to protect the family's property from one of these. When he'd done so, he had endangered a BLM firefighting team camped up on a hill near his ranch. The team was evacuated safely, but the damage was done. Firefighting teams are often made up of local youths, often the children of ranchers, some of them neighbors of the Hammonds. As far as the feds and many locals were concerned, the Hammonds had really gone too far.

Where only warnings had been issued before for the Hammonds' illegal use of fire on the public range, now arson charges were brought for this fire and a previous one from a few years earlier. Steven and his father were hauled into federal court, where, upon their conviction years after the incidents, they encountered what many see as one of the chief blights of the contemporary justice system: mandatory sentencing. In this case they were looking at five years each under guidelines established, as the judge in the case observed, with deliberately destructive arson fires in heavily populated areas in mind. The judge, disturbed by the harshness of the required sentences, chose his last day on the bench to sentence Dwight and Steven to considerably shorter terms, and then headed off into retirement.

The federal attorney's office for Oregon appealed the judge's failure to apply the legislatively mandated punishments. Meanwhile, father and son served out their given sentences, so that by the time the Ninth Circuit had found federal prosecutors in the right, and the Supreme Court had refused to hear the Hammonds' appeal, Dwight and Steven were already back at home. Now they were told they would need to return to prison to serve out the remainder of their congressionally mandated terms. On January 4, 2016, almost ten years after the 2006 Krumbo Butte fire, they were scheduled to report to the small federal facility at Terminal Island, nestled on a pier in the Los Angeles Harbor, amid the giant robot cranes of the ever-more automated transnational economy. To someone like Ammon Bundy, and to many others, this was all incomprehensible. It looked like a clear instance of double jeopardy, and further proof of a federal—and unconstitutional— war on hardworking, hard-pressed, western rural agriculture.

It was this seemingly blatant miscarriage of justice—how could anyone be sentenced twice to two sets of terms for the same crimes?—that had brought Ammon now to the gates of the Hammond Ranch. But the Steven Hammond that Ammon encountered that day was not the fiery Hammond known from the years of his family's angry conflicts with federal land managers. This wasn't the Steven whose family had been accused of death threats. Nor was it the uncle who'd allegedly sanded off the letters his troubled nephew had carved into his own flesh as a sort of makeshift tattoo—a bit of family history brought up during sentencing. As he explained to his dear friends in his New Years' video missive, the Steven Hammond whom Ammon encountered was someone else—a deeply humble, peaceful, people-loving, Christian man.

To Ammon he was also a broken man. The fight had been beaten from him; Steven Hammond had given up on freedom, as Ammon understood it. When Ammon revealed to him his purpose—that he felt he was here to help the Hammond family, that he was *supposed to* be here, that God had brought him here—Steven told Ammon he didn't want the help. The ferocious Steven of the past seemed to have vanished, at least on this particular

November afternoon. One had to just keep one's head down and get through this life, that's what Steven believed, or so Ammon told his friends in his January 1 video. But the two spent the day together anyway, working the ranch, moving cows and feed through the sagebrush and the golden grass, on into the early-November dusk. It was dark by the time Ammon left the Blitzen Valley and headed north, away from Steens Mountain and up over Wright's Point to Burns.

CHAPTER THREE

The Glory in the Wash

The Battle of Bunkerville

UNLIKE STEVEN, AMMON WAS FAR FROM GIVING UP. The next morning he found a more receptive audience in Steven's mother, Susie. "Now Susie," Ammon told his dear friends, "she's got a little more spunk, a little more fight to her . . ." He had a proud story of Freedom to tell the Hammond matriarch, and that November morning Susie Hammond was ready to listen. What a story it was. Full of great American abstractions come to life. Liberty, Tyranny, God, and "the People" swirled about in it, kicking up dust like a herd of the Bundys' near-wild, hearty desert cows. "The People came to our defense," Ammon told Susie. "And because the people came, we now are *free.*"

The story of the Bundy family takes place in another little-known zone of the Intermountain West, the arid lands of the Virgin River Valley, in the far-eastern corner of the Mojave Desert, around the old Mormon settlement of Bunkerville, Nevada. The contemporary American imagination usually passes through the Bundys' corner of the Mojave at the speed of a car commercial, zipping between aerial footage of the canyon country of Utah and Arizona and the gold-plated, glass mirage of Vegas. But people still live out there, and not all of them are retirees, not yet.

This land is part of the "ragged edge" of Mormonism, as acclaimed historian and Bunkerville native Juanita Brooks calls that territory on the southern and eastern borders of the Empire of Zion. The Ragged Edge is a thinly populated territory of rugged landscapes: the inaccessible red-rock canyon country of southern Utah and the Arizona Strip, the sagebrush range lands of central Nevada, and the lesser-known easternmost edges of the Mojave Desert, with its roaring wind and silence, its gas-flame blue sky, and its otherworldly landscape of jagged, alien-looking plant life and brooding stone. These are places seemingly hand-crafted by sublime powers, natural home-lands of revelation, ready-made for the slow cooking of heretical doctrine.

The nation had found out about Cliven and Ammon and their corner of the West in April 2014. Before the Oregon Standoff had come the Battle of Bunkerville, another desert showdown with federal authorities over public land management, this one at the Bundy family ranch near that little Mojave town whose name has since become synonymous with Freedom, or armed fanaticism, depending on who you talked to, or where you stood. The standoff in Nevada had first brought together Ammon and the bearded young man who joined him now in Susie Hammond's living room. Iraq war veteran and Montana militiaman Ryan Payne had driven down from Anaconda to be with Ammon that morning in Burns. Together the two told Susie the tale of their alliance and their victory, and what they felt they could do now for her and her family.

*   *   *

The origins of the Nevada showdown went back at least twenty years, to the early 1990s. The mushrooming of Las Vegas, only eighty miles southwest of Bunkerville, alongside the growth of the vast military bases of the Mojave, had begun to have a troubling impact on the life and habitat of the desert tortoise, a beloved signature species of the zone. In 1991, the tortoise was listed under the Endangered Species Act. In a kind of real estate version of cap-and-trade, Clark County and its seat of power, Vegas, with all its huge development concerns, were able to negotiate a sort of land swap in order to keep the listing of the tortoise from bringing multimillion-dollar construc-tion projects to a screeching halt. Instead, nearby ranchers would be required to move their cattle out of tortoise zones at key times of the year and reduce the numbers of grazing cows.

It must have all seemed logical from the perspective of Vegas to create some tortoise protection zones out there on the federal lands near Bunkerville. The area must have looked basically uninhabited, used only, if at all, by a few holdover desert ranchers, whose barely profitable lifestyles made them seem like living anachronisms—because they were. If you've ever been to the Mojave you know what a marvel it is to even imagine someone trying to run cattle out there. The county's movers and shakers must have felt they were offering these ranchers a lifeline, a way out, a little cash for their allotments and a chance to do something else with their lives—if they'd bothered to think much about them at all.

The effect of the new regulations on ranching in the Mojave was swift. For most local ranchers it was the nail in the coffin. One by one they sold their grazing rights to the county, which added the land to the new tortoise protection zone. But there was one rancher who wouldn't budge: Ammon's father, Cliven. The elder Bundy, stubborn and blustery as the land he calls home, refused to accept the new grazing regulations for his federal allotments. He refused to move his cows, and he also stopped paying for the privilege. Eventually, he also decided that he no longer recognized the federal government's authority over land in Nevada. Sometimes he went even further: "I don't recognize the United States government as even existing," he said at the height of the 2014 standoff at his ranch.

It was in 2014—after a twenty-year battle in the courts—that Cliven had finally found himself facing confiscation of his herd of what federal prosecutors later called his "wild, mean and ornery" desert cattle. Few would know anything at all about this story if it had played out as the authorities anticipated, with maybe a little disruption from the family, nothing an extra dispatch of Bureau of Land Management agents couldn't handle. But that's not what happened, thanks to the internet—and also partly to that intense young man sitting in the living room with Ammon and Susie Hammond, Ryan Payne.

When the government men had come for Cliven's cows, dressed like soldiers in an occupying army, as cops so often seem to do in America nowadays, the first confrontations went as expected—nothing more than some shouty showdowns in the dust between agents and a small band of Bundy family and friends. But then video of one moment went viral, as we say, and everything changed. That incident introduced the right-wing internet to Cliven Bundy's son Ammon, who quickly found himself transformed into a Facebook hero after being repeatedly tased by a BLM officer.

Ammon had leapt into the confrontation when a BLM agent had tackled and tossed his aunt to the dirt. She and other members of the family were trying to stop BLM trucks from exiting an area where they were removing irrigation infrastructure Cliven had installed on his public grazing allotments. The family was concerned that the truck might contain dead Bundy cattle; everyone was amped up and rumors were thick on the ground. The video of Ammon being tased, then stepping back into the confrontation and being tased again, was soon playing on the screens of Patriot types, militia members, and Tea-Partiers everywhere, thanks partly to the presence of a bombastic and confrontational right-wing internet journalist named Peter Santilli, who had traveled to Nevada to document the Bundy cattle confiscation. In a follow-up video later in the week, Ammon showed off the taser marks, fang-shaped, seared into his chest.

In the following days dozens and dozens of heavily armed militiamen from all over the West and farther afield showed up, to defend the Bundys' cattle. In the middle of this effort was Ryan Payne. Payne had been waiting for a moment like this for some time. He had a personal gripe with the federal government and when he began to speak of his recent military experience, it wasn't hard to understand why. "I see this as my actual service," he was to say of his militia work to a reporter in 2016 in Harney County. "I don't believe that my military service was service. I thought it was unconstitutional disservice. I allowed myself to be sent around the world for an unconstitutional, non-declared war—to go kill and help kill people," he said. "It's a horrible thing."

In the years after leaving the military, Payne's experience with government regulations in California had left him further embittered. He'd started a small business building off-road vehicles with his uncle, but then the state changed its rules regarding emissions testing, and the pair couldn't afford to purchase the required testing equipment. "When they redefined the criteria that sand cars and desert race cars fell under," Ryan told a writer for the *Missoula Independent*, "it destroyed turnkey builders like myself, unless you had a giant buy-in." That the new regulations favored much larger, more highly capitalized manufacturers seemed further proof—to Payne—of a rigged system. "And that's what we see in the entire country," he'd told the same Montana writer, "that specific entities are being given certain privileges by government regulation and the inability of the little guy, the small business owner, to really keep his head above water. There has to be purpose in this. They claim to have all the answers, they claim to be taking us down the correct path, and yet it seems like there's a lot of destruction and pain and suffering going on."

Soon Payne decamped for Montana, where he lived off-grid with his family near the old mining company town of Anaconda. There he'd started his own pan-militia organization: Operation Mutual Aid. The group's mission was to create a network of militia members who could quickly mobilize in response to calls from citizens nationwide seeking defense against the violations of what they saw as their constitutional rights. The video of Ammon being tased presented Ryan with his first real opportunity to call this inchoate network into action. Dozens of men began rolling out—tactical gear, weapons, and ammo in tow—toward a confrontation with federal enforcement power out in a corner of the Nevada desert that few of them had likely even heard of before.

The arrival of all these armed militia types changed the situation entirely. Soon a deal was announced: the sheriff of Clark County arrived to tell the Bundys and their allies that the BLM would halt the round-up. But it was too little and too late to satisfy Cliven or his restless new army. Taking the mic on the impromptu stage that Payne and others had built at the militia encampment, Cliven, in his marble-mouthed drawl, began to prophesy and command. He'd had a divine revelation about what was to be done. He ordered the sheriff, standing awkwardly at his side, to carry out God's will and disarm all federal agents in the area. All the guns were to be brought to his ranch. And this was to be done within an hour. That wasn't all. God also wanted the entrance kiosks at the gates of nearby National Park Service–administered federal lands to be flattened. Also within an hour. The commands given, Cliven crossed his arms and waited for their fulfillment. In the intervening hour, the mass of Bundy supporters grew more agitated, milling about in the dust, so that when the deadline passed and Cliven's divine commands went unmet, the crowd was ready to carry out the new plan.

Before the BLM had halted rounding up the Bundy cattle, the private contractor cowboys the feds had brought in had already corralled around four hundred of them. Cliven wanted his cows back and the crowd was ready and willing to make it happen. "Get 'er goin', Cowboys! Let's go get 'er done!" shouted Cliven, as everyone set off for the BLM camp in nearby Toquop Wash.

* * *

While Cliven stayed back at the ranch, his son Ammon had led the surging crowd down into the wash where it cut under Interstate 15. It was a glorious spring day in the desert, the kind of Mojave day when it feels like a body just might drown in the deep blue radiance of noon. All around, the desert was coming to life, the yearly green-up had commenced. It was exactly that time of year when the poor tortoises—forgotten, inadvertent cause of all this human calamity—are out of their holes (what holes are left to them, that is) and methodically munching flowers, their faces and feet stained with pollen and the greenery of the new spring growth. But the tortoise wasn't on so many minds in the wash that day. Abruptly, the scene got frightfully tense. Militiamen with rifles, coordinated by Ryan Payne, got up on the interstate highway bridge above the wash where the cows were penned up—it must have been a strange day to be traveling down I-15 between Utah and Vegas. Some of these armed men lay on the pavement and even seemed to aim their rifles at the frontline BLM agents guarding the gate that separated the crowd from the corral holding Cliven's cows. Folks who were there, on both sides of the drama, say something to this effect: if a car had backfired, there would have been a full-on gunfight. Dozens could have died.

Quickly, an order to retreat came in to the agents on the scene. They pulled back in a defensive phalanx. Then the cry came up to go get the cows. Ammon was there at the gate to swing it open, and out they galloped, raising a great cloud of dust, past the stunned, whooping crowd. The cows thundered off into the desert as the Patriots cheered. Someone raised a banner, thick with anachronism: THE WEST HAS NOW BEEN WON. Behind it shone the blue trance of the desert sky. They'd beaten the most powerful government in the world; their lives would never feel the same.

*   *   *

Bundy supporters who were there that afternoon have described to me something that sounds in their words like a real-life political miracle. Again and again, I've heard how much it meant to have been there on the day that the People backed down the government. In the cauldron of Toquop Wash, the people—with a lowercase *p*—who had happened to be there that day had been transfigured. Now they were *the People*. Or *We the People*, as they began to call themselves.

One man on the scene was a soft-spoken old hippie from a different era of revolution. Neil Wampler is not the sort of person one expects to find in a right-wing milieu like the one that had sprouted near instantly around the Bundy family. But like many involved in the movement, he had his reasons for seeking out new sources of meaning in his life. Now retired, he lives in tranquil seclusion on California's rural central coast, but alcohol addiction had consumed his youth—especially the turbulent years after his return from the Vietnam War. In that personal epoch of inebriate haze, he'd missed out on much of the political struggle against the hated, overbearing federal government that had sent him to Southeast Asia. (Though his personal experience of the conflict, he is quick to point out, was much less traumatic than many, he regards the war to be one of the greater moral abominations in modern history.) Neil's addiction had led him lower than most ever get— most who survive, anyway—but after a prison stint, he'd reentered life sober, as a father and an artful woodworker. He'd quietly dedicated himself to high-end cabinetry and furniture-making for decades until his retirement, when that video of a Nevada cowboy being tased by body-armored federal agents found its way to his screen. Soon he was in his car headed southeast. Not long after his arrival, he found himself standing in the wash under the blue flare of the Mojave sky as Ammon took command of the moment, earning his permanent loyalty and admiration. "He is, to my mind," Neil told me of Ammon, "one of the greatest Americans."

After Bundy Ranch, Neil was ready to follow Ammon pretty much anywhere. There was just nothing like it. The victory they won that day against overwhelming power had reoriented his being. "All we had was our butts," Neil said, against all that federal weaponry and authority—"and we won." He and his new comrades seem to have had a direct, brief experience of what, in political theory terms—terms foreign to the Bundy Revolution—is called Constitutive Power. This is the power to institute nation and law that in a modern democracy is supposed to be invested, in the final instance, in the citizenry. It's related to Popular Sovereignty, the name in political thought for the ultimate rule of the People that is central to all notions of democratic republican governance. Constitutive Power and Popular Sovereignty, when they descend from their throne in the lofty realm of political ideas, manifest in human bodies and experience primarily as *feeling*. It's a rare emotion. If it is sustained and successful, it is called Revolution. The only people I've ever met who speak of events in their lives the way Neil and other veterans of Bundy Ranch speak about their moment in the wash are friends of mine from other nations who have experienced actual popular revolutions, or other massive protest actions of overwhelming success. There may be no nonreligious social experience that can be more sublime than this—no mass-cultural modern feeling more stuffed with meaning and mattering than being the Sovereign People in the flesh. Many, like Neil, who were there in Toquop Wash that day were going to want, very badly, to feel this way again.

*　*　*

It was the emotional power of this transformational event, and the dedication of the people it had galvanized into a movement, that Ammon and his friend Ryan now offered Susie Hammond. Unlike with her son the day before, the power of the story proved affecting to the Hammond matriarch. Susie, said Ammon, "began to get hope." And through her, he added, her husband, Dwight, also began to get hope. Hope that these two strangers in their living room could make something like what happened in Nevada happen for them: that *the People* might come, and that when *the People* came, Dwight and Steven might also be *Free*.

CHAPTER FOUR
———

The Education of David Ward

IN THE COMING WEEKS, BUNDY AND PAYNE began to gather their network—and to call the Revolution to Burns. Soon individual Patriot types and groups of militiamen began appearing around town. Little by little, the people of Harney County began to notice what was assembling around them. "We got an education here in our little town," Samantha, owner of a café on Burns's main drag, told me one summer afternoon, months after it was all over. "We didn't know about constitutionalists or chem trails, or Agenda 21, or sovereign citizens or . . ." she continued, counting off all the new right-wing subcultures and conspiracy theories that the newcomers had taught her and her neighbors.

Strangers stand out in Harney County. Burns and its companion town, Hines, form a small western settlement—population around five thousand—of lumber-town houses fanning out from the intersection of a pair of two-lane highways connecting the Snake River Plain of Southern Idaho to the Cascades, and the Columbia Plateau to the Great Basin. North of Burns, the Great Basin ends, and sagebrush gives way to fir and pine forest. Most of the remaining two thousand residents of the county live west, east, and south, out in the high desert, spread across an area the size of the state of Massachusetts. They live on small and large private lots, on ranches and in small settlements, scattered among millions of acres of public land (75 percent of the county is federal land, which still leaves 230 acres of private land per person in Harney County, though the divisions of that land are hardly even). Somewhere out there is the geographic point farthest from an interstate in the entire continental United States, a fact locals point to with pride. It is a

33

big, lonely place, and its isolation has been a strongly determining factor in the economic, political, and cultural life of the region. I've never been anywhere in America quite like it.

Architecturally, Burns's cattle-town origins show through on Broadway, its principal street, where a few old brick buildings host the usual hodge-podge of local businesses. During and after the occupation, mainstream media outlets liked to represent Burns's considerable economic woes in visual shorthand with shots of empty downtown storefronts. The town has been in deep economic decline since the end of its multi-decade lumber boom in the 1980s, but these days Burns's downtown buildings are actu-ally mostly occupied, and you have to look around a little for an out-of-business sign. There's a little movie theater: *The Revenant* and *The Hateful 8* were playing at different times during the occupation. Up the street there's a café and a Chinese place called "Hilander Restaurant" in homage to Robert Burns, the town's namesake. It was frequented by Ammon during his time in the county. There's a stationery store full of optimistic Christian kitsch, a Thai restaurant furnished more like an antiques store than an eatery (it took me a week to understand that there was food some-where in there). There's a bar and a bank or two, and a used bookstore run by an old hippie SoCal refugee and his majestic cat. There's even a yoga studio. Still, with all these establishments, no matter what time of day it is, it is a little unusual to look up and see another person walking toward you down the sidewalk. At night, Broadway is as quiet as the sagebrush, maybe quieter.

The convergence of people that began in November 2015 might have felt like an invasion even if all the newcomers had been friendly, well-mannered tourists, intent only on exchanging a few pleasantries about the landscape before handing over their cash. But the people materializing around Burns stood out for other reasons: many were armed; some were abrasive in their manner; still others were openly unhinged.

Samantha remembered her first encounter, that November, with the Bundy Revolution. "A crazed, toothless guy from Alabama" who'd ridden the bus all the way to Burns had come into her café to tell her about the meaning of her Christmas tree. She and her husband had just put it up, and had noticed a man pacing out front, examining it through the window. Eventually he'd come inside to give his verdict. "I like your Christmas tree," he'd said. "You know if you'd have decorated it with all white lights, I'd have known you were with the government," the stranger had continued. "And that's," Samantha said, "when our education began." The man had started telling her right there about Agenda 21 and chem trails. "We didn't know what we were in for," she added.

Samantha is a fifth-generation Harney County resident—though she pointed out to me, as she caught herself volunteering the info, that before the Bundy Revolution came to town that she wouldn't have thought to lead with such a biographical detail. "I never would have done that before," she said, "and now I do that."

Samantha totally seems like a descendent of pioneers. Beyond her no-nonsense, small-town affability, like lots of folks in the county, she exudes an uncommon fortitude. Nonetheless, she told me, the whole thing had really gotten to her. She was far more wary of strangers now, she noted—of me, for instance. In the past she wouldn't have needed to suss out, of a stranger like myself, who I was and what I was up to here in her town and her café, as she had just caught herself doing. The mood Ammon had brought to town had been sharply paranoid. She'd even—despite her family's five generations here—been accused of being a paid outside agitator from Portland. Now she too had become more suspicious of others and she didn't like this at all.

As things heated up, many more odd encounters were to take place with the strangers summoned by Payne and Bundy's internet calls to action—and many were less comic than Samantha's Christmas-tree story. Some of the newcomers were openly armed; Oregon is an open-carry state and Harney County a gun-friendly territory, but open carry had been uncommon around town until November 2015. Some locals, including federal workers, reported being followed by strange men, shouted at from truck slow-rolling past their doors, harassed on their own doorsteps, or waking to find their tires slashed. Some received threats, some moved away and have never returned; but in that month leading up to the occupation, no single resident was subjected to as much pressure, or threatened with as much retribution, as Harney County sheriff David Ward.

It was Ward who was the first real student of the Bundy Revolution in Oregon—but he wasn't a very good pupil, at least not in the judgment of his would-be professors, Ammon Bundy and Ryan Payne. Long after the occupation was over men and women of the movement would still be taking to the internet to blame him for everything that was about to go down in Harney County. If only Ward had had the courage or the intelligence to apprehend the simple, providential truth of Ammon's constitutional message, the argument goes, he would have stood like a true American, a real sheriff, and agreed to protect the Hammonds. If he had done so, the Hammonds would have stayed free, and Harney County would have had the honor of becoming a beachhead of liberty, a beacon in the remote West illuminating the dark night of federal tyranny that had otherwise enveloped the continent.

Ward noticed very quickly the intensity of feeling that was being deployed in his direction, first to sway him to Ammon's side, later to vilify him as a government collaborator. Emotion was key to how Ammon operated and to how he succeeded. Emotion and the internet. As Dave came to see it, an alarming level of unwillingness to look into news stories and claims circulated on social media was causing a new kind of damage to democracy—and to social life—in his country and his community. This has come to be an accepted truth since the 2016 election, but in late 2015 Ward and the people of Harney County were getting an early crash course in the new forms of American public life.

*　*　*

Dave had read a bit about the Battle of Bunkerville. "So on November fifth, when I get a call from Ammon, I recognized the name; it made the back of my hair stand up. I thought, 'What's this guy doing in my community?'" He asked Ammon to come by in the afternoon so he would have time to do some more research, and what he learned alarmed him even more. He had only four deputies in 2015, and he and these deputies were charged with policing a territory two thirds the size of Denmark—and of considerably rougher terrain. He knew how ill-prepared he was for anything like Bunkerville; he would learn soon enough that his visitors knew this as well.

David Ward had been in plenty of alarming situations before. He's got the weather-ruddied face and the affable demeanor of the Oregon farm boy he was and still is, but his extensive military background means he's also seen combat and been in the middle of insurgencies and societal breakdowns as far off as Somalia and Afghanistan. But never, he told me, had he experienced anything like the persistent level of fear that Ammon and Ryan's friends were to bring to Burns by the end of the year. "Those guys are in love with the Revolution," Ward told me. "I've been threatened with revolution and civil war I don't know how many times. They were trying to re-create the steps, including the shot heard 'round the world."

What was about to happen in Harney County was a kind of proto-guerrilla insurrection—a real one and a staged one. It was both things at once: an extended protest that borrowed the form and lingo of insurrection, and an insurrection that cloaked itself in the language and form of protest. David Ward was in a better position than most to understand this, but he wasn't the only one. It's something forgotten by those of us who haven't served in the military—that this country is now full of men and women with close personal knowledge of contemporary guerrilla insurgency. Everywhere you go, if you are in a crowd, there's a good chance that someone around you carries inside them that strange experience of having been, in their own bodies and their own lives, the military extension of our turbulent society—of its imperial police power. When Ammon showed up at the sheriff's department that afternoon, he wasn't alone; he'd brought his friend Ryan Payne. Now two of the three men in Dave Ward's office that day had been partly formed by such hard experience.

While Ward managed to mostly get along with Ammon—"Ammon, he gives threats and ultimatums, but he's personable"—the relations between him and Payne were more strained from the start. "Ryan would try to stare a hole through you," Dave told me. The two veterans seemed to have learned very different things from their military experiences. Payne, from all his statements on his service, seemed to have learned the hard way not to trust power, especially the greatest powers in his own society; Ward had learned to believe in the power of breaking bread with everyone.

Dave likes to talk about the importance of sitting down face to face, sharing food and speech. It was something he'd find himself urging his neighbors to do over the coming months. But breaking bread with Ammon and his friend Ryan did not work; the conversations, he said, went only one way. "I tried to reason with them. I told him, 'Listen, this is the issue you have: it is with *mandatory sentencing*. Since the sheriff doesn't write the law— the sheriff only enforces the law—a more appropriate place to take this up would be with your legislator.' Bundy's stance was to get mad."

Ammon was not here to discuss different approaches to the issue, but to educate Dave on his duties. His main argument, about Dave's obligations as a constitutional sheriff, was, to Ward, one of the most baffling in the repertoire of the Patriots who would soon swarm his town. "How many times does the word *sheriff* appear in the Constitution?" Ward asked me. It was a rhetorical question. The answer is zero.

The Constitutional Sheriff

It's not that Ward hadn't heard before of any of these far-right notions regarding the power of the sheriff. These ideas had flickered along the margins of American rural life for some time. He'd become more personally aware of the dogma when he'd first assumed his office. It started with his wife coming home confused after a neighbor had asked her what it felt like to be married to *the most powerful man in the county*. David Ward was now the highest elected law enforcement authority in the county, which meant, to those who thought like Ammon, that he had joined the ranks of the most powerful and legitimate legal authorities *in the nation*: the county sheriffs of America. The current popularity of the idea was partly the work of a leading western Tea Party figure, Richard Mack. Mack, unsurprisingly, was also a sheriff.

Actually, he was an ex-sheriff, having been voted out of office when his Graham County, Arizona, constituents evidently tired of all the time he was spending on the national political circuit. In the 1990s, Mack had gained notoriety when he won a lawsuit that he'd filed against the federal government over new gun laws enacted under the Brady Bill. This victory, won in the Supreme Court with the help of the National Rifle Association, had allowed local law enforcement to refuse to carry out the background checks enshrined in the Brady legislation, and made Mack a hero on the Second Amendment circuit. When his activism cost him his sheriff seat, he'd faded into the right-wing wallpaper until the frenzy of political mobilization that had coalesced as the Tea Party had brought him back onto the national stage. The way Mack and so many in his world saw it, with the election of Barack Obama, the federal government was out of control and the Constitution in jeopardy. Liberties were being threatened: "socialist" healthcare plans were about to be imposed on the people; clearly Second Amendment rights would soon be under attack. After that, who knew what would be next? Once they were disarmed, how would the People defend their rights? He did what many ambitious people do in moments of real and perceived crisis: he looked for a solution and found himself—or his former office—to be the answer. Writing from what he called "complete discouragement and feelings of hopelessness" at Obama's election, Mack put forward a dramatically titled manifesto, "The County Sheriff: America's Last Hope." This pamphlet became one of the central texts of the Tea Party, as Mack emerged as one of the movement's main voices in the West.

To Mack, the power of county sheriffs results from their direct election by the People. The sheriff, he says, is "the only official who reports directly to the power source. In other words, he's not a bureaucrat, he wasn't appointed . . . he reports directly to *We the People*. And so he is sovereign in that regard because he reports directly to the other sovereigns." To Mack's mind, this means the sheriff has an authority when it comes to the law and the Constitution that even federal law enforcement officials—none of whom are directly elected—lack. *We the People. Sovereigns. The Power Source.* These words and phrases place us firmly in the rhetorical territory of the Battle of Bunkerville, as Constitutive Power descends from the lofty realm of political ideas to light up the bodies of the Patriots in Toquop Wash.

* * *

Actually, these notions of the sheriff's special powers weren't new at all, and Richard Mack had not invented them; he'd only helped wash the dogma of its ugly associations. A little research had led Dave easily back to the origins of the constitutional sheriff—in the doctrine of the violent, virulently racist, and anti-Semitic world of the Posse Comitatus, one of the more frightful political phenomena of the American postwar period. While the coincidence of resurgent anti-federal sentiment with Obama's presidency had its own racist elements—the birtherism of Sheriff Mack and his ally, Arizona sheriff Joe Arpaio, come to mind—Ward believes that folks in Harney County spouting the ideas of Mack and Ammon were unaware of their frightful provenance. In a nation of amnesiacs, Mack's intellectual laundry operation—to whatever degree it had or had not been intentional—had proved effective.

The phrase *posse comitatus*—"power of the county" in Latin—refers to the legal authority of a sheriff to assemble a group of men to enforce the law. The movement—which emerged from the anticommunist John Birch Society milieu on the West Coast during the white panic of the civil rights era—takes its name more specifically from a significant piece of nineteenth-century legislation, the Posse Comitatus Act. That act, of June 1878, put a celebratory capstone on the freshly dug tomb of post–Civil War racial progress in the South. The grueling presidential election of 1876—among the most controversial and contested in the nation's history—had been finally resolved when Democrats agreed to accept the election of the Republican candidate, Rutherford B. Hayes, in return for the withdrawal of federal troops from the

South. (Some of that withdrawn military power would be used within two years against the Native population of what would become Harney County.) The removal of federal enforcement power effectively ended Reconstruction; the disenfranchisement of Southern blacks now began with the birth of the era known as Jim Crow. The Comitatus Act formalized the withdrawal of the army, restricting the use of U.S. military forces in future domestic law enforcement. The "power of the county," in the South of 1878, was the power to enforce white supremacy.

The twentieth-century Posse Comitatus movement reached its peak of influence in the 1970s and '80s, during the now much-forgotten catastrophe known then simply as the "Farm Crisis." The movement's conspiratorial theories of a New World Order—convened by the Rockefellers, evil Jewish bankers, and a corrupt federal government—gathered traction among desperate white farmers in the Midwest and the Great Plains, who found themselves caught in a perfect storm of crushing interest rates and the fickle economics of Cold War politics. The stagflation crisis of the '70s had combined with the devastating effects of a Cold War embargo on the sale of grain to the Soviet Union to provoke a foreclosure epidemic that rivaled that of the Great Depression in parts of the Midwest. In the face of this existential threat to their being and livelihoods, some farmers had turned to the rabid hatred espoused by the founder and main mouthpiece of the Posse Comitatus movement, William Gale.

While its power would peak in the Midwest, the Posse had originated in the California pulpit of Gale, an anticommunist white supremacist preacher graced with cinematic polish. A World War II officer and son of an Eastern European immigrant, Gale had gone from raising a handsome family of chipper, aspiring show-business performers in the sunny utopia of 1950s Hollywood—John Wayne had tried for a time, unsuccessfully, to court one of his daughters—to become the founding figure of perhaps the most toxic distillation of anticommunist paranoia, anti-Semitic conspiracy theory, and antiblack civil rights backlash to emerge in America in the postwar period.

By the 1980s, Gale's ideas were being spread widely by word of mouth, by pamphlet, and by audio recordings of his sermons, taped in his small congregation in the western foothills of the Sierra Madre. In 1982, a popular country station in rural Kansas had begun broadcasting Gale's sermons into the nights of the plains. In his smooth Hollywood voice—the now mostly vanished accent of what is today already a largely bygone time and place, the California of John Wayne, Ronald Reagan, and Richard Nixon—he openly called for antigovernment insurrection and racist violence against "black beasts." "Yes, we're gonna cleanse our land," Gale told his listeners. "We're gonna do it with a sword. And we're gonna do it with violence. 'Oh,' they say, 'Reverend Gale, you're teaching violence.' You're damn right I'm teaching violence! God said you're gonna do it that way, and it's about time somebody is telling you to get violent, whitey."

"Arise and fight," he added. "If a Jew comes near you, run a sword through him."

There was a personal history behind all this hatred; no one knew it at the time, but Reverend William Gale was of Jewish ancestry himself. Gale's father was a Russian Jewish immigrant, a refugee who'd fled the rural pogroms of the Pale of Settlement for a new life in America in the late nineteenth century. Now the words of the son revived the ugly ghosts of czarist-Russian anti-Semitic rural incitement that had spurred so many peasants to run his own ancestors through with swords and whatever else they'd had at hand. Even the sunny amnesia of California—New World Homeland of Forgetfulness and the Future—hadn't fully erased the terror of Gale's ancestors. Instead, in the recesses of the man (and of his time) it had mutated and thrived. Horror never seems to go away completely: it returns with subconscious stealth, contorting into baffling new shapes. In America, the powerlessness and trauma of those who'd fled the Old World of Europe could all too easily, over the generations, take on new life in the hateful forms available in the various currents of white supremacy that have coursed through our national life and psyche from the very beginning. It's part of that continuous cycle of violence that makes up so much of what we call History.

Despite the vitriol of the extended white backlash of the 1970s and 1980s, much of the dogma of Gale's late-night broadcasts had been too extreme to survive long in the light of day—especially once Posse followers became involved in bank robberies and acts of violence against law enforcement. Still, some of the Posse's main ideas about the Constitution had survived, absorbed into the militia movement of the '90s. Chief among them was the fanatic, mystical understanding of the U.S. Constitution and the role of the county sheriff at the core of Gale's sermons. "You're either going to get back to the Constitution of the United States," Gale told the Kansas night in one sermon, "or officials are gonna hang by the neck until they're dead." This wasn't just rhetoric; it was a policy proposal. Gale gave specific instructions for what should be done to a sheriff who didn't stand up for his people and that sacred document: lynching. "Your citizens—a posse—will take him to the most populated intersection of the township and hang him by the neck, take the body down at dark, and that will be an example to those other officials who are supposed to be your servants that they are going to abide by the Constitution."

As the militia movement reemerged during the Obama years, these old Posse notions, stripped by time—and Richard Mack—of overt white-supremacist content, were put to new use in what now called itself the Patriot movement, whose leaders tend to take pains to separate themselves from openly racist individuals and ideology. (Mack does his best to push the process further along; if you look up a Richard Mack speech on YouTube, chances are you will quickly find a video of him talking about Rosa Parks, and how she wouldn't have had so much trouble if only she'd had a constitutional sheriff to help her.) Nowadays right-wing "Constitutionalist" positions, moderated and scrubbed of Jim Crow, William Gale, and Posse Comitatus contamination, don't immediately sound—at least to an untrained ear—of an entirely different order than the stances taken by eighteenth-century patriots against newly intrusive British imperial policies. Before taking the final step of advocating outright independence, Samuel Adams and so many of the other colonial radicals and Whigs of the 1760s and '70s had spoken in a compelling idiom of egregious *Constitutional Violations*, and *Natural Sovereign Rights of the People* to resist *Unconstitutional* laws imposed by a distant, out-of-touch, *Overreaching Tyrannical* authority. Cleaned of its disquieting origins, the idea of the constitutional sheriff was shuffled into the deck of Patriot dogma and, in that world, dealt out mostly as an accepted fact. There it took its place alongside familiar Second Amendment rhetoric and a hard stance against the perceived "war" of urban elites and distant, unfeeling bureaucrats on the life of rural America.

Growing Their Turnips

David Ward, for one, wasn't buying any of it. He was still shaking his head two years later at how many people had uncritically bought into the notion of the constitutional sheriff. He finds the logic of it all baffling, and profoundly unconstitutional. "If the sheriff is the be-all and end-all, there's no need for us to have lawmakers. Based on their own argument I should have been able to arrest 'em, lock 'em down, and hang 'em for treason—just as sheriff."

That it all came out of the vile racist milieu of the Posse is something he thinks most people haven't put in the time to uncover. He sees Mack's and Ammon's references to civil rights heroes as clumsy attempts to further distance their movement's ideas from that freshly buried, disavowed racist legacy. He also sees the citations of the civil rights struggle as an effort to turn attention away from an issue a little closer to home for the Bundy Revolution: Cliven Bundy's widely circulated comments on freedom and slavery, captured on video in the days after the showdown in Toquop Wash.

Cliven had been giving one of his rambling informal addresses to a group of supporters under a tree out on the ranch one day in the spring of 2014. His monologue had turned to the oppressed condition of the American persons he referred to collectively as "the Negro." It turned out, oddly enough, that young Cliven had been in Los Angeles in 1965 and personally witnessed the Watts Riots. The way he had seen it, he told his followers, Watts had been an uprising for freedom and against bureaucracy. But then he had some more to add, further observations about "Negro" life. "I would see these little government houses," he said, describing driving through Las Vegas and North Las Vegas, "and in front of that government house the door was usually open and the older people and the kids, and there's always at least a half dozen people sitting on the porch. They didn't have nothing to do, they didn't have nothing for their kids to do . . ." What Cliven had seen on his drive-bys sounded an awful lot like good old-fashioned family life, old folks taking care of children, but it had bothered him, evidently, and as he held forth about it to his own extended family gathering, his imagination veered ever whiter, as he went sailing all the way around the racial American bend.

"And because they were basically on government subsidy, so now what do they do?" he continued. "They abort their young children, they put their young men in jail because they never learned how to pick cotton." It would seem like maybe that would have been ugly enough, but Cliven had still more. "And I've often wondered," he mused, "are they better off as slaves picking cotton, having family life and doing things, or are they better off under government subsidy?" A muffled voice off camera seemed to second his comparison. "Yeah," Cliven continued in response, "they didn't get no more freedom, they got less freedom, they had less family life and their happiness—you could see in their faces they wasn't happy, sitting on that concrete sidewalk. Down there they was probably growing their turnips! So that's all government, that's not freedom."

Growing their turnips. Cliven had held up yet another mirror for White America to drown in. To drown in and disavow. The fact that he was essentially regurgitating whole the more subtly racist anti–Great Society ideology of large swaths of the elected right wing of the last forty to fifty years wasn't going to help him any. He hadn't used the right code words. Even Sean Hannity of Fox News, who for weeks had been presenting Cliven as a hero in the struggle against an overreaching federal government, denounced him in the strongest language.

His son Ammon, with his open, empathetic manner, had proved a better public face for the movement. Not only was the Bundy patriarch's visage now synonymous with racism, but Cliven's is simply not the face of a messiah. He regularly looks as if he's contemplating a rock of dull pain in the center of his own skull: brow furrowed under his hat, his face is often bunched up in irritation—perhaps with the sun itself for all those summers it's tried to boil him and his cattle alive in their skins. Not so with Ammon. Eventually Cliven's inspired, bright-faced son would even be found citing, alongside Holy Scripture and the Constitution, the example of Martin Luther King Jr., carrying a marked-up copy of "Letter From Birmingham Jail" to conversations with the media and referencing the reverend's famous ideas about civil disobedience.

Dave Ward was unimpressed. "They are grasping at straws with Dr. King and Rosa Parks, using the Jedi mind trick to get them away from Cliven's comments. They say he's from another generation. Listen, my dad's eighty, I've never heard anything like that. That's the household Ammon and Ryan [Bundy] grew up in—and that's what he said to a reporter, to a camera. Imagine what was said behind closed doors in that house."

Clearly Ammon Bundy and Ryan Payne had not found an eager pupil in David Ward. The November 5 meeting had been, it seemed, something of a disappointment to them. As the conversation came to a close, the men assured Ward that they could bring thousands of people to town, something Ward knew would easily, instantly, overwhelm his tiny department. "We won't be able to control what they do," Dave remembered Payne saying of this invisible force. Soon after showing Ammon and Ryan out, the phone in his office rang. Sheriff Richard Mack was on the line. He wanted to talk to Ward about this Hammond case he'd been hearing about recently, and see if he could offer any advice on what could be done. David Ward's education was now fully under way; from here on out, the pressure would not let up.

A Cult up in There

On November 19, Ammon asked for another meeting with Ward. This time he brought more friends. Along with Bundy and Payne were a number of militia leaders from Oregon and Idaho; most of them were armed. While he noted all the guns with understandable alarm, Ward chose not to remind the men of the no outside firearms policy as he ushered them into the department's law library for a sit-down. "I was there to defuse the situation," he said. He wanted to avoid provoking an endless and irresolvable debate about the Second Amendment. Instead, he called for a little backup in case things went wrong. "All I had was one of the guys from the jail," he said. "I asked him to come in with me and stand in the corner and watch my back. Those guys aren't trained for a situation like that, but none of the deputies were available." Dispersed across the county's six and a half million acres, none of his four other deputies were anywhere nearby. "All I had was a retired cowboy, who was real good with a peashooter, in case it all went sideways."

Unless you've spent time around serious militia folks, it is difficult to understand just how much boisterous strut and military posturing they bring to every space they enter. It's as much in their carriage and in the language—full of the acronyms of their organizations, and military jargon and procedure—as it is in the arms they demonstrably and dutifully bear. The lingo alone is relentless. Nobody seems to ever research anything in the world of the militia; they "gather intel." Nobody goes to a protest action; they join up with "the boots on the ground."

Now here they were, inside the sheriff's department. These were most of the main militia characters who would play a side role in what would remain principally Ammon Bundy's show. They went around the room, Ward remembered. Each of the visitors "gave their resume, what they would bring to the table—basically telling me how tough they were."

One of the most outspoken of the visitors was Brandon Curtiss, leader of the Idaho III% militia. Curtiss was a small man in stature, but his presence was large. He had a big, square-jawed jar of a head, which he carried about that fall with the brashness and confidence of the ex-cop he was. In Ward's memory, Curtiss now told him, " 'What we do in this community will make Bunkerville look like small potatoes'—that's pretty close to a direct quote. And then he said, 'We're going to bring so much more to this community than you and your four deputies can handle.' And nobody in that room disputed him at all."

It wasn't all tough talk and ultimatums. There were moments of levity as well, self-conscious humor about the amped-up rhetoric of the scenario. One came between Dave and Ammon. Bundy was again exhorting Ward to rise and be a constitutional sheriff. "Ammon was saying, 'You have to wake up, Sheriff! You need to stand up! Your people are being oppressed!' He was getting worked up," Ward remembered. " 'Sheriff,' he says, 'we've had how many conversations? How many hours? Your words have not changed!'

" 'Well, in all fairness,' I said, 'I've talked with Ammon for eight hours now; Ammon's narrative hasn't changed either.' Then they all laughed—Ammon had a big old laugh, and he slapped me on the shoulder."

Despite the moments of good humor, the gathering was mostly an unnerving experience. "It was like a cult meeting up in there—I don't know how else to describe it," Dave told me. Up to November 19 he had hoped, somehow, that it could all be worked out in conversation, especially with Ammon. "The fact is, I didn't want trouble with Ammon. He seemed like under other circumstances he could be a likable guy. Up until then he just seemed misinformed."

After that meeting Dave came to understand that Ammon was not merely misinformed. "Ammon—it's strange," he added. "When you look him in the eyes, behind those eyes there's a naive innocence. But when you deal with him long enough you realize there's some creative genius there too, and some smooth-talking leadership."

*   *   *

After November 19, Ammon was also under pressure. At the meeting, Ward told him that he'd been informed by the Hammonds that they intended to report to prison as planned and were not interested in any scheme to interfere with their scheduled surrender. Around this time, Ammon also spoke with the family by phone and received the same message—with added details, he alleged, about how the federal government had produced enough fear in the heart of the family to drive a wedge between them and the hope of freedom he believed he and his friends represented. In that conversation,

Ammon said that Dwight had told him that the U.S. attorney's office had informed the family's lawyer that if they continued to associate with Ammon and friends, they would be detained early and placed in a less-desirable prison. This threat had been enough, Ammon claimed; the family let him know they would no longer be working with him and his allies. A few weeks later that rejection would be made more public, in a published letter from their attorney, disavowing Bundy and his friends and their efforts.

This was a difficult moment, but Ammon was not quite ready to pack up and go home. Having known only victory thus far, the Bundy Revolution was a feeling that needed to grow. Besides, Ammon was still certain that the Hammonds really wanted his help—or at least needed it, even if they said they didn't want it; the efforts of the feds to separate him from the family only confirmed that his foe was tyrannical. But without the private or public support of the Hammonds for being in the county, he and his friends looked more and more like invaders, outside agitators preaching what was hard to not see as open insurrection. It really didn't look good—as Ammon's own allies in the militia movement had begun to point out. These included the immensely influential founder of the national Oath Keepers militia, Stuart Rhodes, who had great sway over the militiamen who had already begun to come to Burns in support of Ammon's initial efforts to convince Ward of his constitutional obligations.

Under this new pressure, Ammon's strategy evolved in two directions. If the Hammonds had withdrawn their support for his more radical efforts, now those efforts became about more than just the Hammonds. At the same time, Ammon and his friends would need to reestablish local legitimacy—both in the eyes of Harney County and, maybe more importantly, in the eyes of the national Patriot community. That wider community was essential; if Ammon was to accomplish another miracle like the one of Bundy Ranch, he would need "the People" to come.

CHAPTER FIVE

The Beautiful Pattern

"Then We Must"

EACH SEPTEMBER, THE HARNEY COUNTY Fairgrounds Memorial Building
hosts exhibits of the local citizenry's best efforts in arts and crafts. The
stalls behind the building are filled with the year's prizewinning animals.
To the north, the fairgrounds grandstand rises over the rodeo arena. This is
the scene of the yearly fair's main events—horse races and all manner of
rodeo competition. Here men are thrown from bucking bulls and stallions.
Others leap off speeding horses, tackling calves and wrestling them in the
dust. The cowgirls and rodeo queens, all rhinestoned out in pink and
turquoise, whirl back and forth on their horses, making tight turns between
barrels and parading at a breakneck gallop before the crowd, with the banners
of the local sponsoring businesses—car dealership, print shop, feed store—
fluttering behind them.

On a winter night it's all very different. The parking lot of the hangar-like
Memorial Building is crusted over with ice and the silence of the stars. The
cold and the dark gather at the metal walls. But inside on December 15,
2015, despite the stark fluorescent lighting and the seasonal chill and gloom,
those who'd come to hear the evening's presentation—most too cold to take
off their winter coats—could still warm their hearts at the slow fire glowing
in the center of the room: Ammon Bundy.

Thanks to YouTube, we can all watch along from multiple angles as
Ammon sells revolution to his audience: fifty or sixty people, maybe fewer,
huddled around fold-out plastic tables. Ammon's up on some kind of holiday

stage set. Its decor offers a touchingly familiar—community center or grade-school lobby—shabbiness. White fluff is stuck here and there to represent snow. Wreaths are laid around holes cut into the drywall behind him; through them you can see twirling ceiling fans, battleship-gray walls, and more tubes of fluorescent light. The humble surroundings only add to the emotional intensity of Ammon's message this evening: up on that cheesy Christmas stage he's a real buckaroo of the heart, with the cowboy hat and boots, and the tears and cadences of sincerity to prove it.

It's a masterful performance: Ammon at his artlessly artful best. He's no yeller or haranguer; it's always that same tone of concern, delivered through heartfelt personal testimony. Land, the Constitution, his family's story, the Founding Fathers, the Hammonds—all of it is transmuted into emotion and then interwoven in the spell of urgency he casts on the room this night. Pacing the stage, making eye contact with everyone, he weaves all this feeling, along with himself and his listeners, into a grand narrative of American apocalypse and redemption, a tale, he informs his listeners, in which they have the potential to play an indispensable role.

His narrative tonight is made of many stories. He begins with an outline of the Hammond case—as he sees it—and then he tells the story of his own family: how once they were like the Hammonds but now are free. He talks about the Nevada court cases, the years his family and his neighbors struggled with the new grazing rules brought on by the tortoise crisis, how one by one all the neighboring ranchers gave up. More than once he dwells on these fellow ranchers who would not stand with Cliven and the Constitution, a detail that makes his voice vibrate with loss and disbelief. "And now, those ranchers' children, every single one of them, had to move to the cities. And they don't even know where their meat comes from. Their grandchildren don't even know where meat comes from," he adds, with incredulous sorrow. (The little bit of extra emotion here may be even more personal than it seems. Ammon Bundy himself hadn't directly lived from the land in a long time. While the ranch had remained in the family, he personally had been working and living elsewhere—running his own truck fleet maintenance business for years.) The Bundy story Ammon is telling is also a warning to the rural folks in the room with him tonight. "My dad begged 'em to stand. Every single one of 'em that would not stand on the constitutional principles, which I'm speaking about today—every single one of 'em lost their ranch. And there was only one rancher standing, one rancher left: that was my dad."

As Ammon continues, he gives the crowd a full course of Bundy peda-gogy. This night we move beyond the idea of the constitutional sheriff, to what are the core texts of Bundy dogma: the enclave clause and the property clause of the U.S. Constitution. It all boiled down to this: *the federal govern-ment had no right to own all this land.*

Walking back and forth on the stage, gesturing, sometimes taking out his Constitution, touching it, putting it back in his pocket, Ammon keeps moving like a preacher, or an inspirational entrepreneur deep in the throes of his own TED Talk. He explains that his father and his friends, as they were being hounded out of business by the new priorities of the feds (and Las Vegas and Clark County, though Ammon never mentions them), found the solution to all their problems right there in front of them, in their beloved Constitution. Article I, Section 8, Clause 17.

In Harney County in the coming year, those six words were to become a refrain that would either elicit knowing nods of the head or eye rolls and groans. In the coming weeks, Bundy adepts would regularly remove their Constitutions from their shirt pockets, maybe whap them in emphasis, open them up, and read the clause out like a passage of scripture. *Case closed.* The federal government, by its own founding charter, Ammon had taught them, had a very limited right to own a very limited amount of any land within a state. This meant that states like Oregon, where more than 50 percent of the land was federal, or Nevada, where it approached 90 percent, were essentially *occupied territories.* If local or state governments wouldn't stand up to stop this injustice and take back what had been taken from them, then someone else would have to do it.

"Whose ultimate duty is it?" Ammon asks the crowd. "The People's," a male voice says somewhere down there, off-screen. "It is the People's," Ammon repeats, seconding his good pupil. "If they will not do it, *then we must.*"

Article I, Section 8, Clause 17

Formally, what Ammon is doing is a very old move, terrifically Protestant, really. He's taking the holy words of the original document, that secular scripture with all its sacred aura, out of the hands of the priests—in this case, lawyers, judges, and bureaucrats—and returning it to the People, all the while filling the room with the Majesty of Law revealed. There's an evangelical quality to the performance that's no small part of Ammon's appeal; his illuminated readings of the Constitution take the form and, at moments, have the affective power of religious revival. As the evening wears on, the atmosphere of theo-legalistic magic in the room only gets thicker.

At one point in the evening he draws an imaginary line on the stage, illustrating the difference he sees between the unfreedom that the federal government has established on public land in the West and the freedom that exists on private property or on land controlled by one of the sovereign states. Back and forth he steps, between Tyranny and Freedom, across that magic invisible line, a border that divides not only imagined legal jurisdictions but also fundamental states of being. On the federal side, according to Ammon, there was no freedom; because of the government's misuse of it, the Constitution no longer applied and the People were subject to the tyranny of "territorial law." On the other side, where individual property and state's rights obtained, the People's Constitution was in effect, and Freedom still (precariously) reigned.

Ammon's little dance on the sad Christmas stage is legible because all of us understand the sovereign magic of a borderline—its absurdity and its terror. If you've ever been to an unfenced national border, it's been made even stronger for you. On one side of an invisible line is one nation, on the other side there is another. This, despite the bare fact that both sides are of the same landscape, the same earth, which is wholly indifferent to such human pretensions. My own experience of such borders has always occurred in deserts, where the presence of geologic time makes the puny aspirations of human creatures all the more piteous. That it is *illegal* to step across this invisible line without proper permission is so contrary to the evidence of the senses, so wholly imaginary, so vainglorious, it can make you laugh out loud. Yet, at the same time, we've all learned enough about the Law, and the force it keeps in reserve, to fear it—even those of us who are fortunate enough not to live furtively in its shadow, subject to profiling and deportation. Approaching a borderline of any kind, one will likely experience a tingle of holy dread, and perhaps look around—is anyone watching? Even if there is no law enforcement anywhere in sight, even if there are no visible cameras to be seen, no fences, no walls, the Aura of the Law will still be present. It is in us always, in our fear, as we watch ourselves through its eyes.

This night Ammon proposes something powerfully liberating. He is saying that all this awesome legal magic, this fearful presence of the Law inside us, belongs, in the last instance, not to the Law, not to the federal government, but to the Sovereign People—and therefore to the persons in the room with him. Sovereignty is *theirs*, Liberty is *theirs*, and, most importantly, the Constitution is *theirs*—not just to admire and be thankful for, but to *interpret and enforce.* Tonight Ammon and his friend Ryan Payne are asking no less. They, the People, must become the reality effect of the Law.

*   *   *

Watching Ammon's inspirational performance, it can be easy to lose track of the fact that the Bundy family's immediate legal argument doesn't make that much sense. The enclave clause—Article I, Section 8, Clause 17—on which rests much of his justification for the people of the western states to take the law into their own hands, doesn't say what Ammon feels it does. Here is the clause in its entirety. It's part of a long litany of things "The Congress shall have the power" to do.

> To exercise exclusive Legislation in all Cases whatsoever, over such District (not exceeding ten Miles square) as may, by Cession of Particular States, and the Acceptance of Congress, become the Seat of the Government of the United States, and to exercise like Authority over all Places purchased by the Consent of the Legislature of the State in which the Same shall be, for the Erection of Forts, Magazines, Arsenals, dock-Yards, and other needful Buildings.

This does not lend itself so easily to Ammon's exegesis. The ten-square-miles "gotcha" that Bundy and friends would cite is generally understood to refer specifically to the District of Columbia. Beyond that, the clause is about other government buildings, offices, ports, and garrisons, and about *"exclusive" legislative power* over these. Most of our public lands are not under exclusive federal jurisdiction—they are not "enclaves"—but are rather under simultaneous federal and state jurisdiction. This is even true of most military bases at this point. The federal government's right to own or not own land is not mentioned here at all. Unsurprisingly, the Supreme Court has repeatedly rejected enclave-clause arguments against the federal government's right to land ownership. Most recently, in a case from the 1970s that began in a conflict over management of a federal grazing allotment, New Mexico tried to use the enclave clause to argue that the federal government had no right to impede its program to round up the wild burros that a recent federal law had ordered the U.S. Department of the Interior to protect. The Supreme Court rejected the state's logic. Still, Ammon and friends, by no means easily discouraged, argue that if other kinds of federal lands are not explicitly named in the clause, then there can be no other such lands. They simply do not exist—as Ammon's father had said, in the heady days of the Bundy Ranch standoff, of the federal government itself.

While the enclave clause is the central text of the Bundy tutorial that the folks at the fairgrounds are receiving on the night of December 15, Ammon also makes idiosyncratic use of the so-called property clause (Article IV, Section 3, Clause 2). By limiting, in his interpretation, the clause to its application to territorial law, which he must do—otherwise it's fairly damning to his enclave-clause argument—Ammon finds a way to use this passage to explain the "tyranny" that ensues when the Constitution is no longer the ultimate arbiter of law in the land. Here is the property clause itself, in its entirety:

> The Congress shall have power to dispose of and make all needful Rules and Regulations respecting the Territory or other Property belonging to the United States; and nothing in this Constitution shall be so construed as to Prejudice any Claims of the United States, or of any particular State.

Mainstream arguments against Ammon's enclave-clause interpretation generally cite this clause as constitutional recognition of the federal government's right to ownership of property other than that explicitly described in the enclave clause. It helps Ammon's contrary interpretation that when he reads the property clause out loud that night at the fairgrounds, he stops early on, at the word "Territory," and closes his Constitution—erasing more than half the clause, and all that might seem to contradict his claims.

And his claims are drastic. The feds, Ammon says, are—in defiance of the Constitution—*using territorial law on public lands*. This also means, according to Ammon, that "you are no longer protected" by the Constitution when you are on federal public land. This is what his invisible line, and his ritual hopping back and forth across it, between Freedom and Unfreedom, was meant to illustrate.

Understanding what Ammon is doing with this argument is key to understanding the legalistic magic at the core of the Bundy insurrection, as well as the faith that Bundy Ranch was truly now the Freest Place on Earth.

The misreading of the property clause helps to slingshot Ammon and all his friends and family well beyond the wicked perversions they see in the recent federal government's misuse of the Constitution into something much grander: the secret American formula for the creation of Freedom.

The Beautiful Pattern

Ammon and his family and many of his friends believe that through the proper use of the same legal magic it now abused, the United States had, in the past, successfully taken land and turned it into Freedom. This magical interpretation of history (a history actually founded on the taking of land by force from the continent's Native inhabitants) prepares the way for the onto-logical and legal transformations that Ammon and his friend Ryan Payne were to attempt in Harney County that winter. As Ammon explains to the small crowd in that big, cold room at the fairgrounds, it's all about restoring what he sees as "the growth pattern of this country"—which is, in Ammon's vision, "a beautiful pattern," whose ultimate purpose is the creation not just of prosperity but also of Liberty. Given the precarious state of American freedom in the West, *We the People*, Ammon believed, were going to have do it now for themselves.

Ammon, patient pedagogue, explains it all to his audience:

> The growth pattern of this country was that you had the states, they were sovereign independent states, and they united together. The growth pattern is you have territories that were not states—that territory is under the jurisdiction of the federal government, and as Article IV says, that they make all the rules and regulations—but as soon as that territory gets populated enough to become a state and as soon as they're enacted into the union as a state, no longer at that moment does the federal government have the right to exer-cise territorial law. No longer. Now, that state is fully protected under the U.S. Constitution, and the people become sovereign and have their rights within the state. That's the growth pattern, and if we didn't have these—I guess, wicked men, if you want to say—call it what you want, it's a *beautiful pattern*. Because what can happen is our territories—we can obtain land, whether it's through a war or whether we purchased it, we can obtain land that could be a

territory. The people can go in and begin to populate that territory, and it can become a state. We could do that across the whole continent, across the whole world. Right? And make people free across the whole world. That was the intent.

This is a very creative interpretation and an emotionally powerful one. It's also historically inaccurate, reading, anachronistically, the full-blown imperial rhetoric of Manifest Destiny from the nineteenth century backward into the more modest eighteenth-century intentions of the Constitution. In doing so, it also reverses some of the central purposes of that document and the men who wrote it, purposes that anticipated and contradicted Ammon's purposes centuries in advance, by giving the federal government, among so many other things, the authority and power to crush the very sort of rural revolution he was proposing tonight. Reading the words of the founders themselves, the conclusion is inescapable: one of the primary instigating impulses for the creation of the Constitution was to establish a federal power strong enough to directly put down spontaneous rural insurrections against perceived overreaching and oppressive government policies. As much as anything else, it was a fear of surplus popular sovereignty in the years immediately following the Revolution—expressed both legally in the new state assemblies and extralegally in militias and mobs—that drove the political elite back to Philadelphia to draw up a new plan of union in 1787. Their name for what they most feared in their contemporary political world is a word that almost all of us today, whether we find ourselves in the right, left, or center of political life, speak with veneration: *Democracy*. Not so for the Founding Fathers, who often equated the word with the frightful rule of the mob—on the streets and in state governments—which the Constitution was explicitly written to curb.

That is not at all how Ammon understands that sacred document he carries in his shirt-front pocket; but, in engaging in a part-willful, part-inadvertent misunderstanding of American history, Ammon Bundy is far from alone. Contemporary American life is full of such misunderstandings. We might ask how it is that Alexander Hamilton, a man who despised the rabble and their democracy and made it his life's work to centralize financial, political, and military power in the hands of an elite financier and governing class, came to be the hero of a tremendously popular hip-hop musical. Or consider how the contemporary Tea Party, dedicated to the idea that America was founded on opposition to "big government" and taxes, has loved to trot out images and impersonators of George Washington at any opportunity. This despite the fact that Washington famously saw among the greatest immediate purposes and achievements of the Constitution—aside from its creation of federal power capable of crushing populist rural insurrection—the authority it gave the new federal government to levy and collect taxes directly from the American populace. The Constitution has long been an object of fantasy. As with any holy scripture, we are all able to find support in its pages for whatever we want to think. Americans have been doing it almost since the ink was dry.

Just like Americans have always done, Ammon was reading his own history of America backward into its foundational text. And now he was calling the citizens of Harney County to action in defense of this interpretation. What he called "a beautiful pattern," and its restoration, was Ammon's answer to everything, starting with the local issue that had brought them here that night: the Hammond family. What's happened to the Hammond family, he says, is simply "a jurisdictional issue." Because Oregon is a state, it is not possible for the Hammonds to have violated federal land-use laws, because *there can be no such federal laws* in a state. If the Beautiful Pattern and, with it, the proper alchemical power of individual state sovereignty were restored, the Hammonds' problems would simply vanish—and with them, all the problems of Harney County. Economic and political freedom would be instantly recovered. A stand for the Beautiful Pattern would take care of everything Ammon promised: no more regulations, no more ranching or drilling restrictions, no more EPA. All it took was the people standing up and saying, "This is not a territory"—and federal property would be federal property no more. And with that, a greater change would come, that change of feeling and of being that he and his friends had experienced down in Toquop Wash, outside Bunkerville, on April 12, 2014. "It puts the power back into the people's hands," Ammon says to his rapt audience, "and it creates freedom, and we saw that at the Bundy Ranch. We have that example that it can be done."

It's witchy stuff—and it includes a convoluted emotional time travel that has become increasingly standard in the supercharged politics of the nation. 2016 was going to be a back-to-the-future, make-America-great-again kind of year. But unlike Donald Trump's slogan, Ammon's Beautiful Pattern is not just another name for the idealized past; it also names the imperfect past's dream of an expansive future. In a nation where people of all political stripes increasingly have a hard time imagining any kind of positive future at all, this is powerful magic—at least for those who somehow imagine that things like Manifest Destiny and the American Revolution might *belong* or *refer* to them.

* * *

All this thick temporality and power is flowing out of Ammon as feeling on the night of December 15. By the end of his big pitch to the people in that hangar down at the fairgrounds, it is beginning to leak from his body. Hot, salty tears spill down his face as the big-hearted rancher's son conjures once more the Battle of Bunkerville, making sure the people in the room know the extent of the miracle in the wash and what it effected in the life of his family, as he prepares what amounts to nothing less than a plea for open insurrection.

"We are free to ranch," he intones, as the tears openly flow. "We are free to move about. We are a free people on that ranch. And that's because we stood on the correct principles and the people came around us, they defended us. And we went to ranching, and that's what we're doing. I'm pleading with us, with you today, to do the same thing."

He is ready now to make the first public local articulation of an impulse that would soon morph, in a little more than two weeks, into the armed takeover of the Malheur National Wildlife Refuge. He pauses a moment, as his eyes move about the room making moist and earnest contact with the People one by one.

"It is now that we must stand. And if we do it right and if we do it now, we don't have to do it with bloodshed. We do not have to do it with anything but honor. But if we do it right, we can restore the Constitution back to this county, and it can be an example for all the other counties across the nation."

At this point his voice begins to crack with the intensity of what he is proposing: "I'm telling you I know—I know with everything that's inside of me: that the time is now, this is the place, and that *you* are the people."

Committee of Safety

After his teary final pitch, Ammon yields the floor to his friend Ryan Payne. Slowly Payne circles the room, pacing among all those fold-out tables as he reads aloud from that other foundational document—the revolutionary one— the Declaration of Independence. When he finally ascends the sad Christmas stage with its wreaths and fraying cotton fluff, he's reading the most famous lines: "We hold these truths to be self-evident, that all men are created equal."

His dramatic entry aside, Payne is not a natural public speaker. He lacks the ease and charisma of his friend Ammon, but shirt tucked in, pistol, as always, on his belt, he soldiers on. Ryan is here to give the nuts and bolts of what he and Ammon are proposing—that the people in this room begin the process of forming a new governmental body for the county this very night. To this end, in an awkward PowerPoint presentation—he has no projector, so it's just him reading slides from his laptop—Ryan unveils a key mechanism of American colonial insurrection for immediate repurposing: the Committee of Safety. It's a form ripped from the pages of the nation's foundation, modeled along the lines of the self-organized committees of colonial America, many of which had strong roles in the rebellion against the crown. Looking more like a night-school instructor than a militia man this evening in his khakis and button-down, Payne outlines the colonial-era history of the Committees of Safety, going all the way back to the seventeenth century, to tell his audience how a Boston committee once arrested a particularly unpopular British governor during the Restoration.

From here Payne goes on to give the room a full serving of contemporary militia ethos, with its apocalyptic communitarianism. His own organization was originally called Operation Mutual Aid, and sometimes Ryan sounds like all he wants is to reinstitute neighborliness, albeit a heavily armed one. "We lose sight sometimes in trying to satisfy ourselves of the importance of coming together in order to pursue our happiness. And so when we get wrapped up in our own individual pursuits, we begin to ignore each other . . . As a people right now we are more disconnected than we have ever been. We are relying on interactions through social media and electronic means, especially the younger generation, my generation. And we're not communicating with our neighbor anymore. We're not talking to each other, we're not addressing each other directly," he laments. When he goes on to ask the crowd to close their eyes and imagine disaster in their community, and how they and their neighbors might respond, his friend Ammon interrupts. Disaster preparedness is not the real purpose here tonight, and the energy of the meeting is beginning to slacken. Leaping back up onto the stage and pointing to his watch, Ammon abruptly cuts off Ryan's presentation. The People have the info they need, and it's time to get down to the business at hand—a vote to form the committee and elect its officers.

If there had ever been any doubt about the revolutionary character of what Ammon and Ryan were proposing, what Ammon says next should have wiped it away. "I'm not going to dance around what we're talking about here," he says to the room. "We're talking about removing these unconstitutional agencies from Harney County." Now he's showing all his cards. "We have across the U.S. a people that will stand with you. I've already explained that, and I am confident in that. But the thing is, it's not necessarily right for us or the people to come in here and make a stand without the people forming and being in control of it. That's what this Committee of Safety is."

Ammon has given a very compelling performance to an audience disposed to hear his message. Soon the votes are counted and the committee is born—and no one seems to be in opposition. Next, officers are nominated and, without much ceremony, selected. It's disorienting to realize what's just happened. Here in their own community hall, Ammon had succeeded in convincing these people to create what pretty much has to be called a provisional revolutionary government—or at least a precursor to such a form. In the days that followed, members would find, somewhat to their surprise, that their brand-new committee already had its own website—full of facts and links about its powers, origins, and purposes, along with statements they hadn't yet approved. The newly elected officers would have to get the password from Ammon.

CHAPTER SIX

Oath Magick

"Daddy Swore an Oath"

As December wore on, more denizens of Ammon's Patriot FaceWorld were trickling into the county. Some of these folks were of considerably different temperament than mild-mannered Ammon. Jon Ritzheimer was one of the more widely known and more troubling of these newcomers. Before coming to Burns, the young Iraq War veteran had ended up on the national news for leading an armed protest outside a Muslim community center in his home state of Arizona. At the rally he'd sported a FUCK ISLAM shirt, the principal product of his online business, Rogue Infidel. In the coming months he'd recant on the shirts and claim, in emotional videos posted to the internet, to regret the whole thing. It wasn't that he'd mellowed, exactly; around the same time he'd also been making threats to personally arrest a Michigan senator who'd supported the Iran nuclear deal, an act he promised to follow up with more arrests, including a citizen's arrest of the president if necessary. A scroll through his internet videos reveals, unsurprisingly, an emotionally volatile man. Sometimes he's ranting, angry and shirtless, at the camera, but in other videos you can find him in happier moods, like the one where he cheerily shoots up a Koran—with a pink rifle, for the added humiliation factor—alongside his friend Blaine Cooper. Cooper, originally named Stanley Hicks, had made his own contribution to the mini-genre of social media Koran-desecration videos; in his, he'd wrapped some Koran pages in bacon and "roasted" them. Next he shot the whole book with a compound bow and burned that too. By December, both these men were being seen regularly around town. Ritzheimer was spotted following a BLM employee in the Safeway; his unidentified companion shouted threats of following her home and burning down her house. Dave Ward reported being followed by Ritzheimer and Cooper around another store; at the time, the sheriff was Christmas shopping with his eight-year-old son.

While Ritzheimer seemed to cause plenty of turmoil in person around town, the true focus of his public engagement remained where all the real action was, in the new incubator of all America's ugly and unruly feelings: the World Wide Web. In the weeks between his arrival in town and the Bundy Revolution's big strategic move into the Harney Basin, he shot a number of videos. These were some of the strangest, most emotionally extravagant, and, in the case of one video in particular, most watched documents of the entire occupation saga. This is no small feat; he had a tremendous amount of competition. The hours of web documentation shot at Malheur, if anyone were ever really able to gather all the footage and splice it end to end, would likely rival or even surpass the actual event in total duration.

A video from late December went viral and made Jon Ritzheimer a favorite target of comedians and internet wits during the early days of the occupation. His gift for high drama made him irresistible; that gift is on display from the moment he hits record. Even before he begins speaking, he's pulling back his head, breathing in deeply, trying to contain all the emotion. He's in the cabin of his truck, so the sonic effects of all this feeling—and all this breathing—are amplified. (Parked cars make excellent impromptu sound booths, and are a favored location for Patriot video-missives.) "This is going to be one of the tougher videos I've had to make," he begins, already struggling to get the words out, eyes already tearing up. As we "eavesdrop" on this video he's posted for the wide world to watch, Ritzheimer directly addresses his family, telling his wife how proud he is "of the mother you've become" and explaining to his daughters how "Daddy swore an oath," which is why he's been away so long. "You are only three and five now, and you have no idea," he says, shaking his head with the weight of it all. There's more silence, more tears, a heavy, dramatic sigh, and another look away before he turns back to the camera and brandishes his pocket Constitution. "Your daddy swore an oath," he repeats, wagging the pamphlet in the foreground. "He swore an oath to protect and defend the Constitution against all enemies foreign and domestic. And that's why he couldn't be with you on Christmas."

It can be hard not to laugh when he lands on *Christmas*—hard not to laugh at all the staged feeling, no matter how genuine it may also have been. As Ritzheimer's holiday message found its pathways through the ether, many would be laughing—a lot—and passing it on. Some people didn't just laugh. The internet responded rapidly with the giddy malice of parody; the imitable form of Ritzheimer's video made it all too easy. In early 2016, men responding to the hashtag #DaddySworeAnOath hopped in their own cars to make their own oaths: pledges to be a better lover "to your mother"; to return books to the library; or to go down to the strip club "to give these dollars to Sinnamon with an *S*." The parodies were heavy on the silences, the breathing in, the tearing up. Across America, thanks to Ritzheimer, men were sitting alone in their cars and pretending to have feelings.

Parody aside, the level of overwhelming emotion in Ritzheimer's many online communiqués makes it hard to be a witness to him: it's a little like watching a stranger in desperate mourning, or a child in the throes of feelings he can't control or understand. It's easy to imagine Ritzheimer as a child. He's a small man physically, overtaken at times by tears, storms of rage, spasms of righteousness and puerile obscenity. His shiny, egg-shaped skull adds to the impression; it seems a full size too large for his body, like many a screen actor's. And while Ritzheimer may not be the most articulate speaker, his many silences are pure theater. Throughout his "Daddy Swore an Oath" video, his face shifts in anguish or disgust as words fail him yet again, or as he performs the full weight of the failure of language to express the size of what he has to say to us. Sometimes it's simply because he seems to never have learned all that much about what was actually behind the particular cause he'd so forcefully embraced. He runs out of details very quickly. It didn't really matter though. He had just enough talismanic syllables—*Freedom, BLM, Tyranny, Oath*—to get him out of his sinkholes of silence and on to what seemed to be his true point: his death. *I'm ready to lay down my life* was the main message I heard in Ritzheimer's Malheur missives. *I'm ready to die. Are you?*

*   *   *

It's disorienting to recognize how, in writing this book, I've become entirely used to watching men publicly declare their readiness, even eagerness, to die. Sometimes, as I peruse the hours and hours of video of the occupation, I don't even notice that it's happened again—the pledge is so constant. Ritzheimer supplements the weight and meaning of his own oath with the oath from the final lines of the Declaration of Independence, the part right before the unrolling of all those glorious, foundational white men's names: "We mutually pledge to each other our lives, our fortunes, and our sacred honor," he reads. Having joined his troubled American life, ritually, to those of the most magically significant of all Americans, he stares again in silence at the camera, eyes reddened, before closing the pamphlet and turning away.

I asked David Ward about all the oath-taking going down in Harney County that fall. He's a man familiar with oath magic. As a sheriff and a military veteran, he's taken some very solemn oaths, but in the fall of 2015, all this oath-taking had started to seem to him like the liturgical magic of some kind of death cult. The Bundyites, he thought, "were setting up Ammon as a prophet." As a devout Christian, he'd begun to find this very troubling. While he had still taken all the official oaths in question, something about it all didn't seem right to him theologically. One passage in particular from the scriptures gnawed at him. He quoted some of it to me, and later I looked up the rest. It was from the Gospel of St. Matthew:

> But I tell you, do not swear an oath at all: either by heaven, for it is God's throne; or by the earth, for it is his footstool; or by Jerusalem, for it is the city of the Great King. And do not swear by your head, for you cannot make even one hair white or black. All you need to say is simply "Yes" or "No"; anything beyond this comes from the evil one.

He'd also tried to remind Bundy supporters—who often harangued him about his oaths as a sheriff and soldier—that, leaving points of Christian doctrine aside, the oaths in question didn't really say exactly what Ammon and Ryan said they did. For one, the military oath of service included a key passage about swearing to heed the orders of the president. "Those guys didn't like Barack Obama, so they leave that part out."

The Great Unfuck

There's another, less-known video of Ritzheimer's from around this time that I actually enjoyed watching. The more I watched this one, the stranger it got—I found it had effects well beyond Ritzheimer's Patriot intentions. Its lack of deathly oath magic was a plus—nobody swears any oaths or promises to die. Also, Jon's outdoors in this one, and that seems to be a good thing for his mood.

He's pulled his truck out into the desert and parked it under an especially craggy and regal-looking butte, its coating of snow only adding to its aloof, aristocratic air. Dressed in desert combat fatigues, Jon has an assault rifle slung across his back. He's not alone this time; another camo'd-out dude is standing in the snowy sagebrush holding up a big colorful map of the United States—yellow, pink, green, and blue. A third compatriot, Arizona militiaman Joe O'Shaughnessy, watches in the foreground, bemused, as Ritzheimer launches into his routine. Let's call it the *Great American Unfuck*, because that—*unfucking*, as he'll explain—is what he and the boys are here to do.

First, though, he needs to locate himself, and all of us, on the earth and on the map. To *unfuck*, you've got to know where you stand. He's pointing at the sky, seeming to use the sun to orient himself in relation to the map, even as we see the sun is shining dimly behind him, smeared and grayed by a thin layer of cloud. "We're here," he says. "Yeah, we're here in Oregon, and the mission is to *UNFUCK allllll* of this."

As he says this, his gloved hands sweep diagonally southeast across the continent. "So . . . I'm hoping the rest of the militiamen and everyone out there is ready cuz, uh," he concludes, "we're going to *initiate this mission*."

Next, pleased with himself, he just does it all over again. "We're here in Oregon," he repeats, to the chuckles of his buddies, pointing to the sky again and then, again, the map. "Yep," he says, as if confirming that they definitely aren't lost. "We're *here* in Oregon, and we're gonna unfuck *ALLLLLLLL this*." Again, his dark-gloved hands move like cloud shadows across the map, gliding west to east across the continent, pulled by his elongation of "*ALL*" until the spell is complete, punctuated by the sibilant precision of "*this*."

I say "spell" because, however improvised and dumb whatever it is Ritzheimer and friends are doing, and it is both, this is some kind of rite, and all who watch are participants in its hokey witchery. Magic is always at least a little hokey, but the more I watch, the more it occurs to me that whatever is meant by *unfucking* has also got to be some seriously occult stuff. *An undoing of the fucked?*—it certainly *sounds* elemental. Then there's this: in the movement Ritzheimer traces across the map, he's recapitulating, in reverse, the arc of Manifest Destiny, the path of Ammon's Beautiful Pattern, the old route of the Oregon Trail. What would unfucking this entail—its dis-conception? I know he means something else, maybe the opposite—more like a reenactment, a *restoration* of Ammon's Beautiful Pattern, but it's not really what he's done.

At this point my cinema-colonized imagination takes over: all those would-be pioneers who died out there along the way—do they spring back to life in some other universe, reassemble out of the dust into coherent flesh, walking backward, zombied-out, to the east, as Jon traces the great messianic reversal, and rewinds America, erasing it? As I hit play again and again, another witchy thing is happening to me. It takes a while for me to notice, but with each viewing, the silent world around Ritzheimer and his friends gets more present. Soon my attention is riveted to the craggy rim of the basalt bench. That butte lurking above them begins to leak in from the background to take over the whole frame. By my fifth or sixth time through the clip, I'm not listening to Ritzheimer at all anymore. More than that, it's like I actually can't hear him, or even see him. Fucked or unfucked, all I see is stone.

Harry Reid and the Solar Chinese

Folks in Burns probably wouldn't have found such pleasure, or such magical relief, in Ritzheimer's video unfucking in December 2015. Around town, he and his friends were only more present. And then in very late December, maybe the single most obnoxious—and proudly so—figure of the Bundy Revolution rolled into town to join them. Patriot internet broadcaster and all around man-child of the American Apocalypse, Peter Santilli had driven all the way from his hometown of Cincinnati to document the launch of what he called Operation Hammond Freedom. It was time for others to do the same, was Santilli's message. "You need to get in your car and come out here," he told his followers. If you had any objections to the idea, you could just "shut your cake-hole!" It was time for real patriots to "staff up" and get to Oregon to protect the Constitution.

Santilli is what they call a shock jock; he's got the liquid-gravel radio voice and the endless reservoir of verbal energy, antic perversity, and masculine rage that the gig entails. His programs are a frantic outpouring of indignation, banter, conspiracy, obscenity, sarcasm, puerile goofery, and doom. His obscenity can also veer from the infantile aggression and predictable misogyny of the genre into the sort of explicit violent fantasy that gets you investigated by the Secret Service. Before Bundy Ranch, he was best known for some especially vile comments he'd made about Hillary Clinton; in the middle of a rant, he'd fantasized in detail about executing Clinton for what he saw as her many crimes (Benghazi, etc.) by shooting her "right in the vagina."

It's not hard to imagine how Santilli was to become perhaps the most actively detested of the men the Bundy Revolution brought to Burns. During his time covering the Malheur events, Santilli was everywhere. He got himself thrown out of a community meeting for interrupting a speaker; sheriffs escorted him to the door while the crowd cheered. During his livestream from another town hall gathering, Santilli interposes his own face in the screen and begins miming fellatio while a local woman is speaking emotionally about her community. In another video he mocked the granddaughter of Judge Steve Grasty, the county's highest official. Mimicking the tears the teenager had cried when she'd spoken out at a community meeting about the occupation's atmosphere of fear, Santilli accused her grandfather of having "prostituted" her for his political aims.

It was not much talked about in the coverage of the occupation, but the at times insufferable macho posturing that came to town with the Bundy Revolution and its militia friends was another thing people in the county recalled about the occupation. It seemed that some of the unsolicited education Burns was getting that fall and winter was in the ugly, persistent role that misogyny plays in the lives of men seeking to matter.

Beyond his ugly shock-jock antics, Santilli was a populist wild card of the right-wing variety that mainstream America would learn more about in 2016. He'd been a major player in the Bundy Ranch standoff. His footage of an early confrontation between the BLM and the family—the one where Ammon's aunt had been thrown to the ground and Ammon repeatedly tased—had gone viral in Patriot World. Maybe more than any other single piece of media, it had been responsible for drawing the hundreds of militiamen and other Patriot types to the ranch in April 2014.

Outrage at police violence gave a hint of a different sort of antiauthority coherence to Santilli's politics. In 2015, he'd traveled to Baltimore to document the African American community uprising against police abuse in the aftermath of the horrific beating death of Freddie Gray. His livestream footage of young unarmed protesters fearlessly confronting phalanxes of heavily armored police made for genuinely stirring viewing. Not all his white political allies in the Oath-Keeping militia milieu were happy that he'd chosen to support a black uprising against law enforcement, but he was undeterred. It seemed that, to Santilli, most events of the current day were confirmation that a mass roundup of Americans was impending, if it hadn't already begun. Soon, no matter who you were, *they* would be coming for *you*. "Where are your rights?" the intro to his program asks. "They are wherever you are willing to draw a line and say, 'You cannot come across this line or I'll kill you': that's where your rights are." In the world of his broadcasts, the time for such showdowns had already arrived. To Santilli, Harney County was the latest battleground in a rhetorical war against the rule of government, big business, and the military-industrial complex—what he called the New World Order.

Along with the far right's antic-aggro drive, Santilli brought to Malheur its seemingly inexhaustible engine of political folk expression: conspiracy. As Samantha, the café owner, had learned, conspiracy was a huge part of the Bundy Revolution. Santilli wasn't the origin of all the different conspiracy theories she'd counted off on her fingers, but he was a one-man distribution center for many of them. What's *really* going on? he asked of the world. The answer, Pete told his audience, was that it was even worse than they thought. And it was about time they did something about it.

* * *

Conspiracy is a hard thing to talk about. Too easy to legitimize, too easy to dismiss. Regardless, the famous "paranoid style of American politics" is not going away. Not least because many conspiracies of our day are founded on gross distortions of buried intimations about the real cruelties and indifferences of our global economy and political order. Take, for example, a favorite conspiracy of Santilli's Patriot milieu—let's call this one "Harry Reid and the Solar Chinese."

It goes something like this: Reid, the immensely powerful (now retired) senator from Nevada, along with his eldest son, are hooked up with the powers that be in China to get a hold of the Bundy Ranch in order to put in huge industrial-scale solar projects. The whole protecting-the-tortoise business was fake; everything was fake. It was all about Harry Reid's land grab. That's why the feds rolled into Bunkerville in 2014, that's why Cliven and his boys were hauled off to prison two years later, and—somewhat contradictorily—that's why Reid got his pal Obama to designate Gold Butte (which encompassed some of Cliven's former grazing allotments) as a national monument a month before Reid retired to private life.

Factually, it's nonsense. Harry Reid was never personally trying to take Cliven Bundy's grazing lands. Neither was he, as one Malheur occupier told me outside federal court in Portland, personally paying environmentalists to protest Ammon and his friends. There are substantial environmental and cultural reasons to protect Gold Butte, many of them involving the local Moapa-Paiute tribe that Reid has worked closely with over the years. And the desert tortoise really is in need of protection—if we want it to survive—as are the fragile habitats of the Mojave.

Yet the theory wasn't invented wholly out of nothing; conspiracy theories are often founded in nuggets of fact, around which fears and desires congeal. Reid was actually involved in a large-scale Chinese solar project in Clark County, and some of the details about how that deal was negotiated did bring serious scrutiny. But the project in question never went through. It was dead by 2013, a year before the Bundy Ranch standoff. The land was nowhere near Bunkerville in the first place, but 180 miles away, in Laughlin, Nevada, near Reid's hometown of Searchlight.

Still, the theory bloomed—based on old articles about the Laughlin project and spread diligently by conspiracy theorist Alex Jones's InfoWars channel. It's not hard to understand why. It's a lot easier—and faster—to say that Harry wants Cliven's lands for the Chinese than it is to say that Harry Reid and the courts and federal agencies and others in power don't seem to care so much about tortoises and their habitat when it comes to getting approval for large-scale solar projects or Las Vegas real estate development. It's easier to say Harry wants Cliven dead or in prison—because $$$, because Foreigners—than it is to say that in the shifting priorities of a vast, complicated society and global economy, Cliven and his way of life have become anachronisms that the powers that be, of whom Harry Reid is but one fleeting face, have determined can no longer be indulged. It's a lot easier to say that Harry Reid is stealing Cliven's land for the coming Communist New World Order than it is to say that, in the current dispensation of the world, Cliven Bundy is not, nor will ever be again, a priority. Easier to say that this is a corrupt federal land grab than to accept that the land had never really belonged wholly to Cliven in the first place, and that his rights to its use came from an older dispensation. Human dispensations always change, and when they do, what happens is rarely entirely just or fair. "It's a situation where not everybody gets what they want, and so a lot of the decisions that we make are compromises," a BLM official would say to reporters from *Frontline* years after the standoff. There were winners and losers, and the

Bundys were the losers. But all that is too vague and sad, and it takes a hell of a lot longer to explain.

I'd venture that's the real cultural function of conspiracy theory; it compresses the indifference of an incomprehensibly vast set of economic and political priorities into immediately understandable shapes crafted by desire. The dark desire *They* have for *You*. How much better to believe that Harry Reid *wants* Cliven—even if what he wants is his imprisonment or death (the irascible Reid has called the Bundys and their supporters "domestic terrorists," a scary thing to be called in post-9/11 America). Better that than to accept that the contemporary world and its globalized economy have no real interest at all in the Bundys—nor much use for so many of the people who would come to see themselves reflected in their struggle. Better to be wanted badly than not wanted at all.

The sad and often crushing truth is that part of becoming what we call an adult in our present world order is accepting the extent to which we are absolutely replaceable in the global economy—if there is any place for us in that impersonal edifice at all. In a mass cultural and political order that has tended more and more to frame human meaning mostly or exclusively in economic terms, it quickly becomes visible that very few of us—individually— matter much. In his amped-up, hyper-macho articulation of the Bundy struggle, Santilli, like other conspiracy theorists and right-wing shock jocks, spoke directly to some of those out there among us—largely white and male, perhaps underemployed or divorced or both—who find themselves bitterly hanging on to the last threads of a privilege that was always tenuous at best, folks who have never fully accepted what is so difficult for all of us to accept: ultimate systemic indifference to our individual lives. For Santilli, the next step was clear: after waking to the dark truth of the plot against you and your fellow Americans, it was time to stand up for Liberty, to make your worthless life matter. *Put your life on the line and be a patriot. Shut your cakehole and come to Burns.*

People People

By December 30, Santilli was set up in town, having made the drive from Cincinnati in impressive time. On December 31, he conducted an intensive interview with Ryan Payne from his cramped wood-paneled room at the Silver Spur Motel. Surrounded by western kitsch, Payne and Santilli sat facing each other, passing masculine intensity back and forth. In Harney County, Payne explained to his eager interlocutor, the federal government's abuses had reached a crisis point.

"Now, once it breaches the county level of protection, now the Constitution is in full violation. *We the People*'s government at all levels has now turned against the People." Payne explained. But all hope wasn't lost, he added. "Now when they [county government officials] don't uphold that oath to defend the Constitution and uphold it, then the People are not left without remedy. We don't have to forever—you know—take it in the rear from the federal government . . ."

Excited, Santilli can't hold back. "You know what, that's a great point," he interrupts. Apologizing to Payne for butting in, Pete takes over. "What made Bundy Ranch successful, when We the People stood up and we realized that that remedy—OK—it's a peaceful remedy, it's a self-determination where we step out there and say the whole system has broken down, we're the last line of defense here. But we were ultimately the most powerful people out there in the dirt at Bundy Ranch." Pale and stern, Ryan blinks and nods along while Santilli talks on, gesturing and rocking slightly in his motel room chair. "When you just said that it actually gave me— I literally felt energized when you said that," he continues. "When our elected officials don't defend and protect us and do their job as per you know what they were elected to do . . . that the buck doesn't stop there, it's We the People that are going to be holding them accountable. We'll step in and we're the most powerful entity. And they need to recognize that. But that should give a sense of empowerment of We the People in the United States of America. We should feel really good about that."

"Yeah, absolutely," Payne responds.

*   *   *

Despite all this talk of feeling good, every time I watched them, Pete and Ryan made me very sad. I'd like to stop them there, freeze them all on the verge of what they were about to say and do next, freeze all of us, the whole American machine at the edge of 2016. But I can't—nobody can—so I vanish them instead, into their surroundings. It happens easily because the setting is so deeply familiar to me. My attention wanders from their emotive bubble into that room at the Silver Spur. It might easily have been the one I stayed in during the days immediately after Payne and Santilli were taken down by their federal nemesis and hauled off over the Cascades to prison in Portland. All the rooms at the Spur are essentially identical. The wood paneling, the western-kitsch feel—it's a little like another home for me at this point. I know what it smells like in those rooms, what it feels like to sit in those chairs they are sitting in. So it's easily done: I leave them in their Silver Spur, and I go to my own—to my rooms, and my own memories of Burns and Harney County.

But when I do this, I keep touching down on another evening of my own in the Spur, this one from the long fall of 2016. On this night, I was especially drained from a day of awkward interviews and a long trip out into the basin, and I found myself zoning out in front of C-SPAN 2, or maybe it was C-SPAN 3. I've never watched C-SPAN anywhere else but the Spur; something about the fatigue brought on by my days in Harney County—pursuing the repercussions of what Ammon and Ryan and Pete and their friends had brought to that place, a place where I also felt a bit like an invader—left me craving the tedium and pedantry of those bland policy symposiums offered on the upper C-SPANs. Maybe others would choose the Weather Channel or a shopping network in such a state; for some reason, it was policy programming I needed to soothe me into my fitful dreams.

Mostly I wasn't paying attention to what was happening on the screen, which was the point. And then suddenly I was. It was a conversation at one of the think tanks—Brookings?—that seem to provide all the content for those second-string C-SPANs. I can't remember who the host was, but the guest was high up in the World Bank and he was talking about the future. He had been asked about technological change and employment and economic and social policy. He was saying something like this: Let's look at an example, total automation in trucking is coming soon to the United States—twenty years maybe, maybe sooner, maybe a little later, but it will come. The man had a soft southern European accent, which made him sound gentle and informed as he estimated a conservative number of people who would lose their jobs: a million, at the very least. We're not just talking about the drivers, he was saying, but about all those whose work services them. What are those people going to do? You are not going to be able to retrain them for other work—many will be in their fifties or older. They will never work again. You are going to have to take care of those people.

Who did this guy imagine he was talking to? This *you* he was addressing implied a *we*, an American *we*, whatever that might mean. And not just a *we*, but a generous, benevolent one, gifted with foresight. *We?* I said back to screen. *We* aren't going to take care of *anyone.*

I guess, at their best, Ammon Bundy and Ryan Payne felt differently? They sure loved to say *we* anyway, especially as shorthand for *We the People*, though I'd venture that many of us would think that we aren't necessarily wholly included in that *we* of theirs. We'd probably be right, but not to their minds. They meant all Americans, they would say, all the People. And they really loved to say *People*. You can hear the way their mouths linger in pleasure with the word as they enunciate it—especially Ryan Payne. It's in the second, unstressed syllable that the word really gets mushy, primordial with the swamp power of human coexistence. The first syllable is dragged out, but the emotion is all in the second—like the second unstressed syllable in *mama*. *Ma* is just a shout, a hailing—*hey, Ma, I'm home*. But when the second, unstressed syllable arrives, and we say *mama*, these two syllables together make a doll's mouth as the word faces itself, a wet, closed circle and an image of a world. It's almost the same with *people*. Say it and the word peoples a world.

Freedom, the People, America, We. All of them are mostly words, words that point to things that always seem on the way, never quite here, or too vast to ever wholly experience; they remain mostly things we say. Our experience of them is largely the feelings of possibility and imminence the words put in us, as they vibrate and then vanish from our flesh. When we say them in rooms with others, maybe sometimes they conjure larger, collectively meaningful feelings of nation, tribe, bodies politic—imaginary worlds made of real, living meat. In Harney County that December, some of those worlds, as they say, were about to collide.

Back in the future, at the Spur, flailing with impatience and irritable despair, I dug around in the sheets for the remote, found it, and switched off C-SPAN 2 with relief. But it wasn't enough; I needed to move. I got up and went outside. As I stepped out of the room, the thin door swung open to the rough carpet of the outdoor balcony and I breathed in the tinge of woodsmoke in the bracing air. The deep blue cool of autumn had come to the high desert. Across the courtyard from me, on his own balcony, was another man, a guy from the road crew staying there that night—the only other guests in the place. This man was still wearing his yellow safety vest, leaning on the balcony rail, smoking and looking up at a passing cloud, pushed by silent winds high in the air above us. As the cloud crossed over the moon, the moon vanished and the cloud began to glow from within.

Revelations

The day after Payne and Santilli's animated colloquy in the Spur, Ammon Bundy sat down at his desk and recorded his final plea to his internet community. Now he gave his internet followers the whole story of his divine inspiration and subsequent involvement with the Hammond case, and intimated that the next day, a new, grand stage in the struggle would begin. The details remained mostly secret. A select few of his friends, however, already knew much more about the plan. In mid-December, Ammon had gone back to the newly elected officers of the Committee of Safety with a dramatic proposal for how to restore the Beautiful Pattern in Harney County. An armed occupation was what was needed, Ammon said, and he had the perfect place: the Malheur National Wildlife Refuge. (One of the committee's officers later denied this version of the events, which Ammon was to give under oath in federal court.) According to Ammon, the committee rejected the idea, and so he had put it away, but not for long. On December 29, he proposed the action again, to a small group of trusted out-of-town activists at the home of a local supporter. Before beginning the meeting, Ammon asked all the participants to leave their cell phones and laptops in another room. He spoke to his friends of the hard stand that the Lord had revealed to him and with which he had struggled so mightily. Again he put forward the idea of taking over the refuge. This time the response he got was much more positive.

Blaine Cooper, who attended this private session, later described it in court testimony. "The idea," Cooper said of Ammon's proposed occupation, "was to stay there as long as it took"—as long as it took, that is, to re-adjudicate the refuge land and give it back to the People. The men also discussed plans to post security at the front gate, logistics concerns, and what to do if counterprotesters arrived. Most of those in attendance agreed to the plan. One man, Arizona militiaman Joe O'Shaughnessy, dissented but agreed to provide medical support and act as a buffer. Only one person rejected the idea outright: Oregon militia leader B. J. Soper refused to participate. Soper's objections aside, this was now the plan—the secret plan. They left the exact day of the takeover to be decided.

As for Dwight and Steven Hammond, they had only a few days of freedom left. On January 4, they'd be reporting to federal prison in California. To show support for the family, Oregon and Idaho militia leaders, out of the loop when it came to Ammon's occupation plans, had announced a march and rally for January 2 in Burns. This meant that many Bundyites, all also unaware of Ammon's plans, were on their way to Harney County, or thinking about it—if they hadn't already arrived. On New Year's Day, Ammon sat down in front of his computer and made his pitch to those *Dear Friends*. All his feelings—and God's feelings—about the Hammonds, all the "shadows and types" of revealed history, now poured out of him and into his vision of We the People out there watching in the gathered ether. The Constitution was hanging by a thread, he insisted. The time to act in its defense was tomorrow, January 2. The place was Burns, Oregon. "I ask you now," Ammon said to his comrades, to "come to Harney County and participate in this wonderful thing that the Lord is about to accomplish."

CHAPTER SEVEN

Ye Olde Castle

Crossing the Rubicon

THE WONDERFUL THING THE LORD IS ABOUT *to accomplish*. Ammon was proposing much more than he let on in his "Dear Friends" video address, and his online followers knew it, even if they didn't yet know what "it" was. He wouldn't publicly announce the location of his proposed hard stand until an hour before the scheduled march, at a diner that doubled as a cluttered antiques emporium, not the only such establishment in Burns. The name of the diner, Ye Olde Castle, added a little more grandeur and kitsch to what was about to unfold. There, in a back room secured at the last moment for the occasion and hidden away behind all the twentieth-century bric-a-brac—gumball machines and old phonographs, antique prams, and red wagons dangling overhead—Ammon finally unveiled the plan the Lord had revealed to him back in early December. Clustered around the table was a group made up mostly of out-of-towners. Some knew the Bundy family well; others in attendance hardly knew how they'd ended up in the room at all.

*   *   *

As Ammon prepared for the Lord's revelation and put out his final call to the faithful, Robert "LaVoy" Finicum was already on his way north to join him, bringing Ammon's brother Ryan along for the ride. Finicum, a rancher and therapeutic foster care specialist from the canyonlands of the isolated

Arizona Strip, had befriended the Bundy family in April 2014. Maybe no one was a prouder veteran of the standoff at the ranch than LaVoy; it had totally realigned his priorities and set him out on what would prove to be a one-way road to Malheur.

Once in Oregon, Finicum almost instantly emerged alongside Ammon as the other public face of the occupation. And what a face it was. Polished by wind and sun, its skin always seemed pulled a little extra taut around the hard insistence of his skull, as if expressive of the ideological intensity of this otherwise genial and welcoming devout Mormon cowboy. Unlike anyone else who'd join the Bundys in occupying Malheur, LaVoy was an actual practicing cattleman, and he liked to dress the part—down to the revolver and the fringed and silver-studded leather chaps. His experience of the Battle of Bunkerville made for a very different narrative from those broadcast on the news and on the social media outlets of the militia types who'd been there. For Finicum, the event had unfolded on horseback, to the tempo of a slow, determined trot, powered by the measured nonviolent resistance of himself and his fellow horsemen in the wash. In LaVoy's story, the riflemen on the bridge above them were merely a backdrop to what had predominantly been a cowboy's stand for freedom.

That was the name, *One Cowboy's Stand for Freedom*, he'd later given the website for his own Bundy-inspired struggle, a fight he'd unilaterally initiated with the Bureau of Land Management—this in spite of the fact that, as LaVoy himself said, he'd never actually had any problems with the agency. The Finicums lived in one of the more isolated corners of the American West; the Arizona Strip had always been a place where people—including, famously, polygamist Mormon heretics—went to be left alone. In such a geographically and culturally remote zone, it would have been easy for LaVoy to assume that he'd be left at peace to roam the red rock, alongside his family and cows, for the rest of his days. It would have been easy to assume that regulatory problems of the scale that Cliven had faced—with the Bundys' proximity to Vegas and the issue of the desert tortoise—would never reach him and his family. But that was not how LaVoy Finicum thought. That it was even possible for what had happened to Cliven to happen at all, that there was any chance of it happening to himself or any other rancher—this seems to have been too much for Finicum to countenance.

Maybe he was right. Maybe he really wasn't as protected out there on the Strip as it looked at first glance. A number of national monuments had been declared in the red rock country at the end of the previous Democratic presidency, and it was easy to imagine—correctly, it would turn out—that, with the close of Barack Obama's second term, more monuments would be designated in the West. Sure, the government said that monument designation would change nothing with respect to grazing rights—but why would they bother changing the status of the land if they weren't eventually going to change its environmental regulations and uses? Surrounded by so much federal land, reliant on it to run his cows, the potential precariousness of his situation had, by 2015, clearly made itself deeply felt. That year, in an intimate video address, Finicum announced his own Cliven-inspired refusal of BLM authority over his grazing allotments: no longer would he accept federal dominion over his Natural and Constitutional rights. In this and subsequent videos, LaVoy proved himself to be an appealing rural malcontent: folksy, self-effacing, sincere—and always steadfast and militant. His videos had garnered him a following in the Patriot and libertarian spheres of the internet well before Malheur turned him into an icon.

In "LaVoy vs. BLM part 1," as he called his first video, viewers were introduced to Finicum in full buckaroo mode: a kerchief wrapped round his bald pate flows down in a stream of colors from beneath his cowboy hat; throughout the video you can hear his spurs jangle and scrape. He's got his black-and-white cow-dog Diamond with him too. Handsome and alert, she pants beside him. The two are getting older, LaVoy tells us, but she loves it out here, just like her master. Out beyond LaVoy and Diamond you can see their world. "It's good out here," he says, inviting us in. The valley is rimmed by buttes and ridges, festooned in juniper and pinyon. Beyond it you can see more buttes and canyonlands rolling away to the horizon. The camera's mic picks up a gentle breeze, and off in the distance a few of LaVoy's cows are munching away. It does look good out there, damn good. The lushly green high-desert meadow is rich with the kind of grass that better ranching practices—promoted by the BLM and employed by conscientious public-land ranchers like Finicum—have begun to bring back to some of the valleys of the Strip after a few generations of overgrazing. "See the grass?" he says. "Look how thick it is, look how green it is. And we're in late summer." He hasn't grazed this public land pasture in six years, he tells us. "And these cows"—the camera now swoops more closely across more of his cattle—"are fat and sassy and looking good!" And then he's off on a lecture about his grazing rights, how he owns this *grass* (not the land!), which all leads, soon enough, to Article I, Section 8, Clause 17—which is where I usually get bored and go back to the beginning to watch him pet his dog and point out the mountains and the grass and the trees and his fat and sassy cows all over again.

Why do I bother with this cowboy kitsch? Why am I drawn back to hear LaVoy Finicum talk about his life again and again? I've watched it at least a dozen times. It is beautiful out there, but that's not why I'm watching. I'm watching LaVoy Finicum talk about his life because LaVoy Finicum isn't alive anymore. The first time I saw his video was the day he was shot and killed by Oregon State Police officers, a little more than four weeks after he'd rolled into Burns, strolled into Ye Olde Castle Family Restaurant and Antique Emporium, and sat down at a table in the back room to listen to what his friend Ammon had in mind.

*   *   *

One of the last people to enter that room was an ex-Mormon turned Messianic Jew named Brand Thornton. An HVAC specialist by trade, Thornton traced his family's history in the Las Vegas area back multiple generations. Like Finicum, Thornton is a westerner through and through, a dedicated hunter and adventurer of the Intermountain West. Spend some time with him and before long you are off on a colorful narrative of one of his hunting expeditions, tracking—or failing to track—a bighorn ram or a pronghorn antelope through the midday heat of the desert sun and under the cold wheeling stars, over rock, through dust and sagebrush, until the glorious moment of the kill. The walls of his Vegas town house are covered with taxidermied heads, each an epic yarn in itself.

But Thornton is not just a jocular sportsman. Another proud veteran of Bundy Ranch, he is also an amiable ambassador from what they used to call the "paranoid fringe." Thornton seems more like a far-out Jeff Bridges character than a maniac conspiracy theorist. Style makes a difference. Since meeting Brand one afternoon on the steps of the Mark O. Hatfield federal courthouse in Portland, I've spent hours engrossed by his emphatic effusions, in which tales of hunting and desert exploration mingle with sagebrush libertarianism, New Age Kabbalah, right-wing conspiracy, and the nineteenth-century messianic utopianism of Joseph Smith and the early Mormon Church. In the middle of all this, he can drop lines of scripture— Old Testament, New Testament, or Latter-day Saint—with the ease of a seminary-educated preacher. But whether he's explaining the workings of messianic time, describing his flight from government agents, detailing the moment of death of an ancient bighorn ram (a shower of ticks came clattering off its freshly lifeless body), or rhapsodizing about his pigeon stew (city pigeon is much tastier than mourning dove), Brand always seems to be enjoying every meaning-filled minute of what he believes to be the final days of human history.

Heeding the calls to action from the Bundy family, he'd arrived in Burns a couple of days before LaVoy Finicum and Ryan Bundy. He recalls that the week had been madly cold—to him anyway, a lifelong native of southern Nevada. In the Quonset hut lent by a Burns resident friendly to the cause, he'd shivered through the nights, wrapped in everything he could find. By the day of the march, he was ready to get it all over with and head home. But an intervention that he'd come to see as possibly divine had led him into the inner sanctum of Ye Olde Castle just as Ammon laid down all his cards.

Brand had been milling about in the cold in the Safeway parking lot waiting for the march to begin. Bored, he'd approached a group of militia organizers and been told to go away, that their conversation was confidential. That's when a mysterious blonde-haired stranger gave him a sign. The unknown woman had come up behind him (he never saw her face) and pointed over his right shoulder at the restaurant on the other side of the parking lot. "You're wanted over there," she'd said. Without even questioning her—which was strange; "it isn't like me at all," he told me—Brand walked over and followed a man he recognized as Jon Ritzheimer into the restaurant and down a hallway to a locked door. Ritzheimer knocked, the door opened, and the two men were ushered inside.

"I don't think they would have let me in if I weren't behind Jon," Brand told me, "I wasn't part of the insider crew." Later, when he told everyone about the blonde woman in the parking lot, they all thought he was crazy. No such woman knew about this meeting, they told him. In the intervening months, Brand tried—without success—to find out who she might have been. He's come to think the stranger may possibly have been an angel.

* * *

Ammon poured out his heart and plan to the small crowd gathered around the table: the assembled were invited to head out into the basin and take over the Malheur National Wildlife Refuge, a place most of them had never heard of—and to which Ammon himself had still never been.

A hand went up—it was LaVoy Finicum's. LaVoy later recounted this moment, for the media man of the Oath Keepers militia, in a video filmed on the occupied refuge. " 'Ammon,' " he recalled saying, " 'are you telling me that all these years we've been trying to draw a defensive line—getting pressed here, stepping back, pressed here, stepping back, we keep losing ground—are you now saying that this is a peaceful step forward *to reclaim?*' "

Yes, that is what he'd meant, Ammon said. "I says, 'Well, that's what I thought you meant,' " recalled LaVoy.

Finicum was ready right then to sign on—and so was Brand Thornton. Brand was ready before he really understood what Ammon was even proposing. "I was the first person to tell Ammon I was with him," Brand recalls proudly. "My heart said yes immediately, and I knew—instantly I knew . . . Once the Spirit comes in you, you have a choice: I recognized it and I had to make a very quick decision to go with it. You have to decide quickly in this kind of circumstance," he elaborated, "so you don't lose the Spirit . . . I knew what I was up against . . . I had to make a quick decision before fear entered my heart and pushed out that revelation."

As Brand and others in the room understood it, God couldn't act in the world without humans receiving the Spirit and choosing whether or not to follow. It was up to everyone at the table to decide for themselves, as Ammon had put it the day before in his "Dear Friends" address, "whether this is a righteous cause or not, whether I am some crazy person, or whether the Lord truly works through individuals to get his purposes accomplished." Free personal agency was of profound importance. "Stand, because when you stand others will stand with you, and God can't stand with you if you don't stand. Once you stand you can expect the hand of providence to be over you," is how LaVoy had explained the matter at the dramatic end of his 2015 video "LaVoy vs. BLM part 1," before rising from his cowboy crouch and vanishing off-screen, spurs clanking. All this theology raised the stakes for folks like Brand and LaVoy; their immortal souls hung in the balance.

The decision had been easier for Brand because he hadn't taken the mortal dangers of the expedition all that seriously, not at first. Engrossed as he was in the phenomenology of spiritual inspiration, he didn't understand why there seemed to be so much tension in the room now about whether or not to follow Ammon. He remembers one couple whom he assumed from their dress and manner to be local ranchers. They hadn't wanted to sit at the table with the others and had stayed back leaning against the wall during Ammon's appeal. As soon as Ammon's plan was revealed, they'd gone out the door. Another man whom Brand recognized from Patriot circles, the Idaho militiaman and

Bundy Ranch veteran Eric Parker, didn't go so quietly. Brand remembers him objecting strenuously to Ammon's plan. "He was totally against it," he told me. There was much to object to. Ammon didn't have the support of the locals, he didn't have the support of the sheriff; he didn't have any legitimate business doing what he was proposing. Brand remembers Parker even saying that Ammon was no better than the feds who'd locked up the Hammonds. "He was practically screaming at Ammon. He was shaking, he was so angry—and pointing his finger." At the time, Brand couldn't figure out what all Parker's intensity was about. "Color me stupid, but I didn't get it . . . like 'what's with all the drama with these people?' " As far as Brand was concerned, Ammon, whom he remembers mentioning that the refuge workers would be on vacation, was just talking about "an extension of what we were doing here in town." It might be a little dangerous, but protests always were. "We'll go out to this place, and we'll leave when the workers come back. I was *really* naive," he added, chuckling at himself.

After the meeting broke up, Brand joined the others who'd agreed to head out to the refuge; this vanguard called themselves "the tip of the spear." They assembled in the fairgrounds parking lot on the edge of town, without Ammon, who headed over to the march to round up more supporters. After they'd kneeled in prayer to consecrate their intention, LaVoy pointed at the road to Malheur. "Gentlemen, that is the Rubicon, and once we cross that there's no turning," the cowboy had proclaimed. Brand was baffled by LaVoy's intensity, but he also began to wonder something else: "What does he know that I don't?"

The Trump of God

As he drove out from the fairgrounds parking lot, Finicum took up the rear in the caravan. With Ryan Bundy in another vehicle, the long drive out alone to the refuge gave him plenty of time to think. As he headed over the basalt butte of Wright's Point and then dropped down into the wide-open heart of the basin, the sagebrush rushing past, he began to meditate on what he'd just signed on to do. Unlike Brand, he'd fully digested the implications of Ammon's proposal; it was no small thing—to take over a federal facility. As the full gravity of the decision began to weigh on him, he'd been given a sign: an enormous bald eagle was sitting on a fence post in a snowy field of sage, surveying the highway. As the convoy sped past, the eagle sprang into flight, spreading its majestic wings. He knew he had made the right choice.

*   *   *

Alone, at the front of the caravan, Brand Thornton had ended up being the first of the occupiers to arrive at the refuge headquarters. He climbed out of his truck and walked right into the compound. Around him the red-roofed, stone-block WPA-era buildings stood totally silent in the snow. When he turned and began walking back through the line of trees toward the parking lot to wait for the arrival of his comrades, he saw them approaching—and carrying long guns. "I began to get very worried then," he told me, "so I blew the shofar."

As readers will have gathered, Brand is a bit of a Mormon mystic, from the same desert fringe as Finicum and the Bundys. But unlike the leadership of the occupation, he had turned his back on the church some time ago; for him it had become hopelessly corrupt and corporate. In recent years he had stumbled on a new religious practice—or as he would say, it had called out to him until he was no longer able to push it away. At the center of his new faith was the shofar—the Trump of God, as Brand also called it, the old antelope-horn instrument of the ancient Israelites, the kind they'd been blowing since the time of Moses and Aaron. The signs for Brand had started on television. "Every time I turned it on, someone was blowing a shofar—it'd be a documentary and then, the next time, a scene in *Exodus*." Finally he gave in and ordered one of his own. His trump came, via the internet, direct from Israel—blessed by a rabbi. Since then, the shofar had given new focus to his religious thoughts and ideas; it was his ministry now, as he described it.

The day I met Brand, shofar in hand, on the steps of the federal courthouse in Portland, he told me about the breed of North African antelope—koba—whose horn his trumpet is made from. There's nothing like it for the production of sounds, he assured me. Its reticulations led to sound implosions, which themselves created *new matter*, he said. "I'm telling you, it creates new reality." He'd taken it to Bundy Ranch and blown it there in the wash before the standoff, as a prayer for protection and blessing. He was certain that what had happened that day was a miracle and wondered if his horn had helped summon it. Reminiscing about that day, Brand likes to quote a line of scripture from Numbers: "When you go into battle in your own land against an enemy who is oppressing you, sound a blast on the trumpets. Then you will be remembered by the Lord your God and rescued from your enemies." Whatever you thought of Brand's notions, some new reality had indeed been born that day in Toquop Wash, and the people of Harney County were about to learn all about it.

Now Brand stood with his shofar on the slope over the refuge headquarters compound. To his south rose the great snow-blanketed fault-block mountain of Steens. To the north were the Blue Mountains, to the east and west were desert sage and grasslands, interrupted by the jutting shapes of dark basalt buttes. Under the looming fire tower, in the waist-high, snow-wigged sage, he unleashed a blast of sound straight from the deserts of the Holy Land. As he'd done at Bundy Ranch, Brand blew the shofar as a plea for protection and blessing—and for something else as well. He was doing it to soothe himself and to soothe all the others. The shofar, Brand said, brought a kind of quietness and peace. It created what he called "perfect stillness." A stillness that made him think of pine cones, living pine cones. It was like "the perfect stillness between the cones touching noses," he told me. Stillness is what he needed now. It had finally become clear to him what all the drama back in Ye Olde Castle and in the parking lot had been about. As the men went from building to building, Brand watched. "If they took anyone into custody, I told myself then, I was out of there. I wouldn't stand for that. No one was being taken prisoner." The shofar, he was certain, was his best way of making sure this didn't happen; in the end, thankfully, no one was there. In the meantime, LaVoy Finicum had also arrived. He'd parked his vehicle to block the front gate. Pistol at his side, he now waited for whatever it was that was coming next.

General Ammon Takes the Day

Back in town, Ammon had just snatched the moment from the hands of the militia leaders who'd organized the day's official events. The march had begun in the Safeway parking lot with a series of speeches delivered from the back of a flatbed truck. The Safeway lot—at the center of town, a few blocks from the courthouse and a block off Broadway—is as good and central a public square as Burns can really offer. After the speeches, the crowd of a few hundred, most from out of town but with a few dozen locals mixed in, had proceeded past the sheriff's office—where they'd deposited pennies on the doorstep to show contempt for Ward and his refusal to stand. After this, they'd moved on past the Burns home of the Hammonds to deposit flowers on their snow-laden front lawn. When Dwight and Susie came out to say hello, it had turned into a somber meet and greet, full of hugs and tears. News cameras showed up and got some words with Dwight, his eyes red and wet. At his age this sentence was about it for him; his life, he felt, was pretty much over. "But it's not about me," he said. "It's about America."

Slowly the marchers had made their way back to the Safeway parking lot, their circuit through town complete. There they were met by Jeff Roberts of the Oregon III% militia. Roberts was yet another middle-aged bearded white man with a pronounced drawl—and a cheerier manner than his militia compatriots. He greeted the crowd, congratulating them on having taken this first step and inviting folks to stick around for a follow-up meeting down at the fairgrounds.

As he continued with the usual end-of-rally pleasantries and announcements—remarkably similar, whatever the cause—Roberts seemed to glimpse something out of the corner of his eye, some new reality hovering up there just above him to the left. It was Ammon, perched on a snowbank, poised to steal the day. If a bit anxiously now, Roberts went on reassuring the locals that they were in the driver's seat—"Goodness gracious, guys, thanks for coming out . . . Nobody is here to push an agenda"—when a voice in the crowd interrupted him: "Hey, Ammon. Let 'em know what's going on."

Suddenly all eyes were on Ammon Bundy. His speech was quick and to the point. "Those who understand what has happened here"—he paused for a second—"those who don't should probably go to the fairgrounds. But those who know what's going on here and have seen it for many, many, many, many years, those who are ready to actually do something about it, I'm asking you to follow me and go to the Malheur National Wildlife Refuge and make a hard stand." Now it was all out in the open. "Follow me," he shouted, leaping off the snowbank. As quickly as he'd appeared, he was gone.

Ammon's timing had been perfect. Anyone who's been involved in protest, left or right, has experienced that little eddy at the end of the march—when we all vow to keep educating and fighting, maybe chant a few more of the same old slogans before dribbling back to our lives. In that moment at least once, we've all felt that deflating recognition that this march, like all the previous marches, has meant little and will likely mostly come to nothing.

In that moment we'll have yearned, whatever our politics, for something else, anything else, to *finally happen.*

Neil Wampler, for one, had been ready for something to happen. As always, he'd admired Ammon's leadership instinct. "A little-recognized side of Ammon is his generalship," he told me. "He grasps the dynamic of the moment, the powers in play, makes a decision, and proceeds."

General Ammon's first casualties that day were from among his own allies, the militia leaders who had organized the protest march, many of whom had been with him for the meeting with Sheriff Ward. In the day's video footage, you can see Jeff Roberts trying to explain to the confused crowd that he and the other militia groups gathered there in Burns will not be going with Ammon and do not encourage anyone else to do so. "Well, if Ammon's fighting, I'm fighting," a man's voice can be heard saying in response. Roberts nods his head grimly in silence as he turns away, his American flag dangling in a blurry stream of color over his back.

* * *

Later at the fairgrounds meeting hall, where those who hadn't chosen to follow Ammon had reconvened, many weren't taking the turn of events so quietly as Roberts. Thanks to the multiple hours of post-rally footage, you can—if you can bear the militia posturing—watch in real time as Brandon Curtiss, B. J. Soper, and other militia leaders, along with apocalypse shock jock Pete Santilli, attempt but fail to reclaim the day that Ammon has just spirited away. As we enter the scene, Curtiss is running around with the microphone, barking militia jargon, as if somehow he were in charge of this mess. Then Santilli gets the mic and does the same, at one point trying to get the crowd to vote to collectively detain Ammon. Somebody yells out that that would be kidnapping. "It's not kidnapping!" Santilli yells back, though obviously it is. Quickly Santilli backs off the idea, saying he only wants to talk sense into Ammon, whom he loves like a brother. He's interrupted by another man in the audience, visibly angry, who is not buying any of it. He challenges Santilli, insists that after all the time he's spent with these Bundy guys, it's impossible he didn't know this was coming. "You know what, come here, dude, come here!" Santilli demands. "Come look me in the eyes, come over here. Come over here. I am going to tell you something right now—may a bolt of lightning strike me, okay?—that I did not know." Disgusted, the man backs down and walks away, joining the stream of other folks already headed for the door.

But Santilli is not deterred; the man is nothing if not inexhaustible. Soon he's trying to rally the crowd for some kind of vote—about what exactly, it's hard to understand. He seems mostly to be proposing an impromptu plebiscite on the necessity of his own reporting. Everyone needs to trust him to deliver the truth. And they need to vote on this, or that seems to be the idea. The militia leaders have retreated into a huddle, and for a while it looks like the meeting belongs to Santilli. But then another local man interrupts Santilli with another pointed challenge: "Why are the people that called this thing standing over here talking to each other, and we have a news reporter taking over and manipulating the meeting—we have a news reporter asking locals to take someone into custody?"

"That's not what we're doing," Santilli protests again, though, of course, once again, it's exactly what's been going on. Finally he takes the hint and steps aside, but not before suggesting that anyone who isn't happy with his reporting come outside and kick his ass in the parking lot *right now*.

Then somehow it gets worse. Brooke Agresta, Curtiss's girlfriend and fellow Idaho III% leader, takes the mic and begins to harangue the crowd. She seems aggrieved that they have been questioned at all. Everyone needs to know that she and the other militia leaders had just been securing their families so they could continue to stay here and sacrifice and stand for the community (which, arguably, had never—Ammon's Committee of Safety aside—invited them to do anything of the sort).

And it's just then that, improbably, Ammon steals the day all over again. A woman interrupts Agresta's speech about her own bravery and commitment and hands her a phone; it's playing a brand-new video—from Ammon, now out at the refuge. The room grows silent. You can feel the tension as they hold the phone to the mic so the room can hear the first Bundy missive from Occupied Malheur.

"We've basically taken over the Malheur National Wildlife Refuge. This will become a base place for patriots from all over the country to come—and we can house them. We're planning on staying here for *several years*." On the audio you can hear the crunching under his feet as he gestures in the snow under a blindingly blue sky.

Agresta's and Santilli's eyes begin to pop. Next to Agresta, B. J. Soper begins scratching his head in exasperation while the silence around him thickens. Stunned, the militia simply yields the floor. After a bewildering bit of last-minute Save the Hammonds Sovereign Citizen legal pedantry, led by a truly far-out dude in a big white cowboy hat with the vacant, fanatical eyes of an alien abductee, the meeting drizzles to an undramatic close. As the remaining locals head for the exits, Curtiss is still begging them to stick around for a follow-up meeting of the Committee of Safety that Ammon and Ryan had instigated just two weeks before. No one seems interested. Whatever the day's deity was going to accomplish, he wasn't doing it here with Brandon Curtiss and the militia. He was out there in the basin with his personal revelator Ammon Bundy and his motley squadron of dear friends.

CHAPTER EIGHT

Necessary Bodies

Stasis, Refuge

AND THEN NOTHING HAPPENED—for a long time. And while nothing was happening, everything happened. The occupation was a holding pattern, an eddy of time, a stasis that was also a whirlwind of activity, logistics, theatrical posturing, and rhetoric—circled by photographers, reporters, and television news crews.

Payne and Bundy had chosen the refuge neither at random nor for purely rhetorical purposes—the accommodations at the headquarters were perfect for a long-term stay. Wildlife refuges, often operating on tightly constrained budgets, rely heavily on the donated time and labor of loyal volunteers; to house all these volunteers, refuges often have kitchen and bunkhouse facilities. As "a jewel" of the refuge system—especially beloved among the far-flung and devoted birder communities of Oregon and the nation—Malheur's facilities were extensive. These facilities could also house fire crews during fire season, when the brush of the steppe grew crisp. The arson charges that were sending the Hammonds back to prison had nothing to do with the lands of the refuge or the Fish and Wildlife Service, which manages them, but the agency that had been involved was the BLM, and the BLM had no facilities of this quality and girth to offer, so the refuge it was.

The compound was also exceptionally well situated. The refuge headquarters was both near and far from Burns; out of the way of the town's daily life but still close enough for regular trips. From there, the crew could head out on its educational missions to Burns and throughout the basin, retreating to the refuge for safety at night or in moments of rising tension. It was the perfect location for a guerrilla base. The Bundy Revolution did have, in Ryan Payne, a military strategist with considerable firsthand experience of insurgency, even if it had come entirely from the other side of this kind of conflict. Perhaps Payne had found a way to apply the lessons of what he called his "unconstitutional disservice" in Iraq to what he saw as this "constitutional" service on the home front.

The refuge's geographical importance also went way beyond the strategic concerns of what was, in the end, a short-term propaganda war. It was here, on the lands of the refuge, that all the runoff of the mountains and the surface water of the Harney Basin pooled—expressing itself in the refuge's effusions of bird and aquatic life, and in the natural grasses that made such great forage for wildlife and for the region's cattle. Ammon and his friends had seized territory of immense value; the interwoven land and water of the refuge were not only the economic and ecological but—as Ammon and friends would soon learn—the historical and spiritual heart of the region.

"We Need Bodies"

The location also made for great TV; the amount of footage that would be shot at Malheur is too vast to catalog. The landscape and buildings of the refuge would soon become familiar characters in themselves, visual shorthand for the frightening new realities of 2016. The fire tower on the hill above the headquarters rose more than eighty feet above the sagebrush against a background of ever-shifting—charcoal gray or radiant blue—winter skies. The structure, for decades an innocuous local landmark, became, in the constant stream of footage and photos from the occupation, a portentous figure of impending calamity. Journalists' cameras zoomed along the watchtower, hoping to catch a good image of one of the Bundy crew in armed surveillance of the high desert and marshlands that unfolded in all four cardinal directions beneath their feet.

From the hill beneath the tower, one could easily survey the entire headquarters compound. Under clusters of cottonwoods, bare of leaves in the winter cold, the WPA-era red-roofed stone buildings of the refuge hunkered in the snow. North of the compound stretched alkali grasslands traversed by the channelized flow of the Donner und Blitzen River. Here the river was in the last stretch of its journey, carrying water off the back of Steens into the belly of Malheur Lake. The lake itself was barely visible that winter; always fluctuating in size, it was now extremely shallow and shrunken and had retreated far to the northeast across the flats.

Around the refuge, the basin distances, the snowy sagebrush, and the ever-shifting winter weather provided stark and moving backdrops for portraits of the occupiers. Maybe the single most photographed of them all would be an Oregon pipe fitter named Duane Ehmer. Ehmer joined the group in the first week of the occupation and quickly earned a role as a set piece, a one-man float in the daily parade of the Bundy Revolution. Every day, in his leather jacket with the Stars and Stripes emblazoned across the back and carrying another flag on a pole in his free hand, he rode his horse Hellboy back and forth through the sage while photographers snapped picture after picture. If you've seen just one image of the occupation, chances are good that it's a photo of Duane. He became a kind of color guard for the leaders, accompanying them on horseback up the hill from the headquarters into the ever-growing circle of jostling reporters, camera crews, and photographers at their daily eleven A.M. press conference.

*   *   *

Openness to the news media became a hallmark of the occupation and its carnivalesque "come one, come all" atmosphere. "Sunshine is the best disinfectant," Ammon Bundy liked to say. But not all the occupation's vanguard were for it at first. Brand recalls a conversation on January 3, the occupation's first full day, about letting reporters onto the compound. There were many objections; Brand remembers Brian "Booda" Cavalier's as the strongest. Cavalier, a hulking, tattooed man with a grin, a gut, and a belly tattoo to match his nickname, had become the Bundy family's lead security guy in the wake of the standoff at the ranch. He was adamant in his disapproval of letting the press and the public in. "It's a security nightmare," Thornton recalls him saying. But Brand was equally steadfast in his argument. "I told them those people up there have no less of a right to be here than we do. If we don't let 'em in, it'll just look like we're hiding something." After a moment, Ammon agreed. "You know, Brand's right," he said. And so the parade of media visitors began.

Soon after this conversation, on the very first media tour of the liberated refuge, LaVoy Finicum led a group of reporters through the snow to what he called "a cook shack." Inside, in the spacious, double kitchen, a Utah woman, Shawna Cox, who before the month was out would film LaVoy's last moments on earth, was making soup out of a mountain of potatoes. In another clip from the same tour, Ken Medenbach, who, two weeks later, was to be the first of the occupiers arrested, showed off his new sleeping quarters. "It's like a giant college dorm, I suppose," he told the camera, looking around admiringly, his laptop behind him, open on his bunk.

In the soundscape at Malheur, the desert silence was soon replaced around the clock with the constant rumble and hum of news trucks. From here on out, the media would be regularly invited down into the compound to film the vanguard of Malheur moving about their new daily routines and going on about government oppression and Article I, Section 8, Clause 17. Letting the media in served the Bundy Revolution beyond the need to maintain transparency and rhetorical consistency. As news footage and other images of the occupation spread from those satellite trucks, joining the homemade Facebook and YouTube videos of the occupiers and their supporters, fascination with the event grew. And the more this fascination grew, the more real a territory the newly liberated zone of Malheur—"the Second Freest Place on Earth"—became. This served Ammon and his friends' most immediate strategic need: the need for more people. "We need bodies," Ammon pleaded in one of the very first videos shot from the refuge, shortly after his arrival in the liberated compound on January 2. All this news footage allowed the occupiers to more widely broadcast the accommodations and the relative comfort that awaited the bodies of Malheur. Soon more bodies would be on their way.

* * *

Everyone who came to join Ammon at Malheur came for different reasons, out of different needs. Duane Ehmer's were among the strangest. I'd come to know and like Duane over the course of many conversations during the Malheur trials in Portland. He's an army veteran; he suffered significant hearing loss during his service and often needed a hearing aid for testimony in court. His hands are gnarled from years of hard work as a pipe fitter and blacksmith. I've been told he also makes his own armor for the Renaissance Faire circuit, where he's said to participate in jousting tournaments. I never would fully understand how Duane had ended up at Malheur—and not just ended up there, but become an icon of the whole event as well as one of the only people to be found guilty by a jury for his involvement. He told me his main concern regarding land-use issues was that the way things were going, soon federal public lands would be privatized and he would lose access to the forests and mountains for his favorite leisure activity, hunting big game, especially predators like bear and cougar. He was also concerned about the rights of the local Paiute people and their claims to the lands of the basin. How he'd ended up hooked in with Ammon Bundy and the anti–federal land movement was something he could never quite explain. Each conversation with him on the subject soon hit a wall and veered off into some other topic, like his horses, or welding and pipe fitting, or the nefarious conspiring of Harry Reid, who, Duane suggested, had paid the environmentalist protesters who came out later to Malheur to oppose Ammon and his friends. This last one was despite the fact that Duane himself had actually befriended some of those protesters. In fact, he twice mistook me for one of their leaders; I evidently wear the same style cap and facial hair as Kierán Suckling of the Center for Biological Diversity, whose threatened lawsuit was held by some to be what had forced the BLM to honor its commitments to tortoise habitat and round up Cliven's cows in Nevada. During a break in the fall 2016 Malheur trial, Duane showed me pictures of himself hanging out with the counterprotesters. In one, he's hanging out with a smiling young woman up in the watchtower, looking out over the basin. She'd loved it up there, Duane recalled, and was always asking him to take her up again. He beamed with delight at the memory.

Others who showed up, heeding Ammon's call, weren't quite as good-natured as Duane, nor did they provide instant iconography, the way Duane and Hellboy did, trotting slowly through the sage. But their stories and reasons for coming could often be nearly as baffling. While some who joined Ammon were long-term, committed Patriot activists, even land-use activists, most knew nothing about ranching. Outside the Bundy family, LaVoy Finicum would be the only currently practicing rancher to join the occupation. Some knew very little or nothing about the Hammond case, or about the issues surrounding public land in the West. Some came powered by the conspiracy litany of Satan and Hillary and uranium. Many came because of the vague but powerful allure of Freedom and "taking back our country." Neil Wampler recalled with amusement the first question he received from an enthusiastic newcomer one morning at Malheur: "Who are the Bundys?" a young man had asked him. But they were all bodies, enthusiastic ones—and enthusiastic bodies were what was needed most of all.

As the first weekend of the occupation came to an end, more and more media appeared from across the nation and the wider world; and by Monday, the small flock of reporters Finicum had led down through the refuge head-quarters just the previous afternoon had grown massively. In the first of what would be many daily press conferences, Ammon, LaVoy, and Shawna Cox, backed by a phalanx of other occupiers, stepped up to the cluster of micro-phones set up near the main gate. Reporters and photographers swarmed them, circled around behind, jostling for positions and camera angles. Visibly nervous, Ammon began by thanking the fourth estate for caring to come report on the events. He then got to the first order of business, an item of what he called "housekeeping": the group's name. "Many of you have asked us for—what is our name?" he said, cracking a smile. "Other than just 'citizens that care,' we didn't really know what to say. But we felt that we'd give ourselves a name so at least we could be reported that way and we could be more organized in that effort, and that would be Citizens for Constitutional Freedom. Our purpose is to restore and defend the Constitution."

* * *

Out of the press's need for a single political subject, the Citizens for Constitutional Freedom (CCF) was born. Called now into existence by the grammatical exigencies of journalistic prose, what exactly did this subject want? Now that it *was*, the CCF would have to speak; it would need to declare. What would restoring the Constitution mean? What were their demands? The press wanted to know. They didn't have demands, the CCF insisted. All they wanted to do was get down *to work*.

Again, dozens of cameras captured the moment. Some of the photos taken this day would become the enduring images of the short-lived CCF, especially of LaVoy and Ammon. Ammon is dressed as he was in the Safeway parking lot, and as he would be on what seemed like every day of the occupation: in the same wide-brimmed brown cowboy hat and blue-and-black-checked wool winter coat. LaVoy is wearing his own even wider-brimmed beige cowboy hat, along with a camo-patterned hunting coat, and—in a touch that highlighted his grandfatherhood—a pair of truly enor-mous earmuffs. His ruddy face seems even redder, more wind polished out there in the Oregon steppe. Standing behind them are some of the other better-known figures of the occupation. Booda Cavalier, the family body-guard, is bundled up in a scarf, stocking cap (with an image of a sniper on it), wrap-around shades, and a big winter coat—you can hardly make out it's him in there. Blaine Cooper, Ritzheimer's Arizona buddy, is dressed up in his full military outfit; he was partial to costume changes, switching between full military gear and civilian clothes that made him look more like a fashion model, or the TV anchorman he seemed to aspire to be. But the only other member besides Finicum and Bundy to address the press during the conference is Shawna Cox, Cliven Bundy's biographer. Face flushed in the cold, her long hair batted about by the wind, she takes the mic to read aloud the group's December "Redress of Grievances" petition regarding the Hammonds. At moments her voice trembles in the winter gusts surging across the sage, adding to the elegiac effect of the performance.

The reading of the petition felt like a parting of ways with the Hammond cause, which would no longer be the main focus of their effort. In a few hours, Dwight and Steven would be reporting to the federal prison at Terminal Island, at the end of a pier in the middle of the Los Angeles Harbor. They were slated to spend the next four years there, in the shadows of the passing container ships, some looming as high as twenty stories—yet virtually unmanned—as they glided in and out, back and forth, in their endless, near-automated parade across the Pacific.

The White Horse

As the Hammonds receded into the distance, the CCF's new, larger project emerged. Though there would be much talk and emotion about the father and son here at this first press conference, the CCF was out here in the basin to do something else, to restore the lands of the refuge to the People, its "rightful owners." And not just the lands of the refuge, but all the public lands of the county. As the scope of their ambitions grew over the coming days and weeks, they would begin to speak of extending this work—what they called the *unwinding* of land transactions—to all the West and the rest of America. The unwinding the CCF was calling for was absolute. It was nothing less than what Ammon had described at the December 15 meeting, when the Committee of Safety was formed: the restoration of the Beautiful Pattern, the freedom-producing operation of American Providence. It was Bundy Ranch, and it was much more. The public lands of Harney County would be taken out of what Ammon and his friends understood as the realm of "territorial law" and brought properly under the jurisdiction of the People. Freedom and prosperity would be the immediate result. Soon,

Ammon promised, the county roads would be full of logging trucks, the ranges full of cattle, and the restaurants full of hungry diners. As for the people, they would be free, free to finally live without fear.

The grandiosity of this project was impossible to miss. So were its messianic undertones. It wasn't lost on many observers that the three occupiers who stepped up to the mic at the first press conference—Ammon, Shawna, and LaVoy—were all devout Latter-day Saints. Among those who noticed were the highest officials of their faith. The very day the CCF was born, the Church of Jesus Christ of the Latter-day Saints officially denounced the group's efforts. The church's terse statement was an absolute rejection of the occupation as well as the use of church doctrine they had detected in Ammon's communiques:

> While the disagreement occurring in Oregon about the use of federal lands is not a Church matter, Church leaders strongly condemn the armed seizure of the facility and are deeply troubled by the reports that those who have seized the facility suggest that they are doing so based on scriptural principles. This armed occupation can in no way be justified on a scriptural basis.

Among the many scriptural allusions and citations in Ammon's missives over the previous months had been words from a piece of formally disavowed Mormon doctrine known as the White Horse Prophecy. Regarded by the contemporary church hierarchy as based in part on actual statements of Joseph Smith but largely apocryphal in much of its wording and content, the prophecy is still cited with real reverence in the desert lands of Mormonism's ragged edge. The actual text of the prophecy was written down many years after Smith's death by a close associate who claimed to have received it directly from the prophet. Much of its content is concerned with the future of the Mormons in America, something of pressing concern to Smith in his own latter days. The Latter-day Saints had narrowly escaped wholesale massacre in Missouri, and would soon be staring it down again in Illinois. In the prophecy, Smith is said to have claimed that the church would come to move to the mountains of the West and establish itself there in strength, as the allegorical "White Horse" of his vision. In little more than a year, Smith himself was dead, lynched by his gentile neighbors. Soon after, the Mormon faithful would begin moving west together en masse.

They'd keep going, until they'd passed beyond what was then the border of the United States, settling near the shores of the Great Salt Lake, in one of the transformative events of American western expansion.

The prophecy also had something to say about the Constitution, tying together the future of the church and the future of the nation's foundational text. One day, it declared, there would come a time when the Constitution would *dangle from a thread*: the duty to restore it would fall on the Latter-day Saints. In this coming time of crisis, as Brand Thornton emphasized to me, the Saints would no longer preach the Book of Mormon but instead preach the Constitution. Perhaps Smith had already been contemplating his ill-fated leap into national politics when he received this prophecy; in his short-lived presidential candidacy of 1844, he ran as a defender of the nation's founding document. As Brigham Young said of Smith during the brief campaign, "He it is that God of Heaven designs to save this nation from destruction and preserve the Constitution." Smith's candidacy wasn't to survive into midsummer; by July 4, he was dead, mobbed in Carthage Jail. Young's words, however, have survived. They could easily be repurposed to sum up how Ammon Bundy was seen by many in the movement that now had its eyes trained on Malheur.

Out there on the Bad Luck National Wildlife Refuge, it seemed that perhaps the day of the prophecy had finally come. Here they were, the faithful and their allies. And here was the Constitution as well; almost everyone at the refuge seemed to have a copy in their shirtfront. It was always the same pocket-size edition, annotated by the far-right Mormon scholar Cleon Skousen. Everywhere you looked, it seemed that the tiny dead eyes of George Washington stared back at you from the cover. If the church hierarchy would not acknowledge the divinely appointed task of preaching the Constitution, then it would be up to Ammon, LaVoy, Shawna, and the motley troupe of saints and gentiles of the brand-new CCF to do God's work instead.

Workloads of the Saints

There was more to restoring the Constitution than just citing the enclave clause to anyone who would listen. This was going to be hard work. LaVoy and Ammon were anxious to communicate this to the baffled, attentive media. In their first press conferences, the word *work* and phrases like *go to work* and *we have a lot of work* were percussive refrains that pounded cadences of urgency into their speech. However much work they were actually doing, they sure sounded like they were working a lot. They certainly *looked* like they were working. Shawna and Ammon carried around laptops—there was a lot of free product placement for Apple on the refuge, as there always is these days on Planet Earth. Ammon and others were often taking important-looking calls as they hurried back and forth across the snowy paths of the refuge—and there likely were lots of files in those refuge offices they were working in, plenty of documents to attend to. The message was clear: this wasn't to be just some kind of sit-in. While they were protesting, the heroic producers of the Bundy Revolution would also be working. As LaVoy put it at the first press conference, on January 4: "We have come here to work. We haven't come here to sit as children and stamp our feets and demand that certain things are met. We're gonna go to work. We're going to try to help restore these ranchers."

Another word, besides *work*, that was heard constantly from the lips of the official CCF spokespeople was the verb *unwind*. "We're going to get to work unwinding the unconstitutional land transactions," said Ammon. What that would mean, and who exactly the rightful owners of the land might turn out to be, was never clear. On one level, the owners seemed to be simply the People. The refuge, Ammon made clear, to his mind, did not belong to the feds; it belonged to the People—and much of the CCF's rhetoric was devoted, and would continue to be devoted, to general promises to get the people of Harney County their lands back. At the same time, the CCF, and especially Finicum, emphasized the existence of a group of one hundred ranchers they claimed had been dispossessed in the past by the creation of the refuge. It was unclear who exactly Finicum and Bundy might mean, but if there were a hundred such people, most of them would have been dead for many years. To make things more complicated, most or all of those who had lost claims to the refuge would have been late nineteenth- or early twentieth-century homesteaders squatting in the dry bottoms of the refuge's lakes. In the end, they'd lost their decades-long legal battle, first with Pete French's P Ranch and later with the federal government. They'd lost, but also they'd won; the court had ordered generous compensation in recognition of their long tenure on the land. Some of the descendants of these evicted but well-rewarded homesteaders still ranched in the basin and would come out in the next few days—against Ammon and the occupation.

There was also the question of the single largest land transaction made by the refuge: the purchase of the whole Blitzen Valley from the Swift company. Were God, Ammon, and his friends really here to give the entire Blitzen Valley—more than half the land of the refuge—back to Swift, which, eagerly cutting its losses, had sold it to the government in the 1930s? To make the issue more complicated, Swift was now owned, in the twenty-first century, by a Brazilian conglomerate: JBS S.A., the world's single largest processor of beef and pork, with more than forty billion dollars in annual sales. "Unwinding" something like this was going to be a complicated task, with or without the help of the Lord—especially for Ammon, whose political worldview did not seem to make space for even the existence of multinational corporations. In all the hours I have spent listening to Ammon Bundy, I have personally never once heard him utter the word *corporation*. His Reaganesque worldview seemed only to accommodate the existence of the People and oppressed producers, like his dad and the Hammonds, on one side, and the bureaucrats of the wicked, overreaching federal government on the other. This vanishment of corporations seemed more evidence of the near-total ideological victory corporate libertarianism had achieved across wide swaths of the American right by the twenty-first century. Here were Ammon Bundy and his Dear Friends, popular rebels, God-inspired militants of the Sovereignty of We the People, seemingly unable to even perceive—or articulate—the existence of corporate money and power in American public life. This, a mere five years after the Supreme Court had given the legal fiction of corporate personhoods nearly limitless free-speech power to flood elections with cash in its ironically named *Citizens United* decision.

"Rain Follows the Plow"

Few knew more about how difficult—or impossible—Ammon and LaVoy's fantasy of *unwinding* would be to accomplish than Dan Nichols. Nichols is a Harney County rancher whose family has roots in the basin going back to the 1880s. Not far from where the Hammonds bought their ranch in 1964, his family's lands fold back into the canyons at the base of Steens Mountain. Besides ranching, Nichols was also a county commissioner and had been one for well over a decade. He sympathized with some of the sentiments being mobilized out at the refuge; there was "too much damn regulation," as he put it. But when he went out to the refuge on January 5 to pay Ammon a visit, it was to ask him to go home. It was then that he got his own education in the Bundy Revolution.

After a conversation with a group of local ranchers and occupiers, Dan asked to speak to Ammon alone. Bundy agreed. Once they were by themselves, he asked what exactly Ammon thought he was doing out there, and why he had done what he had done. "He said it was 'spiritual guidance.' Well, OK, I said."

It is hard to convey in writing the totality of dismissal that "well, OK" can carry in the western, Missouri-twinged twang of a cowboy like Nichols. As for the rest of the meeting, it was pleasant enough, Dan told me. "We had a nice, cordial, respectful discussion. Didn't agree with him about a thing he said." Dan noticed quickly that all Ammon's information on the county seemed to come from one angle. "He'd been reading too much on one side of the Hammond issue and just assumed that everybody would get on the bandwagon and help destroy public property."

"The whole thing was done under false pretenses in a locale that didn't want it," he added. "Harney County—we can take care of ourselves." Dan had heard that Ammon had promised he would leave if the people didn't want him there. So now he told him that the people didn't want him there. "I told him get the hell out of Harney County. He said he couldn't do that. I said, 'That's going to be your loss.'"

Dan noticed that Ammon's plans and purposes seemed to be constantly shifting. "The Hammonds turned themselves in, so then it was the ranchers. When I talked to him, it was the county supposed to take over the land and we'd all get rich. I said, 'Ammon, how is this going to work? Have you done any studies? Have you run the numbers?' He said, 'I don't need to—just look at all the range and timber, all this wealth we can free up.' I said, 'Ammon, every *blade* of grass in this county is *already adjudicated.*'"

It seemed that Ammon had never recovered from his first vision of the basin—and the lushness he saw there when he had compared it to the hardscrabble desert of his family's ranch in the Mojave. In a larger sense, he was also reviving an old and persistent delusion about the potential fecundity of the arid Intermountain West: climate denial has a long history in America. The new nation, it was held, would make the desert bloom and yield just like the well-watered lands of the east. The period of zealous western expansion following the Civil War had even seen the emergence of a remarkable scientific theory of human-caused climate change. "Rain follows the plow" became a slogan of later nineteenth-century settlement, a bit of now blatantly faith-based science deployed to overcome skepticism regarding how exactly the dry lands of the West were to support the grand extension of American agricultural life and democracy. The theory, propagated by early climatologists and land speculators alike, held that the very efforts of settlers to open the soil would bring clouds and precipitation. Some versions of the theory even held that the plow was frosting on the cake; just the atmospheric agitation caused by the movement of all these passionate pioneers, all those restless American bodies headed west, would be enough on its own to bring clouds and rain. Impatient, some even took to dynamiting the air to hurry and augment the effects. If you listened closely, the providential certitude of these nineteenth-century speculators and pioneers was audible in Ammon's bewildered and bewildering reply to Dan Nichols. Why would Ammon need to run the numbers when he could tell how rich the land was just by looking at it? Why would he even be here if God hadn't meant for him to accomplish precisely this?

If you listen closely enough, you can also hear Dan Nichols shaking his head. After his meeting with Ammon, he, too, got down to work. "I went back to town after that and I ran the numbers. How much money for the schools, roads, the hospitals? I figured if we told the federal government we didn't want 'em around anymore, they'd probably stop giving us money for other stuff; maybe I'm wrong, but I don't think so. Anyway, turns out with those three we'd already be in the red."

Dan is a tall cowboy with a mustache the nineteenth century could envy—and his politics often match his throwback appearance. He is comfortable in the language of the right and the idiom of the Trump Revolution that was to overtake the country in 2016: people are angry and tired, he says; they want change, he says. But one thing he says that many folks don't realize "is the extent to which we're all subsidized in one way or another." Especially in a poor rural region like Harney County, all of Ammon's unwinding was likely to mean only a whole new level of financial ruin.

But, as Dan and others began to suspect, this wasn't really about local economics, or about Harney County at all. Something else was behind this: *feelings.* Feelings about government and also feelings about property, prosperity, land, and work. As the historian Patricia Limerick has put it, the history of the West cannot be understood without understanding the attachment to property as a class of feeling in itself. We live in a nation that has made a secular religion out of prosperity, whether or not it personally eludes many of us. In 2016 at Malheur, this feeling also attached to a different kind of need: the drive to be involved in something of meaning, something urgent. Dan was to be reminded of this urge when he returned home after running all those numbers. Not all of the Bundy Revolution was as amiable as Ammon. The word had gone out on the internet that Dan had told Ammon to get out—and the hate mail had already begun.

"After having a pleasant conversation with the Bundys, I went home and checked my email and my phone messages. It was all hate. You know—'if you weren't so corrupt' and 'stupid, gutless, corrupt politician selling uranium to China.' What brought it home to me is, I went to the enemy camp and had a respectful conversation, and came home and found myself accused of everything in the book. People think they are experts on everything and feel comfortable accusing anybody."

He even took to calling back some of his attackers. "I'd call them up, and they'd be shocked: 'You rotten politicians never called me before!' There were phone calls from clear across the United States. People are tired of the status quo, tired of it and mad . . . It's kind of a riot mentality," he added. "People are angry and looking for something to participate in themselves."

Restless Bodies in the Postwork World

If Ammon and LaVoy and company weren't really going to do all these things they were talking about—if all the work of unwinding was a mirage—and if there really would be no possible legal redistribution of the adjudicated grass, then what kind of work were they constantly getting down to? Maybe more to the point would be a different question: Had they taken over the offices of the Fish and Wildlife Service in order to mount what increasingly seemed like formal parodies of a workday? Why? Why did the "Second Freest Place on Earth" need to be seen primarily as a *workplace?*

Maybe it was because so many of these bodies coming to Malheur were bodies in need of more meaningful work—work and that feeling of purpose, that something-to-participate-in that Dan spoke of. If the conspiracy-minded in the Patriot milieu were continually arousing paranoia among the Bundyites by suggesting that the New World Order would soon find a place for them in detention camps allegedly being prepared at this very moment by FEMA, Ammon and LaVoy had a more positive remedy to feelings of uselessness among their followers.

The success of Ammon's occupation, and his whole public manner, evinced an understanding that the continuing economic crisis going on in the "jobless recovery" lives of many of his followers was also an emotional and psychological crisis—a fundamental crisis in value for these citizens of a country that has a hard time understanding what a person, and especially a male person, is for if not for work. If, in 2015–16, Donald Trump was gathering huge crowds of the white and disaffected in arena-size orgies of resentment, Ammon was doing something much smaller and subtler but also simultaneously grander, more resonant with theological meaning. Here on the eve of the allegedly impending epoch of total automation, he gathered the pain and purposelessness of his followers into his family's cowboy struggle. With his earnest voice and open face and gaze, he pulled them in and then directed them onward and outward, infused with the guiding energy of Providence, toward the restoration of Freedom and the Constitution. In doing so, he offered them tremendous purpose, a role in a grand American dispensation, redolent of the new secular mission for the Latter-day Saints foretold by Joseph Smith's White Horse Prophecy. To come to Malheur was to participate in the narrative fulfillment of America, here in the fraught and portentous final days of the fullness of times. That grand restoration, Ammon and LaVoy wanted the world to know, would not take the form of waiting around for the millennium to come; it would be work. The occupation would be a work site, a job provider, even if much of the work seemed at times like a parody of labor—even if the real job seemed to mainly involve just being a body, a body in community with other bodies, both on the refuge and across the internet, in the agitations of the extended, ecstatic communion of Malheur.

CHAPTER NINE

Rightful Owners

To an American historian like Patricia Limerick, what was happening out there in the Harney Basin in the first week of 2016 may have been intriguing, but it wasn't exactly new. So much of what Ammon and LaVoy were talking about—all this unwinding and reclaiming and restoring—placed their revolution in what Limerick, in her work, has called the "unbroken" continuum of the history of the American West. Out here things aren't ever as new as they might seem; the conflicts of the present are often uncanny refigurations of the same old conflicts that have characterized the region since the beginnings of white exploration and settlement.

When Limerick eventually came to Harney County herself, drawn there, like all of us outsiders, in one or way another, by Ammon's passion, she made a witty proposal to the large, enthusiastic crowd gathered to hear her speak at the Harney County Chamber of Commerce. Whenever anything like this happens, she told the crowd, whenever anyone wanted to do something like what Ammon did, "they should really give us historians fifteen minutes with them first." Fifteen minutes to explain the ongoing struggles they were enmeshed in, the unbroken history they were proposing to break with. Fifteen minutes to explain how all this had happened before. Patty was being ironic, of course. And the crowd would enjoy the catharsis of laughter often that night, over the course of her energized, masterful performance. It had already been more than a year since the end of the occupation, more than a year since the cops had taken Ammon away in a high-speed caravan, over the mountains, to the steel, glass, and concrete of Portland. It was more than a year since LaVoy Finicum had looked up, through the pines from the roadside snowbank where he lay in the Malheur National Forest, and breathed his very last. More than a year had passed, but the occupation was still fresh in the hearts and minds of the bodies assembled there that evening, and the chance to laugh together in public was clearly a cause for collective relief. The welcome refreshment of laughter came at least partly because everyone in the room knew how hard it was to imagine Ammon being talked down by anyone, much less a historian with a nuanced argument about the complex and intersecting patterns of American history. Already in the first week of the occupation, despite his calm demeanor, Ammon had looked emotionally ravaged—the mission had devoured him. At that point, on the other side of his friend LaVoy's Rubicon, no exorcisms of reason were going to set him free.

*   *   *

That's how Charlotte Roderique had seen it anyway, and she said so, back on the morning of January 6, 2016. That day, Roderique was speaking as the voice of the Burns-Paiute tribe at a press conference the tribal council had called, at the Gathering Center on their tiny reservation at the north edge of Burns. To Charlotte's mind, there was no use in talking, not with someone like Ammon—his mind was made up. "They have already decided what they want to do," she said in response to a reporter who'd asked what she'd like to say to the CCF. She wasn't here to give advice or admonish the occupiers. It was too late for that—from her point of view, the inevitable consequences of the forces they'd stirred up were already in motion. If anyone knew just how far in over his head Ammon had gotten himself, it was Charlotte.

In January 2016, Roderique was the chair of the tribal council of the Burns-Paiute tribe—a position she'd held for five years. Now in her seventies, she had played a key role in her early twenties in the negotiations that had finally gotten her band of Northern Paiute federal recognition. The tribe called themselves the Wadatika—"eaters of wada," or seepweed, a plant that grew only in the marshlands of the basin now entirely within the boundaries of the refuge. The land where Ammon and his gang had hunkered down, the land they proposed to legally unwind from the feds and "give back" to the ranchers and "the people" had been at the heart of the lives of Charlotte's people for a very long time. So long it was hard to hold in the mind. "We were here before the volcanoes at Diamond Craters," Charlotte told the reporters that morning in the Gathering Center—speaking of the eerie landscape of volcanic craters and lava flows to the southeast of the refuge headquarters.

"I don't think these people knew what they were getting into when they went down there," Roderique added. I'd hear variations of this over and over from folks in the tribe and across the county. Dan Nichols put it more bluntly, using the same phrase for Ammon that he also sometimes used for environmentalists who attacked ranchers: "They didn't have a clue." Beyond the complexities of the adjudicated grass, beyond the formidably independent spirit of the place—beyond the fact that the last ten years had seen a quiet revolution in the way federal agencies, local government, ranchers, loggers, and environmentalists saw and treated one another—Ammon and company truly didn't have a clue about the deep history of the territory they had come, lit up by God, to save. That cluelessness imbued many of the Bundy crew's basic pronouncements with an irony that wasn't lost on everyone, certainly not in Harney County. To Steve Grasty, the county's head executive, what was coming out of the occupied refuge about local history was especially ridiculous. "Just totally ignorant," he told me. "I mean, he makes the comment 'Well, this needs to go back to the rightful people.' Oh really!—well then I'm gonna see if I can get adopted into the tribe."

In short, the press was to get itself quite a history lesson on the morning of January 6—a very different sort of earful from what reporters had been getting down at the refuge. Charlotte and her colleagues walked them back in time, to the nineteenth century and further—way further—back. Recent archaeology had suggested continuous human occupation of the basin going back *fifteen thousand years*; the areas around the refuge had been occupied by the ancestors of the Paiute for thousands of years at the very least. Everywhere around the refuge headquarters, along the meander lines, and in the sage lands and marshes around the lake, evidence seeped up—in the forms of material artifacts: points, spearheads, grinding stones. Countless bodies had been buried in the earth there as well, centuries' worth of dead.

The Wadatika, of course, hadn't been pried from these homelands willingly. The story of their violent, forced exile and their ongoing refusal of that exile ran straight up against Ammon's dream of the Beautiful Pattern, undermining his narrative and the Malheur operation differently, and more obstinately, than any other opposition the gang were to encounter in their time in Harney County. It was the Wadatika who understood immediately that what we were really watching at Malheur was not just a protest about federal overreach or public land management—struggles the tribes knew about as much as, or more than, anyone. Ammon's occupation was also, from the perspective opened by the tribe on January 6, a kind of ceremonial land grab, a historical reenactment of white settlement. It was Manifest Destiny, restaged with the unnerving gravity of unconscious inevitability on what was, essentially, a massive Native American graveyard.

The Extreme Grandma

Charlotte Roderique has a favorite nickname, one given to her by her grandkids when they were young. "Extreme Grandma, they called me," she said, chuckling. The kids were referring to her tenacity outdoors. She's a deadeye shot, she assured me, and has spent years of her life traversing the desert and forests of eastern Oregon and northern Nevada.

She's also from another time—something she brings up a lot these days. She recalls a very different Burns—the one of the 1940s and '50s, when they still drove cattle into town and shipped them out by train. The rail line is gone now, as are the stockyards, but in those days, the yards were packed with cows, and the auctions were a big part of the life of the town. The bars were full of cowpokes and buyers. The cowboys often drove the cattle into town by foot, she told me, from all the way across the basin—from even as far as Wagontire, she said, referring to the sagebrush settlement, at least sixty miles from Burns, with a current listed population of two. She knows just how far and hard the journey out there was back then; she'd often accompanied her uncles when they headed out into the desert to round up wild horses to sell for "whiskey money." "That's what people said to tease them," she said. "And that's exactly what it was," she added, chuckling. Through her big granny glasses, Charlotte Roderique's eyes often glitter with the kind of ironies, gleeful and harsh, that come from a life attentively lived.

Charlotte remembers when traditional Paiute religious practices were still banned, and her aunt and uncle held ceremonies in secret at night, with blankets over the windows so the Indian agent down the road wouldn't be burdened with the knowledge of what was happening right under his nose. She remembers her uncle's neighbors coming to him for traditional medicine. Behind the barn he'd shove an awl up their noses; the bright red blood might run, but their pounding headaches went away. She remembers her mother being sent from the high desert of Burns all the way to a sanatorium in the rainy coastal lowlands of Tacoma for her tuberculosis—the worst possible climate for the ailment—because the local hospital didn't admit Indians, even though her mother worked there as a nurse's assistant. She remembers being shipped out herself, at age five, to a boarding school over the mountain, until her mother recovered. And she remembers those drives with her uncles, rumbling through the sage after the wild horses—eight years old, riding on the roof of the truck with her dog and nothing but a chain to hold on to. "No child seats in those days," she recalls, laughing.

She also remembers when Indians were finally allowed into the bars, and then, after that, into the schools. She also remembers how, years later, when she was in her twenties, her own tribe called on her, because she was the one in college, because she'd been out in the world—and, most importantly, because she was the one with a typewriter. The machine was key; her people needed someone to prepare all the documents as they made their final push for federal recognition. She recalls her gnawing anxiety over getting all the translations from Paiute just right, spending days obsessing over each page. And she remembers when they sent her, terrified by the responsibility, to a conference in the Dakotas and then for the final negotiations with the federal government in Minnesota. But now they had their tribal recognition, and their little reservation, and their Gathering Center, where she explained her people's history to the horde of reporters on the morning of January 6. Above her head a documentary about her people and their land—"this country," as Charlotte called it—played in silence, while on the loudspeakers the sounds of different tribal leaders from other towns and reservations joined the livestream, interrupting her talk with the beeps, whispers, and robot whistles of our new millennium.

The tribe had called the press conference to give their side of the story—"a brief background of what we've endured over the years," as Roderique put it. "For them to come and say we're going to give it back to the rightful owners," she added, chuckling and launching into one of her signature grandma-style digressions, "I was laughing . . . I told one my friends . . . I am sitting here trying to write an acceptance letter for when they return all the land to us." The room filled with laughter while Charlotte smiled, sparkling a little with silence and irony. "We know they didn't mean us," she added. "We know they meant themselves."

History Lessons

Behind Charlotte's stories are much older memories, much longer stories, of the people who, with her help, finally gained federal recognition in 1968. The tale of the modern Wadatika begins far earlier, in stories of a subsistence culture developed over millennia, through a living and reverent collaboration with the sage lands, salt flats, marshes, and mountains of the northern edges of the Great Basin. These times, which must once have seemed destined to last until the very end of days, were interrupted—first gradually, and then with abrupt violence and terror—by the cataclysm of European invasion and settlement. First came the trappers, wiping out all the beaver in the Harney Basin and much of the rest of the Intermountain West. These first adventurers were followed by waves of disease that augured further waves of death and displacement in the coming years of white invasion and settlement. The Paiute of the Great Basin, like other groups, met each incursion first with tactics of evasion and then with attempts at coexistence. Later, when the tipping point was reached, there was resistance, warfare, and inevitable defeat—a defeat the Wadatika have never accepted as final. The post-settlement years have been marked by an awe-inspiring persistence and dedication on the part of the Burns-Paiute to the lands of Malheur. "Tenacity" was the quality Charlotte applied with pride to her forebears. "We're the ones who came back," she told me, referring to what is often called the Paiute Trail of Tears, a brutal forced relocation of the Wadatika and other Northern Paiute bands in the late 1870s. "Nothing could keep us away."

*   *   *

Far west as they were, the catastrophes of white settlement came relatively late to the Wadatika of the Harney Basin. The first written record of white travel through what is now Harney County comes from Peter Skene Ogden, whose trapping forays in the 1820s provided initial reconnaissance to Europeans on much of the region, from contemporary Oregon down into Nevada and Utah. He didn't enjoy his first trip into the Harney Basin so much; it was a cold, lean fall by the alkaline lakes, and the waterfowl, though plentiful, were "shy." The party wasted precious ammunition trying to kill swans to get themselves a meal; they fired a hundred shots at least, he wrote, and not one hit home. On this mission, Ogden failed to find the Blitzen

Valley, just a little to the south, or the springs on the south end of the lake, where the refuge headquarters now lies. If he had, besides finding more food and water, he also would have found the true targets of his expedition: beaver. Ogden was in the employ of the Hudson's Bay Company, and had been sent to trap out all the beaver of the West in order to kill off American interest in the region. He'd kill plenty of beaver in his day—so many that even he, not a man recalled for his conscience, wrote of regretting it—but the beaver of the Blitzen Valley would be left to future expeditions. He was to leave a more symbolic and differently lasting legacy. On his map of the region, Ogden left a mark of his dismay: over the heart of the basin, where now Ammon and his friends were hunkered down, he wrote out a single word: *Malheur*.

Thanks to Ogden's notes we also have our first record of a white encounter with the ancestors of the Wadatika. Here he is, stunned by the size of the population gathered in the traditional camps at the basin's lakes: "It is incredible the number of Indians in this quarter. We cannot go 10 yds, without finding them. Huts generally of grass of a size to hold 6 or 8 persons. No Indian nation so numerous as these in all North America . . . They lead a most wandering life."

While historically the description of the lives of Great Basin Native peoples as "wandering" has often been used to undermine claims to ancestral homes, it is hard to imagine a kind of life with a more intimate tie to land than that practiced by aboriginal desert cultures like the Wadatika and their other Paiute, Shoshone, and Bannock relatives. The Wadatika followed a life of seasonal movements that themselves were part of a reverent, ceremony-filled attention to the places that had sustained their ancestors for millennia. The archaeological record marks out the shape of a mind-boggling persistence of habitation and life practices. This often happens in the deserts of the West, where human temporalities hang out with geologic time. People here, right here, hunted mammoths—and they were still here when the mammoths were gone and the land turned to desert, and they themselves turned to new hunting techniques—like those used to catch rabbits in expansive nets in yearly drives, or the ritual magic used to charm herds of antelope so that they entered willingly into earthen pens. In one of her sardonic asides during the tribe's news conference, Roderique suggested that if the tribe were feeling a little more generous today—they weren't, but if they were—maybe they should go down there and teach the Bundy crew how to do one of those Wadatika rabbit drives. The occupiers had just sent out a plea for snacks and warm clothing; they could probably use the meat, she mused—and the fur.

Traditional Wadatika culture traveled an internal map of the edible roots, seeds, and beasts of the basin and its marshes and buttes, as well as the foothills and forested slopes of the mountains at the basin's edge. That map was kept alive by tribal traditionalists like Charlotte. Given an interested listener like myself, her conversation quickly veered into gastronomic geography. In imagination I followed her words through the landscape, from food source to traditional food source—camas, chokecherry, salmon, bitterroot, elk, deer, antelope—snacking all the way. As harsh as it seemed—and was—this wild, lonely-feeling place had been an edible, provident world.

The circular movement of the traditional Wadatika year had been powered by pulsations of contraction and diffusion, as social patterns and rituals followed the food. They came together in large groups to winter in temporary villages, near lakes and springs in the basin; and in the height of spring, in camps on sunny hillsides and meadows, when the fresh roots of certain key plants, like bitterroot, were tastiest. These root-gathering camps were also times of joyous assembly, days of dancing, games, footraces, and later, with the coming of the horse, equestrian races as well. Afterward, small family-based bands would disperse into the mountains to pick summer seeds and berries and track game, all returning later to the lakes to gather other plants—including their namesake wada seeds in early fall. It was a richly varied life, if one lived always at the edge of subsistence. At its center was an intimate relation to all the spaces through which the people moved. Rituals for passing through the different landscapes of the region are still practiced by members of the tribe to this day.

The first catastrophic disruption of this traditional life came after Ogden's expedition and those that followed it in the 1830s, when waves of disease swept through the basin. Much of that dying happened near the present refuge headquarters, Diane Teeman, the tribe's archaeologist, explained to me, when life was at its hardest and when the people were gathered in the greatest numbers in their winter villages. When it came to the years of death that inaugurated the Paiute catastrophe, she quoted Peter Skene Ogden's amazement at the Native population of the basin in 1826. "The fact that there were really so many of us," she added, "that so many of us died—this is something that I think continues to be too painful for most people to face. The erasure of that dying is almost complete." Many of those who died were buried right there, in that land chosen by Ammon and the boys as their own winter camp, where they now hunkered down with their donated supplies.

*   *   *

The nature of European conquest of the Americas has meant that there are precious few written records by Natives who witnessed the first cataclysms. The Paiute catastrophe is a marked exception: it unfolded throughout the infancy, childhood, and youth of one of the great figures of the nineteenth-century West, Paiute activist and author Sarah Winnemucca. Winnemucca's English-language autobiography, *Life Among the Piutes*, was the first book published by a Native American woman in the United States. In its opening pages, she recounts how interwoven her path to authorship was with white settlement and its disastrous impact on her own immediate family. In adulthood, as the tribe's translator, she was also on hand when the Beautiful Pattern came for their Malheur Reservation—to once again steal Indian land and turn it into Freedom—only a few years after it had been granted to her people as a permanent refuge and home.

Sarah was the daughter of an important Northern Paiute leader, Winnemucca, and the granddaughter, on her mother's side, of another Winnemucca, an equally influential leader, called "Truckee" or "Captain Truckee" by whites. The elder Winnemucca had received his white world name—*truckee* is a Paiute word translated by Sarah as "alright" or "very well"—from the explorer John Fremont, whom he had befriended, guided, and fought alongside during the war with Mexico. Truckee/Winnemucca had seen the coming of whites as the completion of a Paiute prophecy: the reunion of the squabbling children, white and brown, of the parents of the human race. He had also come to identify the true source of the power of his long-lost "white brothers" in their communications technology, the "talking rags" they used to bridge great distances of time and space. Before dying in old age of tarantula bite, Sarah's grandfather had sadly lived to see his hopes for peaceful coexistence crumble. Nonetheless, at his request, he was buried with his favorite talking rag—a letter of praise from the great explorer Fremont that his granddaughter had watched him brandish often over the years whenever he encountered whites.

It really had been a magic talisman. For one, it had kept the whites he'd encountered from killing him; other family members and friends without such talking rags had not been so lucky. Fremont's letter had also had the secondary effect of procuring gifts of exotic sweets for the terrified young

Sarah. It being a book of memory, and Sarah having been very young in these first years of white invasion, there is much attention in the opening pages to the experience of tasting sugary snacks and cakes for the first time. The little girl had never known anything like them, and they delighted her—though everything else about white people continued to terrify. Much of the early narration is devoted to her fear—screaming, or hiding her face in robes anytime whites came near, and berating her "bad grandpa" for allowing them close. They looked like owls, she thought, when she finally saw them, the men anyway. Their faces were covered with feathers, and their eyes were white. She understood only later that the feathers were facial hair, and that the white eyes were in fact blue. By then whites had given her more substantial reasons to fear them, firing on and killing members of her extended family who were fishing in one of their usual spots along the Humboldt River. She also learned very young about the sexual predation that accompanied the arrival of the Beautiful Pattern. When camped out near a white settlement where her grandfather had left her, she witnessed her mother, her uncles, and her older sister subjected to regular nighttime harassment by men demanding that Sarah's sister be given to them. The abduction, rape, and murder of Native girls would be a source of serious violent conflict between Natives and whites in the coming years. Before the arrival of European Americans, the Paiute had had no reason to fear sending their girl children on gathering expeditions. Soon after settlement began, this became a horrible risk—adding both to the generalized climate of terror and to the horrible food shortages the bands began to suffer. The violence only got worse over the years. By the time Sarah reached full adulthood, her mother had been killed and her infant brother pitched live into flames by zealous Nevada Volunteers during the so-called Snake Wars.

Still, as an adult, thanks to the efforts of her grandfather to make sure she received schooling and learned the art of letters, Sarah's relationships to whites had grown more complex. Her skills led her into a public life as a theatrical performer and an advocate for her people, and also to teaching and other government employment. A large portion of Winnemucca's book is dedicated to her service in Oregon, giving us a firsthand Native account of the brief life of the Malheur Reservation and the crisis that led to its dissolution.

Samuel Parrish was a rarity: an Indian agent who doesn't seem to have treated his position as an occasion for graft or an opportunity to indulge a sadistic need for absolute power. Much beloved by Sarah and the people of

the Malheur Reservation, he was able to persuade the Paiute, suspicious of
white ways, to embark on the difficult work of sedentary agriculture in that
hard land. Even the radically traditionalist shaman Oytes, a stubborn practitioner of the pan-tribal Dreamer sect, which rejected farming and the owning
of property, would come, under Parrish's influence, briefly to the plow.
(Oytes, I was to discover, was an ancestor of Charlotte Roderique; she had
grown up being told by her aunt and uncle that some of the rites they practiced had been passed down to them from their militant relative.) These
good times under Parrish on the reservation—of relative autonomy and
safety from immediate violence from whites—would come to form, in Sarah
Winnemucca's mind, the ideal solution for Indian woes. But these halcyon
days were not to last.

A gold rush in the Blue Mountains north of present-day Burns had
birthed the boom town of Canyon City, where the population had swelled
from zero to ten thousand in one summer. (The current population is
669.) With all the miners came a need for beef, and ranchers were eager
for ever more grazing land in order to provide it. Settler pressures finally
led to Parrish's removal and the installation of a new agent, William
Rinehart, a Canyon City merchant. Rinehart was notoriously hostile to
Native populations—he'd fought against the Paiute as a volunteer. The
new agent immediately reversed Parrish's policies, which were founded
on the notion that the reservation belonged to the Indians. Not anymore,
Rinehart announced; the land was the government's now, as was all its
bounty. Soon the Paiute faced winter starvation on their own land. Whenever
they left the reservation to seek food sources in the wilderness or at army
outposts, Rinehart flew into vindictive rages. He took to physically abusing
his charges as well. Over a pair of days, he brutally beat one child he found
impertinent, and imprisoned and threatened first to shoot and then to
hang another boy who'd mocked him. Oytes arrived the next day with Egan,
probably the most influential of the Wadatika leaders, to confront the agent
about his abuses and to demand, again, access to the wheat the Wadatika
had themselves managed to harvest from this dry land. Egan had a special
reputation for inspired eloquence, and if Sarah's translation of his words
that day is accurate, that reputation was well deserved.

> Did the government tell you to come here and drive us off this
> reservation? . . . We want to know how the government came by
> this land. Is the government mightier than our Spirit-Father, or is

he our Spirit-Father? . . . His white children have come and taken
all our mountains, and all our valleys, and all our rivers; and now,
because he has given us this little place without our asking him for
it, he sends you here to tell us to go away. Do you see that high
mountain away off there? There is nothing but rocks there. Is that
where the Big Father wants me to go? If you scattered your seed
and it should fall there, it would not grow, for it is all rocks there.
Oh, what am I saying? I know you will come and say: Here, Indians,
go away. I want these rocks to build me a beautiful home with.

The Paiute Trail of Tears

The situation was no longer tenable; in the summer of 1878, Egan, Oytes,
and many of their people were pulled into the revolt of their neighbors and
relatives, the buffalo-hunting Bannock of Idaho. The movement of thousands of adults, children, and horses during the Bannock-Paiute War—
across arid steppe and pine-forested slopes—was breathtaking in its
momentum and scope. The logistical talents of the Bannock and Paiute
bands, under the resigned command of Egan, befuddled the army pursuing
them, under the perhaps equally resigned leadership of General O. O.
Howard. Howard, for whom Howard University was named, was a former
head of the Freedman's Bureau and took a more compassionate view—
sometimes—of the Republic's undercastes. Sarah Winnemucca was at his
side as interpreter. She had thrown in her lot with the cavalry—ironically,
the only branch of the white world that had shown her people any kindness
or mercy until now. Sarah's choice has earned her an ambivalent reputation
to this day. Her logic, as she saw it, was simple: victory for the Paiute was
clearly impossible, and war was futile. All she could do was try to prevent
wholesale slaughter.

   In the end, Sarah was unable to save her friend Egan. When the Bannocks
and Paiutes reached the Umatilla homeland near the Columbia River,
Umatilla leaders, feigning willingness to join Egan in flight, killed him for
a reward. His head was taken as a souvenir. After much travel, it ended up
in Washington, D.C.—until 1993, when the Wadatika were finally able to
bring the reluctant war chief's head back home.

   What followed the final surrender of her people was, for Winnemucca,
perhaps even worse. Howard, despite his sympathies for what they'd suffered

under Rinehart in the last years at Malheur, was resolute in his determination to punish the rebels, and to defend his reputation from charges of being soft on Indians. No distinction was made regarding the roles of individual bands in the war, or even whether they'd participated at all. With the single exception of Sarah's father's group, all were to be deported. They'd be marched in chains, as prisoners, more than five hundred miles across frigid mountains and steppe, through deep snow and storms, from Fort Harney to the Yakama reservation on the Columbia Plateau.

All Sarah's efforts had resulted in a total betrayal. When she returned, ashen, from the fort commander's office to deliver the harsh sentence to her people, her friends and cousins turned their backs on her in silence. Although she herself was free to go live where she liked—a small token for her service to the army—Sarah accompanied her people anyway, on what was for many a death march and has since become known as the Paiute Trail of Tears.

The story of this forced deportation, its refusal, and the subsequent tenacious return of the Wadatika to Malheur is the foundational story of the modern group that today calls itself the Burns-Paiute tribe. Their attachment to the land, the gravity with which it drew them back, is the force that has animated and defined them as a people. This wasn't abstract history; it was family lore. Most everyone in the tribe had ancestors who'd been marched out and who had, somehow, found their way back to the basin, to this land that belonged to them, because they also belonged to it.

"I Got a Question for the World"

The emotional intensity of this living history surfaced at the January 6 news conference when tribal council sergeant-at-arms Jarvis Kennedy stepped to the mic. Kennedy and Roderique would be the two Wadatika leaders who would take the largest public roles in the tribe's opposition to the Bundyite occupation. While Charlotte would be widely quoted in the coming weeks, as she staked out the tribe's positions in legal and political terms, Kennedy's rawer words from the news conference would soon go viral, passed around and embedded in links that granted the recently elected council member an instant fame with which—like most inadvertent internet celebrities—he struggled at times to contend.

The first thing anyone notices about Jarvis Kennedy is that he's a big dude—he's got the build of the football player he was in high school. Now in his early forties, he's still suffering from the injuries; I've seen him whistle with the effort of holding in the pain from his knees and back. The second thing you notice about Jarvis are the tattoos, the ones on his face: eagle feathers dangle down from his right eye. He's a tattoo artist, a painter, and a creator of contemporary ceremonial costume—"powwow gear," as he calls it—of stunning sculptural complexity. From the moment he took the mic on January 6, he had the room's attention. And then he started talking. Once he did, everyone could feel just how much Jarvis Kennedy was feeling that day. Soon many others, linked to this moment in time and space through their screens, would be feeling it as well, and passing these feelings around.

"I got a question for the world out there," he said, in his gravelly east Oregon accent. Jarvis's voice mixes the flattened vowels of a Paiute accent with that Missouri twang, so common to east Oregon, that came with its white settlers and stayed—even though Jarvis, like many or most of his neighbors, Paiute or not, had never been much east of Idaho. "I got a question for the world," he drawled, "because all the eyes are on this little tribe right here . . ."

"What if it was a bunch of Natives went out there and overtook that or any federal land?" he continued. Charlotte, at his side, cracked a tiny smile, sensing where he was going. "What would the outcome be? Think about that. What would happen? Would they let us come into town and get supplies and re-up?" He dangled a long, long pause, as he slowly opened his hands in a questioning gesture. "Tell me. I'm asking *you*. Think about that."

His questions hung there in the silence, made more poignant by Jarvis's direct address of the crowd of mostly white reporters. Everyone knew what he was really asking; he didn't have to say it. What would happen if *we* went out there and finally took *our* land back? If *we* finally took back what *you* know is *ours*, what would *you* do to *us*?

It was a powerful question, and different from the vaguer ones already circulating in left-leaning media: What if these occupiers had been people of color? What if they had been Muslim? Unlike these hypotheticals, Jarvis's questions emerged directly from the land of Malheur and his tribe's history. Among those who seemed to hear what he was asking was the FBI. Just beginning to establish its presence at a command post at the Burns airport, between town and the refuge, the agency would take pains moving forward to keep the tribe in the loop. Out on the refuge, the Citizens for Constitutional Freedom would hear Jarvis's questions too, and as the occupation went on, persuading the Paiute to enter into a dialogue would become an increasingly important part of LaVoy Finicum's public workload. Up into the last few hours of his life, Finicum would be trying, and failing, to bring the Wadatika to his side. His efforts, made in a series of videos recorded on the refuge, would be wholly wasted on the tribe. The occupation, with its reenactment of the settler land grabs of the nineteenth century, had dredged up way too much history. On January 6, as Jarvis continued, he challenged the members of the media to experience that history directly as emotion.

"We weren't removed," he said. "We were killed and ran off our land. Marched in the snow out there, hundreds of miles." The feeling grew thick in his voice. "When they finally let us go, we didn't have no place to go. Our land was already taken . . . They gave us ten acres at the city dump." (This bit of charity had been bestowed by the new town of Burns, decades after the displaced Wadatika had trickled back to the Harney Valley.) "Think about that," he continued. Charlotte, grown graver, was now nodding at his side. "Think about those little kids back in the day, marching home. Those elders. Would you want to be out there? Walking, marching?" As he pointed out the window of the Gathering Center, it was no longer the imaginary snow back then that his forebears had been marched through in chains—it was the snow out there right now: miles of frozen, snow-blanketed sagebrush, stretching north toward the mountains, the snowed-in peaks and canyons, all the way up to the Columbia River and the wind-whipped plateau beyond. Returning to the more limited present of the Bundy occupation—the heroism of its "hard stand" now deflated—Jarvis's speech took another blunt turn: "We don't need these guys here. They need to go home."

Jarvis spoke that day as both a tribal leader and a member of the community of the county. As his moment at the mic went viral, it would have a notable effect within that larger community. "We, as Harney County residents," he'd concluded, "don't need some clown to come in here and stand up for us. This community's hardworking. We make something out of nothing here. We don't got no jobs here, but we don't need them to back us up. We survived without them before, and we'll survive without them when they're gone. They just need to get the hell out of here—sorry."

His grim visage, with its severe frown and those eagle feathers inked down his cheek, made for a compelling expression of determined local opposition for those drawn to the anti-Bundy side. For the first time in local history, a tribal leader had become—instantly—a face for the political feelings of many in the rest of the county. Whenever I was in public with Jarvis in the aftermath of the occupation, I saw the effects his words had

had—neighbors thanked him for saying what they couldn't. Waitstaff made sure he had what he wanted. In the summer of 2016, he ended up in the hospital, and a nurse he'd never met before had scolded him for not warning her in advance that he was coming, so a more appropriate welcome might have been prepared. He couldn't have, because he hadn't known in advance, Jarvis explained: he'd come in for acute appendicitis. In early 2017, the Chamber of Commerce of Harney County would name him "Man of the Year"—the first tribal member to ever receive the honor.

All the attention and celebrity gave Jarvis a new role in the community. In the spring of 2017, Steve Grasty told me that Jarvis—whom he now called by his nickname, JJ—had just posted to Facebook about the long exclusion of Wadatika from the schools and asked all his non-Native friends to think about that too. But all the emotions had had an effect on him, the attention had seemed to wear him out. By 2017, he'd be looking for options to move away. The occupation drama had been fatiguing from the very beginning. "It gets tiring. It's the same battles that my ancestors had. And now it's just a bunch of different cavalry wearing a bunch of different coats," he'd told CNN in an interview shortly after he took the mic at the January 6 press conference—right before his words went viral and his face became a meme.

Kafka's Ghosts

As Jarvis's moment at the mic was distributed across the internet, a new aspect of the standoff was emerging. This was a battle of political feelings, and it was to be waged more extensively on social media platforms than it would be in any direct face-to-face confrontation. It's no wonder Jarvis was soon exhausted. Ammon, too, had already begun to look deeply drained. The new era of internet politics can wear a body out. Especially if it is you who's been weaponized, whether you've chosen to do it to yourself or not.

Franz Kafka, a man especially attuned to fatigue, as well as the vampiric tendencies of modern life, had some characteristically gloomy and comic apprehensions about the new communication technologies of the early twentieth century. They made him question the dangers present in a much older technology, the one he had dedicated his life to, that same one that Sarah Winnemucca's grandfather had identified as the true power source of the invading whites—what he'd called their "talking rags," their writing.

"The easy possibility to write letters must—seen theoretically—have brought a terrible disruption of the souls into the world," Kafka wrote in a letter to Milena Jesenská. "It is communication with ghosts, and not just with the ghost of the receiver, but with one's own ghost as well, which develops under the hand in the letter one is writing ... Writing letters means to bare oneself in front of the ghosts, which they are greedily waiting for ... Because of this plentiful food they multiply so outrageously." Kafka's ghosts were insatiable, and the living stood no chance. "Humanity," he conceded, had tried, inventing high-speed transport like the car, train, and airplane "to achieve the natural communication," but it wasn't enough. "It's too late, apparently they are inventions made while falling, the opponent is so much calmer and stronger, and invented after mail, the telegraph, the telephone, wireless telegraphy. The ghosts won't starve, but we will perish."

Many in Harney County in 2016 might have agreed with Kafka as they watched the internet mobilize the old talking-rags technology of writing to spread rabid feeling and conspiracy theory among their townspeople. Thanks to Facebook flare-ups, old friends, people who would never have uttered an impolite word to a neighbor face-to-face, railed against each other in the most vicious terms in the privatized public sphere of the internet—reaching through time and space to stir feelings in human bodies not directly present to their own. It's as if Kafka's ghosts were now in charge, and not just in Harney County. All the software gathering us up, the algorithms sorting us, coding and placing us in each other's "feeds"—perhaps these were Kafka's "ghosts," hard at work on a contemporary realization of the writer's dystopic bureaucratic vision: the data-driven automation of social and political life and feeling.

But there were also other ghosts involved. These ghosts were properly ghosts: the disembodied angers, fears, and dreams of the dead, circulating on social media platforms as intense emotion in the present. The agitated spirits of the Republic—or at least the residual feelings they have bequeathed us as our collective inheritance—had found a new form of life on the internet, new ways to enter human bodies and multiply, manifesting poignantly in culture war battles, and recent struggles over the undead legacies of slavery present in issues of police violence, and the controversies attending the removal—or not—of Jim Crow–era Confederate statuary. American ghosts were also active in the dreamtime of the social platforms of Malheur. In the FaceWorlds of what was already being called "The Oregon Standoff," nineteenth-century visions of the Mormon millennium marched beside the conflicted aspirations of 1776. With them came Ammon's Beautiful Pattern and the hardscrabble dreams of restless homesteaders. Now these were joined by the refusal of the Wadatika of Harney County to ever give up their claims—moral, legal, spiritual, and historical—on the land of their ancestors, this wide-open, windswept country to which they, like no one else, belonged.

CHAPTER TEN

Zion's Camp

The Unburial of Zelph

IN 1834, JOSEPH SMITH WAS LEADING AN ARMY of Latter-day Saints west from the fledgling Mormon capital of Kirtland, Ohio, to the Missouri territory when he halted the march, gathered his fellows around him, and performed an impromptu ceremony over a hilltop Native American gravesite. Zion's Camp, as the force had dubbed itself, was on its way to intervene in a growing conflict between a new Mormon colony and other white settlers at what was then the far frontier. For the moment that would have to wait. Some of the faithful had spotted what looked like shards of human bone on the surface of one of the many mysterious human-made earthworks so common to the region. The following words, attributed in scripture to Joseph Smith himself but actually culled together after the fact from the accounts of those present and published after Smith's death, describe what happened next:

> The brethren procured a shovel and a hoe, and removing the earth to the depth of about one foot, discovered the skeleton of a man, almost entire, and between his ribs the stone point of a Lamanitish arrow, which evidently produced his death. Elder Burr Riggs retained the arrow. The contemplation of the scenery around us produced peculiar sensations in our bosoms; and subsequently the visions of the past being opened to my understanding by the Spirit of the Almighty, I discovered that the person whose skeleton was before

us was a white Lamanite, a large, thickset man, and a man of God. His name was Zelph. He was a warrior and chieftain under the great prophet Onandagus, who was known from the Hill Cumorah, or eastern sea to the Rocky Mountains. The curse was taken from Zelph, or at least, in part—one of his thigh bones was broken by a stone flung from a sling, while in battle, years before his death. He was killed in battle by the arrow found among his ribs, during the last great struggle of the Lamanites and Nephites.

After Smith had spoken his words over Zelph, the other faithful swarmed his remains. Brigham Young carried off the arrowhead that seemed to have brought poor Zelph to his mortal end. Other members of the church elite carried off pieces of the skeleton itself as relics.

The Treasure of Cumorah

On January 6, when reporters, fresh from the news conference at the Wadatika Gathering Center in Burns, arrived at the refuge for the CCF's daily eleven A.M. press conference, they asked Ammon Bundy about the tribe's rejection of his claims to be working on behalf of the historical, rightful owners of the lands of the refuge. Ammon at first clearly didn't know what to say. He was exhausted. He and his friends had been up all night at the front gate awaiting a rumored final showdown with the FBI. This new element seemed to take him entirely by surprise. "I really don't know anything about that," he said. "That is interesting and they have rights as well. I would like to see them be free from the federal government as well," he added. If the entrance of the Burns-Paiute into the dispute surrounding the occupation troubled the Latter-day Saint leadership of the Bundy militia differently than any other opposition they encountered—and it did—perhaps some of the deeper reasons could be found in the grand story their prophet Joseph Smith had made about the American continent and its Native inhabitants.

Mormonism was a radically New World Faith, a remaking of Judeo-Christianity for a different continent. As such, it was deeply concerned with that continent—its history, its peoples, and its land, down to the dirt and rocks. Faced with the evidence that this New World was not at all new, but ancient, Joseph Smith and his followers had looked into the earth and found not the past of Native America but a version of themselves. The evidence for this seemed to lie all around them. Mounds, like the Illinois mound from which the remains of Zelph were extracted, were also common across the region of western New York where the holy scripture of the Latter-day Saints was first revealed to young Joseph. There, and across the frontier lands of the Ohio and Mississippi Valleys, puzzling earthworks and funereal hillocks covered the landscape. Some were found to contain ornate metalwork and figures of startling realism—too advanced, many settlers believed, to have been made by contemporary Natives. Frequently, these mounds also contained human remains, sometimes in great quantity. Some of the dead, like Zelph, appeared to have perished suddenly and violently, sometimes en masse. The group burials and mysterious artifacts convinced many settlers that they walked on an ancient land, haunted by a vanished race that had been wiped out in some kind of cataclysmic war—perhaps by the very contemporary Indians whom white settlers alternately feared, romanticized, and despised.

Despite plentiful evidence of cultural continuity, most whites of the day held that the civilization that had built the mounds had to be unrelated to those contemporary people who were still stubbornly occupying so much of the coveted frontier land of the restless new republic. It wasn't just creative young rubes like Joseph Smith who dreamed up or subscribed to existing imaginary histories for the bones and artifacts hidden in all that American Dirt. Luminaries of the new nation also endorsed theories of earlier, whiter inhabitants of the New World. These included frontier war hero (and shortest-serving American president) William Henry Harrison and long-time New York Governor DeWitt Clinton, who conducted his own investigations of burial mounds in western New York and wrote a scholarly paper on the topic.

Like their colonist forebears, white citizens of the new republic were obsessed not only with the mysterious burial mounds of the past, but with the origins of the present-day Native peoples that they lived alongside, and alternately traded with and fought. These theories tended to involve a biblical genesis, sweeping indigenous people up in the totalizing millennial arc of Christian history. Whether American Indians were seen as figures of Edenic nostalgia or children of Cain, marked and driven naked over the earth, early European Americans found ways to incorporate Natives into the Bible. Many of the great early Anglo-American theologians were convinced that Native Americans were lost Israelites but nobody was to take it as far as Joseph Smith. Despite—or perhaps because of—his humble origins, Smith was endowed with an uncanny gift for intuiting and channeling the dreams and desires of his age. With his young man's imagination, he was able to unite different white fantasies about the aboriginal peoples and mysterious earthworks of the New World in a new Christianity, custom-made for the American frontier.

As a boy and young man, Smith had already distinguished himself as an inspiring teller of tales. His mother recalled him regaling her and others for hours with detailed narratives of the lives and cultures of the mysterious vanished race of people that had preceded them in this landscape, so visibly molded by past human hands. He was also, if less successfully, an avid treasure hunter, who passed his free time digging in the lands that surrounded his family's farm. In his adolescence, his treasure hunting became something of an employment, though never very profitable. It gave him a reputation as a bit of a charlatan in the region and, upon his marriage, he swore off the pursuit. But those childhood stories and all that digging were not entirely behind him. In his early twenties, they became the foundation of what he first seems to have imagined as a profitable literary work, a "lost" epic, whose sales might save his family's farm from the latest epidemic of foreclosures blasting the region. It wouldn't save the farm, but Smith's Book of Mormon quickly became the foundation of a brand-new religion that would sweep him and his family along a path that he himself at times confessed to find scarcely believable.

The composition of the Book of Mormon was an extraordinary occult literary performance in a century and a nation obsessed by such things. In the nineteenth century, enormous audiences composed of all classes of society would flock to see performances by renowned mediums and mesmerists. Séances were another popular entertainment. Literary artists live-composed works, dictated to them on stage by the dead. Meanwhile, everywhere, especially along the frontier, in the passionate revivalism known as the Second Great Awakening, Americans were giving themselves over to spontaneous possession by the Holy Spirit: babbling in unknown tongues, weeping, rolling on the floor, and even leaping up and barking like dogs, or running off into the wild night in pursuit of glowing visions in the starry frontier skies. The Awakening had been especially strong in the zone where Smith grew up, which came to be known as the Burned-Over District, exhausted as ground for fresh revivalisms, its denizens having already undergone too many paroxysms of faith.

In such a time and place, Smith's extravagant literary techniques and claims, risible in our own day, were right at home. Firstly, he claimed not to have written the text but to have been a mere vehicle for its arrival: the prophet was the translator, not the author, of scripture. The Book of Mormon, he swore—and he was the only person to ever gaze directly on the original script—was written in an unknown ancient language and alphabet. Fortunately it also came with a decoder kit: two magic seeing stones with names straight out of the Old Testament—Urim and Thummim. The book itself, as befit its discovery by the young treasure hunter, was made of gold, with gold-leaf pages bound by three rings. Joseph had found it, he said, buried in a great hillside on the turnpike near his family's farm outside Manchester, New York. The hill, called Cumorah, was believed by Smith and many of his neighbors to be yet another ancient burial mound. He'd been guided there by an angel, he said, who'd begun appearing to him in his adolescence.

The composition of the English-language version of the book was a collaborative effort. Using the two seeing stones, he dictated the translation to his young wife, Emma, and a pair of early acolytes. Smith's scribes marveled at how the tales delivered by the new prophet confirmed and elaborated on all their widely held suspicions about ancient America. The story began back in the Holy Land, with the prophet Lehi who, at the command of God, led his family and his followers on a sea journey to the New World. Conflict between Lehi's sons Nephi and Laman split the Israelite settlers into factions. One, called the Nephites—the followers of Nephi—remained God-fearing and therefore "white." The others, followers of Laman, were given "skins of blackness" as a marker of their sin. Centuries of conflict followed, before a brief reconciliation brought on by the preachings of Christ. This peaceful interregnum ended in another schism, which led to two centuries of fratricidal war. The dead in many of those burial mounds of North America were understood as being mostly Nephites, slaughtered in battle with the Lamanites who had eventually wiped out their white brothers—a divine punishment for the Nephites' abandonment of God and Christ. And so it was that only red men had remained when the gentiles of Europe arrived on the shores of America.

In his holy tablets, Smith had extracted—from land otherwise poorly equipped to dispense anything but debt and misery on small farmers—a treasure much grander than mere economic subsistence or the elusive promise of mineral wealth. From the ancient dirt, he'd dug up a past that pointed to a Future for this new nation: an American Story that was also the destiny of humanity. Most of all, he'd dug up a feeling, a Big American Feeling, where Freedom found its messianic fulfillment in the completion of all human time. The story of the Book of Mormon gave structure to the feeling, and so the feeling endured and grew, driving his followers, through wilder and wilder lands, ever westward.

*   *   *

"Feeling" is another word for the human experience of the passage of time. Whether in terror, boredom, pain, bliss, dread, or mirth, feelings are how the movements, tiny and grand, of our fleeting lives register themselves as meaning in the meat of our bodies and in the more secret substance, the soul stuff, of our interiors. The power of the dispensation that Ammon had been raised in had taught him what it meant to live fully in a great millennial arc of feeling. It had taught him how a single narrative could gather other stories to it, weaving bodies and souls into an enduring accomplishment.

In America, nobody had ever done it quite like Joseph Smith had, and Ammon was a child of his prophet. He owed even his name to Joseph Smith. In the Book of Mormon, it was told how Ammon had gone out as a missionary among the Lamanites, how he'd taken on the duty of guarding the Lamanite king Lahoni's livestock, how he'd stood up alone to the vicious rustlers and protected the flocks, alone miraculously defeating them, cutting off the arms of each and every marauding thief. This miracle had converted the Lamanite king, whose people would afterwards be known no longer as Lamanites, but as Ammonites.

These stories had propelled Ammon's own ancestors west, across the plains and the mountains, after the assassination of the prophet in the midst of his presidential campaign. Hurried on—by faith on one end and persecution on the other—they crossed the Rockies to establish Zion in the deserts of the West. In wagons they came; and then, when Joseph's successor, the organizational genius Brigham Young, decreed that wagons were too expensive, they'd come on foot, from the end of the rail line in Iowa City, pushing all their belongings in a wheelbarrow of a new efficient Mormon design. They'd built their Zion—and into its lonely, wild, and ragged desert edge, Ammon's grandparents and parents and then Ammon himself had been born.

Now here he was in 2016, a desert gatherer of souls himself, a storyteller—and even, some hinted, a prophet, touched by the revelations of Providence and by God's urges to complete Smith's later prophecies and save the Constitution. In the new Zion's Camp of Malheur a brand-new band of Ammonites had been assembled, Necessary Bodies lit up in the flesh by

Ammon's words and the American story he was telling: from here on out they would all be making it and telling it together.

The Community and the One

When I first began to follow the occupation of Malheur in early January of 2016, I was appalled by the CCF's rhetoric of assault on federal public land—one of the few aspects of our current national dispensation that I personally value without ambivalence. But I was also certain that at least some of the ebullience they emanated must have come from the basin—that public land on which they found themselves: the brooding buttes, the fragrant sage, the mad surging weather; all that distance. But that wasn't it at all, they told me when I finally caught up with them. Sure, it was an interesting place, even pretty at times. Sure, they liked climbing that fire tower and looking out at the views. But what they had really found there was something else: each other. *The community*, they said. *The only one I've ever known*, said one. *All for one and one for all*, said more than one, more than once. *You can't understand it*, they said. *You can't really know it unless you were there.*

One of the many occupiers who spoke to me with fervor about the feeling of community at the refuge was a young former marijuana-dispensary worker turned full-time libertarian activist named Matthew Deatherage. His ideal society, he told me, was "probably tribal." For Deatherage, his time at the occupation had been a revelation. "Honestly, it was the first time I ever felt community," he would tell the jury in federal court in Portland, after it had all come to an end. He said the same to me on the steps outside the courthouse on another afternoon, where he stood, as he had most days of the trial, with a colorful flag draped over his shoulder. It wasn't an American flag, or a Gadsden flag, or even the new banner popular with his friends, a black-and-white flag bearing the cattle brand of LaVoy Finicum, the now-martyred cowboy hero of Liberty. The flag running down Matthew's back, flapping in the small gusts of the passing rush-hour traffic, was from another world: it was a Tibetan "war flag," as he called it. The struggle for the liberty of Tibet was close to his heart, along with other causes that might surprise readers unfamiliar with the collage of issues that energized the denizens of Malheur. For Matthew, marijuana legalization and the reform of drug laws and prisons, as well as the wider introduction of Montessori education and, through it, freethinking into the American populace, all linked nicely with the restoration of the Constitution advocated by Ammon and friends. Like Ammon, he felt that the simple restoration of the Constitution would remedy seemingly intractable social problems such as poverty and homelessness, an argument he was making that fall in his Ron Paul–inspired campaign for mayor in his hometown of Coos Bay, Oregon.

When I asked Matthew why the community had been so strong on the refuge, he spoke of the total absence of private property lines and, with that, the absence of neighbors. "I think what people call community now isn't community. They don't look to help each other—they look to what they can get from each other. It starts in the public school. Kids aren't nurtured to see what kind of special thing they each bring; they're just taught to want to make money." It was money he saw as the root of the problem. "It pacifies people," Matthew told me. "That's why I've chosen poverty." Wealth, he thought, should be held in common for the common good.

It was one of his favorite things about the occupation: they'd lived all those days without money. OK, sure, the people who'd donated stuff had bought the food with money, so they weren't *totally* outside the system, but for a few precious days out in the wind and the sage, they had lived an economy apart, where Matthew could feel for a moment that his activity wasn't, as he put it, "contributing to the war machine."

Opposition to the military-industrial complex was not uncommon among the Malheur occupiers, in spite of the presence of heavily armed militia types and others demonstrably committed to exercising their Second Amendment rights. A few of the Necessary Bodies were veterans unhappy about what they ultimately felt had been "unconstitutional disservice," as Ryan Payne put it. One of these was Neil Wampler.

Wampler had taken up his favored role of cook. "It's good to be the cook," he explained. "Nobody messes with the cook." On his breaks he'd chat quietly with other occupiers or visitors, often about his favorite topic: U.S. history. To Neil, the occupation seemed to be the revolution he and his hippie friends had dreamed of. He felt that what he was now a part of was something like the march of the veterans on Washington during the Great Depression—or the 1969–71 Native American takeover of Alcatraz Island. He was here to participate in the endless American fight for liberty, a struggle that had not at all ended with the nation's founding; even back in the very first years of the republic, "the federal bastards" had gone and passed the Alien and Sedition Acts, as he reminded me.

Neil took a more circumspect view of the carnival. More discipline would have been better, he thought, but what they needed most were bodies—even if some had to get the story of who the Bundys were from the bemused old man smoking outside the cook shack. He had maybe the best name for the whole crazy thing: our *Rural Electrification Project* he called it, glinting a bit each time he said it, in enjoyment of his own wit. He was likely going a bit over the heads of most of his comrades. Few in his audience would have known much or anything about FDR's Rural Electrification Administration, or that it had operated in the same era as the Civilian Conservation Corps, whose jobs project, in the days of the Great Depression, had gathered up the energies of under- and unemployed men to build things like the compound of the refuge headquarters, where they all were now staying.

Ammon's and his friends' New Deal was offering something more than work, or infrastructure. The Rural Electrification Neil was referring to was largely, or mostly, about feeling. As the Necessary Bodies arrived, they came in all kinds of different states, some eager, some wary, some boisterous and ignorant, others drunk and ornery—but they all, as far as Neil could tell, left "jazzed up" with the feeling of the place—that spirit that was circulating there, amplifying itself. This electrification—you could sense it—was spreading outward from the refuge.

It had worked that way for him too. The whole movement had lit him up and changed his life. Reaching for how to describe it, he kept falling back into what he called "all the clichéd words: *transformation, growth.*" He had felt himself "becoming a part of life in a very real way." He'd "always been a loner kind of person, but now these barriers started coming down. I've never felt so alive and full of fight: I can't recommend this life enough."

* * *

But wait a minute. Wasn't this stand for freedom supposed to be all about individuals, property, cowboys? What was all this utopian sounding communitarianism? Rural Electrification? Yes, Neil was being ironic, but still, weren't these people the sorts who ranted against Obamacare as socialism? Listening to so many of the Necessary Bodies, it sounded like the real purpose of all this was their community, that the real plan was *them*—their simply being there together. Could this possibly be?

If you listened to the more official statements of the occupation's leadership, the answer to these questions was most certainly *no*. This was all about Article I, Section 8, Clause 17. It was all about property rights and the individual, not the social joy and sense of community to which the occupation had given shape and location. Indeed, at times it seemed that LaVoy Finicum—like Margaret Thatcher famously before him—didn't even believe in the existence of society in the conventional sense. Instead he spoke of the plight, agency, and heroism of the lone entity he referred to sometimes simply as *the One*.

The official politics of the CCF were libertarian to the core, a kind of cowboy Ayn Randianism—of which Finicum and Ammon's brother Ryan were maybe the most zealous advocates. LaVoy's appearance got more elfin every day in Oregon—with his earmuffs and his wind-polished red face shining there under his not quite ten-gallon hat—but his statements grew no less militant. In his vision, the respect for private property governed all human relations as well as all relations between humans and the natural world. That principle—and the gun that every good property owner carried to keep his fellow men in check—created the proper conditions for what Finicum considered neighborliness. With our guns in our holsters, LaVoy preached, and our property lines drawn, neighborliness could reign.

It was a startling vision of individualist society—the antithesis of Matthew Deatherage's imagined moneyless community—but it may be no less utopian. The actual history of the West, as Patricia Limerick has pointed out, is inseparable from the ongoing failure to adequately wrap Finicum's concept of private property around the region's forbidding landscapes and resources. Grazing rights, mineral rights, hunting rights, foraging rights, logging rights, and water rights—again and again have come up against the limits of their descriptive power and practical use, as generations of settlers have attempted to mold these abstractions to the dry, unyielding, rocky realities of the arid West. Rain has never literally followed the plow, and rarely has it done so figuratively either. The ghost towns that form a staple of western tourism are one material reminder of the land's resistance to our American hopes and ideas. But somehow it doesn't matter; all those ghost towns—those would-be object lessons—have instead become glittering fetishes, scattered across a treasure map of the Old West, only adding to the appeal of a fantasy like Finicum's. Indeed, LaVoy was already, in life, a bit like a western specter himself: a real Ghost Rider in the Sky—and not just because he looked and talked like a character torn from the mythic pages of western literature or lifted off the silver-studded screen. In the months before Malheur, LaVoy Finicum had made his own contribution to the genre.

If God's feelings had led Ammon to write his way into providential clarity and jump-start his mission to Oregon, the experience of Bundy Ranch and the need to further articulate the vision growing within LaVoy had turned him into a literary artist. In the wake of Bundy Ranch, he'd written a genre-bending, post-apocalyptic western novel. And then gotten it published. In *Only by Blood and Suffering: Regaining Lost Freedom*, Finicum reimagines the red rock country of his childhood in a fantasy frontier state, clearing it of government power and of most modern technology—except high-powered assault weapons, sniper rifles, and lovingly described semiautomatic handguns—through the plot device of an atmospheric nuclear blast. Shortly after the book opens, America is hit, presumably by Russia, with an electro-magnetic pulse bomb attack, which permanently disables nearly all vehicles, computers, and the power grid, adding to the chaos of the total economic and social meltdown already under way. In this brave new world, Finicum's hero and avatar—a diligently prepared rancher named Jake Bonham—leads the armed resistance of heroic individual "producers" (ranchers of Utah's Long Valley) against a cadre of weak townspeople, hell-bent on appropriating their property. The townsfolk have abandoned the proper strictures of Finicum's neighborliness, having been seduced into a tyrannical, resource-sharing communitarian arrangement by a local high-school football hero turned diabolical federal agent. This agent is a leading figure in a deep-state shadow government called simply "the Society."

In its standoff with the Society, the isolated ranch of the Bonham family becomes another desert outpost of the Freest Place on Earth. But while the standoff at the Apocalypse Ranch of Finicum's imagination mirrors those at Malheur and the Bundy Ranch in many ways, marking out a sovereign territory—an *unfucked zone*, as Jon Ritzheimer might have put it—in a sea of tyranny, what it is decidedly *not* home to is a millenarian commune. Finicum's literary ranch is not the compound of a one-for-all-and-all-for-one brotherhood of the kind I kept hearing about from Malheur occupiers. That type of sharing is limited exclusively to the bosom of family—the family of the One—in their armed redoubt. Even in the aftermath of nuclear war, it is private property and individual rights that govern all relations—a message reinforced in a number of dramatic, didactic, and sometimes grisly scenes throughout the novel. Violators of these principles meet a stern judge in Bonham, a self-appointed magistrate unafraid of making recourse to the terrifying remedy of the noose.

Yet, if property was LaVoy's truth, within the enchanted circle of the Malheur occupation, it was share and share alike. A few minutes with many a veteran of Malheur could easily have you convinced that while Finicum and the CCF presented daily doses of Cowboy Libertarianism at the refuge gates, what was actually being practiced down on the compound was something a bit more like voluntary religious socialism. *Community, Brotherhood, Love*: these were its terms.

To Live the United Order

Like everything at Malheur, this paradox had deeper roots. During the standoff at the family's ranch in 2014, Cliven Bundy had made much in the media of his family's claims to its water rights and its long-standing priorities to graze the land of what was now called the Bunkerville allotment, a swath of desert running south from Bunkerville to Lake Mead. His family had ranched this land since 1877, Cliven argued, long before the BLM or federal grazing allotments had even existed. The reporters who looked into Cliven's story about his personal 1877 water rights were confused: local records show that his parents had purchased the ranch and begun grazing the allotment in 1954. Some assumed the old rancher was demented or lying, but Cliven actually had a historical, if convoluted, basis for the claim, going back to the foundation of Bunkerville, in which his maternal ancestors had been key participants.

Bunkerville's first pioneers had been a band of eager, millenarian Mormons relocating from southern Utah. They'd followed the Virgin River down from St. George in order to "live the United Order," to consecrate what property they'd brought with them to the Lord and to their community, and thus to live in pious, industrious anticipation of the ushering in of the "dispensation of the fulness of times." This was a moment in Zion's history to which Brand Thornton's Latter-day Saint nostalgia was tuned. The Mormon Church, he felt, had begun moving down the wrong path when it had turned away from its nineteenth-century dream of the United Order, Joseph Smith's vision of a communal church modeled on the lives of the apostles as described in the book of Acts. The result had been its inevitable slide into the corruption and banksterism of the present day.

Leaving aside the thorny issue of the Southern Paiute Moapa Band's far deeper ancestral ties to this land, Cliven's asserted family rights seemed to go back to that utopian moment in Mormonism—not to the property claims of any particular legal individual, but to a history of use first established by a fervent community of faith. Insofar as Cliven's claim of continuous beneficial use of the open range back to 1877 arguably did exist, it did so partly through this community—which would have held that the rangelands belonged not to any of its individual members, nor to the federal government, nor to the people of Nevada, but to God.

The community itself had been both a shocking success and an acrimonious failure. The diligent founders made the desert bloom with their industry; their hand-dug irrigation projects resulted in massive crops of sugarcane, wheat, and other grains within a year. But the community's spirit had not held together long. Soon the quarrels that plague so many utopian collectives hit the new community of Bunkerville, and after two successful years, it began to fracture under the familiar sorts of interpersonal pressures. Some of the Saints weren't pulling their weight, it was charged; as their descendent Cliven Bundy might describe it, there was too much freeloading going on.

* * *

The Malheur occupation hadn't lasted long enough to blossom into a full-blown experimental community—a historical phenomenon as essentially American as the Constitutionalist emphasis on private property and rights—but even during its brief tenure, it had begun to experience some of the challenges of a self-constituting and relatively structureless society. Brand told a harrowing story of his front-gate guard-duty work during the occupation—an illustration of just how hairy the enforcement of the come-one, come-all policy could be. One afternoon, a notably drunk local man had driven up to the gate seeking entry and the chance to bring in some supplies and fraternize with the denizens of the Bundy Revolution. Obviously loaded, he'd also been visibly armed—with a pistol on his hip and an AR-15 leaning against the front passenger seat. It, Brand noted, was loaded too—a big old banana clip locked in place. Brand decided for himself then and there that while he had no authority to prevent anyone from visiting the refuge (he'd helped make the determination that no one really did), he wasn't going to allow this drunken visitor to walk around with a loaded rifle. "I was going to wrap him in a bear hug if he went to pick up that long gun," Brand told me. As the man stumbled out of his car, beer cans spilling out all around him, he didn't reach for his rifle, and Brand breathed a sigh of relief. Many days had brought moments of tension like this. For Brand the question of what to do about these unhinged visitors was among the scariest and prickliest things of the occupation. But there really were no rules of exclusion and no official leaders, so it was up to each of them to improvise their own reactions as best they could.

Yet, somehow, to their minds, it had all worked. As Neil Wampler reminded me and anyone who'd speak to him about the occupation, they'd had not one fatality, not one gunshot injury, not one shot fired in anger—not from *their side*, not in Oregon, nor anywhere else. Brand saw this as miraculous proof of the efficacy of the reticulations of his shofar in calling God's protection down upon them. "It was an organism," Matthew Deatherage said, shaking his head in continued astonishment at his memories, ten months after it had all collapsed in chaos and panic. To his mind, it was the government that blocked the existence of more ethical communities in the first place. "The government might kill you if you tried to form a commune," he said, and his experience at Malheur seemed to bear this out.

Mostly, despite all the talk of death and martyrdom that also marked the occupation, the fact that potentially lethal punishment had loomed on their horizon seemed only to have fed the vitality of their community of feelings. "You can't understand it unless you've lived it," Brand told me. "We all thought that any moment we could be killed." But they wouldn't be killed. Instead their community would grow and change, flocking from courthouse to prison to courthouse: a flash mob, one journalist would call them. *They* would live, it was *the One* who would perish.

CHAPTER ELEVEN

It's the Economy, Stupid

The Suicide Belt

WHEN HE LEAPT OFF THAT SNOWBANK IN BURNS, Ammon had invited his followers to dwell with him inside of a grand and powerful narrative. Now that story was unfolding daily beneath the phantom—increasingly real—of sovereign federal power. Federal Death loomed in the imaginations of the Necessary Bodies of Malheur, charging the world around them with thrill and dark portent. It all alarmed Montana journalist Hal Herring tremendously on his visit to the occupation. The air of mass suicide underlying the whole endeavor was something he couldn't take lightly. Suicide rates were rising all over America. They were rising in just about every demographic, but they were especially high among middle-aged white men who, in 2016, would account for seven of every ten self-inflicted deaths. In the Intermountain West, which people had been casually calling the Suicide Belt for some years now, the suicide rate was considerably higher. In 2016, Herring's home state of Montana had the highest rate in the nation.

The figures were bleak, but, for me, maybe the most unsettling thing about looking through suicide rate reports is the regular insistence on measuring the human loss in dollars. The economic loss caused by suicide in 2016 in Herring's Montana was estimated to be $253,380,000. I knew that those kinds of economic numbers were created to convince people that it was worth it to spend money to lower suicide rates, but why did it take that? Maybe this kind of logic had something to do with why people were dying. Hadn't the world taught them that the economy was more important than their individual lives? Isn't becoming a contemporary American adult a continuous process of learning to accept that really, in the larger scheme, nobody much mattered, that anyone was replaceable, that even in death, especially in death, you were a statistic, at best an argument for a policy intervention?

Sometimes researchers tried to explain the data a little more, narrativize it a bit—why were white men in the West the most successful at offing themselves? Discussing the western Suicide Belt, Nevada sociologist Matt Wray told the story like this: "The Intermountain West is a place that is disproportionately populated by middle-aged white men, single, unattached, often unemployed, with access to guns." Economic despair, the story goes. Loneliness, the story goes. Just you and the sagebrush, just you and the pines. Just you in your trailer and nobody's around and you know you are worthless, because, according to the real God of America, the Economy, *you are worthless*—and so you grab a gun. You have a lot of them lying around; now you put one in your mouth. If this was the story, and in the big, sociological picture it was, then it looked like Ammon was making an intervention that the larger society simply was not making. Need meaning? Need to feel like your life matters? Why not take a stand for freedom? No wonder you feel so bad: the Constitution is hanging by a thread! *Your Constitution!* But don't despair. It's not too late. If we act now, if we act today, *there is Hope.* The Beautiful Pattern can be restored. Prosperity and Happiness! Come on down: see what the Lord is about to accomplish. See what the Lord is about to accomplish through *you*.

Nothing made this more meaningful than the possibility you might die trying, a martyr, a patriot, live on the internet, under the watching eyes of the world. Everyone, for a moment, would know you'd been here. Everyone would know that Daddy took a stand.

* * *

Hal Herring also saw suicidal undercurrents in the economic platform of the CCF. If the Bundy Revolution got what it wanted, he noted, it would very likely be the final nail in the coffin for ranchers like the Bundys and LaVoy Finicum. Massive private interests were poised to grab up the public lands of the West. Among them was Ammon's own beloved Mormon Church, whose economic activities had already made it one of the largest private landholders in America. Millions of acres of available western land had been bought up by a few private interests in recent years: the billion-aire Koch brothers and the Mormon Church were just two among them. Here Ammon's and LaVoy's inability to account for global capital had them living in another century. Herring broke it all down: "Buyers, in a world packed and competitive beyond the imaginations of those who set aside these unclaimed and abandoned lands as forest reserves and public-grazing lands in the early 1900s, are now everywhere, planet-wide. As Utah state Rep. Ken Ivory, when he was president of the American Lands Council, famously said of privatizing federal lands, 'It's like having your hands on the lever of a modern-day Louisiana Purchase.'" By some esti-mates already one fifth of the wealth of the world was held in American real estate. Capital everywhere wanted in on that market. Add to the mix the potential value of water rights in an overheating world and the picture got only more dire.

Ammon and friends claimed they weren't advocating privatization; they said they wanted only to return the land to local control. One had to wonder if this claim was entirely true: "unwinding" sounded an awful lot like privatiza-tion. Still, even if you took them at their word, the CCF's local and state control platform, as Herring pointed out, would be a disaster for public land and for small-time western ranching. Cash-strapped states and communities—often bound by law to balance their budgets—would inevitably sell off at least some territory to make ends meet. That land would simply not go to smaller holders. There were too many big buyers out there in the global economy. But even without those contemporary buyers and their capital, small-time ranchers would never be able to afford the amount of range they would need to carry on. Land like the sagebrush steppe of the Great Basin, or the desert terrain of the Virgin Valley the Bundys called home, has never provided enough forage for small holders to be able to afford the quantities of land, or the taxes on it, that it takes to keep a cattle operation precariously afloat.

No matter how you broke it down, small ranchers depended on public land; without it they'd be finished. It was federal power—for all its flaws—that had helped keep that land available up till now for use by the ranchers whose plight the occupation had made its central cause. The Bundyites, pumped up on the energy of their messianic commune, were advocating for policies that would in all likelihood bring an economic end to the pictur-esque lives of cowboy freedom they idealized. Along the way, if they were victorious, they'd also deprive themselves and the rest of us of perhaps our single greatest public good. Precious ecosystems and water all over the American West would be turned into the private wealth of absentee and overseas landlords while the rest of us lost access forever to the meaningful intimations of peace, freedom, and spiritual connection that public land provides to its millions of users.

It was too much for Hal Herring, and he left in disgust. "I went to the Malheur looking for kindred spirits," he wrote. "I found the mad, the fervent, the passionately misguided. I found the unknowing pawns of an existential chess game, in which we are, all of us, all now caught." If the Bundy Revolution and its corporate co-religionists succeeded, Herring prophesied, "the unique American experiment in balancing the public freedom and good with private interests will be forever shattered, while a new kind of inequality soars, not just inequality of economics and economic opportunity, but of life experience, the chance to experience liberty itself. The understanding that we all share something valuable in common—the vast American landscape, yawning to all horizons and breathtakingly beautiful—will be further broken."

"A Place Called Hope"

We assume that we know exactly what we mean when we say "the economy": some combination of jobs, unemployment, taxes, public and private investment, inflation, the stock market, the prime lending rate—and everything else that is involved in the distribution and production systems of our world. The Hammonds, cause of all this drama, were now planted in the middle of the sort of scene that often serves as a stock image for what we understand "the economy" to be: the massive, heavily automated Port of Los Angeles. Images of ports, as well as factories and farms, are never so present on the nightly news as during presidential election years, like 2016. Presidents rise and fall, the wisdom goes, on the strength of the economy, and of the political messages—and of the feelings—they are able to pin to its circulations. "It's the economy, stupid," as James Carville, Bill Clinton's take-no-prisoners strategist, had phrased it for the edification of staff working on Clinton's successful '92 campaign. But the way Carville's phrase was taken up as a kind of meme in the pre–social media world of the '90s suggests that what circulates in economies is always much more than just goods and services. An economy is, in the last instance, a gathering up and distribution of bodies *and of spirit*. It's a machine also made of feelings, and, up until 2016, perhaps nobody in our era had understood that better than Carville's candidate Clinton.

"I feel your pain," Clinton had said in 1992 while he and his image circulated throughout the nation, from town hall to factory to small-town diner. As Clinton moved in the body of the people, on display were his famous skills for making everyone in whatever space he entered feel personally connected to him. He combined the communication talents necessary for making a set of neoliberal economic ideas seem comprehensible with the emotional—and theological—instincts it took to link those ideas to messianic feelings of American purpose and redemption. "I call this approach a New Covenant," he said in his famous nomination acceptance speech in 1992, repeating the phrase again and again, before closing with what became another of his signature lines, punning with the name of his Arkansas hometown: "I still believe in a place called Hope."

There are few politicians more hated in the ranchlands of the ragged edge of Mormonism than Bill Clinton. Clinton's designation of the Grand Staircase–Escalante National Monument was seen by die-hard, long-term Bundy supporters like Shawna Cox as an instigating moment for their movement. The Hammonds' conflicts with the federal government had exploded in the first years of the Clinton administration, which is also when the Bundy family's struggles had begun. And yet, in his style and in his talents, Ammon Bundy resembled Bill Clinton more than any living right-wing politician who has crossed my American screen since the death of Ronald Reagan. When it came down to it, Ammon was also proposing a New Covenant. With the return of constitutionality, he promised, would come a new economic distribution of matter and spirit; vibrancy and purpose would be restored to the forgotten, irrelevant lives and bodies of the Suicide Belt. *I feel your pain*, Ammon said, in his own words, reflecting that pain in his face (and with the suffering of his family), while also turning it, with the preachy magic of his constitutional seminars, into a word even bigger than Hope—the biggest American word: *Freedom*.

The Hand of Providence

I don't know if you are old enough to remember Bill Clinton's rousing 1992 Democratic Convention address, the one in which he accepted his party's nomination. It was Clinton at his most masterful; it may have been his greatest speech, alongside the one he gave for Barack Obama at the Denver convention of 2012. The '92 address perfectly combined a technocratic authority with preacherly waves of emotion, feelings about the dreams of hardworking Americans, feelings that can still induce a strong emotional response more than two decades later, even in viewers and readers like myself, as wary as I am of all the Third Way rhetoric, ideology, and policy of the Clinton years.

"I call this approach a New Covenant." It's powerful stuff, especially when you have the skills to deliver it in the humble demeanor of a man folks could actually think to call "Bubba." He was the first truly post–Cold War president, the first executive elected into the new era of Western globalist triumphalism. Throughout the nineties, centrist leaders like Clinton would tell us that our unfettered financial sectors and globalized economies would solve our social problems, restoring hope, and that we'd all feel good together soon. It was LBJ's Great Society, as if wholly revised by Goldman Sachs with a little bit of Divine Providence thrown in to leaven the mix. Capital would now be freed to go where it needed to go, and subsequent growth would now distribute, thanks to a more nimble economy, goods and opportunities to all who needed them. This was what political and economic theorists call neoliberalism—a doubling down on the belief that markets, if allowed to function optimally, would bring universal prosperity and happiness. Those it would elude would be the ones who simply weren't willing to work for it, or so the logic went.

In the next two decades the dream fell apart. By 2008 one of the supreme proponents of this worldview confessed just how faith-based the whole thing had been. Under questioning from Representative Henry Waxman, Alan Greenspan, deregulation guru and head of the Federal Reserve Bank from the tail end of the Reagan administration through the Clinton years and into the second term of the George W. Bush administration, confessed that, yes, he, supreme rationalist, had functioned all this time according not to a coldly rational and scientifically tested set of proven objective economic laws, but rather to a system of belief. Waxman asked him about his earlier admission that he had based his decisions over the years on what he called an ideology, an ideology that, he confessed now, was flawed. "Remember that what an ideology is, is a conceptual framework with the way people deal with reality," Greenspan said. "Everyone has one. You have to—to exist, you need an ideology. The question is whether it's accurate or not. And what I'm saying to you is, yes, I've found a flaw." It wasn't really Greenspan who found the flaw. The whole economy had found it: it had just crashed, and only a massive infusion of government bailout money would save us now from another worldwide Great Depression. The crisis had been brought on partly by some of the policies pushed for years by Greenspan, policies that had been foundational to Bill Clinton's New Covenant.

"You found a flaw in reality . . ." Waxman suggested, perhaps ironically.

"Flaw in the model that I perceived as the critical functioning structure that defines how the world works, so to speak," Greenspan answered.

"In other words, you found that your view of the world, your ideology, was not right. It was not working," Waxman paraphrased.

"Precisely," Greenspan replied.

* * *

Greenspan's ideology is also a kind of shadow theology. All our theories of economy are shadow theologies in one way or another—our ideas of what an economic dispensation is are inherited from the core theological debates of early Christianity. *Economy, oikonomia* in Greek, was originally a term referring to the organization of goods within the household, in the private sphere, as survives in uses like *home economics*. It was appropriated into theological discourse in the debates that proposed to settle the controversy over the multiple natures of the Christian God. The Holy Trinity, as the early fifth-century theologians put it, was an economy through which God was distributed. God was both a singularity and a plurality—a circulation between three entities: the Father, the Son, and the Holy Spirit. Through the Holy Spirit, the providential economy of God also operated on earth, in human affairs, guiding humans toward correct choices while not depriving them of the personal agency they needed for their eternal salvation. This is how Ammon Bundy and his brother Ryan described the action of the Holy Ghost, as well as how Ammon described his own theories of leadership and education. God governed the world not as an autocrat but instead through his divine economy.

This hand of Providence, so important to the thinking of Ammon's own descriptions of how he and the occupiers had come to Malheur, was also the inspiration for perhaps the single most influential economic idea ever: Adam Smith's foundational idea of the invisible hand of the market. Greenspan's ideology, and Bill Clinton's, had, when stripped down, really been a restoration—and a drastic fundamentalist expansion—of faith in the action of this providential hand. Neoliberalism was based on the trust that the selfish actions of free individuals produced beneficial results for an entire society more effectively than direct attempts at amelioration—to a degree far beyond what Adam Smith himself would have likely supported. In the 1990s, a centrist consensus had emerged in the Western world around these beliefs. Some spoke of things like the end of history and even politics, of a New World Order in which good governance became, simply, efficient apolitical management, and the rest of the folks settled down to the good life. The whole ideology of the era boiled down to something like Carville's snarky little slogan: "It's the economy, stupid." As the years rolled on and the stock markets rose, not so many in the new consensus had bothered to wonder if it was possible that the economy itself, made of people, as it was, might prove in the end to be as stupid as we were.

A Place Called Punishment

As it turned out, economies could be stupid too. Much of what Bill Clinton had dreamed of—a neoliberal economic dispensation that would reward the hardworking middle and lower-middle class—was pretty much dead by 2016. On the other hand, aspects of the New Covenant were still very much with us. One was the internet, produced by an explosive synergy of capital flows, entrepreneurial "energy," and rapid technological advances. Another was our vast American economy of punishment, the flip side of our fraught economy of mattering. Bill Clinton hadn't invented the War on Drugs or the War on Crime: these were Nixonian tactics, deliberately calibrated to appeal to white voters and punish black communities. Still, despite his antiracist convictions and feeling for the poor, Clinton had doubled down on crime—in some cases, looking at the statistics that emerged from the nineties—literally. Under Clinton the federal prisoner population doubled, mostly due to drug offenses. In another telling statistic, his administration cut seventeen billion dollars from public housing, while adding nineteen billion dollars to the federal budget for prisons. A long-term side effect of the bipartisan mania for punishment was a bonanza in the growth of perhaps the ultimate dystopian figure of neoliberal governance: the for-profit private-prison sector.

The human costs of the recent American mania for incarceration have yet to be fully tallied. Most of us—some of us much more directly than others—have a sense of lives unfairly, unduly derailed, but the full scale of it eludes us; it's too large to hold this catastrophe in the mind. Differently hidden is the presence our carceral culture has in the unconscious psychic life of the nation. To political theorist Wendy Brown, one of many disturbing political characteristics of neoliberal America is our cultural, economic, and psychic investment in punishment. The redemption Ammon seemed to be offering, in which the otherwise Unnecessary Bodies of the faithful could be transfigured into sites of patriotic meaning, seemed to me to ultimately rest on what Brown has described as a *psychic economy of punishment*—a circulation, in which, she argues, "freedom is nowhere to be found." As Brown explains it, a political subject, like an injured or forsaken child in a family, easily ends up unconsciously substituting punishment for the love and acceptance withheld in the imaginary space of the Nation—a space in which they nonetheless, regardless of their feelings of ambivalence and injury, must have their being and live their lives. In other words, it's better to be wanted badly than to not be wanted at all. The phrase names an unconscious structure of feeling that has gathered more valence in a neoliberal world, where more and more feel, not without reason, that their lives have become increasingly disposable.

Of course, *actual* punishment is unpleasant for most people, so what Brown describes takes place mostly in the murky, confused realm of fantasy identification. Most of us will do what it takes to stay out of the eye of the State, or any other entity, for that matter, when it seems to be in a punishing mood—which doesn't mean that many of us don't enjoy consuming scenes of torture, or the fantasy deployment of high-tech, deadly police and military force. (Or low-tech force, as in *Cops*, regularly the most popular reality show in the Clinton years.) The Necessary Bodies of Malheur, on the other hand, were disconcertingly eager to place themselves right in the sights of the Law. And for a few weeks at the beginning of 2016, this terribly excited the rest of a nation that also had its gaze trained upon the bull's-eye of Malheur.

*   *   *

Punishment was actually what had started it all off—the mandatory sentences reimposed on the Hammonds. In one way, symbolically, the occupiers had initially offered their bodies in the place of Dwight and Steven. Now it had all morphed into something much grander, as the foot soldiers of the Bundy Revolution hunkered down on the old WPA compound and called forth the magisterial violence of the modern state. It was as if they were inviting the abstraction of their Nation to finally appear and use their bodies as a site on which to manifest its Sovereignty in all its Punishing Glory, like they were summoning a neglectful or sadistic God, an iteration of the old desert one who'd given Abraham the famous command to sacrifice his son Isaac. If they couldn't restore their Constitution and their country, at least they could be American martyrs, slaughtered by their Big Bad American Daddy—in real time on Facebook Live. The suicidal-seeming bravado of the Ammonites had troubled Hal Herring deeply, and he'd left the occupied refuge, certain that someone was going to be sacrificed before this was all over.

But it wasn't just the Bundyites who were invested in the American Economy of Punishment. At Malheur, seemingly everyone wanted to see somebody punished. The Patriots wanted to punish the feds and their supposed liberal enablers, and seemed to crave punishment and victim attention for their own forgotten-feeling selves. The way they courted confrontation and the possibility of lethal retribution was startling—but so was the eagerness of many, expressed in the various righteous or vituperative idioms of the internet—to see them get what they were perceived to be asking for. Out in the ether, strangers wanted to punish the Ammonites for their criminal offenses (though it remained strangely unclear for the moment, beyond misdemeanor trespassing, which actual federal laws they had violated) or for the whole racist, unfair ontological order and history we've inherited, and which the occupiers seemed to so many of us to stand for.

The calls for the violent removal of the occupiers, and even for their deaths, came fast and thick. Sometimes these were uttered in the subjunctive phrasings of an understandably frustrated moral language—*What if they were black? What if they'd been Muslim?*—voicing impatience with the strategic patience of the FBI. The agency's strategies would pay off in the end, but in the moment it seemed to many to be yet more evidence of the drastic and persistent inequality in the distribution of the violence of law enforcement across the country, the latest proof that some folks—white ones—still mattered more in America. When a black child could be shot for playing with a toy gun, it was easy to understand the outrage stirred up by the sight of white men with guns occupying a federal facility—even if the white impunity attributed to the occupiers would prove to be largely illusory.

I understood the basic logic of the subjunctive calls for their removal. In conversations I, too, had joined that chorus, deploying my share of "what if they were" and "would" clauses, angered at the shortsightedness of the occupiers' actions, at the blind historical offense they were giving to the tribe, the only rightful owners I could see. It made it all the worse that they were doing all this in the name of a foolhardy political program that would, if achieved, likely end in stripping the American people of much of the priceless public land of the West. I wanted the Ammonites out of there. I wanted their terrible ideas about public land off the news. But over time I also began to wonder about what I was saying—and about how I was saying it—whenever I uttered a "what if they'd been" phrase? Was this a call for justice or just for more killability? Hadn't I been horrified, in 2013, to watch Boston's police deploy martial law–like conditions, armored assault vehicles, and militarized tactical squads on the streets of an American city in the search for one immigrant teenager, the sole surviving Boston Marathon bomber? Was I really calling for similar federal units, now bivouacked out at the Burns airport, to stop holding back? Did I want them to rush in and rain death down on the Bundyites—who had actually killed no one, assaulted no one? Did I want this just because I found the land politics of the occupiers to be foolish or dangerous or offensive? What was most disturbing was the kind of pleasure it clearly gave me. To be able to invoke such violence privatized it, made it possible, in fantasy, to imagine that it was mine to compel. It felt good to feel that powerful for a second without having to examine the source of the power. It felt good to feel, briefly, that the FBI was on my side and that America was for me and my priorities. It felt similar, I bet, to what the occupiers felt, invoking the Founding Fathers and the Constitution to bolster their own vision of a more just world.

The ugly trolling language that was also being directed at the occupiers gave me additional pause—was I part of the same current as the folks who patrolled Facebook and the comments section of YouTube videos and news articles boasting of how if they were president Ammon and company would already have been shot, or gleefully forecasting prison rape, or offering the occupiers cyanide capsules—or vodka, so that they might get drunk and shoot each other? At the same time the more righteous subjunctive mode never stopped making sense to me when I heard it in Jarvis Kennedy's voice. It was different when Jarvis used it. In his phrasings the abstract rhetoric of *what if* clauses was historically grounded in what had happened to the Paiute when they'd tried to make a stand here for their liberty and self-determination. The particularity made all the difference—pointing at what seemed to me to be the core offense of the occupation—one that seemed more historical and spiritual than specifically criminal—that this stand for "Freedom" with all its Tea Party, Constitutionalist, and Libertarian bluster, was really also a blithe reenactment of white settlement. With their guns and their bravado, whether they understood it this way or not, they were doubling down on a vast historical crime. That the settler idiom of the Beautiful Pattern seemed, for the moment, to be the main one in which the occupiers could conceive and speak of human freedom just made the whole thing seem more deeply—and dolefully—American. As an early observer of the occupation, scholar Jedediah Purdy, pointed out, the trouble with the Bundyites' use of arms wasn't about white impunity exactly, but rather the historical meaning of the use of those arms—"It is too much to call the occupiers 'domestic terrorists,' as the Oklahoma City Bomber Timothy McVeigh or the Klan were," Purdy wrote in the *New Yorker*, "but it is also obtuse to ignore the special comfort that certain white men have using guns as props in their acts of not-quite-civil disobedience. After all, guns were how they acquired their special sense of entitlement to public lands in the first place."

But more nuanced voices like Purdy's were drowned out in the heady days of the occupation. For the moment everyone seemed too caught up in the Economy of Punishment, waiting for the hammer to fall, and it gave an unpleasant image of a version of that imaginary thing a nation is. With the extra help of the internet, all of us who'd been caught up in this story were now gathered and held together in awful anticipation of an impending national ceremony of punishment and sacrifice: the yet to come final raid of the feds. In the hum of the news trucks and the glow of our screens, here we were, both divided and together—plugged into what exactly? Was this what being a powerful country was all about in the end—the worship of violence? Maybe it was. Maybe this was just the truth. Maybe all nations are structured around regular ceremonies of sacrifice in some way or another, around the honoring of war-dead and other martyrs, and around the regular punishment of selected victims—foreign and domestic. In such rites the life and death power of the State can periodically manifest its awful majesty while allowing us (or some of us) to identify in our various ways with its glory. But the faith in a better kind of national community that America continually demands—or claims to demand—of its people doesn't abide well with such macabre understandings of ritual statecraft. Could a different economy other than that of punishment finally emerge from the political morass of our present—a national dispensation of coexistence that actually honored the best in human notions of Liberty? It was hard, watching from

Malheur, to see how that might happen. And yet, at the same time, events out at the Bad Luck National Wildlife Refuge—and other events to come in 2016— seemed to make clear just how much the survival of the American nation will depend on it.

"LOL Economics"

What we were left with in America, two and a half decades after Bill Clinton had announced the coming of a New Covenant, was the world's by far highest prison population, an ever-widening gap between the superrich and everyone else, soul-crushing debt for students and working people, millions of people strung out on opiates, endless-seeming wars around the world, and the increasingly calamitous results of impending—and already happening—climate change. In exchange for all this we'd gotten a world-wide social mind that allowed us to share all our ugly feelings instantly.

All that capital that had been freed up in the '90s had helped give us the tech explosion and all the privately owned, data-gathering social media plat-forms, where more and more of our social lives took place. It was on these platforms that the occupation also took place; even in Harney County the occupation seemed to happen as much on social media as it did in town or in the desert. This meant that the whole event naturally partook of the web's familiar mix of outrage, self-righteousness, fear, sadism, absurd humor—and even a little bit of pornography.

The laughter and terror of Malheur made for a rich figuration of our wider cultural and political moment. If this is our apocalypse, it is going to be a silly one. It's going to be a smutty one too. By 2018 we'd get the terror of a mistaken incoming *this-is-not-a-test* missile alert in Hawaii, communi-cated by error statewide through everyone's cell phone—and shortly after, *the laughter*, when the pornography site Pornhub released its minute-by-minute usage numbers for the same moments in space and time. Thousands and thousands of Hawaiians—the People, the data seemed to intimate—had plunged from the last moments of their lives right into internet-enabled masturbation. It all seemed yet more proof that the internet, a machine for the continuous co-presencing of the illusory totality of human existence, had discovered its apotheosis in pornography. This, the Porn Web said, was humanity: an infinite-seeming assemblage of hot and bothered bodies, contorted in every imaginable aspect of desire. When the occupiers plugged their Rural Electrification Project into its wider circulations, it was only a matter of time before they found themselves splattered with obscenities.

The immediate cause was a widely circulated list—including French vanilla creamer and other risible condiments—that the occupiers had broadcast to the interweb as a part of a poorly phrased supply request for "snacks." Mockery of the plea became a news item of its own. Some of the occupiers even enjoyed it. Duane Ehmer, laughing about it a year later, told me a friend of his had made him a Gadsden flag with the "Don't Tread on Me" slogan replaced by the words "Send Snacks." Other forms of mockery were less friendly and more obscene. Hundreds of cocks, big, fleshy, plastic ones, and tiny, gummified edibles, were shipped to them by the boxful at the address the occupiers had provided with their call for supplies.

It wasn't a surprise which of the Necessary Bodies placed himself in the eye of the dickstorm. Here he was again, Jon Ritzheimer, not in his car this time, nor out in the desert with his map of Unfucked America. This video missive was shot in one of the generic, fluorescent-lit common rooms of the refuge headquarters. On a fold-out plastic table he'd assembled a mountain of recently received packages, including one particularly large, fleshy dildo. As usual, Jon was worked up. "This one was really funny," he says, with bitter sarcasm, "a bag of dicks." In his hand is a plastic sack of candied genitalia. He complains about the haters who spend their money on hate instead of doing good, and then, with familiar dramatic flair, sweeps the whole table of its heap of gifts. "So we're going to clear the table," he says, staring into the camera, delighted with the convergence of figurative and descriptive language. "We're going to continue to do work and do good for our country. We're not going to be deterred."

The internet could not have been happier. Soon, very soon—instantly, maybe—many more dicks were being conjured out of the social vapor, shipped from warehouses, loaded on trucks and planes; they were all heading to Oregon to join the revolution. Commentators asked themselves if maybe what Jon had wanted was more dicks: why else would he have made such a display and broadcast it to the web? Whether he wanted them or not, he got 'em; soon, the rumors said, the occupiers had begun opening and discarding the packages in town, before bothering to cart them out the thirty miles into the basin.

Meanwhile, the Bundyites had what they thought was the perfect response to their trolls. Patriot movement supporter Maureen Peltier, who hadn't joined the occupation but would emerge in the coming months as one of the most tireless of the Ammonites, posted the naive comeback. The crew out at the refuge, she wanted the haters to know, were just going to sell all these dildos and candy cocks on eBay and make a profit to support their occupation. "So, keep sending stupid shit," Peltier wrote. "It's gonna turn a dime for them. LOL Economics!" she closed.

"LOL Economics" was exactly where we were—it was a better name than any I've ever thought of for the dark and antic mood of the internet dispensation. Peltier didn't understand the half of it; neither did I. Her visions of eBay resale were quaint: there was no secondary market for these gag gifts. I had no idea myself until the occupation that anonymously shipping your enemies bags of gummy, sugary, edible genitals was a mini, mostly automated industry. All you need to do is go to BagofDicks.com or any of the other similar sites. You could probably ask your own robot personal assistant to do it for you. You wouldn't even need to look up from whatever else you were doing. "Alexa, send the militia in Oregon a bag of dicks," you could say, and Alexa would likely handle all the logistics, find you the best deal, look up the address of the refuge, and secure the fastest shipping.

Where the Costumes Are Kept

Out on the refuge, the Bundyites made such a layered image of our moment in history that sometimes I wondered if Ammon was right: maybe God had guided him there, just to give us this freaked-out picture of our past and present as they mingled in the manic Now of the web. Here was so much of the history of the American Thing, a settler story, but restaged for the internet, on sacred Native ground. Here were a bunch of wannabe heroes on a divine mission, looking for a sense of power in their world, channeling the Spirit of '76 and mixing it with the legends of the West. And here were so many others—the rest of us—watching them, having feelings about them, and hurling these feelings at one another, alongside what we would soon enough come to discover were the fabricated personhoods of Twitter bots and social media operatives, faked-up voices of We the People, invisible companions in the scrum, egging us on.

Given all this, it didn't seem too strange when, on the second weekend, as if downloaded from the internet, the pages of history, or a Tea Party rally, the very man depicted on the cover of all their pocket Constitutions walked out of the freezing fog into the compound of the liberated refuge—or the "Harney County Resource Center," as the Ammonites had now rechristened it. It's like the whole thing had been a séance meant just to summon him. Every day they were walking around with his face sticking out of their shirtfront pockets. No wonder he finally showed up. But unlike the stiff, waxen Washington in the painting reproduced on the covers of the Constitution they all carried, this George Washington came in full military dress. He wore the blue and the gold; his buttons shone, lacy cuffs sprouted from his sleeves.

Malheur Washington didn't just look the part—he seemed to stay in character the whole time. Neil remembers him that way anyway. But then again, so much was going on, he couldn't really be sure, he said—maybe he dropped the act at some point. Duane Ehmer did recall that he'd somehow gotten some information about the man inside the costume: that he'd come from somewhere far away, that he'd flown in, and then driven, and that maybe he was a schoolteacher; but then, as he thought about it, he added, he really couldn't be sure. The whole thing had been like this; it was often difficult to believe any of it was happening. But the father of the nation had in fact been there. Some had shaken his hand, touched him; there were pictures to prove it, and those images of his visit soon began circulating on the internet. On the day I saw them, I knew for certain that I, too, would be traveling to Malheur.

* * *

It was on January 10 that he appeared in my life, on my screen. The most famous, the most Necessary American Body of them all. So necessary he'd even been turned into money. Washington wasn't just the face of the one-dollar bill; he was the face of all money—ironically, since the man, like his whole class, had hated the idea of paper currency. It made him a kind of cartoon god of the great circulations of the economy. Now we even make his money-face talk—what an indignity really—in all those car and furniture commercials for Presidents' Day and the Fourth of July. It would mortify him endlessly if he weren't already so stiffly, so gloriously undead.

I've pulled up one of the pictures of his Malheur visitation as I write this. I'm looking at a middle-age white man in an amazingly well-tailored costume; this thing looks custom-made. He's also got a big tricorn hat, with a white-powdered wig poking out from under it. Lots of shiny brass, white gloves. There's a sword—scabbarded, strapped to the waist. The hilt is dangling at his belly. There he is in the snow, one foot forward, presenting himself as if for a duel. Behind him stands a white pickup truck and one of the stone buildings of the refuge. The sky is gray and there's snow everywhere, so his clothes provide most of the color in the picture. The eye contact he's making with the AP photographer who took the shot broadcasts a firm, uncompromising nature, as does the tilt of his frown, which seems judicial in its measured but absolute severity. He's carrying a book in his hands. I can't make out what it is, but I suspect it to be the sort of text upon which one might swear a binding oath.

*   *   *

Karl Marx spoke of revolutionary dress-up in a piece that yielded one of his most famous bon mots, on the repetitions of history. "All great world historic facts and personages appear, so to speak, twice," he wrote. "The first time as tragedy, the second time as farce." At Malheur, we seemed to have gone way deep, deeper than the nineteenth century could possibly have imagined, into the spectacle of farce. Even with death and punishment impending, and the mood growing a bit darker day by day, it never stopped feeling like a carnival, until the day it did.

In Marx's essay "The Eighteenth Brumaire of Louis Bonaparte," which begins with his famous Hegelian witticism about repetitions, he addresses the uses of historical costume and rhetoric in both the French Revolution and in the self-coup that brought on the nineteenth-century reign of Louis Bonaparte. To Marx's view, it had been necessary for the practitioners of bourgeois and reactionary revolution to dress up their relatively prosaic aims in the grand feelings and outfits of times past. His later contemporary Friedrich Nietzsche also broached the issue of historical cosplay. To Nietzsche, the modern European "simply needs a costume; he requires history as a storage room for costumes. To be sure, he soon notices that not one fits him very well; so he keeps changing . . . It is no use . . . it 'does not look good.'"

Nietzsche had not lived to see this fine-lookin' fella at Malheur, or experience the absurdity and darkness of internet culture, but his point is well taken. He goes on, in the same passage from *Beyond Good and Evil*, to give us a little bit of his typically nihilistic hope: "Perhaps this is where we soon will discover the realm of our *invention*, that realm in which we, too, can still be original, say, as parodists of world history and God's Buffoons—perhaps, even if nothing else today has any future, our *laughter* may yet have a future."

But soon Nietzsche's laughter dribbles off into befuddled silence, and now I pick up another image. Here on my desk I've got my own copy of the annotated Constitution so many of the male occupiers carried over their hearts. The first thing I notice is that the picture of Washington on the cover of the pamphlet seems to be an image not of a living body but of a statue. It's not even a photograph of a statue but rather a digitally reproduced painting of a statue that I don't believe exists. It's an image of an imaginary wax-museum sculpture. The face is a dead mask—its unseeing eyes meet but don't meet mine. The right hand is permanently stretched out toward me. It offers me a plume so that I, too, might take the sacred oath and bind myself forever to the great document laid out in the picture's foreground on the table between us.

It makes sense that it's not the "real" George Washington pictured on the cover, but rather an image of an image of the idealized image of him we've all internalized. After all, both here and at Malheur, it's not the real George who's returned, but his dead image that has come to life. On the back cover of the pamphlet, undead Washington, this unseeing representation of the representation, is also offered to us as a personal witness to our commitment. There is a line where one can sign the following pledge with that proffered plume:

> I, as one of We the People of the United States, affirm that I have read or will read our U.S. Constitution and pledge to maintain and promote the standard of liberty for myself and my posterity, and do hereby attest to that by my signature.

Beneath the signature line is the reproduced signature of a solitary witness—again, it's Washington. All the millennia of the witchy European oath magic that grounds the West's fraught relationship to law and language comes pouring through this somnolent mountain of kitsch. Somehow this silliness is also deathly, necro-social seriousness—an oath witnessed by George Washington, no less. What kind of outcast would the person be who signed this and then turned his back (or her back? Are women allowed in the club?) on the true Constitution? Would they find themselves outside the magic circle of (white) American being—sliced off from We the People, to wander, unprotected, killable, in the wilderness?

* * *

The actual, historical George Washington had not even wanted to go to the Constitutional Convention in Philadelphia in 1787. He was worried, as usual, about his reputation. Washington thought it would look bad that he'd just turned down an invitation to the convention of the Society of the Cincinnati, the new association of military officers of the revolution, who would be holding their gathering in Philadelphia around the same time. He'd turned the Cincinnati down because the group had become a problem for him—and his image. They'd decided to become a hereditary order—firstborn sons would have membership bestowed upon them. Many in the country were crying foul as they witnessed unfolding before them what they saw as the birth of a new aristocracy. Not wanting to be seen as condoning this reinstatement of primogeniture, viewed by so many Americans of all classes as a primary example of the corruptions of the old colonial order, Washington also wanted to avoid giving offense to his officers, who largely adored him. He'd simply begged off the whole thing, citing his health. How could he now attend the Constitutional Convention, he asked James Madison, without giving offense? Besides, the last attempt at such a thing, held the year before in Maryland, had been a total failure. George Washington was not a man inclined to donate his prestige to failures. He simply wouldn't be able to come. But the organizers of the convention had had a feeling that all the popular and legislative unrest of the new states might change Washington's mind. They had waited before asking him for a final reply to give him a chance to digest the news coming in from around the nation, especially the news from Massachusetts, where the western countryside—maybe even most of the state—now seemed to be engaged in open insurrection.

Their instincts were right. It was rural insurrection against government overreach that brought Washington around. He was moved to act by what he saw as the need for a powerful centralized authority to crush such insurrections, and a strong national government able to move power a bit further from the people, and thus get economic policy mostly out of their hands. In this he was of the same mind as the other gentlemen of the convention. Like his fellow "Founding Fathers," as they would come to be called, he came to Philadelphia motivated above all by a need to restrain the *excesses* of democracy. "Our chief danger arises from the democratic parts of our constitutions," Edmund Randolph had said in the opening address of the convention. "It is a maxim which I hold incontrovertible, that the powers of government exercised by the people swallows up the other branches. None of the [state] constitutions have provided sufficient checks against the democracy." The American Revolution needed to be brought to a tidy end. The remedy, a new constitution and a powerful central government, would be far in excess of the mandate of the convention itself, which had been presented as an effort to merely reform the old Articles of Confederation. The delegates knew just how much they were overreaching, and thus their work was done in total secrecy. Care was taken to shutter the windows against eavesdroppers, despite the stifling heat of the Philadelphia summer. The birth of the Constitution was a stealthy and a sweaty affair.

Washington likely wouldn't have been there presiding over that stuffy chamber if it hadn't been for the rural rebels of Massachusetts and his alarm at their audacity and disregard for order. He came to Philadelphia to help make sure that things like the future Malheur uprising could be easily suppressed. If he hadn't come, not only wouldn't he have been on the cover of the document poking out of the pockets of the Bundyites, but there very likely would not have been any such document. Despite all the compromises and concealments made to avoid alarming people about the restraints on their local sovereignty the new Constitution threatened, it is very difficult for historians to imagine that the charter would ever have been ratified without Washington's participation and the magisterial aura of his approval.

In a story full of historical ironies, this was perhaps the deepest one: the Constitution, which the occupiers adored and adorned themselves with, had been deliberately conceived in the desire to restrain people very much like them. Not just to restrain them, but to create a government with the might and authority to crush them—to kill them if need be. Here they were, as if dancing in the punishing shadow of that power, with its charter pressed to their hearts. And somehow it was all making them feel fantastic, electrified, reborn, *free.*

CHAPTER TWELVE

By Other Means

A Good Day

THE SAME WEEKEND THAT GEORGE WASHINGTON strolled out of the mist onto the compound, some other self-styled ghosts of the revolutionary era appeared, but in more menacing contemporary gear. When today's militia movement mobilizes, it's not with muskets and tricorn caps but with AR-15s and ballistic vests, walkie-talkies, and that indispensable Blackwater strut. Tired, evidently, of their irrelevance and exile to town, the various groups who'd been left behind by Ammon's revelation mobilized to the refuge, rolling up just in time to hijack the CCF's daily eleven A.M. press conference.

Hijack was their word for what Ammon had done to them. Feelings were still hurt, evidently. "We kind of feel our event was a little hijacked," one of the leaders, Joseph Rice, said to the reporters, about the January 2 Hammond support march, while explaining why they'd felt it necessary now to pay this dramatic visit to the occupied refuge. The men of the militia didn't want to be exiled to the sidelines anymore. "We're playing a very significant role," Brandon Curtiss insisted. It would never be exactly clear what that role was. The militia leaders claimed, in spite of all their attention-grabbing weapons, to be providing a de-escalating buffer between all parties. If their real purpose had simply been revenge for Ammon's hijacking, now they would have it.

Soon LaVoy Finicum emerged, bursting into the press conference scrum. He thanked Curtiss for coming, pointing out in his affable drawl that there was much work Curtiss and friends could do here—like taking out the trash—before formally asking for all the long guns to go away. "My concern," he explained, "is that there's long guns here, and that's what always gets out in the media—is people packing long guns." It was already too late; the damage was done. By the end of the weekend, photos and video clips of a long-bearded militiaman were circulating everywhere. In the images, this unnamed man appeared in tactical gear holding a semiautomatic rifle, while sometimes using his free hand to move reporters back and create a bubble of security (or significance) around Curtiss, Rice, and the other militia leaders. Despite the fact that this militiaman never joined the Ammonites at Malheur, these images quickly became some of the most iconic of the occupation, rivaling all the artful, melancholy shots of Duane Ehmer riding Hellboy through the sage. There was nothing for Ammon, LaVoy, and friends to do but move on—and so they did.

*   *   *

On Monday the CCF invited the press to go on a little field trip with them, so they could stage a bit of theater of their own for the glowing screens of the worldwide dispensation. If, the previous week, they'd set the conversation with their January 4 press conference, now they began week two of the occupation by ceremonially cutting a Fish and Wildlife Service fence that separated the property of a local rancher, Tim Puckett, from the refuge range lands. The backstory for how Ammon had supposedly been invited to intervene on behalf of the Pucketts was murky; reporters quickly ran up against Ammon's go-to, brush-off compliment: "That's a good question." Soon enough, Mr. Puckett himself would emerge to put the fence back up and contradict all the crew's justifications for their action. The fence hadn't impeded him from anything, he said; he had no grazing contract with the refuge, had never grazed there, and had no need to do so. But by then it was Wednesday, and the week's first images were already old news. More importantly, the conversations they'd started—on the occupiers' terms—had been going on for days, and none of them involved the militia's visit or long guns.

This is basic campaign strategy. Every campaign strives to get out there on Monday and set the terms of the conversation for the week. Once you've done so, you don't look back. You don't respond to criticism of Monday's words and images—Monday's over. The fence-cutting ceremony contained all the central elements of the story Ammon wanted the occupation to tell. Here were images of the Necessary Bodies getting back to work, unfettered by the federal government in this new outpost of the Freest Place on Earth. They weren't just getting back to work; they were getting back to basic ranching work. Here they were, ranchers, and play ranchers, out in the Wild West, homeland of freedom, while journalists swirled about them, documenting their every gesture and word.

Along the way, LaVoy and Ammon got to give the cameras some folksy lessons in the basics of the cowboy life—which involves a fair amount of work with fencing. Ammon taught reporters how his father had taught him to wrap wire once it had been snipped. And here was LaVoy, holding up the day's basic tool—"rancher's pliers"—explaining all the different functions of the contraption. A kind of cowboy Swiss Army knife—it was good for clipping, twisting, removing staples, and all manner of manipulations of barbed wire, that most elemental of cattleman's technologies.

Once the pliers had been introduced, the tool could now be passed, sacramentally, to each of the Necessary Bodies who'd come out in trucks with Ammon and LaVoy. One by one, they took their turn at the fence line. Here were Blaine Cooper and his friend Jon Ritzheimer—both reported to be on disability—being restored, thanks to the Bundy Revolution, to productive, meaningful work. Or at least to the representation of such work. "For the Constitution!" Cooper shouted, as the wire snapped, turning the exertions of his body into words. This was real political theater—a screen-ready ceremony of Rural Electrification. Quickly it was compressed neatly by the media, into brief, entertaining video clips, which could be easily passed on via Facebook and other platforms. Far-flung viewers could participate passively in the rite, watching as the boys cut the fence and opened a magic gap in the snow, a passageway for the invisible transcendence of Liberty. "We wanted to make sure that the gate was big so everybody could see the gate was big," LaVoy told reporters, grinning.

The photographers and videographers on the scene were caught in the rite that had been staged for them—you can see them in one another's images, turning this way and that, trying to capture the new absence of fence. But there was nothing there—just cloudy sky and yellow-gray tufts of grass poking up out of the crust of snow. Looking satisfied, LaVoy gleamed, ruddy in the cold. "This is a good day," he proclaimed.

"Our Time Now"

This Bundyite political performance was also an oblique—and likely unintentional—piece of historical reenactment. The history of the West is full of fence-line drama—Harney County is no exception. The Hammonds' long showdown with federal authorities had first escalated into open conflict at a refuge fence line near their ranch more than twenty years earlier. The occupiers' fence action had taken place very close to the most famous fence-line confrontation in the county's history, the one between Ed Oliver and Pete French that had ended in French's death back in 1897.

Oliver and French had already entered into the occupation story a week earlier, when Oliver's great-granddaughter, a local rancher named Georgia Marshall, had invoked her ancestor and French at the first emergency town hall meeting in Burns, in a performance of searing rage that had gone viral across the matrix. A small, bespectacled woman in her early sixties, Marshall began her moment at the open mic quietly, but after invoking Oliver and staking her claim as an old-timer in the basin, all her feelings had come uncorked. By the end of her moment up there in front of her community, her voice had risen to an unnerving scream of curselike intensity.

But it wasn't a curse Marshall was delivering. It was a plea, an angry plea to move beyond the weight and the anger of the past. While she had begun by invoking the old fence-line violence from some of the worst days in the history of the county, from there she'd ascended to these heights of public feeling to make a plea not for the rights and claims of the past, but for the difficult work of the future.

"Let's not destroy what we are doing because we think we have to make a stand for everything that's happened in the goddamned past," she implored the room. "This is our time now. It is not what we did one hundred years ago, or sixty years ago, or thirty years ago. It's our moment right now. We don't know our future. But I'll tell you what: it's better than what we had. So let's try to keep going. Let's not get caught up—like I'm pissed as hell right now. And my boots are shaking. But I'm proud of who I am. I'm proud to be a rancher, and I am not going to let some other people be my face. I am me. This is my home," she'd concluded, screaming, as the room split open into cheers and hoots and applause.

Her husband, Gary, had been, for years, a central figure in a partnership that had made Harney County, as she put it, "the poster child" for a new kind of rural West. The High Desert Partnership, begun in the collaboration of her family with the then new assistant director of the refuge, Chad Karges, had brought together ranchers, federal agencies, loggers, environmentalists, the Wadatika, the county, and other local stakeholders in consensus-based work, to collaboratively devise conservation plans for the basin and the forest, plans that everyone could agree to. And it had been working—slowly, but with real achievements. New respect had emerged between former antagonists; and out of that respect, the recognition of common goals. Only in a world so polarized, so alienated, could something like what Marshall was talking about sound so much like a miracle. But in that world it was, and many in the room knew it. They also knew that one of the biggest dangers to that fragile spirit of collaboration that had been growing in the county was emotion, and particularly the hard feelings of the past.

But the past was always there; its presence was physical. It was in Georgia Marshall right now as she stood in front of the huge crowd filling that same hangar down at the fairgrounds where Ammon had delivered his Beautiful Pattern speech less than a month earlier. The past was the emotion that was gripping her. The past was her shaking boots, her trembling feet and legs, and her voice as she described her feelings. It was all making it very hard to focus on the present, not to mention the future. It had been hard, in the moment, in her quavering voice, to even get out the words.

Face-to-Face

What Georgia Marshall had asked her neighbors to do would remain much easier said than done. Harney County had become a real-world outpost of the internet. All the old feelings and old dreams were whipped up now in a circulation that also briefly made Ammon's economic prophecies come true. The streets were busy again; the hotels, the bars, the restaurants were full. But not with new, thriving working-class neighbors, not with loggers and ranchers and mill workers, but with out-of-towners, reporters, feds, and militiamen. And as soon as the story moved on, this economy it had gathered up would move on with it, leaving the town as quiet as ever on the surface but with all its unprocessed feelings, its historical and economic wounds exposed, and old friends wondering if they'd ever find a way to speak to one another again.

Sheriff Dave Ward urged his townsfolk to get off the internet and talk to one another face-to-face before more friendships were ruined by that blanket permission to hyperbole, rage, and pettiness that social media seemed to bestow on everyone. Like Georgia's plea, it was a simple-enough request, and yet in the atmosphere of 2016, in Harney County and America, it sounded almost messianic. Maybe it was. Maybe the idea of the people finding each other is always messianic. Ryan Payne had made his own militia-inflected version of Ward's plea at the meeting that had birthed the Committee of Safety. The two were far from alone in hoping that if only Americans could turn away from their screens they might finally see one another. The words of Saint Paul came to mind: "Now we see as through a mirror darkly. Then we shall see as if face-to-face."

This kind of ultimate face-to-face community of truth that Paul's words seem to so many to suggest is always imminent, never arrived. In order for that ultimate community to finally take place—or to take place in imagination—the spell of the world as-it-is must be broken in some way. In America, by 2016, social media had become a very good name for that spell.

* * *

Dave and the highest official of the county, Judge Steve Grasty, seemed sure that the majority of the county's residents were not for this madness at the refuge. Along with the rest of the county government leadership, they were doing their best to find ways to make a stage where the people might appear to the world and to one another and make their feelings known. At the first town hall meeting—in which Georgia Marshall had briefly taken flight—the sea of hands that went up to vote to ask the Bundy Revolution to leave had seemed to represent a near unanimity. It was decided then and there that David Ward would go out to the refuge to ask Ammon and company to pack up and go home to their families.

The next day, Dave called Ammon and invited him out to a conversation on the paved road east of the refuge. Ammon agreed. Ryan Payne came along. These three had already spent so much time talking. Their lives were intertwined now and would continue to be. The face-off was shot with multiple cameras by a film crew: it gives a freaky intimacy to a viewer's voyeur access. This effect is compounded for me by the familiarity of the landscape. That curve in the road where they are standing, I know it. The butte just beyond Dave, I know it too. From there the road bends and plunges on into the basin lands, past more basalt escarpments and bowls of yellow grass.

They are standing out there, in the winter wind, on the lip of that world. Dave's ruddy face is bright with life in the cold. Ammon, looming over him, seems to be trying to scrunch his body into his pockets for warmth. Around them several deputies watch, one filming with his smartphone. Dave is making his pitch, his last one, an offer of safe passage out of the county and the state. He couldn't promise the feds wouldn't charge them for what had happened down at the refuge, and he makes that clear, but he could escort them all safely from the state. Now was the time, he was saying. Your work is done. The occupiers had already started so many conversations, good conversations. "I've talked to senators, congressman, governors," Dave says, giving credit to Ammon and Ryan. Why not leave, before all the good they'd done was erased?

Ammon is quiet and, for him, a bit severe in the cold, nodding, unsmiling, as the sheriff makes his pitch. Payne is more worked up today—leaning in with some 1776 talk about a free state and the rights of the people to have their petitions heard. Dave shrugs; that's not what he's here to talk about, he says. He's always felt comfortable with the two of them, but reminds them of their own words, how it would take only one crazy person for this all to go wrong. "That could happen in any community, in any area," Ammon argues, "that could happen even if we left."

They aren't really talking to each other. Ammon and Ryan keep returning to their Redress of Grievances while Dave keeps coming back to his pitch. You can see it register in Dave's face that this proposal will go nowhere. But he keeps trying. The offer itself seems generous, and unlike other proposals cops might make, this one was genuine. Dave really was empowered to escort them out, but it's too late for his offer—it was always too late. Ammon and the sheriff part brusquely, shaking hands. This was a revolution now and it wasn't over yet. There were people coming by the refuge all the time. Ammon had come to understand those visitors, not Dave, as the real voice of the county. Walking away, he passes a camera. His eyes are steady, his face cold and set.

Once in a Lifetime

What was happening in Harney County was getting more intense by the day. The conflict was taking on an aura of symbolic warfare. In that warfare, different visions of the People surged up and dissipated, weaponized, as different sides jockeyed for legitimacy. Meanwhile, federal law enforcement was assembling, awaiting its moment and mandate to act. Burns's little airfield glowed all night. It could be seen for miles, a glaring cloud of activity in the usually dark night of the Harney Valley. It was becoming hard to believe that there was any way this was going to end well.

One iteration of We the People had flocked to the refuge. Another, larger figure of the People appeared, divided, in the increasingly combative town hall meetings in Burns. Meanwhile, out at the edge of town, a third, older, more originary figure of the People was assembling. After the news conference of January 6, the Wadatika had stayed on the edges of the conflict, but by no means entirely out of it. Tribal leadership continued to put pressure on law enforcement, pressure that would increase as the occupiers themselves drew more attention to the artifacts present on the grounds of the refuge. The tribe's rebuke of the occupation also buoyed the wider anti-occupation sentiments of the community. Jarvis and Charlotte had become heroes across the county as well as further off in the national circulations of the matrix. "I thought the tribe was really positive," one local rancher told me, "really powerful for them to have a news conference and say for all the wrongs [committed by the federal government], we still think they'll do a better job than you would."

The occupation had also had an emotional effect on many tribal members. The neo-homesteader claims of the Bundy Revolution couldn't help dredging up historical memories of all that had been taken before, and all the violence that had attended the whole history of white-Native relations in the lands of Malheur. One tribal member, Leland Dick, a popular figure on the reservation and in town—he'd been a basketball star on the Burns High School team—was unreserved about the rage the occupation called up in him. He soon became one of the more public faces of opposition to Ammon and friends in the county—and he didn't keep it to Facebook. Finding a crew of out-of-town Patriots and militiamen eating in the McDonald's one day, he went up to them and began snapping pictures with his phone. The men stood and surrounded him. Eventually, an older tribal member had ushered him out before the confrontation could escalate. Nobody had doubted Leland's willingness to take things further.

Other tribal men, especially the men it seemed, were also having trouble managing the feelings that the occupation had roused in them. "It was like another coming of the cavalry," tribal member Drew Beers told me. "It was hard for me to directly protest or get directly involved because I would have probably gone too far. It would have brought out too much anger for me, and I would have done something that would've been bad for the tribe, so I stayed away from the refuge . . . I probably should have gone out there to see it . . . but I had to stay away.

"It was so easy to get riled up and let the anger go," he added. "But you have to calm down."

A group of the men had decided that they needed to do some gathering of their own, to find some focus for this historical rage. In lieu of setting up armed checkpoints, as some had suggested, they settled on the idea of mounting a night watch over the little village of the reservation. On a knob, along a low ridge up in the sage, over the street of one-story homes and scattered tribal offices, Jarvis, Leland, Drew, and others spent many nights with a bonfire raging, singing songs and talking while they watched to make sure no one from the Bundy or militia camps tried to enter their community and stir up trouble. From the ridge they could also see the military encampment of the FBI out on the airfield to the east, glowing through the freezing fog all night.

With all those feelings, it got heavy up there sometimes, singing on the hilltop in the firelight. One night Jarvis had gotten a strong intimation of a presence gathering in a semicircle behind them. It was the tribe's dead; they were there—he was certain of it. Others had felt it too, he told me. Drew was also there that night. He hadn't had the same mystical experience that Jarvis had—he hadn't directly felt that presence. But he believed Jarvis had and on reflection thought it likely, logical even, that the spirits of the People would have joined them in that moment. "They were probably there," he told me; "we were all together, in good spirits, trying to heal."

*　*　*

Meanwhile, back at the refuge, the occupiers had convinced themselves that local sentiment was almost wholly on their side. At the same time, they were working hard to try to improve their numbers. Seemingly dearest to LaVoy's and Ryan Bundy's hearts were plans to get ranchers from the county, and from around Oregon and the rest of the West, to converge on the refuge and together cross the Rubicon by renouncing the management of federal agencies and beginning to ranch in Freedom. To that end, the two traveled far and wide in Oregon and much farther afield, all the way back down to Utah and Arizona, looking for fellow ranchers, eager to stand with them. One from New Mexico had committed to come to the refuge and ceremonially renounce his federal grazing contract.

The crew kicked off week three of the occupation with a Monday-night presentation for ranchers at a local hot-springs RV resort in the small settlement of Crane, north of the refuge and southeast of Burns. Here they revealed this new turn in their plan, something at least one of the ranchers in the room recognized was a road map for regional insurrection.

They showed a short video. Finicum exhorted the room a bit. The gaunt cowboy sounded a little more scripted and fanatical than usual. "When will you stand up," he demanded to know, "if not now? Do not worry how big Goliath is. You must be willing to put everything on the table—for freedom. If you are not willing to put everything on the table for freedom, are you worthy to have freedom? . . . Will you have the courage to stand up there and cancel that agreement between you and the federal government and say I do not care how big Goliath is? If I be only one, I am yet one and I shall stand. I promise you that if you stand, others will stand with you. If you stand, God will stand with you." As LaVoy went on it only got grander—and darker too. "There's much I have to live for that I don't want to lose. I have nineteen grandkids, and two on the way. My daughters all made a quick trip here because they didn't know if they'd see their dad again. But they stood beside me. They hugged me, they cried, and said, 'Dad we're proud of you.' You want your kids to do the same. It's not for your grandkids to do, it's not for your children to do, it's for you in this room to do now. If you do not do it now you will have lost your opportunity in the course of the history of the world."

One rancher stands up, seemingly made nervous by the stark sacrificial tenor of Finicum's rhetoric, and presses about the legal ramifications for himself and his family. He wants to know what kind of support they would really have—noting that the Hammonds are presently in prison. Eventually Ammon takes back the reins and tones things down. Yes, in a situation like this, it is necessary to stand so that the law may follow—he cites Rosa Parks—but the ranchers who did stand would not be standing alone. The effort would be collective. There was a long-term local plan, the crew revealed as the presentation went on, to allot each rancher their federal grazing area through the county government (though the existing county government was opposed to the entire Bundy operation). If the ranchers would stand, the crew promised their support. Not forever, Ammon qualified. Eventually they'd have to do for themselves. But at the beginning they could count on the support of the men out there at the refuge to shield them, as had happened at Bundy Ranch.

Ammon outlined the strategy. The idea was to "take the usages that are already adjudicated, identify them so they're clear, document them in the county record, and to begin using them as a free people and with the defense of the people in Harney county and around the nation to make sure you're not violated and abused. It's a once-in-a-lifetime opportunity. It will never happen again, I promise you. It will never happen again. Next time that this happens—or that you have an opportunity—it will be war . . . Right now we have an opportunity to do this peacefully. You'll be an example to other counties around you that are already right on the verge."

Another local rancher demanded to know where the rule of law was in all this. Aren't we a nation of laws? Scott Franklin stood to ask. No, Ryan Bundy replied. Not with the Constitution in violation. Not with the law of the Constitution being broken. Who decides what the Constitution says? Franklin asked. Doesn't the Supreme Court decide that? pressed the rancher. Isn't that how it works? No, replied the Bundy brothers, echoed by a few voices from the crowd. It was one of the more radical elements of the Bundy Revolution, part of the populist and evangelical tenor of the movement, which held, among so many other things, that the Constitution belonged to the people, and it was their duty to determine what it said.

"There's a lot of what-ifs," Ammon said, as a final pitch. "But what if this just happens to work." As the long meeting finally comes to a close, all are invited to show up on Saturday for the renunciation ceremony with that rancher from New Mexico. (He'd be joined, it was said, by another local rancher as yet unnamed.) Ryan Bundy closes the meeting with a prayer. A prayer of thanks, it also includes an entreaty. "Father in heaven," Ryan intones, head bowed, "we want to be free."

War by Other Means

"War is the continuation of politics by other means," wrote Carl von Clausewitz, arguably still the Western world's preeminent military theorist. This may be so, but the inverse often seems to have as much descriptive power. If what was happening in Harney County was a political struggle, it was also a kind of cold war, waged, for the moment, at the symbolic level with words, ritual, and theater.

Whatever it was, it had all weighed awfully on Steve Grasty, the county judge—an arcane Oregon designation that meant he was essentially the head executive of the county and the chief of its three-person legislative branch, the county court. Months after it was over, I visited him at his house, west of town, on a rise in the juniper and sage. We sat on his porch looking north toward the site of the biggest military battle ever fought in Harney County, the fight in 1878 at Silver Creek between groups of Bannock and Paiute warriors, making a run from Steens and the U.S. cavalry. Egan was wounded here, and in a few weeks he'd die, betrayed by the Umatilla he thought were seeking alliance with his people. You could still easily find cartridges from that fight out there, Steve told me, before mapping out for me what Harney County's cold war of 2016 had looked like from where he had sat.

While the conflict had quickly acquired a media name, the Oregon Standoff, it wasn't called this in Harney County, where people spoke generally of "the Occupation." Besides, *standoff* was not really accurate as a name for what had gone on. Steve mapped it out differently. He had seen the whole event "as a group of circles," he told me. At the center were the occupiers: "Bundy and friends, not very many, although people came and went." This circle was "surrounded by a circle of militia who at least said—as I watched their actions, that wasn't true—but they said they were there to prevent bloodshed." This group was in turn surrounded by law enforcement. "But what no one ever talked about or recognized was that all of that was surrounded by us." It was that last circle that was of the biggest concern to Steve. "I mean, I'm not embarrassed about this—and I think most guys in the county would tell you the same thing—there's enough guns in that house to start a small army," he said, gesturing at his home. "Apparently, our goal in life is to see if we can have more guns than the other guy. I have no idea why I have as many guns as I do, but, man, I keep buying 'em. So you have this culture of guns, firearms—but then you bring into it this outside culture of people who are open-carry with a clear intent to intimidate."

Steve was at the political center of the county, the one that no longer exactly held; by placing yourself in his role, it's easy to imagine what he most feared—and what he began to hear rumors of. He recalled an especially harrowing visit from three local residents. "I had mothers, three of them, in my office, saying, 'You gotta help. Our kids are going out there, and they're gonna take these guys out. They're sick of it' . . . And I'm going . . . whoa, wait . . . That's why I got so passionate through the whole thing."

If violence erupted, it was hard to say how many directions it would be erupting in, and what kind of conflict Steve might be looking at. Local residents including the tribe against occupiers and militia? Local residents against local residents? Feds and state cops against everybody? All of the above? Once the shooting started, who knew how it would end?

CHAPTER THIRTEEN

Sacrifice

The Restless and the Dead

BY JANUARY 18 THE POLITICAL THEATER of the occupiers had realized one of its most important goals. Despite all the chaos and the public mockery, the Necessary Bodies of Malheur had incontestably established the terrain of the "liberated" refuge as a second Bundy Ranch, an imaginary *and* real zone, outside the purview of government power. The more the occupation went on without violent intervention from the authorities, the less audacity it required of outsiders to come and join. Right up to the day the FBI took Ammon and the other leaders away, newcomers were still arriving to join the party.

But beneath the festive atmosphere, the occupation had been growing more tense in both the interiors and intersections of the layered circles Steve Grasty described. On the night of Tuesday the nineteenth, at what was to be the last of the public meetings in Burns about the crisis, some of the occupiers witnessed just how intensely their actions had divided the local community. Despite their firearms and seats high in the bleachers in the Burns High School gymnasium, the occupiers received a fair amount of real opprobrium that night—along with some expressions of gratitude. One after another, townspeople took the microphone. While some voiced support for the occupiers, and many confined their comments to emotional declarations of support for the Hammonds, others looked directly at Ammon Bundy and friends, seated scowling in the upper bleachers, and demanded to their faces, in front of hundreds of witnesses and dozens of cameras, that they just go home. Each cry of "go" received especially resounding applause.

This was the third town hall meeting. Contention in the community had been growing since the first meeting, when an overwhelming show of hands, nearly everyone in the room, had voted to ask Ammon to leave. What Steve Grasty saw at this third meeting would lead him to question the safety of holding any more public meetings of any kind. This was the first time that the occupiers had been present. Ammon and a few others, including his family's informal bodyguard Booda Cavalier, had arrived late, walked across the gym floor, and taken their seats high in the bleachers. This, for Steve, became one of the emblematic moments of the whole saga. "I can be naive, and maybe I can be proud sometimes of being naive, so it took me a while, but eventually I realized what they were doing: they were taking defensive positions. I realized then, counting law enforcement, there were at least seventy firearms in the room." This was all happening in the gym of his community's high school. It had been far too easy to imagine how quickly it all could have gone wrong.

*   *   *

LaVoy Finicum didn't attend the last town hall meeting on the night of the nineteenth, but in his novel, *Only by Blood and Suffering*, his fictional avatar, Jake Bonham, attends a community meeting very much like it. Bonham, wearing a vintage revolver on his hip and carrying an AR-15 rifle and more than two hundred rounds of ammunition, enters a fraught, literally post-apocalyptic meeting of his rattled fellow townspeople. The meeting also takes place in a high school gymnasium, this one in the old Latter-day Saint town of Orderville. (Like Bunkerville, the original community of Orderville had been consecrated to the voluntary socialism of Joseph Smith's dream of the United Order, lasting ten years until internal strife and enforcement of a federal anti-polygamy act brought it to an end.) Bonham, too, takes up a defensive position on a seat high in the bleachers. From this perch he listens with open disgust to local leaders discussing an involuntary emergency allocation of local resources in the aftermath of the Russian attack that has put the whole continent off-grid. Bonham doesn't listen for long. When he's heard enough, he rises from his seat and hijacks the whole meeting with his AR-15, leading ranchers, farmers, and other allied defenders of private property and the Constitution out of the hall and into the parking lot and the bracing air of Freedom. It's the first act of the local civil war that takes up the remainder of the novel. So much for politics in the world of Patriot fantasy.

But back in the so-called real world, the combat in Harney County was taking place mostly in the political realm. The next night it was Finicum, not his more muscled avatar, who took political action to address an unsettling problem for the occupiers: the stubborn opposition of the Burns-Paiute tribe.

*   *   *

The tribe's inconvenient recalcitrance had surfaced again at the opening of the last community meeting when a local man tangled with tribal council chair Charlotte Roderique over the occupiers' stated desire to "return" the four thousand plus artifacts stored at the refuge to their "rightful owners." The artifacts had become a flash point, thanks to a widely reprinted AP piece that described how the tribe had filed demands for action with various federal agencies, including the FBI, citing concerns related to the possibility of Archaeological Resources Protection Act violations. The tribe had expressed anxiety for the thousands of objects stored on the refuge, and the potential ease of their monetization through the flourishing internet market in Great Basin artifacts. It hadn't helped the occupiers' relation with the tribe that Ryan Bundy, interviewed by the AP for his response to the tribe's actions, was quoted in the article as saying the tribe had "had a claim to the land, but they lost the claim."

The artifact issue seemed to trouble the Bundy crew more than any of the other community rejection they encountered the night of January 19. It looked to have bothered LaVoy Finicum most of all. On January 20, the night after that raucous town meeting, he recorded the first of what was to be a series of videos addressing the tribe and the question of the artifacts. Finicum had lived and worked among Native people most of his life, and now his video efforts aimed to bring his own political dreams of a white and Native antigovernment alliance—a solidarity imagined intimately throughout his novel—into play in the lands of Malheur. The Wadatika, unsurprisingly, were to read his first video missive differently. It was an offense and, for the more traditionally minded among the tribe, a literally fatal mistake on Finicum's part; disturbing objects crafted and handled by the dead was something never to be undertaken lightly.

The Artifact Room

Finicum's confusion and sincerity can make his January 20 video painful viewing. In it we watch LaVoy as he goes through the boxes of artifacts in what looks like a dark basement. As always, he's wearing his big cowboy hat, his face under it stretched ruddy and bright across the firm insistence of his skull. He makes clear that this visit is being staged as a reach-out to the Paiute, "the rightful owners" of the objects in the room. "We're looking for a liaison," he says, "because we want to make sure these things are returned to their rightful owners." He continues about the room, pointing out artifacts, enumerating the wrongs they've suffered. Of special outrage to LaVoy is the rodents' nest that's been discovered in one of the boxes. "So the way I understand it," translates Blaine Cooper from behind the camera, "[is] that the BLM or whoever is in charge of these Native artifacts [it was the Fish and Wildlife Service] just kind of boxed them up and let 'em just rot down here." LaVoy, meanwhile, keeps moving through the basement, picking up and putting down ancient points and tools. As he does so, to the traditional sensibility of the Paiute, to whom his video was addressed, he was also unsettling all the volatile spiritual residue left hundreds or thousands of years ago by who knows how many thousands of Native dead. But Finicum and friends are moving in a different time. With quiet outrage, LaVoy, checking the artifact tags, establishes that sometimes for decades this stuff has "just been sitting down here . . . locked away for nobody but for them [the feds] to look at whenever they came down here." Satisfied he's made his case, Finicum wraps up, reiterating his plea for dialogue, even going so far as to declare a willingness to hear about the Paiute claims on the land— claims that Ryan Bundy had recently dismissed—before the video concludes with a demand, this time from Cooper: "The rightful owners need to come back and claim their belongings." It sounds like the Paiute are about to be evicted from a storage space.

Of course, it wasn't going to be that simple. The boys weren't going to pack up history and hand it off "respectfully" to the "rightful owners." Neither was the tribe overly concerned about dirt or animals mingling with the objects. "It's not just the artifacts," Charlotte Roderique told me weeks after it was all over. "We're in the dirt. Our history and culture is in the soil." The problem for Charlotte and her tribe wasn't so much that there was dirt on the artifacts, or that animals had been in the boxes where they were stored, but that the artifacts were out of the earth at all, and being rifled through on the internet by a man whose words and actions, despite his assertion of his desire to be respectful, were nowhere near appropriately reverent.

* * *

If you view the artifact video with a traditionalist Wadatika perspective in mind, it gets freaky. It's like Finicum is surrounded by so many ghosts that he can't see them. It's like he can't see them because they are everything. They are the air he's breathing, the ground he's walking on; they are what's stored in the boxes stacked on boxes stacked on boxes, seeping from the objects chipped by hand, used and discarded for millennia by the people known as Wadatika and by their ancestors. It's the nightmare of the settler, repackaged as Stephen King horror; he's about to be ambushed by the silence of the dead. And he can't sense that silence, because he's the one talking, telling his own story about how horrible the dirt and animals, how horrible for the poor artifacts, this sacred property, to sit in a room undisplayed since as long ago as 1980—a timeframe with no significance when one considers the epochal timescape of Native presences and absences in the land of Malheur. And this storeroom of artifacts—this is nothing: the ground of the Harney Basin he's walking on every day is full of these "belongings." They are buried in the dirt and marsh muck, and just lying about on the surface. Nobody will ever be able to come by and pick it all up. You can't just leave history out on the stoop for the rightful owners—it's everywhere, it's in everything. He's surrounded by relationship, and he's also in one—one for which he's not going to be able to dictate the terms.

The dead weren't the only ones getting restless. Neither were the Wadatika the only ones watching. After Finicum posted his video, the law enforcement response to the occupation took a major strategic turn. The very next day Ammon Bundy found fourteen messages on his cell phone from an FBI agent who identified himself only as Chris; it was the first contact he'd received from federal authorities. From this point forward, the pressure was on. Drones and piloted aircraft began to buzz the compound regularly, as the formidable military presence of the FBI out on the Burns airfield shifted into a more active mode.

Communities of Dirt

I first talked to Jarvis Kennedy on the phone a few days after the FBI had surprised Ammon, LaVoy, and the rest of the leadership on a snowbound road in the Malheur National Forest. "You know," he said, "we don't think it's a coincidence that Finicum died. No disrespect. We feel for his family. We didn't want that to happen to him. But you can't go messing with objects like that without protection. Whenever we find anything," he explained, "we bless it, say a prayer or sing, sprinkle some tobacco or sage on it, and return it to the earth, because it's ours but not ours. I think that's hard for people to understand."

Often the explanations of cultural practices and feelings that I've received from tribal members in Burns are punctuated with variations of this last phrase: "I don't know if you can understand that"; "it's hard to explain"; "it's hard for people to understand." These refrains, usually coming at moments of intense interest for me, moments when I feel very much that I understand what is being said and am eager to learn more, have reminded me to be skeptical of how much I think I do understand. Inevitably, there is much I do not. There was much here LaVoy didn't understand either, which is partly why he was able to imagine that something like a dimension, threaded through the land and through the Wadatika, could somehow be boxed up and handed over.

The basic misunderstanding involved with the artifacts at Malheur extended well beyond the specifics of the Bundyites' relation to the Wadatika—it is the source of ongoing conflict between tribal relations to ancestral lands and the economic, scientific, cultural, and theological views that underpin all the private and governmental institutions with which tribes have to negotiate. Tribal archaeologist Diane Teeman told me that, for her, the land feels more like a relative than a good she could own. "It's a family relationship. Ownership doesn't describe that. You can't own your relative. Everywhere around here, all the dirt I dig up in my garden, my ancestors are woven through that, and that land is woven through me. I don't know if people can understand. It's hard to explain."

Her traditionalist relationship to land has informed her non-Western approach to the Western discipline of archaeology. "It's a *community* in the dirt," she told me. "I use that word. And when we dig, it's an offense against that community. It's why I became an archaeologist, not so much to participate in this particular knowledge-gathering system of the West, but to minimize the offense that archaeology is to these communities in the soil." She recognizes this as a somewhat quixotic position. I was struck by how it was also a very practical one, devoid of any of the absolute, all-or-nothing, "when will you stand" purity LaVoy and the Bundys espoused. Archaeology is here to stay for the moment. It has tremendous power over how the meaning and value of lands immeasurably precious to the Wadatika are culturally and legally determined at local and national scales. Diane saw no choice but to participate and hope that something like what she calls "real collaboration, not just adding an Indian or two to your team," will keep happening.

The Wadatika had found this kind of real collaboration over the last two decades in the relationship the tribe enjoyed with the Fish and Wildlife Service archaeologist on the Malheur Refuge. Diane hoped that, as this kind of collaboration increased, it would form part of a larger development of more robust transcultural knowledge-gathering practices that might, with changes in laws governing artifacts, eventually lead to some or all of the artifacts stored on the refuge being returned to the dirt communities from whence they came. This is an ultimate goal that can be very hard for people outside her perspective to understand. In the larger culture, *artifacts* are things that belong in museums, carefully cared for, curated, cleaned. If there is dirt on them, then they are dirty, disrespected. This is how LaVoy had seen the artifacts stashed in the basement room on the refuge. To Diane's mind, on the other hand, what was important was not the dirt or the rats, but that the objects were still on-site, still close to the dirt they'd come from. If they were to be transferred to a museum collection and "properly" cared for, legally returning them to the soil would become even more difficult.

*   *   *

In her scholarly work, Diane talks about the inadequacy of Western ideas of property and of the sacred when it comes to describing Paiute relationships to landscape. Compared with the vocabulary she offers in its stead, the language of God and Law can seem both pompous and impoverished. While the typical ethnographic description of a "nomadic," "foraging" culture like that of the Northern Paiute might present their concept of land owner- ship as nonexistent and their religious practices as "animistic," Diane proposes a different understanding of landscape as a palimpsest of ever- shifting relations—so that, in her words, "an action on a landscape is not only an action on prior acts and events but also the people who were involved in those activities."

Thinking like this can also make Diane's gardening complex. And not only because the dirt is like a relative, shot through with the material traces of her ancestors. Our conversation turned to Oytes, the nineteenth-century Wadatika shaman and Dreamer prophet who'd played a big role in the society of the Malheur Reservation and in the rebellion of the Bannock-Paiute War. There was no strict catechism for Dreamers, but Oytes was known to have strongly rejected agriculture and, with it, private property, as the great

Dreamer prophet of the Columbia Plateau, Smohalla, had also done. The most complete written record we have of nineteenth-century Dreamer doctrine comes from a conversation Smohalla had with a U.S. Army ambassador sent to measure his mind, and perhaps convince the prophet and his Wanapum people to take up farming and ownership of individual plots of land in order to become properly "civilized." Smohalla explained to his guest, whom he'd treated to a salmon feast, that both land ownership and what the white Americans that his people called "Bostons" thought of as being "work" were prohibited to Dreamers. "Men who work," he'd said, "cannot dream."

In Smohalla's vision, those who violated the earth by owning it or digging deeply in it to cultivate specific plants solely for human consumption would lose access to the coming world, when the earth was literally to be overturned and reborn. All the Native dead were to return with this refreshed and plentiful earth, alongside lost populations of animals and plants, as the dream world merged with this one—and purged itself of Bostons. These ideas had made their way down through the Blue Mountains to Oytes. "I think I can see what he meant," Diane told me. "There is something very strange, kind of absurd, about taking one part of the earth and saying *only* this kind of plant will grow here now, and that this plant's *only purpose* is to be eaten by *me*. I've been thinking a lot about food lately in this way. It does totally go against our sense of reverence and reciprocity. It's so important to acknowledge that nothing exists just for me; if we take a plant, or part of a plant, we always make an offering or ask permission. We need to respect the plant's liberty."

LaVoy Finicum, of course, had a very different understanding of liberty—a somewhat extreme and colorful version of what remains the mainstream American understanding. It is a dispensation that is rarely extended to plants. Liberty is for people and their property—and for corporations and money. To Smohalla and his disciple Oytes, this had been an obvious contradiction: property and liberty were at odds.

Earthly Sojourns, Spiritual Tests

In Mormon cosmogony the earth has a very specific purpose: it exists for human growth. For devout Latter-day Saints like LaVoy, our time on earth—our earthly sojourn—is a test we must pass before continuing on our spiritual way. Liberty—or personal agency—was the other crucial ingredient in salvation. "I believe that the first principal of heaven is personal agency," Ryan Bundy told me, two years after his friend LaVoy's fight for personal agency had taken his life. "A lot of people think faith is the first principal, but before faith you must have the ability to choose. You must have your liberty. We believe that we existed before this life—as spirits, as intelligences—that we dwelt with Him in a pre-mortal realm. It was His design that we should progress to become more like Him. We needed to have a body and experience mortal life—and that's what this mortal life is. We are spiritual beings that are here on Earth having a mortal experience. When you view yourself as a child of God, you begin to have a different perspective."

As far as Ryan was concerned, this perspective meant that "the only legal purpose of government is aiding the individual in claiming, using, and defending his rights." This minimal government wasn't quite anarchism—a charge Ryan and his friends had to continually confront—but it came close at times. It sounded even closer in the interview LaVoy Finicum gave Jason Tatenhove, the heavily tattooed media guy of the Oath Keepers militia, at occupied Malheur. The two men talked of the relation between firearms and freedom in the ideal world they had both found prefigured in the communities formed in antigovernment militia operations like Bundy Ranch and Malheur. As in his novel, Finicum presented a familiar fantasy version of the American frontier, an apolitical world of self-reliant nonrelation, where firearms and fences sufficed to make good neighbors. Regarding firearms, he says to Tatenhove, "One sword tends to keep another sword in its sheath—and that's exactly where all the guns should be, is holstered in their sheaths, and we should all be neighborly, kind, and friendly." LaVoy's smiling, nodding as he says this, in front of the fireplace in one of the older Conservation Corps buildings on the refuge. What appears to be the grip of an antique pistol—or perhaps the handle of a knife—pokes up out of his jeans, over his Southwest Native–patterned shirt.

*　*　*

There was no space in Ryan's and LaVoy's vision for the liberty of plants—or tortoises. Here the earth was nothing more than the stage for a human drama, the drama of salvation. As militant as this Mormon position can seem at first to a nonbeliever, it's really an expression of a basic theological position that underlies some of our most fundamental modern, secular notions of what means and matters in the world, as well as what the world itself is. Joseph Smith's genius had been to create an optimistic American Christianity that coalesced secular and economic notions of progress with a vision of eternal growth. To live in Joseph Smith's story was to live in a certain theologized version of what we call the American dream. That dream, as Americans have been discovering in recent decades, doesn't have much room for concerns about sustainability or climate change. It certainly has little room for a critique of capitalism or the secular religion of growth. Growth, if you listen closely to the politicians and economists on your screen, is what we're here for. *It's the economy, stupid*: we exist to keep it going.

LaVoy and friends had a peculiar relation to that kind of nonspiritual growth. Their Mormon libertarian impulses praised the drive toward prosperity, but their vision of the proper world of freedom was a cowboy's vision—rural, independent, isolated, a world one still moved through on horseback. Ideologically, the Bundyites seemed to have little in their tool kit with which to critique our actually existing globalized economy. I still have never even heard the word *corporation* pass through Bundy lips—nor have I heard it uttered in all the hours of footage that now exist of LaVoy Finicum. Neither do corporations have a role in Finicum's novel—except as gun manufacturers. It's easy to see why: Mormon constitutionalism left him no tools for the analysis of mega-corporate capitalist power, and little to say— beyond reproving its rejection of freedom as he saw it—of the society produced by ceaseless, mindless growth. Still, that society was one LaVoy seemed to have had little interest in living in. He'd recently escaped it, when he and his family had gotten their ranch in the Arizona Strip six years earlier. Unable to contend with contemporary capitalism politically, LaVoy had dealt with it literarily instead, laying waste to our world in fantasy in the pages of his novel.

In *Only by Blood and Suffering*, the Russian attack that sets the book's plot in motion has basically forced Americans back to nineteenth-century life. Unlike most, the novel's hero, Jake Bonham, apocalyptic prepper, has been readying himself for this for years. As Bonham moves through the book's pages, under the jet-free, starry skies of the West, through the juniper and pinyon, and over the red rock, always on horseback or on foot, he often has cause to think of his own ancestors, white and Native, moving over the same land. Sometimes it seemed the true pull of the Bundy Revolution was that it offered a version of this kind of apocalyptic American pastoralism as a way out of America. Here, through ideology, was an escape to the preindustrial past, a move that also short-circuited the nightmare of climate change *and* its right-wing denial. With it came also a dream flight from the prospect of a lifetime of unsatisfying, unrewarding work in the ever-more-automated urban sprawl. When faced with such melancholy prospects, non–Native Americans of all sorts tend to dream of being cowboys—or Indians—or both.

No Longer a Slave

The artifacts weren't the only thing on LaVoy Finicum's mind that week. For much of the occupation, he and Ryan Bundy had been trying to recruit more ranchers to renounce their grazing contracts and join the Bundy revolt. Saturday, January 23, was the culmination of this effort, a renunciation ceremony where participating ranchers could publicly, ritually, cast off their shackles. On the big day, the Necessary Bodies of Rural Electrification gathered with their visitors, scrunched together in the refuge's little picnic pavilion, near the bird-viewing pond. The proceedings began with the Sharp Family Singers, a mother-and-kids' gospel group, known to many of the Patriots from their visit to Bundy Ranch during the heady days of that standoff. Odalis Sharp and her many children had driven all the way from Kansas to lend their holy voices to the cause once again. The Sharp matriarch's eyes seemed lit by an unnerving intensity. No one knew it at the time, but the family was on the verge of breaking apart. One day that coming spring, her children would take advantage of their mother's time in the shower to flee what they charged was her long-term parental regime of physical and mental abuse. On the way out, the kids had confiscated her guns so that nobody would be hurt if a standoff with law enforcement ensued. But that was a few months off still, and today the Bundyites were enraptured in the family's sweet voices. It was a lively show. One of the numbers, a contemporary gospel song, even featured one of the boys doing some impromptu beatboxing. Briefly the concert was interrupted by a double blast of the shofar—from Brand and his adult son, a shofar adept like his father. The youngest of the Sharps, a little boy with long blond hair tumbling out of his wool cap, stood between the father and son, gazing up in wonder at the holy horns.

In the end, only one rancher, a man named Adrian Sewell from New Mexico, had shown up. He signed a renunciation of his contract, which was notarized on the spot. Ryan Bundy, who was the day's MC, pronounced Sewell finally free. "He is no longer a subject, no longer a slave, no longer a serf to the federal government," Ryan explained. Then LaVoy stepped up and presented Sewell with a sheet of names and numbers—the contact info of the People, or at least the persons, armed, Sewell could call to his aid. "Amen!" the crowd shouted—spontaneously and in unison.

No other ranchers joined Sewell, no one from around the West and no one from Harney County. But if LaVoy was disappointed at the showing, he never revealed it. His wife, Jeanette, visiting from Arizona, said in later court testimony that he'd been thrilled with the day, and about the whole occupation—it reminded him of his days as a Mormon missionary on the Lakota reservation in South Dakota. A video camera caught him during the ceremony in a private moment of communing alone with his feelings, smiling, eyes closed as he listened to the Sharps. "Of whom shall I be afraid," the voices of mother and children sang, together for now, folding into one another and rising up as one.

We Are Not Enemies

There were more reasons to be afraid now. Things had definitely heated up. "Saber rattling," LaVoy called it. Around the clock, FBI drones and planes buzzed overhead. Ammon was now regularly on the phone with "Chris" and other FBI negotiators, lecturing them on the Constitution. Ryan Payne, meanwhile, had begun helping his comrades prepare to stand their ground in the event of an FBI assault. An impromptu shooting range was set up out by the refuge's boat launch on the frozen desert marshlands. Occupiers accepted the help of a mysterious, recently arrived Vegas man named John Killman in training uninitiated Bundyites in firearms use and the art of hand-to-hand combat, as well as in the correct way to remove a driver from a stopped car. Killman, it would turn out, was not his real name, and he hadn't just come to help.

The artifacts stayed in the occupiers' thoughts throughout those frantic and festive final days—and not just in LaVoy's. On January 24, Ryan Bundy again involved himself in the artifact conflict when he and Blaine Cooper's wife, Melissa, made a video with an actual Native American person, a visitor to the refuge. In the video, Sheila Warren, wearing a down winter coat and a blank expression, is standing in a room among boxes of artifacts. Bundy, in his broad-rimmed cowboy hat, leans against a wall behind her, gazing off grimly in the opposite direction. Warren informs viewers that she's a duly enrolled member of the Siletz tribe, and then looks around and assures the camera that the artifacts are now "well kept." She also wants us to know that she's been well treated out on the refuge. While only irritating the Wadatika in Burns and provoking a disavowal from her own tribe, this video still played well with its real audience. In the coming days and weeks and months, the occupiers and their supporters continued to cite Warren's visit as evidence that the aggrieved stance of the Paiute had, in the words of one Burns resident, "with all due respect . . . turned out to be a lot of hooey."

Months later I met Sheila at federal court in Portland. In person, the blankness of expression she'd projected in the video from the refuge seemed more like the customary reserve of a carefully spoken, quiet sort of person. In the days since the occupation, she'd become a real Bundyite. During the trial she was in the courtroom most days, lingering on the court steps for the end-of-day informal rally and social scrum. The movement had become a kind of second family for her; she even brought members of her own family to watch the trial and meet the gang. The occupiers were such sincere, good people, she told me, again and again, during a break in the proceedings.

She was eager to learn more from me about the Wadatika—especially Charlotte, toward whom she'd come to feel anger for her perceived role in the eventual takedown of her new friends. But when I relayed what Charlotte had told me about her perspective on the land of the refuge—how for Charlotte and so many of the Burns-Paiute, the Wadatika *were* that place— Sheila's attitude immediately, visibly softened. Nodding, she said that she understood. Her soft voice grew even quieter. She wished that things could have been different. "If they could have talked . . . if Charlotte had gone down there . . ." She felt certain that Ammon and the others would have listened and apologized and gone elsewhere. But it had probably been too late for that, we agreed, nodding grimly.

It was probably too late. LaVoy Finicum, however, hadn't yet given up on his own plainly improbable dreams of a meaningful reconciliation and strategic alliance—on his terms—with the tribe. The day after Sheila's visit, his second-to-last day on earth, Finicum made another video about the artifacts, this one addressed directly to the Burns-Paiute.

In this missive LaVoy is crouching in the doorway of one of the stone buildings of the refuge. He tells the camera about his Native bloodlines:

Comanche and Pima, he claims. He talks about his youth on the Navajo reservation and his time among the Lakota. Moving on from his Native cred, he assures his viewers that their sacred objects will not be handled or mistreated, before turning to today's real pitch.

"It is time," he tells the Wadatika, like he seemed to be telling everyone in his final days. "It is time, Paiute people here of Harney County. It is time for you to throw off the BIA [Bureau of Indian Affairs] to become a completely sovereign independent nation without them." He takes off his gloves; he pivots on his heels. "I believe in the American people," he continues. "I believe in the Native Americans. It is time for them to stand up and throw off the federal government out of their own nations." Now he's reaching his right arm out from his heart toward "you"—*you, Paiute people of Harney County.* "I hope to see *you* soon," he says, drawing out the *soooon* a little, now gesturing toward the camera, now looking down, looking up. The anaphoric refrains drop away. "We'd be on the same side—we . . . we . . . we," he stammers, "are not enemies. That's all I have to say."

*   *   *

The stammered "we" of Finicum's dreams would never be. Later that day a letter from the tribe to the U.S. attorney general and the governor of Oregon appeared in the press. Penned in response to LaVoy's initial artifact-room video, this was not the answer Finicum had been hoping for. In it, Charlotte Roderique demanded immediate action against the occupiers, citing the historic obligation articulated in the nineteenth-century U.S. treaty with the Northern Paiute to ensure the prosecution of "any crime or injury [that] is perpetrated by any white man upon the Indians aforesaid . . . according to the laws of the United States and the State of Oregon." These clauses, sometimes called "bad men clauses," highlight the complex, deeply ambivalent historical relationship between Native American tribes and the federal government, one the occupiers never seemed to understand. While federal forces and policies had been responsible for many of the worst traumas suffered by Native peoples, in the history of eastern Oregon and of the Northern Paiute, the federal government had also often been the only force that stood between tribal groups and settler depredation.

By the next morning, Finicum had given up. Clearly now, despite his efforts to enforce his fantasy of an alliance, he and the Paiute of Burns were enemies. On Tuesday, January 26, Finicum filmed his final video on the issue. Standing in what looks to be the same doorway he addressed the

Wadatika from the day before, this time he begins addressing himself to America—a nation that no longer seems, at least rhetorically, to include the Paiute. "At this point they have made it very clear that they do not want to have any interaction with us," he drawls somberly, looking downward. The artifacts, he promises, will remain safe and undisturbed.

The Body of the Law

Not so long after finishing his final video message, Finicum headed up Highway 205 toward the snowy, pine-forested mountains in a two-vehicle caravan with Ammon, his brother, and a number of other important occupiers. Together they were basically the entire leadership of the group. Despite the tribe's rejection and the increased pressure from the FBI, their collective spirits were high. January 26 promised to be a momentous day, even a tipping point, in their struggle. Today they were headed into what they anticipated was especially friendly territory. They were going to John Day, a mountain town in adjacent Grant County, to attend a public meeting. There they were to speak along with Grant County sheriff Glenn Palmer. This sheriff happened to be an avowed constitutionalist. According to Jon Ritzheimer, Palmer had even asked him and Ryan Payne to autograph his pocket Constitution when they'd visited John Day earlier in the month. The man was clearly not just any old constitutionalist-leaning sheriff; he had recently been voted Lawman of the Year by Richard Mack's Constitutional Sheriffs and Peace Officers Association. Even more importantly, to the horror of law enforcement, the day before, Palmer had spoken out in favor of meeting some of the occupiers' main demands. The possibility of another occupation, and the growth of the Bundy Revolution, was in the air. In John Day, a crowd was already beginning to assemble to hear Ammon and friends speak—but the Bundyites would never arrive.

For the moment, though, they must have felt great—they were the vanguard, traveling with mission, galvanized by it, through that landscape already so conducive to expansive feeling. The territory they moved through could only have collaborated with their feelings. As they came up over Wright's Point, the basalt and sage of the butte top were bewitched with snow and ice. In a few more minutes they reached the end of 205 where, joining 395, it turned up toward the foothills, winding through snowy fields of golden grass into the mouth of Devine Canyon. This part of the ride is intoxicating, the kind of drive that makes you want to sing along with the world. It's especially thrilling in the first moments of entering the canyon. As the road curves, and the canyon snakes up and up into the mountains, its chunky basalt walls rise on both sides with the solemn authority of Easter Island heads. As you move, the walls continue to grow around you to the twisting measure of your ascent. It's one of those everyday sublime automotive moments the American West is so full of, where the world itself seems to expand to the thrill of your own fossil-fueled momentum. It also happens to look exactly like that canyon in all the movies, the one nobody in their right minds ever wants to enter, because they know that, depending on the flick, a band of outlaws or Comanche—or a sheriff with a posse—are waiting up along the rim.

But that afternoon no one was worried. They were westerners, after all; one can drive through such canyons every day in the West, and by now they must all have gotten used to being followed by surveillance craft. Besides, the conversations with the FBI negotiators seemed to have been going well—they'd been on the phone with them, Ryan Bundy recalled, thirty minutes before they headed out that day, talking about further negotiations. In Finicum's truck, contemporary pop music played. (The Patriot movement's favorite cowboy professed a dislike of country music; he preferred Adele.) Ryan Payne rode beside him. In the back seat were Ryan Bundy, Shawna Cox, and a last-minute addition, young Victoria Sharp, the eldest of the Sharp Family Singers. Eighteen-year-old Victoria had been in the shower when the rest of her family had left for John Day to prepare for the opening ceremonies, so she'd hitched a ride with LaVoy. She chatted cheerfully in the back seat with Cox, who had only gone along that day in order to accompany Victoria. Behind them, Ammon and Bundy family bodyguard Booda Cavalier rode in the jeep of fellow occupier Mark McConnell. According to McConnell, who would later turn out to have been an FBI informant, he and Booda jawed on good-humoredly about trifling things while Ammon caught some much-needed sleep, napping in the back.

And then their lives changed forever. As they wound up past the basalt rims of the canyon and into the pine forest, with its deeper drifts of snow, they spotted a line of dark vehicles on the right, idling on an icy National Forest Service access road. The vehicles pulled out behind them, lights flashing, and pulled over McConnell's jeep. Finicum stopped farther ahead in the road's center. Ammon, Booda, and McConnell surrendered, but with Finicum's truck a terrible standoff ensued.

* * *

A new genre of aesthetic experience has emerged in our lives: the police-shooting video. Thanks to media technologies and the diffusions of the web, we can all watch along over the next thirty minutes as LaVoy Finicum confronts Death and the Law, before gathering both into the finality of his body. We can even watch from three different viewpoints. There's the FBI's silent, overhead surveillance-craft video; a video shot by Shawna Cox from inside Finicum's truck; and two other brief, choppy cell phone videos from Ryan Bundy. After a commission of inquiry released Cox's footage, the *Oregonian* newspaper synched it with the overhead surveillance view into one split-screen, simultaneous video, giving two totally different views onto the same passage of time. One is jagged and jumpy, stuffed with human voices and panic, while the other is smooth and silent, gliding over the snowy pines and the tiny mysterious vehicles and their tinier humans.

In the FBI video, we can see Finicum's white pickup stopped on the black asphalt of 395. The road is lined with deep snow and tall, skinny pines. Behind the truck at a distance of maybe fifty yards, we see the black vans and flashing lights of the feds and the Oregon State Police. Among them we can make out tiny body-armored figures taking tiny Ryan Payne into custody. (Payne, assessing the scenario, had chosen to surrender.) It's a dark afternoon up in the winter mountains, already slouching toward sunset—it's hard, in this aerial footage, to tell the difference between the little bodies down there going through the rituals of arrest. While watching the synched videos, it's hard to pay attention to the aerial view at all, because in the superimposed video in the bottom-left corner, from the moment Shawna Cox hits record, LaVoy Finicum is screaming at the Law.

This is not the earnest LaVoy of the artifact videos, or the genial cowboy of his chats with reporters back at the refuge. "You wanna shoot me, you shoot me!" he's shouting as the video begins. He's got his head out his driver's-side window; all we can see of him is the back of his denim jacket and his cowboy hat. "I'm going to meet the sheriff. The sheriff is waiting for us. So you do as you damn well please," he yells, now thrusting more of his head, neck, and shoulders out the window of the truck.

"I'm not going anywhere," he adds. "Here I am, right there. Right there. Put a bullet through it. You understand? I'm gonna go meet the sheriff. You back down or you kill me now."

For a moment, Cox pulls the camera away from the back view of LaVoy's hollering head; now we can see the panicked face of eighteen-year-old Victoria Sharp swiveling toward us. Beside her is the dark cowboy hat of Ryan Bundy; he's listening at his backseat window, right behind Finicum. Then Cox spins the camera so it's looking out through the rear window and the truck's camper shell at the blurry, fluid flash of cop lights. "Where's Ryan?" she says, meaning Ryan Payne, who's now being taken in by the Law somewhere back there behind her. Her voice is cracking a little with fear now because this is all really happening. It's happening and about to happen all at once.

Of course, for the hordes of us who watched it on video, it's also all already happened. Despite the fact that it seems like each week brings a new harrowing video of someone's final moments, every time I watch this video I still can't believe I'm watching, sharing this moment with them. How could anyone belong here with them, inside this—their own stuttering time, stuffed to bursting with dread, defiance, and confusion? To escape, I look away at the snow and the trees in the aerial footage, but their voices draw me back into their cabin and their human commotion. And I never hit stop, except to play it back, to watch all over again as, right there in front of me and right here in my ears, they mull over and then make what most of us would likely regard as an incredibly poor decision.

*   *   *

Inside the idling truck, the plan begins to take shape.

"I'm not giving over . . . I'm going into Grant County and see the sheriff," says LaVoy to his friends.

"Well, if we duck and you drive, what are they gonna do? Try and knock us out? How far we gotta go?" asks Shawna.

"They'll shoot your tires out," Victoria interjects.

"We got about fifty-odd miles," says LaVoy.

You can feel Shawna beginning to recognize the scope of their hopelessness. "Tell him to approach the vehicle," she suggests.

But nobody responds. LaVoy lifts his arm up off the steering wheel, drops it again. Says nothing.

"Ryan's talking to 'em, right?" Shawna asks, trying another hope.

"Is he talking to 'em?" Ryan Bundy asks.

"I can't tell," says LaVoy.

A moment later, Finicum, bafflingly, turns to the stereo and cranks it up: it's been on low this whole time. You can watch his body recognize the song, and then he reaches for it. He wants it somehow, the feeling that it is; he wants it in the air, in his flesh, right now. And as the chorus of the tune begins, he cranks it even higher. And what a number it is: deeply plaintive— it's one of those forlorn contemporary pop hits that fills gas stations, doctor's offices, supermarkets, and fast-food joints with banal, anthemic despair. This one's by a group named A Great Big World. It's called "We Hold Each Other," and its chorus, trembling with warbly studio enhancement, now fills the cabin with its weepy refrain. It's just the four words of the song's title repeated till your heart breaks or you lose your mind.

LaVoy listens in silence. How could he want to fill his being with *this* kitsch *right now?* All this piped-in emotion, knowing what is about to happen, certainly makes me want to scream. But I never do. Each time I watch I'm as silent as the day I watched it during the trial over the mountains in Portland with the jury and the judge and all the lawyers and all the defendants and the U.S. marshals and Lisa and Angie Bundy sitting right in front of me, the song blaring in the acoustically sealed space of the court. The only other sound in that room was Shawna Cox weeping quietly on the witness stand. I think the rest of us had stopped breathing.

Finally someone speaks up—it's Ryan Bundy, in the truck, in the video. "Hey, turn that down," he says from the backseat. Thank god. He's trying to get help on his phone, as is Shawna. But there is no help to be had.

*   *   *

For a moment the thought of help surges in them all, replacing the song, which can still be heard low in the background. Ryan and Shawna paw at their phones, while LaVoy starts shouting at the Law again: "Hey, boys, you better realize we got people on the way. You want a bloodbath, it's going to be on your hands. We're gonna go see the sheriff!"

But already, back in the cab, this plan has hit a fatal obstacle. "I don't have any service," Shawna says. "We have no service here," she repeats, confirming it to herself and everyone.

LaVoy, done yelling at the cops for a second, pulls his head back into the cabin. He is still caught up in their momentary hope, but then he registers what Cox has said.

"Start calling people!" Then his voice gets quieter. "They did it 'cuz there's no service here."

It dawns on Shawna too. "They know it . . . there's no service here. At all."

"We shoulda never stopped," mutters Ryan. "We should never have stopped."

"I'm going to meet the sheriff," says LaVoy, to everyone and no one at all.

"Then we're going to have to duck," says Shawna.

As LaVoy hits the gas, his friends in the back seat hunker down. "Are they shooting?" asks Victoria.

"Get down, honey," says Shawna. "Gun it!" she adds, to LaVoy.

* * *

As they twisted and turned along 395 through the pines, Ryan and Shawna kept checking for coverage, but there is no coverage, not in Devine Canyon, not in this stretch of the Bad Luck National Forest. On their right they passed a snow-filled meadow in the pines. Diane Teeman later told me this was a site she has always associated with good times in the pre-dispossession history of the Wadatika—a summer gathering and celebration place, a site of communal joy, horse races, and feasting. Now the inevitable police barricade, which LaVoy and friends had failed to anticipate, came into view in front of them. "Hold on!" shouted LaVoy. These were the last words he would address to his friends.

Now the truck slams into the snow bank to the left of the barricade— almost running over an agent who'd dived in the wrong direction. Quickly it comes to a halt, its whining tires whirling fruitlessly in the snow. Two shots ring out, striking the vehicle. Immediately LaVoy leaps from the cabin. Watching on the two-channel video you see him suddenly emerge from one video into the other: gone from the truck and the world of his friends, he now becomes the tiny figure down there, spinning in the snow. He's turning back and forth, toward each of the two state troopers who are gingerly approaching him, knee-deep in the snowdrift. He's raising and lowering his hands—and reaching, law enforcement would say, toward the 9 mm pistol found in his jacket pocket. (His friends would say he'd only been trying to keep his balance.) From the audio in Cox's video you can hear him out there. "Go ahead and shoot me! Go ahead and shoot me!" And then they do. You hear the shots, and on the aerial video, tiny LaVoy falls straight back into the snow, one arm stretched up toward the sky. The wheels of his truck are still spinning, they will keep spinning for some time, as he breathes his last there, and dusk falls. They keep spinning on as each of his friends, so tiny down there in the gloaming, are taken, one by one, with ceremonial slowness, into the body of the Law.

CHAPTER FOURTEEN

Camp Finicum

The Fear

I ARRIVED IN BURNS A FEW DAYS after Finicum's death. On the way into town, in the gray-blue gold of a midwinter dusk, I passed the turn-off to the refuge. Out there in the frozen sagebrush were the final four occupiers, an unlikely crew of minor players who had refused the FBI's offer of safe passage out. The cordon of special agents that ringed their doomsday encampment in the refuge parking lot hadn't stopped the youngest among them, Bundyite videographer David Fry, from occasionally livestreaming and posting footage to YouTube. In one video Fry wandered alone behind his camera through room after room of the abandoned bunkhouse. A few days earlier it had housed the boisterous foot soldiers of the Bundy Revolution. Now all that was left was trash and scattered wads of clothing. Only Fry's footsteps and the click and creak of opening and closing doors interrupted the forensic silence.

Burns was also quiet when I arrived; it usually is. In the crusty snow, deer nibbled on bare twigs in front yards. I turned up Broadway, the town's old main drag. Buildings of vintage small-town brick squatted in the ashen twilight. Here and there a shop was still lit, but most windows were dark, their glass reflecting the last light still held in the clouds. The only folks out on the sidewalks were a bundled-up news crew hurriedly setting up in front of the Central Pastime Tavern.

My motel, however, was full. The Silver Spur was buzzing with militia, media, and other Patriot movement folks. (The FBI, I learned, stayed at the other end of town.) The proprietor had a distant but manic cordiality, giddy and wary all at once. His companion didn't bother; she grunted at us all, except when she yelled. By the door of my room, on the snowy balcony, an older, rattled-looking dude dressed in camo and sporting a long, white backwoods beard smoked and guzzled thirty-two-ounce cups of gas station coffee while mumbling to himself. He was very friendly whenever he surfaced from his own reverie and addressed me, though it was hard to make sense of what he was talking about. Something about snow in the mountains, something about my peacoat, which in turn provoked something about the navy, something about the high seas. He fulfilled a certain stereotype of a militia guy, but more of my fellow guests, most of them also recently arrived, were much younger; some sported cowboy hats, but most wore black hooded sweatshirts—all had intense stares. They smoked a lot of cigarettes. There were a number of women as well, also grim smokers, shivering outside their rooms in the morning light while their trucks defrosted in the lot below. One woman had brought her horse.

Meanwhile, the press bustled about with their own sense of mission. There were some TV news crews, Oregon Public Radio, and also a documentary filmmaker. The first night, I lay in my bed listening to him through the thin walls as he paced on the balcony in front of my room. He was excitedly narrating to someone on the phone the tale of how he'd been trapped in John Day on the night of Finicum's death. He'd gone up there to film the public meeting that had never happened and then, with the highway through the forest closed down, he'd had to loop around the mountains to get back to the refuge before the FBI arrived. It had taken like five hours, but he'd made it. The panic there had been wild; he'd gotten some great footage.

*   *   *

A week ago, when the news had come in, the world of the occupiers had changed in a flash. For all their paranoia, they hadn't really been prepared for this. Sure, the FBI had been engaged in a bit more of what LaVoy had called "saber rattling," but it hadn't dampened their spirits. Visitors and new occupiers were still coming—colorful characters among them. (One was a three-hundred-plus-pound weirdo claiming to be Chris Christie's older brother, who challenged, via video, the New Jersey governor to a sumo-wrestling match.) But then the word had come in, and their big tent of feelings had collapsed. Ammon was in custody; the rest of the leadership had been arrested too. Except for LaVoy—LaVoy was dead. Shot with his hands in the air. The freak-out had been immediate and drastic. Mental health was an issue on the refuge to begin with, and most everyone was armed. Now those whom occupier Jason Patrick had called the reasonable people were gone—and Patrick found himself one of the only core occupiers left. Even in the chaos, true to form, one of the first priorities had been to livestream everything—so that the whole world could watch, in real time, as their panic blossomed.

They were clustered now in the kitchen for a meeting, calling in others via walkie-talkie. Many seemed to be in tactical gear—camo and vests and assault rifles everywhere. Some were pacing nervously, others staring ahead, blank with the shock of what had happened. Some wanted to stand and fight the feds; some thought it was time to go home. Besides mocking his comrades for their useless yammering, Blaine Cooper blithely put forward his own plan of action: taking a refuge fire truck and busting out. "If they try to fuck with us," he said, "lay lead down, we'll regroup in Idaho." At another point, another male voice piped up with an even worse idea: what they really needed to do was get out there and start executing people who worked with the feds, start executing their families, show people what the consequences would be. Jason Patrick tried to intervene with reason: "And you think that that's more tactical than just standing peacefully here?" For his part, Jason was going to do what he had been doing from the beginning: standing and defending the Constitution. "We are the David in the David and Goliath story," he argued. "You go guerrilla tactics now and the narrative changes to domestic terrorists." Another off-screen male voice suggested at another moment that maybe none of this was necessary. "We already have our martyr," the voice said. In the end there was a vote, and the vote was to stay and peacefully defend, along the lines Patrick had suggested. Within twenty-four hours, only four of them would remain.

Beautiful Monsters

I spent my first day in Burns talking to strangers, visiting with Charlotte at the reservation, wandering around town in the deathly quiet aftermath of the afternoon's snowfall. When I got back to the Silver Spur in the dusk, the Patriot folks seemed more worked up. There were a lot of people here now, and they seemed to be doing things, though what exactly I wasn't sure. Mostly they were smoking and stamping their feet to keep warm, just as before, but now there seemed to be an aura of extra purpose. Maybe there was reason for some extra agitation: while chatting with local folks in town I had been told that the Pacific Patriot Network militia group had announced some kind of plan for an operation—a "miracle," it was supposedly called—for that Saturday, February 6. The PPN, it was said, was proposing to somehow peacefully pass through the cordon of elite FBI agents who were penning in the final four occupiers and deliver them safely to freedom. It was a vague plan—I guess it was mostly a secret plan. Maybe there really was no plan, but talk of it made the waiting scarier and more interesting. Waiting was all we were doing really—today and every day, as the week ground on.

In the meantime, I was eager to check out the refuge myself—or see how close I could get. The next morning, I drove out toward the basin, a little nervously at first—unsure if there would be roadblocks. It had been more than a week now since the takedown of the leadership of the short-lived CCF, more than a week since most of the remaining occupiers had fled or surrendered, but there were still those last four Necessary Bodies stranded out there on the refuge—"the Final Four," as they would come to be called by their supporters and the press. Ringed in by the FBI in their raggedy camp, they'd even ignored Ammon's plea for them to go home.

On my way out I paused at the top of Wright's Point and stumbled around a bit in the snow among the smooth chunks of basalt. This world I'd entered was mostly lava; I was beginning to understand this, to get a picture of it in my imagination. The whole place was built of molten stone, layers and layers of it, cooled into shape in the atmosphere. And it went down thousands of feet, the whole table of the east Oregon steppe, marked here and there and everywhere by escarpments and buttes like this one, eroded into prominence, or pushed there by seismic forces. It was all frosted with snow and ice right now, sparkling in the morning light. The sage, outlined as if in crystal, bobbed in the little breezes rising off the land below. From up here I could see to the end of whatever this world was. There were a couple of ranches beneath the bluff, but beyond them was just the gold of the basin grasses. In the distance, a sloping hulk of snow marked the south horizon. Soon, but not yet, I'd come to understand that this whole beast was a single mountain, the long western back of Steens, pressed up over millions of years by fault-block action. I got back in the car and slid on down into the basin, driving out along that same raised highway Brand and LaVoy had driven down, also for the first time, just a month earlier, as they and their friends crossed their Rubicon and began the occupation.

Things were so different now—in the human world, anyway, so much had happened. But I guessed it made little or no difference to the land itself, or to the eagle I startled off a fencepost along the road—just as LaVoy had done on his first ride. Maybe it was the same one. Such a handsome monster of a bird, it was hard to keep my eyes enough to the road, to keep my car from ending up down the embanked highway, nose buried in the dirt, tires spinning in the air. Finally I just stopped and watched until the bird vanished in the far reaches.

I was the only customer at the Narrows RV-park restaurant down at the turnoff to the refuge. I enjoyed an enormous chicken-fried steak while chatting with the owner—herself clearly still jazzed up on rural electrification. Soon we were joined by a British photographer, now living in Portland. He told me about seeing LaVoy come running up the day the militia had rolled in with their long-gun bravado, waving his arms—no, no, no. The proprietor interrupted, nodding toward the plate glass. A few SUVs were rolling into the parking lot. Out popped some fit white dudes, in the ball caps and outdoor gear that I, too, had come to recognize as the informal uniform of the FBI. They came into the restaurant, toting a huge laundry bag.

Somewhere out there, five miles down the road, a contingent of FBI agents was camped out, marking some kind of perimeter in the bunchgrass and sage around the refuge. A big LED sign was being dragged into place right now as I watched, flashing text that warned anyone who tried to push farther that they were subject to arrest.

The road was Sodhouse Lane, named after the old northern outpost of the ranch of Pete French. It was near here that Ed Oliver had shot French in the head from behind. Some of the buildings of the ranch were preserved on refuge land under a clump of enormous ancient cottonwood trees, home in warmer months to roosting herons. Two years later I'd find myself there, stunned and somewhat terrified, under those trees. Used to the silent and solitary elegance of herons and egrets, I wouldn't be prepared for the grotesque theater of their family life: the rubbery roar of the gigantic "chicks," punctuated by the clacking of their scissory beaks, high up there in their wide-brimmed, self-befouled nests. But for now, birdwatching would have to wait. The wildlife of real interest for me and everyone else were the Final Four, still holding out in their *Mad Max*-looking campsite in the refuge headquarters' parking lot, where they'd removed to, in terror, after the news of LaVoy's death had come in. We all knew what their digs looked like because, whenever possible, they'd been streaming live what they seemed to be sure were their last moments on earth.

"God Help Us"

I love long, boring videos. The kind where the camera never moves and nothing much happens and then something happens and then nothing happens again for a very long time. If that is a genre of film, that genre might be my favorite. I like videos where the most dramatic changes are often the ones in the light, in the sky. I've been trained to it; I've taught at a famous art school for more than a decade. Little did I know that all that time I was also being prepared to be a student of the Bundy Revolution, and the Malheur oeuvre of young David Fry. At the center of the immense body of work that Fry streamed and posted from occupied Malheur is the footage he shot on January 27 capturing much of that day—its mood of giddy terror and all the pointless activity that accompanied it.

There are hours of this footage, the camera trained most of the time on the yellow upraised elbow of a Caterpillar front-loader and, above it, the low white-and-charcoal sky. It's a beautiful shot, the tension of its angles directing our eyes up into the clouds. The Caterpillar engine rumbles, the faceless voices of the occupiers come in and out, talking about what sound like logistical banalities until you realize those include speculations on things like how likely it is that they'll be able to take down a federal drone with a rifle. At different points, Duane Ehmer and a young Montanan named Jake Ryan get into the Caterpillar and set its arm to work on the refuge earth. The beast drones and bucks. Periodically the screen is invaded by the red and pudgy face of a man who'd become, with Fry, one of the other final four occupiers. Sean Anderson is the only one directly addressing the digital void today. Sometimes he's screaming, calling on the militia brethren he believed or fantasized were out there and on their way. They needed to be quick about it—fast, steadfast, and undeterred. "Don't be afraid of those roadblocks . . . Drive up there and shoot them! They are dishonorable, not following their oath, not protecting American people, good patriots, fighting for our rights! They're the terrorists!" he hollers. "You a militiaman? Come get some!"

At another moment, we hear Anderson, just off-screen, shooting at an FBI surveillance plane; in another he's hectoring a fellow occupier to keep his gun close at hand—you never knew when the final assault was going to begin. And then he's gone; again, for long, peaceful stretches it's just the digger, punctuated by occasional torsos of armed occupiers passing back and forth, as the sky darkens and the horrible day finally comes to an end. Nobody was coming to save them.

* * *

By dusk almost everyone had left. Jake Ryan and Duane Ehmer, despite all that digging they'd been doing, were now both gone. Blaine Cooper, for all his bravado the night before, had fled before the FBI arrived. Jason Patrick was gone too, arrested, like Duane, at the FBI checkpoint down Sodhouse Lane. Most others had been allowed through; some would be picked up and charged in the coming weeks and months. By nightfall only the four remained: Sean and his wife, Sandy Anderson, Wisconsinites recently transplanted to rural Idaho; Jeff Banta, a wiry, enigmatic Nevada man who'd joined the occupation only two days before; and, rounding out the group, David Fry, young tech nerd, amateur documentarian, and perhaps the unlikeliest occupier of all. The darkness now seemed to soothe them. The only images on their livestream were of the fire they'd gathered around. It flickered and cracked, making these nighttime videos a bit like YouTube footage of yule logs, an entire subgenre in itself. Here, instead of Christmas music, we have the voices of David, Jeff, Sean, and Sandy as they loosen up—Fry told a reporter they'd been drinking—and settle into the realization that they are truly the only ones left.

"Funny it came down to this little group," Sean Anderson remarks.

"It really is," Banta drawls in agreement.

* * *

Now Jeff, sounding a little tipsy to my ear, holds forth over the fire, bantering about his life and philosophy.

"I'll tell you my motto: the only way I lose is if I quit. I cannot lose unless I quit," he tells his brand-new friends. "I tell you what: I've got a bank account as big as the fucking sky and I don't want it. I want to go up top. I want to go sit by my God. Fuck this life. It doesn't matter how much money you have. I'm a reality-TV star—yeah, hard to believe, I know. I'm fucking *huge*, the largest in America."

"Are you *the survivor?*" Sandy Anderson asks, laughing.

"I don't know what they call me, because they kind of keep it under wraps, but I'm a—I kind of like to think of myself as Jeff Banta," Banta replies.

"Who?" Sandy inquires.

"Jeff Banta," Jeff Banta repeats.

"I don't watch TV, so . . ." says Sandy.

"Well, yeah, you don't have to follow along. That's fine with me," Jeff drawls back. "For a large part of my life I've gone into every situation alone."

"You don't want this one to be alone too," Sandy posits, somewhere in the dark.

"Not really," Jeff answers, quietly now.

And then suddenly they are all shouting, not in fear but with joy. "WOW!" Sandy effuses. "Oh my gawd, look at the heavens!" exults Jeff. Sandy lets out a long, wordless groan at the beauty of the night sky of the Harney Basin, which has just been unveiled to them.

Up in east Oregon it's a different sky, a glimpse of one from another time. It gets very dark out there, about as dark as it gets in the Lower 48. The black gets sopping wet with that milky starlight, beaming at us from millions of years ago, layers and layers of it landing on our eyes, so that the night sky has a depth I've rarely seen elsewhere. Sometimes when those stars are revealed, if you aren't familiar with it, all you *can* do is shout.

"Lordy, lordy!" hollers Sean Anderson. "We're probably in heaven already and don't even know it."

* * *

All the while, they are caught in another glowing network, being watched and listened to by the watchers and listeners they'd invited. Fry checks out the comment stream and, disheartened, declares to the group that he thinks maybe it'd be better to just turn it off for a bit.

"I'm not going to sit here and look at these," Fry says. "I think half the people are just wanting to see us die anyways."

"Yeah, oh yeah," agrees Sean Anderson, no longer the screaming, suicidal militant of the afternoon. "This is better than anything."

* * *

The peace they found that night wouldn't last. In the light of the next day, things were looking dire again. In a video Fry posted under the title "Maybe Last Dance? Husband and Wife," the encampment already looks like a disaster area. The clouds have rolled back in; the sky is low and dim. There's a tarp up on poles covering a little makeshift cooking area. Stacks of boxes, water, beer, and food are scattered about in the dirt lot. All this disorder is hemmed in by a jigsaw puzzle of muddy vehicles: the wagons had been circled.

From the open door of a white pickup truck, a maudlin song is playing loud, going on about being tangled together. In the shot's middle ground, Sean and Sandy Anderson are embracing, wrapped tightly around each other and so puffed out in winter ski jacket and camo coat that it's hard to distinguish their bodies. They are moving around and around in the staggering circle of a clumsy high-school slow dance. Sometimes Sean sings along, while gazing into Sandy's eyes. The words are love-song words, lyrics about being wrapped up in each other forever. Sean's not a great singer, but he's impassioned. To show more of the scene, or give his new friends some privacy, David Fry pans away from the couple out over the camp and its surrounds. You can see out into the gold grass, across the water of the pond and the river, out toward the far-off lake. Boxes are scattered everywhere, and you can see the lip of the big ditch they dug the day before. The plan had been to use it as some kind of fortification, but by the end of it all, they'll be using it as their common latrine.

The comment stream for this video is a litany of mockery, anger, and abuse. "Fall Back to Dairy Queen," says one. "This is morbid . . . like watching two diseased orcas prepare for spawning," adds another wit. Finally the song ends. Now Sean Anderson is addressing America. "We're fighting for everyone. We're free. We're *the People*," he says to the camera, imploringly, tapping the bulk of his torso with both open palms. "God help us."

Death Magic

We never learned what the Pacific Patriot Network had had in mind for the miracle rescue of these four lost souls. Later in the week PPN leader B. J. Soper changed plans. Now he asked everyone to meet for a rally on February 6 at one P.M. at the improvised memorial that had sprung up at the side of the road on the snowbank where LaVoy Finicum had been killed. The photographer I'd met at the Narrows had told me it was easy to find the memorial—you couldn't miss all the flags, he said—so, with a few free hours on the morning before the scheduled rally, I decided to go check it out for myself. I headed up early, hoping to spend some time alone at the site before the Patriots converged. I wanted to see what magnitude of martyrology was leaking from that roadside shrine.

On the drive up though the landscape, my sense of mission increased. As I emerged from the canyon into the forest, I recognized from the video the access road where the line of FBI vehicles had waited. But then something happened—or nothing happened, actually. There was no memorial. I continued driving, passing out of national forest land into a wide, high mountain valley, given over to a large-seeming cattle operation: dark, shaggy cows traveled in slow circles through the snow, behind big red machines spewing out moist gobs of green and gold shredded hay. I kept going, confused, reentering federal land—more rocky, snow-covered pine forest. After an hour of driving I gave up. As Shawna Cox and LaVoy and the others had discovered, there was no reception of any kind up in the pines of the Bad Luck National Forest, and I needed to get back to town for a phone meeting with Wadatika archaeologist Diane Teeman.

* * *

Death and the dead were the main topics in my conversation that day with Diane. Already a little unsettled by my time seeking out—and failing to find—the site of LaVoy's death, I was primed for Diane's description of the Paiute concept of *puha*, a kind of spiritual substance that also gave a name and form to my own inchoate trepidations. "Because *puha* is the power or essence of each person," she explained, "it's on everything they make or use." This, in traditional Paiute thought and practice, could be a serious problem. The *puha* of the dead was not something to be messed with; it could cause grievous harm, misfortune, illness, and death. Thus, the things of the dead required special attention. "Traditionally we bury people with all their most important possessions—less-important stuff is burned—so that none of it can cause harm to the living, and so that the part of the soul of the dead that must travel to the Milky Way isn't held back."

Puha had played a role in a mysterious ailment that had long afflicted Diane's father, she told me. He had suffered for years, traveling to see Western doctors and shamans on various reservations, before a shaman at the Bannock Reservation at Fort Hall in Idaho had had a vision of a disturbed grave in a mountain pine grove that her father recognized as one he had passed through before becoming ill. She herself had to go through serious spiritual preparations and cleansings in her work as an archaeologist in order to protect herself from sicknesses brought on by disturbing objects crafted and used by the long departed—which was something impossible to avoid in her field.

It was because of *puha* that traditionalists in the tribe were certain Finicum had placed himself in mortal jeopardy in his video from the artifact room. Now, because of his own *puha*—and the evident turbulence of his spirit during his time on the refuge, along with the violence of his death—the refuge itself was a more dangerous site, one that would require serious cleansing before traditionalists like Diane would be comfortable returning to it.

So, it was with even more trepidation that I headed back up the canyon to the site of LaVoy's final breaths. Even before speaking with Diane, I'd had my own reasons to be leery of the martyrology blooming around me at the Spur. In my research into the stories of Malheur, I'd often found that Native thought about Spirit and World seemed eminently more helpful, practical, and sane than many of the understandings I had grown up with. But those Euro-understandings, when it really came down to it, were part of a world outlook that I essentially shared with the bereaved and enraged supporters of the occupation. In the end, it was that outlook that was stronger in me. Despite my fear, I needed to find it, the exact location where LaVoy had expired.

Off I went, driving right back up into the Bad Luck National Forest, trying one more time to find the Patriot Golgotha up there in the pines. This time there was no missing it. Where this morning there had been nothing but a bank of roadside snow and its bland aura of fatigue, there was now a sea of flags and a little wooden cross. People on both sides of the road were stomping in the snow, while others paced, and a few raised more flags in a clump of pine. The horsewoman from the motel rode back and forth on her steed in front of the growing memorial. I recognized many faces from the Silver Spur, but this time they met my eyes with an open hostility that ignited my paranoia about the whole enterprise—this mass bath in the invisible substance that leaks from every site of sudden, violent death. I drove on slowly into that same valley, turned around near the same cows, now huddled in wind-defensive clumps in the snow. Snaking back through the crowd again, I headed back down the canyon in silence—dread having drowned out all sense of purpose.

When I got back to the motel, I found out what was up—why all the glares, and why I hadn't been able to find the site earlier. In an unexpected confirmation of my growing feeling that there was a magic war being waged in these parts, I learned that the original shrine had been removed in the night by unknown hands—presumably to thwart the scheduled rally. An article quoted an enraged B. J. Soper offering a five-hundred-dollar reward for info about who had done it. He'd promised to buy "every damn flag in this town" and rebuild the memorial. It had looked to me that he had.

Ranchers' Lives Matter

It was too much for me, even if I had sought it out: the death magic, the clustering of all those bodies and faces—who were they, and why had they come? It saddened me to see them, clumped like that, trying to get closer, as if the place were a portal to the ultimate moment, the last breath, as if they could touch it, as if they could touch him, poor Finicum, on his back in the snow, looking up, his last vision framed by the dark spears of lodgepole pines, his arm raised at the fading winter sky.

RANCHERS' LIVES MATTER. I'd seen that sign, heard the slogan. Why did it take LaVoy's death for his life to matter? And why did it need to be phrased in this seemingly aggrieved rebuke of the simple, moral assertion of the Black Lives Matter movement? I suppose human significance is irrevocably tied to death, violence—and, in America, to race. Here was the glory machine of our culture stripped bare, revealed in its racialized automation. There seemed to be no escape from the economy of punishment in 2016 America: RANCHERS' LIVES MATTER said that too. The economy of punishment was enmeshed with the economy of mattering, and in American politics, despite all our big democratic sentiments, the possibility of mattering seemed to be something always scarce, never distributed equally across all bodies. The All Lives Matter reactionary panic had been to me one of the most troubling of American phenomena in the troubling years and months leading up to Malheur. I had found it totally heartbreaking—all the more because of how unsurprising it had been—to see so many white folks feel deeply threatened by the unthreatening proposition that black lives mattered *too*. It seemed the assumption was that any increase in the value of black lives would have to be balanced by a drop in the value of those of white people—and some of those folks already felt their value to be seriously waning. So here we were at Malheur with RANCHERS' LIVES MATTER, even though the only rancher here seemed to me to be the absent, dead one. Ranchers are busy people, and also this really wasn't primarily a ranchers' movement. The people who'd flocked to Burns and up to the forest to grieve LaVoy were likely not ranchers or cowboys, but they were rural folk, and almost all of them were white. They'd looked terribly hungry to me in the pines with their crosses and their flags—hungry for meaning, hungry to matter. But death magic will make all of us look like ghouls.

It seemed so much saner, what Diane had described to me—the opposing urge to just leave the dead alone, *especially* those who'd died violently. How much saner to tend to the living, to their healing, in ritual practice—and to let the dead go. Some Northern Paiute had traditionally even buried the dead with their faces covered, so they couldn't return in dreams and afflict the living by staring into their eyes. I made a vow to myself, as I drove away from the clump of mourning Patriots, to leave the dead alone, to stay away from martyrology in the future, away from all such sites, irradiated with trauma. No more of these fetishized sacred zones where bodies became words and feelings—words and feelings that now circulated so easily, weaponized in our social ether. But I was lying to myself, and I knew it. I'd be back to this very site, again and again. I couldn't stay away any more than I could stop hitting play on LaVoy Finicum's final moments on earth, any more than I could stop watching those moments from the air through the eyes of the FBI surveillance craft as the bullets entered him and he fell back into the snowbank in the pines, in that terrifying, absolute surrender to gravity.

Up in the forest, the Patriots continued to huddle around the death site into the late afternoon. But as the winter shadows fell, and the dim, gray sun sank down through the bluing pines, temperatures began to drop. Finally the crowd petered out, returning to bunk down again in town.

*   *   *

Meanwhile, out on the refuge, the martyrology was only getting thicker. The news that B. J. Soper had called off the rescue was not received well by the Final Four. "They said no free Wacos, they killed LaVoy—is there anybody getting justice for that?" Sean Anderson implored on a video that David Fry posted to his YouTube channel. He and Sandy were seated on a makeshift bed in their ramshackle cabin of tarps and ripped camo fabric, heated, it seemed, by some kind of generator hammering away loudly off-screen. "Here we are at Camp Finicum, freest place on earth, I guess," Anderson intoned bitterly. "Here we sit as hostages." Having heard that the U.S.

attorney's office intended to add the Final Four to those to be charged with felonies in the case, he rants on a bit about the Constitution, his wife chiming in with details, before drawing up his own terms for bringing the occupation to a close. "They either let us go, drop all charges, because we're good people, or they come in and kill us. How's that going to sit with America? How's that going to sit with God?"

Celebrations

That night I met Jarvis Kennedy at a big celebratory dinner at the fairgrounds building—the same meeting hall where Ammon had preached the Beautiful Pattern, and where Georgia Marshall had invoked her own ancestry before calling on the assembled to embrace the future and turn away from the past. The room was packed with fold-out tables, where the burger-chomping citizenry sat. At the center was a clump of law enforcement officials—glad-handing, back-slapping men, all congratulating one of their number, Sheriff David Ward, whom the dinner was honoring. No one could deny it had been a frightful ordeal for Ward and his officers—one that was ending much better than it had seemed like it was going to. An hourlong line snaked its way along the metal walls of the fluorescent-lit hall to get to those burgers being cooked up by a crew of cowboys out in the icy parking lot on the biggest charcoal grill I'd ever seen. The line clearly wasn't getting any shorter, so Jarvis and I steeled ourselves and joined in. Death and the dead were still on my mind. As we shuffled along I brought up a story Diane had told me about the repatriation of the head of Egan, the reluctant Wadatika leader in the Bannock-Paiute War.

When he'd been betrayed and killed by Umatilla leaders, one of them had taken Egan's head as evidence and as a trophy. From there, the head had traveled back to D.C. and the secular shrines of the United States, where it had eventually been located deep in the collections of the Smithsonian. Finally, in the 1990s, members of the tribe had won it back and, after much debate about the dangers of bringing such a tormented object into their community, flown a delegation east to get the eloquent chieftain's skull. (How had they cared for the head on the plane? I wondered to myself. Were they allowed to hold it during takeoff? Did they check it? Put it in the overhead bin?) The story reminded Jarvis of the spiritual intimations he'd felt at the vigil he and his friends had kept on that reservation hillside during the tense nights of the occupation. Their bonfire had been up on the same ridgeline with the tribal cemetery, where Egan's head had finally been interred. It had been there, with their backs to the graveyard, that he and his friends had felt accompanied, in their moment of need, by an invisible assembly of their dead. "You felt it, right?" he asked a nodding companion.

There would be so many assemblies in this story—of the dead and the living, in body and imagination. So many flocks. Maybe that's where human meaning is really located in the last instance: in flocking, in the different ways we find to declare ourselves to each other in time and space. I'd see many more human flocks in the months to come. Some would be at these same fairgrounds and in this very room. That fall, a month after visiting the county fair, I'd attend the Burns-Paiute tribe's yearly Reservation Day Festival and Pow Wow, in celebration of the date—in 1972—that the tribe's current reservation had finally been formally established. I'd watch as the Wadatika unfurled themselves to themselves, to the liquid thrum of the drums and the raised voices of the powwow singers. I'd watch as Jarvis himself, alongside his people and their guests, entered this same room, dressed in a powwow costume composed of what looked to be thousands of feathers, an outfit that seemed to transform him momentarily into some kind of mythical being, a bird-man of the sort one might see in a dream.

Meanwhile, back in the present, the flock of neighbors around us kicked its assembly into gear: the speeches had begun. This community was here to pay tribute not only to its cops, but also to itself and what it had done earlier that week, when B. J. Soper's Pacific Patriot Network had staged a demonstration demanding, among other things, that the feds leave Harney County. Out-of-town militia folks and local supporters had assembled en masse at the courthouse that Monday, February 1—but there they'd been met by an even larger crowd of angry locals, protesting them and demanding that the militia go home. Another *We the People* had surged forth that day on the stage of the occupation drama, and tonight, they were here to unfold themselves once more in celebration.

*   *   *

The next day I headed down Highway 205 one more time. I had decided to take the long way home, around Steens Mountain, out to the Alvord Desert, and down the back way to Winnemucca, Nevada. I felt an imaginary line running through me as I drove—the line Finicum and his friends had traveled that last day—only running in reverse, north to south from the national forest to the refuge, passing the new sacred site of the Bundyites where Finicum had expired in the snow, and traversing the ancient sacred earth of the Wadatika, where, if you listened to the tribe, Finicum had contracted that fate. Up again I went, over Wright's Point; again the basin unfurled beneath me, running out toward snowy Steens to the south. I pulled out onto the refuge at an unguarded point and climbed a butte, up through the sagebrush, to get a last look at the marshes, the meadows, and all the distance.

I'd asked both Diane and Jarvis what it felt like to spend time on the land of the refuge, with the knowledge of that sublime persistence of their people in that landscape. Diane had said that whenever she is walking on the land, everywhere she looks she sees obsidian shavings and objects, the whole basin is full of them. "Everywhere I go I feel accompanied," she said. "In this landscape I never feel alone." "Oh man," Jarvis had said, "just go down there to the refuge. You'll feel it when you get there. You'll just see them there."

He was right; if I closed my eyes and looked closely, I could see them. It was like Jarvis had described—there they were, the winter villages, the wickiups, smoke rising from the fires, people in reed boats fishing on the lakes. I could barely see the lake that winter, it was so shrunken. But I could see the dead, or I told myself I could. Sentimentally, I also began to imagine the voices of children, thinking about something Charlotte had told me, about learning as a child to make baskets from the reeds that grew here— baskets for egg gathering. She was taught to whip one together in a few minutes right there in the marshes. (She'd also been taught that if she found a nest she had to leave one egg for the birds and one for the coyotes; only an extra third egg could be hers.) How different that landscape would look to me if I had been taught to weave baskets of the reeds that grew there, baskets for gathering, carefully, mindfully, my food. As I stepped through that big western silence, my thoughts of Charlotte's childhood weaving took on a more metaphorical register: it seemed that *I* could be *reeds*, reeds woven into *space*, that my walking was a weaving of myself as motion into that landscape of basalt and yellow grass. Eventually, if I walked with the proper care, on the other side of it, this thing called I, a simple strand of material in the wind, might be finally, truly *pulled through*. Then only land-scape and distance would be left, there where I was not, in the magic basket of my vanishment.

The problem is that I still seem to be here—right now, for example, on this page, with you; I'm no more gone than the day I was born. Maybe this was also the ultimate problem for LaVoy Finicum: that there is no meaningful way out of this sticky palimpsest of relation—culture, society, history, whatever—that impinges on each of us, all throughout our lives. Maybe there's no way out without a final leap into death. Maybe death is what he'd meant, in the end, by freedom, the freedom of the One. If so, I wondered if even death had worked. Sure, his body and breath were gone, but his story, his words, and his name were still here, entwined with the mess of everyone else, whether he'd wanted to be here or not.

CHAPTER FIFTEEN

Hallelujah

Surrender

THE END DRAGGED ON FOR A FEW MORE DAYS—until, on the morning of February 11, the last of the Final Four, David Fry, stuffed some cookies in his pocket, grabbed a smoke, and stepped from his tent to begin the slow walk from camp toward FBI lines. By the time the final surrender took place, Highway 205 out to the Narrows was lined with cars, reporters, supporters of the occupation, and curiosity seekers. One out-of-town supporter, in camo, flak jacket, battle helmet, and white high-top sneakers, stood on his truck and waved a flag, becoming in the act the signature image of the day: photographers were allowed nowhere near the actual event.

The surrender had unfolded over many hours, beginning the previous afternoon, when Fry, tooling around on an ATV, had come upon an FBI team in the sage and realized that the perimeter was tightening fast. Now negotiation began in earnest. While the holdouts talked on one phone with the FBI, they were livestreamed on another by Patriot activist Gavin Seim. Finally, a time for surrender was arranged—held off until the following morning, so that the Reverend Franklin Graham could be there. Graham is more right wing—hatefully so, I'd argue—than his famous father, but he looked an awful lot like him, and he had that same Carolina accent. His willingness to be on the scene had helped smooth things out, while adding a stately aura of Billy Grahamness to what was shaping up to be an elaborate ceremony. In the meantime, all there was to do was wait: the famous reverend was flying himself into the county in his own jet. He needed daylight to land on the tiny Burns airfield.

Graham wasn't the only right-wing celebrity trying to get to Burns that night, but unlike Cliven Bundy, he would actually get there. Bundy had heard the news, and the word was that he was on his way to Oregon to stop the surrender. "WAKE UP AMERICA!/WAKE UP WE THE PEOPLE! . . . ! IT'S TIME!!!!! CLIVEN BUNDY IS HEADING TO THE HARNEY COUNTY RESOURCE CENTER IN BURNS OREGON," he, or somebody, had written on his Facebook page. Cliven had initially expressed a little doubt and confusion about his sons' actions at Malheur, but since their arrests and the death of his friend LaVoy, he'd gotten more involved. A few days earlier he'd sent Sheriff Ward, along with the president of the United States and the governor of Oregon, a notarized letter imperiously demanding that federal law enforcement clear out. It was also displayed on his Facebook page for the benefit of the interested public. "We the People of Harney County and also We the People of the citizens of the United States," it awkwardly began, "DO GIVE NOTICE THAT WE WILL RETAIN POSSESSION OF THE HARNEY COUNTY RESOURCE CENTER. (Malhaur [sic] National Wildlife Refuge)." He had never been there and, as it turned out, he wasn't going to see the property anytime soon.

With Cliven in the air and on his way to Oregon, the U.S. attorney's office in Nevada unleashed some brand-new indictments—these for the standoff at Bundy Ranch. The Nevada charges were more intense than the charges in Oregon. While Oregon defendants would face single charges of conspiring to intimidate federal employees (and—in some cases—linked firearms violations), Cliven—and eventually his sons, Ryan Payne, and others—would be facing up to fifteen counts each for the confrontation at Bundy Ranch. If convicted, Cliven seemed certain to die in prison, while his sons would be old men by the time they were released. U.S. attorneys would even go on to take a shot at the Bundy herd. Cliven's cows, a later federal memo read, were "mean and ornery," and had been wreaking havoc up and down the Virgin Valley and over yonder to Lake Mead for years now, tearing up golf courses and the like. When Cliven landed in Portland that evening, the FBI—relieved, no doubt, to find the old rancher bodyguard-free and prescreened for weapons—met him at the gate and took him into custody.

* * *

Gavin Seim may have been the perfect MC for the end of the occupation. A young man still, in his early thirties, and a relentless inspirational talker, Seim is well known in the online Patriot world as a proselytizer for self-governance—a "liberty speaker," he calls himself. He's the kind of God-lit, home-schooled white American Christian who still looks crisply showered when he's been living for months on the road, camping out with his own home-schooled family. Even sporting a van Dyke beard, Gavin Seim somehow looks clean-shaven. His voice is the voice of someone who's learned to talk for a living. Every syllable is rounded and projected as he pours forth his gospel, the political theology of a kind of radical Christian libertarianism that sounds, at moments, an awful lot like anarchism, though Seim rejects that label.

His talk is peppered liberally with citations of John Locke; Enlightenment-era notions of *Natural Rights* are Seim's bread and butter. He calls himself "an abolitionist," and in his many videos that seems to possibly entail the abolition of prisons, police forces, gun laws, immigration laws, and even the entire federal government if necessary—anything that stands between the People, true democracy, and God. He prides himself on being a thorn in the side of police everywhere, and is probably best known for his videos of himself chasing cops down to cite them for their violations. (Additionally, he speaks on natural medicines, calls square dances, and—like the true Pacific Northwesterner he is—roasts his own coffee.) David Fry had gotten Gavin on the phone and, right up through the final moments, Seim livestreamed the end of the occupation to the world.

All that tense morning, Gavin had devoted himself to keeping everyone focused on bringing the occupation to an end peacefully, the militant spirit energized but positive. "We got the world watching," he was saying when I tuned in that morning. "When principled people stand, there's no need for blood, there's no need for violence—and that's what we're showing people here." On the line were Sean and Sandy Anderson from the refuge, and young Victoria Sharp, who'd been patched in to offer further encouragement to the Final Four.

Under the chipper Patriot spell cast by Seim and his references to God and the revolutionary era, Victoria Sharp chatted brightly with the Andersons. The couple wanted updates on Ryan Bundy's condition; they'd heard he had taken a bullet in the arm during his arrest. He was doing fine, Victoria assured them; she'd spoken with his wife, Angie, about it at LaVoy's funeral. Sean expressed deep regret at not being able to attend the service, which had taken place the week before in Kanab, Utah. Victoria assured him that the constraints of his circumstances were understood by all, and then asked if she could put her mom on the line. Seim seemed reluctant, but he agreed to let the elder Sharp have her moment. He must have regretted it immediately.

Odalis Sharp sounded like she was in mental agony; it's in the texture and cadence of her voice, as well as her words. "I'm a very transparent lady, OK," she said, before diving into some fiery Bible verses about punishing evil with expedience. "These people have been getting away with this for too long, and right now, we believe someone is even circling us . . . while they are telling you that they're just going to take you guys out peacefully. I don't believe that. I don't believe that for a moment."

"OK," Seim interrupted. You could hear the rising panic constricting his throat as he spoke. "I don't think that's true, with this many people watching. I think we just need to relax. We need to breathe. It's in God's hands."

But Odalis was worked up now; she was shouting, calling not for a stand-down but for an escalation. "People need to get in there and do what they're supposed to do against this tyranny *now!*" she hollered. "Because people are being taken out . . . Victoria is being circled at this moment by the FBI. We believe that!"

"*Mom!*" you could hear Victoria groan in the background, sounding like the teen she still was.

"We're going to stay on message here," Seim cut in again, sounding very worried. And really, it was terrifying. My own heart plummeted as I listened to Odalis rant. It had seemed that Seim's more reasonable, or at least less suicidal, spirit was prevailing and that the last four would probably get out without any shots being fired, without any more martyrs. But who knew how the folks out there in their apocalypse camp were going to react to this holy exhortation. They'd already refused to surrender many times before. Some of Sean Anderson's rants from the refuge had been bizarre and belli-cose, and the emotional stability of the other three had also seemed ques-tionable at moments. I considered closing my laptop; I really didn't want to hear anybody get killed, not in real time. But I kept listening.

Now Seim was trying to limit the damage. "Let's clear up the lines," he coaxed. "Look, we got Reverend Graham on the ground, we got a lot of people watching." But he can't shake Odalis without hanging up on her, which he doesn't seem to want to do. So when she proposed that the family sing a song, he jumped at the offer. *Yes, a song!*

And so then the Sharp family serenaded the Necessary Bodies of Malheur one more time. It was one of the strangest of many strange performances. As the family burst into song, the synergy of all their different connections being beamed in and out through Seim's livestream turned their voices into something wholly alien—silvery and robotic, punctuated with watery gurgles. A hymn from another, nonhuman world.

Afterward all were silent. It had been uncomfortably long since anyone had heard Sean or Sandy Anderson's voices. How had these fragile, well-armed people taken all this madness? But then Sean was there, laughing, and everyone could breathe again.

"I'm sure that was beautiful in person," Anderson said, chuckling, "but on our end on the phone it sounded kind of like the Chipmunks!" Sandy could also be heard laughing in the background. Gavin laughed nervously with evident relief. These were not the voices of people who wanted to die.

＊　＊　＊

Much of the next hour belonged to the flamboyant Nevada legislator and longtime Bundy ally Michelle Fiore. Fiore helped Seim keep the mood positive, as she and the famous reverend, now landed, made their way to the refuge. For those familiar with Fiore's more provocative statements, her demeanor on the livestream was a big relief. In keeping with the aura of her 2016 pin-up calendar—featuring images of herself posed with a different firearm for each month—the Nevada legislator was most famous for advocating bullets in the head as the solution to all manner of social problems. She loved talking about punctured craniums. "If these young hot little girls on campus have a firearm, I wonder how many men will want to assault them. The sexual assaults that are occurring would go down once these sexual predators get a bullet in their head," she'd said, in support of a campus firearms bill. This quote was mild compared with another proposal she'd made, about Syrian refugees. "I'm about to fly to Paris and shoot 'em in the head myself," Fiore had said of Syrians displaced by the horrors of war. "I am not OK with Syrian refugees. I'm not OK with terrorists. I'm OK with putting them down, blacking them out, just put a piece of brass in their ocular cavity and end their miserable life. I'm good with that."

But on the livestream, Fiore was someone else: an insistently upbeat, self-described "motherly" voice of relative sanity—adding credence to wisdom in Nevada that her ugly, more frightful statements were cynically calculated, Donald Trump–like, reporter-enticing sound bites—effective ones, of just the sort that got a Nevada state legislator into the *New York Times*. She kept the occupiers involved in cheery small talk, complimenting them endlessly, chatting about music, reminding them to snack and pee before they surrendered to join her in what she called the day's "adventure." She even started dispensing literary advice, seizing on Sandy Anderson's desire to tell the story of how she's survived this ordeal: "Be detailed, Sandy. Be very, very detailed. Because, you know, think about what book hit the top charts on the *New York Times* bestsellers: that *Fifty Shades of Grey*, and, I mean, that's a pretty *detailed* book. So you be detailed on how you survived. People want to know—people want to know *all* that."

Despite Fiore's cheerleading, the Andersons' spirits sagged when Sean noticed they had only one bald eagle hovering about them that day—usually there were many more. He and Sandy feared this was not a good sign for what awaited them. Even worse were the crows that flew overhead, yammering at them while they spoke. "They're sinister," Sean remarked warily. Sandy piped in with the detail that their flocks were called *murders*. She sounded genuinely worried about it. Fiore, determined to refuse any gloomy talk, was having none of this portent. Crows were cool, she insisted; she liked crows, and not just crows but other sinister winged beasts as well. Her backyard in Vegas, she told the Andersons, was full of two-hundred-pound solid-stone gargoyles, eighteen of them, mounted on pilasters. "Gargoyles!" laughed Sean, humor restored. "That's right—you said you were Catholic!"

The Passion of David Fry

Graham and Fiore headed over Wright's Point, passed the Narrows—now clogged with onlookers—and approached the FBI lines. Now Fiore got off the phone. Her role on the livestream was taken over by constitutionalist lecturer KrisAnne Hall, who would prove less adroit at handling the volatile feelings of the moment.

It had seemed to be going so well. All this buildup and now it was happening, the smooth surrender, the hoped-for peaceful end. First the Andersons and then Jeff Banta crossed out of their camp to two armored federal vehicles, parked in a defensive V. They were patted down and taken into custody. Everything was going exactly according to plan.

And then it was David Fry's turn. And then something was wrong. Fry wasn't moving. Only minutes ago he had sounded supremely chilled-out as he'd given a dispassionate play-by-play of the Andersons' collective surrender. But now he'd had second thoughts—and this change of mind came with a frighteningly swift shift in mood. Now David was shouting. "Unless my grievances are heard, I will not come out!" he hollered at the feds, at the sky, at all of us pinned by our ears to his voice through the internet.

*   *   *

How had it come down to David Fry, a long-haired young man from the outskirts of Cincinnati who had little to no familiarity with issues of public land? Like many Patriots, he was a libertarian. He was pro–gun rights, anti-abortion, and pro–marijuana legalization. Like Brand and Ryan Payne, he called himself a Messianic Jew—but he was also pro-Islam and liked to cite the Koran. The issue that seemed closest to his heart was the death of the oceans, an ongoing catastrophe he worried had dramatically accelerated with the nuclear disaster at Fukushima. Half-Japanese, Fry was also one of the only nonwhite participants in the occupation. He'd clashed with some of the occupiers over their bigotry; he'd been ready to leave over the issue, but in the end he'd thrown his farewell note in the trash. His friend LaVoy Finicum had helped convince him to stay. LaVoy was the main reason he was here in the first place.

In 2015, he'd struck up an inspiring internet friendship with Finicum through an online anti–federal government community. He'd been living at home at the time, working for his father's dental office. Recent scrapes with the law had seemed to intensify his antiestablishment leanings. When his new friend LaVoy had showed up at the forefront of the occupation, Fry had decided to check it out for himself. Once there, he'd stayed, and quickly became the tech guy of the operation. Mainly, he'd hoped that joining the occupation would give him a chance to speak about Fukushima publicly and was frustrated when his interviews with national and Oregon media yielded only mockery. Yet when LaVoy had been killed and most everyone else had left, he felt his media skills were still needed; besides, maybe now there'd be a better platform to address his political concerns. Just a few days earlier, he had posted a video on recent problems with New York's Indian Point nuclear facility. But now, he told Seim, he'd done all he could and he didn't care about his voice being snuffed out. "I already told everybody what I need to say, and I have to stand my ground. It's liberty or death. I will not go another day a slave to this system. I'm a free man. I will die a free man." What David was feeling now, he told Gavin, was *suicidal*.

This is what it had all come to: David Fry, screaming about his grievances and threatening to blow out his brains. When Fry claimed he had a gun actually pointed at his head, I shut my laptop and walked away. After all my recent time with *puha* and death magic, I wasn't going to listen to that gunshot. But after a few minutes, I anxiously tuned back in: Fry was still talking. In custody, a mere football field or so away, Jeff Banta asked now to be moved. He had become close with Fry in their two weeks out there, and he really didn't want to hear that shot he thought might be coming. David was lying on his back in his tent now. He just wanted some space, he told us, he just wanted everybody to back off. At one point he said he was feeling sleepy; he sounded like he might take a nap. It kind of seemed like a good idea—many of us would soon be wishing we could just have napped through the drama of 2016. But David Fry wouldn't be dreaming himself out of the filth of Camp Finicum any more than Americans would be dreaming their way out of the bigger American mess.

At the refuge now, the People were gone. It was down to the One. The Sovereign Power of Government loomed yards away, ready to reabsorb this last square of its confiscated territory. Here was Ammon's Beautiful Pattern, reversed, turned to abjection and nightmare. And what an American nightmare it was. Straight out of the Enlightenment philosophy of John Locke, whose thought had helped lay the foundations of our republic, and whom Seim had been quoting on the livestream that very morning. This whole Bundy thing owed much to a hyper-Lockean logic of sovereignty. The compound had become a site for the manifestation of the Power of the People, a power conjured with the Bundyites' "liberation" of the territory of the refuge. That power was being drained now, in real time, of the very last of its life. As more Necessary Bodies had left the refuge, the size of the liberated territory had shrunk down to this dirt parking lot, ringed in cars and trash. But as long as Fry held out, the militant popular sovereignty of his community was still alive with him; as long he was there, it still, tenuously, existed. As soon as he was gone, Camp Finicum would be just a parking lot again, and the refuge a government facility.

Or that's how it looked, watching from the pages of John Locke. Locke had said that the Power of the People and the Power of Government could not actually coexist. The People's Power could happen only when and where government was *dissolved*. In a sense, the People only really existed as a power in the abolition or constitution of government. Once government was established, in Lockean terms, the supreme power resided no longer in the People but in the legislature. It was *only* in revolutionary moments of abolition and foundation that the People and their power, the Power of the Community, as Locke put it, *took place*. It was probably why Gavin Seim called himself an *abolitionist*, lingering, as he tried to do, in the permanent act of contesting government legitimacy—pulling over cops, yelling at judges, and so forth. But Fry wasn't interested in these sorts of heroics, not anymore. Besides, all the other people were gone now. This wasn't about *them*; it was about him. "This is my stand," he said. "David Lee Fry's stand. I declare war against the federal government."

That war sounded like sacrifice and suicide. The whole last hour of the occupation was horrifying—but the shouting match Fry got into with KrisAnne Hall about the meaning of Jesus's sacrifice was especially so, given that Fry could end the argument at any moment, punctuating it all with a bullet in his cranium. From my own experience as a freaked-out Catholic child, I wasn't sure that David Fry was wrong when he insisted that Christ's death had been a kind of suicide, that Jesus had chosen death and become the example he was by that dying. "Christ is not dead!" Hall shouted back. When David reminded her that she and other Christians called Jesus a sacrifice, Hall countered again that Christ had lived. "Christ lived. That's the point. We are supposed to live. We are supposed to live for his name, for his glory, and for truth. Christ did not die, he lived; that's the whole reason we live." I knew Hall's arguments, I'd heard them as a child too, but my own experience of the terror of God had left me unconvinced. It wasn't just Enlightenment ideas of sovereignty that had brought us to this moment with David Fry; it was the pain theater of the whole Christian thing, the faith that human meaning itself ultimately depended on the introduction of *ideas* into bodies, ideas that arrive in writhing moments of passion, agony, and extinction.

Meanwhile the wind blew and rattled David's tent. Evacuated of all but one of its people, Rural Electrification had been reduced to David Fry's livestream Golgotha. Nothing was left of the Freest Place on Earth but a little dirt patch of martyrology. "LaVoy got *his* on the ground," Fry announced. "I'm going to try to get mine on the ground."

*   *   *

Hall had given up; she was now telling David that there was nothing she could do if he wasn't going to help himself. But Seim kept at him—asking Fry what the real issue was and encouraging him to be candid. Finally he uncovered a lurking fear behind David's refusal to surrender—his terror of prison rape. Seim insisted that prisoners loved Patriots for their courage in standing up to the government, but in the end it would take an agent of that hated federal government to talk Fry down. The FBI negotiator, "Marc," assured Fry that that was not how the federal prison system worked. The serious offenders—the "Big Bubbas," as Fry called them—were kept out of the general population, Marc told him; David had nothing to fear. And then a real miracle happened: David believed him. David Fry believed the man from the government. He'd been saying for the last hour that unless he was allowed to opt out of a system that took his tax dollars for abortions and for killing Muslim civilians overseas, he would not surrender. Suddenly all that was gone. He had only one request now, a simple one. All he wanted from the feds was a single word, to hear them say four syllables of praise: "If everybody says *hallelujah*, I'll come out," Fry now promised. "Will you? Will you do that? Everybody's listening. Everybody's listening."

Marc, inaudible on the livestream, had apparently agreed, because suddenly David was getting ready to go. "I'm getting one more cookie . . . one more cigarette . . . Alrighty then . . ." We could hear what sounded like a tent unzipping and the muffled cry of distant voices. "They're saying *halle-lujah!*" Fry cried triumphantly. We could hear him walking, and the voices of the shouting agents growing nearer. "David, keep walking, my friend—*hallelujah!*" you could hear someone saying. Now everyone was shouting it: *Hallelujah! Hallelujah!* Then he was being patted down and taken into custody—and then his phone went silent. KrisAnne Hall was openly sobbing on the livestream; Gavin Seim, choking up, joined her. It was over.

Still Here

Soon after, I spoke with Jarvis on the phone. I'd wondered what he'd thought of the desperate climax to episode 2 of the Bundy Revolution. He didn't have much to say about the surrender. He was irked about the trench of excrement the Final Four had left behind in the earth of his ancestors, but mostly there was something else he wanted to tell me. He and Charlotte and some others had gone out to the headquarters; the FBI had invited the tribe to be the first civilians to visit the refuge. They hadn't been allowed to get too close to the crime scenes, but they'd gone up on a slope by the watchtower, and they'd built a little pit and a fire and done smudging with sage of all who were present, including a few curious FBI agents. I would have liked to have seen that, the tribe blessing the federal men of violence. "We prayed for their families and for their safe passage home, and we prayed for Finicum and his family too—you know, we didn't want that to happen." And they'd blessed the refuge, he said. "And I sang a song." "What kind of song?" I asked. "A victory song," he said, a little mirth now crackling up at the edges of his voice. "You know, it was like I said in the beginning at the news conference. We were here before you got here, we'll be here when you're gone."

PART II

The Boisterous Sea of Liberty

Opening Arguments

THE BOISTEROUS SEA OF LIBERTY is never without a wave, says Portland's Mark O. Hatfield Courthouse to the world. These words of Thomas Jefferson's are chiseled into the smooth dark stone at the base of the building's steps. It's a masterful act of institutional rhetoric; the phrase is perfectly positioned to preempt and incorporate into the building's aura of legitimated power every act of dissent performed in its shadow. And quite a shadow it is: the federal courthouse itself stretches the confines of the word *house* well beyond bursting. A thirteen-story monolith of glass, concrete, stone, and steel, it has interior halls and foyers filled with speckled marble and granite. It's not a house; it's a formidable Temple of Justice. Still, for seven weeks in the fall of 2016, as the bright end of the Northwest summer plunged into the rain and gloom of fall, the old words of Jefferson took on a daily life that threatened to separate them from the stately rhetorical purpose to which they'd been bound.

The ragged scrum of energy that the occupiers had brought to the refuge rematerialized in Portland on the steps of that courthouse and in the courtroom itself. But as it stepped into this new frame, its meanings also began to change. No longer were these just the colorful or dangerously deluded gun nuts who had held a beloved wildlife refuge with assault weapons. Neither were they just the band of disenfranchised white men who had gone mining for feelings of sovereignty and personal power by restaging white settlement on Native land. Now they were also defendants, facing a sweeping federal conspiracy charge in a justice system many have likened to a conviction-and-incarceration machine. (Or a "predatory judicial industry," as occupier Shawna Cox had called it in a countersuit.) Now they were also standing up in federal court for the right to protest, contesting the state's right to declare which kinds of dissent were allowed and protected and which were not. Things got messy, and fast.

What follows is a travelogue of my time in the Boisterous Sea—which is the name I found myself using for the life of court and the more raucous life lived in its interstices, in its hallways, in its foyers, and on its steps, as well as out in the leafy parks and streets of Portland's courthouse district, bounded by its city hall and its jail as well as the other seats of local and federal governance. It all took me back to my rock in the Mojave, where the sovereign national power of the Marines had interrupted my communion with the unsovereign dreamtime of the earth. Between these two, where was our contemporary public life to be found? Where in our world did the People properly take place? These were and are still my questions. I don't think I've found any definitive answers, but for a few weeks in the fall of 2016—and again in the later winter of 2017—I had a glimpse of another kind of American public life, different from the corporate-dominated one I knew. I saw flickerings of a different kind of nation, a dynamic one that could be lived everywhere, both inside institutions like courts and city halls and also out in the open, in the streets, face-to-face, every day. Weekdays I watched the Bundyites bring their sovereign circus to the courtroom floor. Evenings and weekends I talked with them as they ranted and flocked along the court-house steps and the parks of downtown Portland, coming at times into contact with left-oriented groups and movements with which they some-times sought and mostly failed to find common cause. Some weekends I took trips back to Harney County, where the events of the occupation were still quite raw. Meanwhile, the whole country, panicking harder and weirder each week, was being poured, ever faster, toward Election Day. It was a thrilling and an ugly time in America, a dark time, with many peaks and troughs, but I was grateful to be exactly where I was.

CHAPTER SIXTEEN

Before the Law

Rituals

I DON'T KNOW HOW MUCH TIME you've spent in court. I'd spent little, before 2016. If you aren't a legal professional, and you and your loved ones have been lucky enough to avoid major legal entanglements, it's jury duty that otherwise drags you into the courtroom spectacle. Over the years, the representatives of successive governments have obliged my civic reluctance by weeding me out. In 2016, entering the hallowed spaces of the Law was still a relatively fresh experience for me, especially in that realm, heavier in majesty, of federal court. The ritual of it all impressed itself with an intensity beyond what I'd expected. As I entered court every day, I changed, because entering court changed me, as entering court is designed to do.

It all starts at the front door with the first round of security, a checkpoint like the airport security of old. There's the big scanner, and the metal detector, and the federal marshals, some jocular, some resolutely pissy. The combination adds to the effectiveness of the ritual—obliging you toward friendliness, even when you're being grunted at or chastised. It all keeps you off-balance, reminds you who is in charge. You'll need to behave, ye who enter here. No matter how hard you try, you'll never quite behave well enough.

In Portland, after the first checkpoint, you enter a huge mausoleum-like lobby of smooth dark stone, engraved with more quotes from founding ghosts. George Washington is there, among others. But no one lingers here; everyone's in a rush to be somewhere else. You enter distracted, scrambling to hold your belongings together long enough to get to one of the isolated stone benches in the center of the space. There you frantically reassemble yourself, reattaching all you've removed—belt, shoes, watch, jewelry, phone, jacket, hat. Then you're off into the elevator with the other bodies: in this case, the ragged Patriot crew, smelling a little peaty from cigarettes and rain, bedecked in slogans and flags. (A new symbol had emerged in their iconography: the interlocking *L* and *V* of LaVoy's cattle brand.) Here they were, every day, the bodies of the Bundy faithful, pressed together alongside the bodies of marshals and attorneys—sleeker men and women in suits—as well as FBI agents, gossiping cryptically among themselves or carefully looking away in silence, studying the metal ceiling, staying as far as possible from the Bundyite banter. And then you'd be disgorged onto the ninth floor, where the Malheur proceedings were held. Here was a long, narrow lobby of stone and glass. Floor-to-ceiling windows overlooked the city to the west, which meant, more often than not—this being Portland and autumn—that the elevator had just uploaded you into a cloud. Then, after leaving your electronics with the marshals and passing through another metal detector, you were in—into the hush of it, as Justice opened up its inner sanctum around you. Here the Law, in its interior, manifests no longer in stone, but in blond wood, soft and softening, adding to the feeling of quiet sanctity. No loud talking—and no hats, as one of the more severe marshals would scold me in a whisper, more than once. In all the taking off and putting back on, I would often grow careless; it was hard to keep track of everything.

What it all did—the passage into that muffled land of legal majesty—was make me want to be obedient. By the time I finally got my seat in the gallery, in what can only be described as a pew, I had been transformed. I was now, at least in body, a dutiful congregant of the Law. My slouch vanished; in those first days in court, I moved my head slowly, carefully, like I was balancing it on my neck, like it was made of glass, or like it was a glass, filled to the rim with something I did not wish to spill. If I spoke, even in the breaks, I mostly whispered. And when I stood for the judge or for the jury, I felt moved—I couldn't help it; the whole thing had gotten to me. It got to me every day.

Federal court was not *like* a temple; it *was* a temple. And now the Bundy Revolution was inside. Rural Electrification may have ended in abjection, but the party wasn't over. Here they were, where, if you believed Ammon, they'd always intended to end up. Seven were slated to stand trial in the first of two rounds of prosecution; now they were right in front of me, some within touching distance. It startled me to be suddenly in their presence, to hear their voices, the creaks they made as they shifted in their chairs.

There, right there, was Ammon himself. With no beard and no cowboy hat, he looked more stereotypically Mormon: clean-cut, blond, in a nondescript suit, his earnest face more earnest with more of it in view. After the first days of jury selection, he'd ditch the civilian garb and come to court each day in his prison scrubs, protesting both his claimed status as a political prisoner and the court's refusal to allow him to dress as he desired. There had been a quarrel with the marshals over the formal western wear he'd wanted—the cowboy boots and belt and tie, it seemed, could be construed as weapons. And that's what the fuss unfolding in front of me was all about. Defense lawyers were making arguments on the issue, fascinating—and confusing—ones that were a window onto what the rest of this trial would be like. The problem, according to the lawyers, Marcus Mumford, Ammon's attorney, and Tiffany Harris, the standby counsel for Shawna Cox, was something like this: that sticking Ammon here in this bland suit and "urban loafers," as opposed to his western wear of choice, would seem to jurors like a repudiation of his rural self, and thus of all he'd stood for at the refuge. This, they said, would amount to a tacit admission of guilt before the jury. The judge, Anna Brown, showed herself openly baffled by the whole question. In an effort to resolve the issue, she descended from the bench to look Ammon over herself: "He's dressed better than anyone else in this building," she quipped, adding, with a glance at his feet, "is there any reason he can't be provided black socks?"

Soon defendant Neil Wampler would trade today's pressed button-down for a blue scrub shirt as well, to show his solidarity with Ammon. The prison-issue top was the same color and design as a standard nurse uniform, and Wampler, out on pretrial release, found one easily enough. But that was to come. Today, Neil was sitting at the very back of the courtroom, to the right of the jury box and the table of the prosecution team. With his sun- and cigarette-wizened face and his great shock of white hair, he looked like a man from another century, a frontier face in a daguerreotype. Here also was David Fry. Over the coming weeks Fry would appear exhausted by the long proceedings; sometimes he looked to be napping with his ponytailed head down on the wooden desk next to his lawyer. He rarely spoke to anyone. Neither did Jeff Banta, who was also here, seated behind his troubled young friend, leaning his gangly frame far back in his chair as he perused the scene with skeptical bemusement. Many assumed the Bundyites had no chance in this trial, what with all their livestreamed bravado at Malheur, but Jeff didn't seem worried in the slightest. "I'm stoked," he told a reporter outside court. "We've got this one."

Banta, who'd joined the occupation only the day before Finicum's death, highlighted, with his presence alone, just how many of the foremost of the Necessary Bodies were missing. Seven other defendants in the case would face trial after this one; these included the Andersons, Jason Patrick, and Duane Ehmer. On the eve of the trial, the government had dropped all charges against Pete Santilli, uninterested, it seemed, in dealing with issues of freedom of the press. He was on his way to prison in Nevada now, to await trial in the Bundy Ranch case. Also absent were Jon Ritzheimer, Blaine Cooper, and Ammon's bodyguards, Wesley Kjar and Booda Cavalier. They'd all pleaded guilty, as had maybe the biggest absence in the room that day, the man who'd been at Ammon's side from the beginning of the Malheur adventure, and who'd done so much to summon militia to his family's aid in Nevada: Ryan Payne.

Ryan Bundy, on the other hand, was very much present. His booming voice and austere confidence would stand out every day in the courtroom. This was because Ryan was representing himself, by "special appearance," as he liked to say—a phrase from the eccentric Sovereign Citizen jargon with which he spiced up his motions and court statements. While he generally refused to recognize the lawfulness of the proceedings, in one of the more amusing of his motions he'd announced that he was willing to play the role of defendant or inmate in this juridical show—but not without fair and just compensation. His required fee would be one million dollars. For the same fee, he graciously suggested, he would be willing to consider playing the role of judge, and perhaps the role of bailiff. To make sure he didn't damage himself or the proceedings unduly, the court had assigned him a standby attorney, experienced Portland lawyer Lisa Ludwig, who sat now by his side, often whispering in his ear.

Also representing herself was longtime Bundy friend and Ryan's companion in LaVoy's truck that fateful afternoon, Shawna Cox. Cox had been out on pretrial release since the winter. Her desk was littered with documents, which she perused through reading glasses. Back in February, she'd filed a separate lawsuit of her own, accusing the federal government of "extremely serious public corruption" and "damages from the works of the devil in excess of $666,666,666,666.66." The court had also provided Cox with a standby lawyer, Portland attorney Tiffany Harris. Rounding out the seven on trial that fall was Ken Medenbach, seated at the very back of the room, so neither the judge nor the prosecution nor the marshals seemed to notice what he was wearing when he took off his coat and sat down. It was a custom-made shirt—with special messages regarding that first day's proceedings emblazoned all over it.

* * *

Emblazoned is a word that stands out in my notes from that day. But it wasn't because of Medenbach's shirt; it was because of what was happening in the front of the room. The court had moved on from the issue of Ammon's attire, and now Marcus Mumford, one of Ammon Bundy's two attorneys, was stuck on that word, *emblazoned*; as literally stuck on a word as one can be.

A fireplug of a man—short, but with the burly frame of the farm boy he was—Mumford is a talented courtroom lawyer with a marked disability. He has a profound, very-difficult-to-control stutter. The stutter seemed to grow more pronounced the more heated the contention between Mumford and the court. My notes are full of moments detailing the supercharged weirdness of being in that room, caught in that space of attention with so many others, all of us focused in silence on the spectacle of a single human body struggling mightily to regain the power of its speech. His head thrown back, face turning red, jaw seemingly locked open, as gurgling, painful-sounding clicks emitted from his throat, Mumford regularly gathered the whole room away from the particularities of fact or procedure at hand and into the great human struggle of articulation. It was as if he were a singular embodiment of the tumult and confusion of the Boisterous Sea of Liberty itself. As the trial wore on, it became clear that this was likely also a strategic aim of his performance. The procedures of court, the seamless narratives of the prosecution, and the hush of the room were constantly interrupted by Mumford's passionate arguments, which were themselves then often interrupted by the even stronger disruptive power of his body. At least until the words came tumbling back, and he made his point or simply backed off, saying, after all that effort, "No further questions, Your Honor."

Today he was trying to argue that all the extra security present at the courthouse was prejudicial, especially given the militarized nature of the gear: the ballistic vests, the firearms, the uniforms. The uniforms, he was saying, were "emblazoned"—and this is the word that had caught him by the throat. Finally the whole phrase came loose: "emblazoned 'Homeland

Security.'" It would prejudice the jury against his client, he argued, making him seem unduly dangerous, like a terrorist even. It was a scene that would be repeated pretty much daily: Mumford strenuously objecting to something, arguing passionately but then losing his flow, his whole body pulsing, snagged on a syllable. And the judge, increasingly losing patience with his often repetitive arguments, sometimes growing short with him, even openly angry, to the point where she'd threaten him with fines and contempt—although she would never end up actually sanctioning him in any way.

Female power is still a difficult thing to wield in our world, as political events of 2016 would attest. Judge Anna Brown's whole manner, it seemed to me, partook of a sort of wisecracking-grandmother persona I've seen deployed before by powerful women of Brown's and preceding generations. I'd observed it most recently just a few months earlier, when I'd watched Senator Dianne Feinstein preside over a huge, unruly public meeting and a crew of very talkative—and almost entirely male—speakers. Feinstein chided, teased, and grumped her way through the day, carefully taking up opportunities to rebuke—gruffly, but not too gruffly—just about everyone. Her authority had been near absolute by day's end. As a judge, Anna Brown mixed a meticulousness and enthusiasm for the finer points of the law with a Feinstein-like sardonic world-weariness; it made for another effective performance of power. I found it so, anyway. Brown's large, expressive face, her heavy brow, and her skeptical gaze combined to give the overall impression of someone who had been born already a tad fed up with your shenanigans—and there would be plenty of shenanigans in her courtroom that fall, most, but certainly not all, from Marcus Mumford, his colleagues, and the assembled defendants of the Bundy Revolution.

The Wisdom of the People

As jury selection got under way in early September 2016, Judge Brown was mapping out a schedule that threatened to take the trial up to Thanksgiving. In the coming weeks, she would do much to try to hurry things along, but the jury-interview process—known as voir dire—was not something Anna Brown was going to rush through. She was a member of the Jury Instructions Committee for the Ninth Circuit, and her attention to all matters concerning the jury would be foregrounded by events in the weeks to come.

The first batch of prospective jurors had been seated up in the jury box, and now Anna Brown was explaining to them the jury's exalted role—what would be asked of them were they to be selected, what a precious thing trial by jury was, how essential to the life of our democracy. Whenever the judge spoke with jurors, she took on a different aspect; the weariness vanished. She became an inspired civics instructor and an American believer. It was like she was selling the job, and given the time commitment that would be asked of jurors in this case, it was likely they'd be in need of some encouragement. But it would be worth it, the judge seemed to promise—the role was so important, so vital to the health of the nation—and besides, *this* was going to be a fascinating trial.

At stake, she told the prospective jurors, were some really big constitutional issues: What was protected speech, and what was not? Also at issue was the Second Amendment. What constituted a legitimate exercise of Second Amendment rights? To what extent could they legitimately be exercised in support of First Amendment rights? When did the display of arms fall into the category of threats, violence, and intimidation? Was this a protest or—as the prosecution had charged—a conspiracy to intimidate federal workers?

Those selected for the jury would have to determine together whether the defendants were guilty, beyond a reasonable doubt, of conspiring to impede federal employees of the Fish and Wildlife Service and the BLM—through threats, violence, or intimidation—from doing their work. This was the principal charge against each of the defendants, the only one federal prosecutors had found in their toolbox that fit, to their minds, both the specifics and felony-meriting severity of the defendants' deeds. The alleged conspiracy did not need to have succeeded or even been put into place, Judge Brown explained, but the criminal agreement had to have existed, with the explicit, conscious purpose of impeding government employees. Jurors would be judging the intent of the actors, not only their deeds. In making all these determinations, they would be applying their reason.

The judge liked reason, *reasonable* reason; she loved to say "common sense," and when she said it, she sounded like the very voice of common sense. While she extolled the virtues of the trial-by-jury system, I was convinced; I even felt proud. Erased for a moment were the realities of our justice system—all those Un-Necessary Bodies, warehoused away, so many for nonviolent drug crimes, so many of them nonwhite. Erased was the fact that this trial was itself a novelty. The jury was no longer at the center of the American justice system. Far from it. Few American prisoners have ever met a jury; plea deals, often coerced with the help of draconian mandatory-minimum sentences, are beyond dominant these days—especially in the federal system—where around 97 percent of all cases each year never reach a trial of any kind.

But we'd reached trial, and now it would be up to the jurors to decide what facts, which versions of events, and which of the stories that made up this story were true. All the narrative threads, all the emotions, would be ground down and poured into them, and then they would decide, and then it would be over. If they couldn't provide justice, they would provide finality. Or that was the idea. That's what all this ritual was saying.

What an intriguing burden was about to be placed on these folks—the final twelve and the eight alternates selected in voir dire to represent the Wisdom and Reasonableness of the People. No wonder we all would stand up for them whenever they entered and departed. They weren't an exceptional bunch, but their ordinariness only added to the solemn effect of that rite: the rising we would do for them so many times a day that fall, every time they entered, some making curious eye contact, others carefully averting their gaze as they filed up into the box. Over the next two months, we'd all stand in silence every time the jurors left as well, waiting until the very last one of them had exited through the door, stage right, into that more interior room in the Law where none of us could enter. Each time we stood and watched them come or go, I'd cross my hands in front of me, trying not to breathe too loud, like I'd learned to do as a boy in church. I don't know why I did this, but as I looked around, I saw lots of other folks doing it too. There *They* were, up there, the ritual said. *They the People.* And we down here, saluting them—*Them* who were *Us.*

CHAPTER SEVENTEEN

The Power of the Jury

Biggest Rejects Ever

ONCE YOU START THINKING ABOUT WHAT A TRIAL IS, it really hits you what a peculiar social circumstance you've stumbled into. We'd all be together for weeks, examining one another. The jurors would be watching and listening to the lawyers and the judge and the defendants, trying to determine "the facts," and we'd all be watching them do this, while we also watched one another, and watched one another watching them. The judge wasn't hiding this strangeness; she was celebrating it. It made me look around at the room again, at all the silent faces, all these listening bodies, all the skulls encasing all those buzzing brains, each of us gathered here around the defendants and the lawyers and their conflicting stories, trying to determine for ourselves what was true. Today, in voir dire, we'd even be doing it with the jurors themselves—which of them was hiding something, which of them was lying? It was all making me terribly attentive, the ritual, the quiet, all the soft wood, the judge's careful civics lecture, the presence of all these other people, taking in information, hearing, watching, thinking, all separately, together.

In my notes I paid special attention to what caught the attention of others—especially the defendants. I was particularly curious about Neil Wampler. Well-spoken and well-read, he stood out among the foot soldiers of the Bundy Revolution—but not only for his articulation or his hippie past. I was curious about Wampler's reaction to court because this wasn't his first encounter with the criminal justice system: Neil Wampler was a confessed murderer. And not just a murderer. Decades ago, one horrible night, a young, drunk Neil Wampler had murdered his own drunk father.

In the third week of the occupation, reporters had dug up the story: the Bundyites had a parricide among them. In his drunken stupor, after hitting his father in the head with an eye bolt, young Neil had hitched into town and gone into a store, where he had become distraught and told the clerk to call the law. "I have killed my father," he'd said into the phone. Extenuating circumstances, the details of which Neil wouldn't discuss with others (he said doing so made it seem that he was trying to excuse his actions), had gotten him a shorter prison sentence. He was out in less than five years. Since then, he had lived quietly, married, raised a son, stayed sober, and dedicated himself to what he loved most in the world, the craft of woodworking. Not even the Bundy Revolution lit him up like talk of woodworking, but it was the Bundys who had given him, late in life, an opportunity to make a greater use of himself, an opportunity of a size that he had never dreamed. Now that opportunity had brought him here to federal court, and *that* was something he had no regrets about, as he told anyone who would listen. He was having the time of his life.

Jury selection can be grueling, and we were all getting sleepy, but I watched as Neil snapped back into alertness. He was trying to locate the face of the voice that was now speaking. Now I was too, but I never found it. It was a male voice, from near the front of the room, of a prospective juror. This guy was not feeling as summoned to posture as I had been by the rites of court. He was totally slumped, slouching in his big leather chair up there in the jury box. I could see his shoulders and a little of his back; I could see his gesturing hand, but I never saw his face.

Neil was intrigued, I was intrigued, the whole room was intrigued. We were intrigued because it sounded like what was happening up there was refusal. Judge Brown was handling the entire vetting process, reading out the questions from the attorneys and asking her own. She'd asked this faceless voice whether or not he could follow the dictates of the law even if he felt, that in a given instance, the law itself was in the wrong. Now she asked if he could at least take an oath to follow the law in this case. "I don't know enough about the case to answer that," the man replied.

His answer telescoped the years on me, so that suddenly, in that way a strong memory drops into consciousness, it was me up there in the jury box, more than ten years earlier. I was in Brooklyn, New York, as part of a panel for what we'd all just learned was a murder case—worse, a murder case involving a teen, a girl who was being charged with murder not for actually killing anyone herself, but for phoning in a food order that had led to a man's death. She'd made the call for some boys who had meant to rob the delivery guy, a recent Chinese immigrant who worked, it was said, at the only place that delivered to those projects way out in Brownsville. He'd been robbed too many times already—so he'd made an awful miscalculation. In defense against the pistol the boys had pulled on him, he'd tried to pull out a kitchen knife. You can imagine the rest yourself, and that's exactly how it went: panic, gunshot, flight, bleeding out.

Shaniqua Brown was the girl's name. I've never seen anyone sit so still as she was sitting that day, at the table with her lawyer, a blustery public defender in an ill-fitting suit. He had a ponytail, I recalled, and a big, fat garnet Brooklyn Law ring, engraved so large I could read the inscription. Up against him that day had been a prosecutor with an even greater aura of polish and efficiency than the chief federal prosecutor in the Malheur case, assistant U.S. attorney Ethan Knight. Like Knight, she'd been wearing a high-end, tailored pin-striped suit—that I remember because she was pregnant, and this fancy suit had clearly been cut for this moment. The contrast with the public defender's rumpled disorder was startling. Now, in my memory, the prosecutor was approaching us and questioning us one by one, because that's how they did voir dire in the New York State Circuit Court in Kings County, Brooklyn.

As she worked her way down the jury box, I watched her manner change; she was very good at this. With the older, working-class woman next to me, she got all down-to-earth, calling the woman "honey," like the waitresses do to everyone in Brooklyn diners (or like they used to). She even patted my neighbor on her knee as she looked into her eyes. Had this really just happened? Maybe my eyes had deceived me. Is the prosecution allowed *to touch* the jury? In the moment, I was too shocked by the liberty to even consider the question. And then it was my turn. I watched as the prosecutor's whole aspect changed. She got taller, I remember, instantly. Her posture tightened, her voice deepened, the friendliness drained from her face. I had scarcely spoken when we'd all introduced ourselves earlier. What had I said, I wondered—had I said I was a poet? Maybe that was it—she was narrowing in on me demographically. We're all more predictable than we'd like to think. I was feeling pretty disturbed by these charges against this young woman, a girl, really, for making a phone call. How could this be murder? Maybe the prosecutor simply saw it in my face. Now she was asking me that same basic question. Would I vote to convict if the facts demanded it, even if I felt that the New York State law, allowing murder charges for making such a call, was wrong?

I can't remember what I said, but I think it was something very close to what this guy was saying now, here in federal court in Portland: *I don't know. How could I say at this point?* Whereas Judge Brown had continued, patiently, to flesh out the man's answers for all the lawyers in the room to hear, the Brooklyn prosecutor had already gotten what she needed from me; she moved right along to the next juror. And soon I was moved along—all of us were. Even the jolly bailiff had been stunned, he'd never seen a whole panel tossed before. "You are the biggest bunch of rejects ever!" he'd guffawed, congratulating us, Brooklyn style. He knew we'd wanted nothing to do with that sad murder and the trial of that poor girl. One of our number had even earned us all a vexed lecture on our civic duty from the sleepy-looking judge. This dude had really pushed it; his uncle was a cop but he also hated cops, he'd told the court—so he was double biased, *for and against the police.* I exited the building walking with this same guy, each of us loudly jubilant at our success. But then, as I crossed the gray plaza under the concrete sky, the cold sea air of Brooklyn hit me, and I found myself thinking about Shaniqua Brown. Not thinking really—I just saw her image in my mind, sitting there, alone. I'd remembered her off and on after that for years, until I hadn't anymore. Until today, when she'd returned.

I guess it hadn't mattered in the end. She'd pleaded out, although I wouldn't learn the news until I googled her that night in Portland, thirteen years later. Even with a plea, she'd gotten *fifteen years* in prison; she might still be there, I realized. It was *ten years* more than Neil Wampler had gotten for killing his own father, in an era less deeply invested in the economy of punishment than our own, with its extreme, legislatively mandated sentences; terms disproportionately applied to nonwhite folks like Shaniqua Brown. It wasn't that I felt Neil should have gone to prison for longer—I didn't and I don't—but how had the State of New York, with pride, sent this lost young woman away for fifteen years for confessing to making that phone call? No matter how normalized such things had become, it was still shocking. Who even really knew how she'd been convinced by these boys to make the call in the first place? The full circumstances were never unpacked; no jury ever heard them. The prosecution had won without having to deal with the risk of jurors considering not only the facts but also the prosecutor's decision to apply the law in this manner and in this particular case.

They'd won without facing the danger that even one juror might have questioned whether the law itself was just. This is one way the prosecution wins almost every single case in America today: by never going to trial.

"Jurors, Not Robots"

What that prosecutor had been on the lookout for that day back in Brooklyn was the same thing Judge Brown had been probing for here today: jury nullification. Jury nullification was of special issue in this trial, the judge explained. There was reason for concern that some of the prospective jurors might have been approached by an advocate of this strange phrase that very morning out in front of the courthouse. The man might even have given those jurors a pamphlet on the topic. I knew exactly who the judge was talking about. I had the very same pamphlet in my pocket.

I'd been given it that morning by a frenetic and bearded dude in a cowboy hat. He'd be out there almost every day for the duration of the trial, running up and down the courthouse steps, no matter the weather, seeming to ritually curse the building itself with legalistic and theological imprecations and offering pamphlets to all who headed toward the front doors. He was very hard to miss; sometimes he even brought a bullhorn. If you'd gone up to him and introduced yourself, he'd likely have offered you his hand: "David Zion Brugger, Citizen of Heaven!" he might have beamed.

"We need jurors, not robots," Brugger argued that September to all who would listen—and to many who would not. "Jurors have the law of God written on their hearts, and we know how to judge ourselves and our brethren." Despite his antic and confrontational style—which tried even the patience of his own comrades—Brugger's basic gloss on the history of jury nullification, it had to be admitted, was largely accurate. He had a spiel about it that he delivered while pacing on the sidewalk in front of the courthouse. He had it down—the facts and the ideas, along with compelling details, like the story of the jury in the famous late seventeenth-century English trial of Quaker leader William Penn. Penn had been arrested for preaching a faith other than the official dogma of the Church of England. When the jury had failed to return what the judge regarded as the correct verdict under the law—guilty—the jurors had been fined and imprisoned by the court. Still, they'd refused to give in. Finally a higher court had released them, affirming their liberty to return a displeasing verdict. Then there was the famous case of Peter Zenger, charged with seditious libel for printing criticisms of the royal governor of New York in the 1730s—truthful criticisms about the governor's removal of officials who had blocked his plans to augment his own salary. Truth was not a defense for libel at that time, but Zenger's lawyer had nonetheless argued truth as his defense to the jury: what his client said was true, and how could the truth be punished? The jurors had acquitted Zenger in ten minutes—beginning the long process by which the meaning of *libel* changed to what it is for us today, one where truth is a defense.

In the courtroom the judge was telling the jurors something else entirely—that they were to ignore the human bullhorn outside, and his pamphlet, that jury nullification was not an option. In doing so she was following standards set by higher courts in the United States for many years now. But there was more legal ambiguity to the situation than Brown was letting on. The really strange thing was that, as the law stands, both Brugger and Brown were right.

Judges have the right to tell jurors that jury nullification is prohibited—courts had ruled on this explicitly. And yet the same courts had also ruled that Brugger was correct—that jury nullification was a right, foundational to the system. One key ruling had gone so far as to state that not telling jurors about the right to nullification was necessary for the preservation of the important power of jury nullification. You're forgiven if you're feeling bewildered. It's confusing.

The Nullifiers

One person who didn't feel confused about the matter was sitting at the back of the courtroom pit that day: defendant Ken Medenbach. While the judge explained to the jury that, as far as they were concerned, jury nullification was not an option, Medenbach was sitting in her courtroom wearing a homemade public service announcement contradicting everything she was saying. On his shirt were two of the most famous passages on the subject, one quote displayed on his chest, the other across his back.

Medenbach lives on the dry eastern slope of the Cascades; one of the most dedicated of the occupiers, he was also one of the few from Oregon. He's a chainsaw sculptor and woodworker by trade; he makes bear sculptures, eagle sculptures, furniture, and cabins, as well as signage for people's camps, stores, and RV parks. With the DIY flair you'd expect from the sole proprietor of Chainsaw Creations, Ken in years past had also made himself into a one-man movement for Oregon's sovereignty over its wild lands. Most recently, in 2015, he'd built a cabin, festooned it with signage, dragged it out to some BLM land positioned strategically along a rural highway, plopped it down, and waited for his permitted camping time to expire. At Malheur he'd taken charge of signage as well, which had led to him being the first occupier to be arrested. Eleven days before the takedown in Devine Canyon, he insisted on driving one of the refuge's trucks on a shopping trip to the Safeway in Burns. He'd outfitted it with a new HARNEY COUNTY RESOURCE CENTER sign and wanted the People to see it. The cops had grabbed him while he was sitting in the parking lot waiting for his friends, who were shopping in the store.

The front of Medenbach's shirt bore the words of John Jay, first chief justice of the Supreme Court and one of the authors of the Federalist Papers. Despite his party's eagerness to expand federal power, John Jay was also a man of that revolutionary era—and the sovereign power of the jury to judge both law and fact was an untouchable piece of dogma for him. The quote on Medenbach's chest—THE JURY HAS THE RIGHT TO JUDGE BOTH THE LAW AS WELL AS THE FACT IN CONTROVERSY—was a paraphrase of a longer statement from Jay in the 1789 case of *Chisolm v. Georgia*, a trial concerning the right of an individual to sue a state government.

"It may not be amiss, here, gentlemen," Jay had said to the jury, "to remind you of the good old rule that on questions of fact it is the province of the jury, on questions of law it is the province of the court, to decide. But it must be observed that, by the same law which recognizes this reasonable distribution of jurisdiction, you have, nevertheless, a right to take upon yourselves to judge of both, and to determine the law as well as the fact in controversy." The jury had the power to judge matters of the law, but generally, Jay suggested, it would be best if they refrained from using it. In the years to come, courts would gradually push away from frank acknowledgments like Jay's of the full powers of the jury. By the twentieth century, jury instructions that explicitly forbade jurors from judging matters of law, or basing their decisions on conscience instead of fact, were the norm—affirmed in appeals and Supreme Court decisions. Yet none of these decisions determined that jury nullification was in itself unconstitutional. Some explicitly said the opposite: nullification was constitutional, a necessary feature of the system. Without the possibility of jury nullification, there would soon be no such thing as a meaningful right to trial by jury.

This is the crux of the matter: to close down that possibility of nullification would be to allow the court to second-guess a jury's not-guilty verdict—giving it the power to pick which not-guilty verdicts it felt were based on illegitimate factors and to throw them out. At the same time, what was the point of having laws at all if all jurors in all cases were told beforehand that they could decide cases based on how they felt about the laws in question? Over the years it had all shaken down to a weird stalemate, a gap, a silence—an aporia, as they say in philosophy. It's confusing, for sure, but there's also something marvelous about it. Here lies a method for the silent rebuke of prosecutorial and legislative overreach; this remedy persists in the decisions of court after court. Jury nullification legitimately exists, in other words—but only insofar as it remains, in today's courts, *unsayable*. It lives in the Law as a kind of open secret.

It was this contemporary, more concealed life to which Medenbach's second quotation, stitched over his shoulder blades, under the heading JURY RIGHTS, referred. Ken's back said, THE PAGES OF HISTORY SHINE ON INSTANCES OF THE JURY'S EXERCISE OF ITS PREROGATIVE TO DISREGARD INSTRUCTIONS OF THE JUDGE. This is how it was put by Judge Harold Leventhal, of the U.S. Court of Appeals for the District of Columbia Circuit, in his famous majority opinion on the topic in a 1972 case, *United States v. Dougherty.*

The strange thing is that in affirming the jury's rights, Leventhal and the court had actually not decided in favor of notifying jurors of their glorious prerogative. In fact, they'd decided, 2–1, on the opposite. Like Ken Medenbach's, the case had also been one of protest. In 1969, a group of nine anti–Vietnam War protesters (seven of whom were nuns and priests) had burst into the D.C. headquarters of napalm manufacturer Dow Chemical during working hours. They'd broken windows, tossed out documents, poured fake blood everywhere, and waited for the cops to come and arrest them. In 1972, they were appealing their convictions and asking for a new trial on two grounds: that the judge in the case had refused to notify the jury of its right to refuse to apply the law and that he'd also refused to allow defendants to represent themselves, alleging their disruptive intent. The appeals court would rule in the defendants' favor on their latter contention, tossing their convictions, but it is mostly for its ruling against them on the issue of jury nullification that the case is recalled.

Leventhal, a deeply experienced jurist—he'd worked on the Nuremberg trials—dismissed arguments against jury nullification *as well as* arguments for the need to inform jurors of their right to judge more than the simple facts of a case. The right of jury nullification was crucial, Leventhal said. Jury power was an original part of the ornate system of checks and balances that early theorists, both elite and popular, of republican government had seen as necessary for the restraint of power. If enough juries refused to convict under a statute the legislature had insisted on, or failed to modify or strike, the statute would eventually die, or be altered, by repeal or disuse. Over time something like this had happened with libel. Leventhal reminded his readers that jury nullification had also been central in the popular revolt in the Northern states against the despised Fugitive Slave Act of 1850. In non-slave states, juries had refused to convict persons accused under the hated statute of sheltering escaped slaves or of rescuing them from slave catchers and jails. Eventually many northern states passed additional "personal liberty laws" weakening the power of the federal legislation. In Wisconsin, the state supreme court went so far as to declare the Fugitive Slave Act of 1850 unconstitutional. (While Leventhal didn't touch on the issue, over the years jury nullification opponents have pointed to another piece of America's ugly racist history: the refusal of all-white juries to convict whites for crimes against blacks, especially in the Jim Crow South. Jury nullification advocates counter that these all-white juries, in areas with high African American populations, are examples of institutional jury rigging, not nullification.)

The legality of the power of nullification established, the court's decision took its curious turn. Now Leventhal explained that, while a fundamental right, jury nullification needed to remain in the dark to function properly, a secret remedy hidden in the silent recesses of the law. If it were brought into the light, it would only be abused; abused, its crucial power would be lost. He used the curious example of speed limits. "We know that a posted limit of 60 m.p.h. produces factual speeds 10 or even 15 miles greater, with an understanding all around that some 'tolerance' is acceptable to the authorities, assuming conditions warrant," he wrote. But what would happen if there were no limit at all? Would speeds stay the same? The judge thought not. The jury system worked because, as with speeding, people knew, regardless of what was publicly stated, that they had some flexibility—but the law kept them reasonable in their use of that flexibility. "The jury system has worked out reasonably well overall, providing 'play in the joints' that imparts flexibility and avoids undue rigidity. An equilibrium has evolved—an often marvelous balance—with the jury acting as a 'safety valve' for exceptional cases, without being a wildcat or runaway institution." Informing the jury of its right to interpret the law would undermine the whole system when what was needed was for the jury to act as a crucial check and balance *within* that system. "The way the jury operates may be radically altered if there is alteration in the way it is told to operate. The jury knows well enough that its prerogative is not limited to the choices articulated in the formal instructions of the court . . . Law is a system, and it is also a language, with secondary meanings that may be unrecorded yet are part of its life."

Nullification is one of those issues that pushes juridical writing into the realm of philosophy. Whatever I or anyone thought of their politics, Ken Medenbach, Ammon Bundy, and their friends had a special talent for delivering us to moments like these, the impasses and sticking points of American history, law, and politics. It's true that much of the time—when it came to the law—Ken seemed to be off his chainsaw-carved rocker, an impression he did little to assuage with the motions he'd filed that summer, claiming that Judge Brown was not legally a judge because of an irregularity with her oath of office. Yet, when it came to legal complexities pertaining to the foundation of the republic, Ken Medenbach was not ignorant, and he was often not wrong. Jury nullification was real—a living legal fact—as long as we all agreed not to talk about it. But Ken Medenbach wasn't about to do that—not without a little bit of theater, anyway.

*   *   *

The judge never saw his shirt. Her position, raised at the bench at the front of the room, put Medenbach much too far away for her to make out any of that lettering. But she caught wind of it—it was inevitable. Ken proudly posed for photos and soon those were circulating. The shirt had cost him only six bucks, he said, and he'd paid only twelve dollars more to have all the words stitched into it. Soon enough, he got an email from Judge Anna Brown. If the photos and reports she was getting about this shirt he was said to have worn were true, it was a problem. Jury nullification was not an argument to be presented to jurors, as had been exhaustively established. He wasn't to wear the shirt again, or display any other slogans about jury nullification, or anything else, for that matter. "Very truly yours," she'd signed off—an informal, seemingly ironic touch, perhaps betraying both fatigue with Ken's sovereign shenanigans and maybe a little amusement of her own. Medenbach proudly forwarded the email to reporters.

Ken wouldn't wear the shirt again, but he wasn't done with jury nullification—despite the exhortations of his lawyer, Matthew Schindler, with whom he'd entered into a hybrid counsel agreement. "First day, jury selection, my client comes in, takes off his coat, he has got a jury nullification shirt on," Schindler recalled. "My first comment to him was, 'Ken, you are going to fucking jail,' and my second comment was, 'You realize you don't need jury nullification—you are not guilty.' But those guys, they looked at the realities of the federal system and they thought what we need to do is find a hedge and maybe find these magical unicorn jurors. I worked very hard to disabuse them of the notion that that was even necessary."

Ken Medenbach is not one easily disabused of notions, even by an authoritative and experienced attorney almost twice his size. No matter how needless or harmful his lawyer thought it was, this space—the zone that Judge Leventhal had mapped out in the Dougherty decision, this place of secret flexibility and silence in the joints of the law—was exactly where Ken Medenbach wanted and had fought so hard *to be*. For someone like him, the point wasn't just to find the magical unicorn, *but to be it*. It was the same with many of his friends. Besides, they were right about this one. The jury can judge the law and its rightful application; it's one of the last resorts left to the citizenry—at this point, barely—when it comes to reproving their legislators and executives. When it happens, it happens. In those moments a shadow figure of the constitutive sovereignty of the people takes place, briefly, in secret, outside law and government, and deep in its interior, all at once. It takes its place, for a sequestered moment, as it nullifies, before returning into the courtroom, and pouring its decision back into the Law, which registers and absorbs its act.

Regardless of what any of us thought about it, nullification—as more than mere strategy, almost as a way of life—was at the core of the whole Bundy Project. *We the People, Ammonites, Necessary Bodies*—whatever I called them and whatever they called themselves—the Bundyites were really a confederation of nullifiers, self-nominated "regulators" of government, to borrow the idiom of rural insurrectionists of the colonial and revolutionary era. They sought out gaps in the law, those zones of flexibility Leventhal had written of, and they camped out there, asserting momentary sovereignty. Nullification, it seemed, is what they really meant by *freedom*.

Which explains partly why once we got to court, and there were no more guns, except government guns, and no one was directly taking land away from wildlife, or restaging, yet again, the theft of Native land, it felt strangely thrilling to be around them. Even for someone like myself, who disagreed strongly with most of the ideology they pumped out. Now what they were contesting—the conviction machine of our increasingly juryless federal court system—clearly needed to be contested. It made me uncomfortable, but these people were beginning to make a little sense to me. Out there in the basin, all the stubborn particularities of that land and its communities, its cultural history and ecological dynamism, had combined to make the holy legal abstractions of Ammon and his friends seem violently absurd— because they were. Ammon and friends had known nothing about the place; all they'd had were their feelings and their articles of faith about the biggest of the Big American Words. It had just made the whole thing look like what it, at least partly, was: yet another episode in the generalized madness for God, Property, and Liberty (for some) that had characterized so much human behavior on the continent since the coming of Europeans. But here in court things were different. This was a physical space that, far from resisting grand abstractions, was actually made of them; it was nothing but the institutional materialization of Big Words, the magic and fiction of government and law reified, made *thing*. That imaginary thing was the United States of America; now they were really inside it. The Bundy Revolution had found its way home.

CHAPTER EIGHTEEN

Citizens of Heaven

"i am what i say i am"

THEY SURE WERE EXCITED TO BE HERE, the occupiers and all their jazzed-up friends. It must have piqued the jury's interest. Who really wants to be in federal court? *They* sure did. Here they were in the real homeland of the biggest of Big Ideas: federal court was the place the nation most properly deployed its legitimated sovereignty onto its own people, making use of its power to dispense or deny Freedom. Freedom and Sovereignty. They *aren't* synonyms—but in the world of the Bundy Rebels, the two concepts tended to cross into each other and blur. Bundy Ranch was their "freest place on earth" not because anyone could do whatever they wanted there, but because the Patriot version of We the People—and their cowboy avatars, the Bundy family itself—were sovereign there, or at least seemed to be from 2014 to 2016. There, in the rocky, wide-open desert acres of Gold Butte and the Virgin Valley, government had been *dissolved* and the People had taken its place.

Ammon Bundy's political strategy had been all about finding vulnerable spaces in the legally administered American landscape and standing on them, and by doing so, creating what he thought of as freedom. But it was people like Ammon's brother Ryan, Ken Medenbach, Shawna Cox, and David Zion Brugger who took the Bundy family faith in the people's sovereignty into the mystic realms of what is known by some as the Sovereign Citizen movement.

In the first Malheur trial, no one deployed more sovereign magic than Ryan Bundy. When he had declared himself, in court documents, a "citizen of heaven," when he'd offered to "play the role" of defendant, judge, or bailiff in the theatrical production of the trial for a steep fee, when he'd insisted he was not the legal "person" Ryan Bundy but rather another kind of being—"ryan c., man of the bundy family" (deliberately spelled with all lowercase letters)—he had been employing the open-source idiom of the shadow-world of the Sovereign Citizens.

Journalists and antiterrorism experts alike call that world—it has earned the attention of both—a "movement," but it's more like a tendency, an ever-morphing set of practices in which the strong American urge for militantly absolute individualism meets the equally strong American drive toward paranoid, obsessive litigiousness. The SovCit underground is rich with veins of such convergence. There, constitutionalism and the old common law rediscover their origins in theological magic, while the millenarian Christian antinomianism of centuries past meets the enduring American faith in get-rich-quick tricks and the more mundane wizardry of the legal loophole. What Sovereign Citizens do with all this, more than anything else, is write and file documents—motion after motion after motion—just as Ryan Bundy was doing, to the considerable fatigue of the court. Indeed, the fatigue and dismay of the court seems to be one of the main goals of Sovereign practice.

These filings are often composed in improvised and theologically inflected legalese, deployed in a kind of counter-magic against the official jargon of law and governance. Both magic and the law are spaces where one can be "hanged on a comma," and the SovCit thing always comes down to words, to using the right words, the right sequence of phrases, in the practitioner's quest to separate the living flesh-and-blood body from its subjection to the power of the State. Ryan Bundy's longest motion with the court—his declaration of his Sovereign Citizenship—begins doing exactly this.

> 1. i am what i say i am; i am without evidence to the contrary, therefore it is so; and
>
> 2. i am "man" (the meaning of which word in this case is decreed as follows: "a sacred union between consciousness/spirit, flesh-blood-bone and bio-electricity/energy created by that sound of which in the standard English language is commonly translated as "God" hereinafter-and-before expressed as "God") i am without evidence to the contrary, therefore it is so; and

3. i am the seed of Abram, to whom God said, unto thy seed I have given this land; i am without evidence to the contrary, therefore it is so; and

4. i am ryan c, the man jure divino, created in God's own image, in the image of God he created i (Genesis 1:30 & Moses 2:26–30); i am without evidence to the contrary, therefore it is so; and . . .

On he—or "i"—goes in this manner through ninety-five such propositions of "fact." Among the other "facts" asserted are many supporting the central contention that this speaking and writing entity, "i" (also made known to us in these pages as "ryan c., man of the bundy family," not to be confused with *any other* third-person designation), is independent of legal jurisdiction and even of the name Ryan Bundy: "DEFENDANT RYAN BUNDY is not the property of i," "i" writes. "i am neither 'person,' nor 'child,' nor 'human being' as defined by Black's Law Dictionary, the unholy bible of the Legal Society; i am without evidence to the contrary, therefore it is so."

"i" further declares independence of all institutions and authorities that might impose the status of person upon ryan c., man of the bundy family (except, maybe, an entity called "the republic of nevada"). "i am not a creation of 'Congress,'" the list begins, before getting to the courts, the judges, and the U.S. attorney. The document closes with the assertion that these "facts" will stand proven and confirmed if the court fails to respond (with satisfactory evidence to the contrary, whatever that might be) within ten days.

Redemption

What "ryan c." is doing here is establishing what some Sovereigns have called "redemption," the legal separation of the flesh-blood-and-spirit individual from their government-given identity—namely their name as it appears (printed in all caps) on birth certificates and so many of the other documents, licenses, and contracts that follow a legal person from birth to the grave. "Redemption" is necessary because the Sovereign needs to free him-, her- or "i"-self from the illegitimate legal regime that reigns over the United States and its sheeplike "voluntary citizens." Depending on whom you ask, the United States has been under unconstitutional "admiralty law,"

ruled by a foreign corporation called the federal government, since either
the 1868 enactment of the Fourteenth Amendment or since the United
States went off the gold standard in 1933.

In explicitly white-supremacist versions of Sovereign practice, only those
guaranteed citizenship prior to the passage of the Fourteenth Amendment
are true American citizens. The whole thing seems to have started with Bill
Gale and the rabidly racist Posse Comitatus; but, as with the theory of the
constitutional sheriff, these white-supremacist origins have been occluded
over the years. Contemporary Sovereigns seem more likely to place the
triumph of admiralty law much later, in the midst of the Great Depression.
Here it gets differently nutty, even more theological and litigious. When the
United States went off the gold standard, the theory goes, the government
began setting up secret accounts in the name of every child born in America,
every *citizen* that is, in order to guarantee the new fiat currency of the dollar.
These accounts are opened in the false names printed (in those alarming
capital letters) on our birth certificates, names that each designate the corporate shell identity of a "straw man"—a fake and lucrative legal "person"
created by the State. Conveniently, "redeeming" oneself from the fraudulent
name also, in some schemes, promises the newly freed Sovereign the opportunity to also liberate the money stored in that secret government account.
Get-rich-quick schemes follow. Many in the SovCit world have gone to
prison for attempting to capitalize on redemption in various ways: by printing
and passing notes based on those fantasy reserves in the nonexistent "straw
man accounts"; or for swindling other Sovereigns by selling them (for real
U.S. dollars) the plans and procedures by which their redemptions might be
accomplished. The Sovereign shadow world even comes complete with its
own roving judges, ever ready to hold forth on Divine Law, the Constitution,
the Magna Carta, and the foreign corporate status of the federal government. One of these, Joaquim Mariano DeMoreta-Foloch, had appeared at
the grazing-contract renunciation ceremony at the refuge in the days before
the Devine Canyon takedown.

Really, what can you say but "only in America"? Out of racist repudiation
and economic anxiety, out of conspiracy theories and a zeal for legal scheming,
those who called themselves Sovereign Citizens had woven an imaginary
territory that now hosts groups as divergent as militant white supremacists
and far-out black nationalists. It had even given birth to an African American
empress, Empress Verdiacee "Tiari" Washitaw Turner Goston El-Bey and
her indigenous American black nationalist tribe, the Washitaw Nation. The

Washitaw claim to have arrived in America not with slavery, but to have floated over—much, much, much earlier—with the land that became America when the prehistoric continent of Pangaea split up. In an echo of Joseph Smith, they also see themselves as the builders of all the burial mounds along the river lands of the Mississippi, and as the original rightful owners of all the lands of the Louisiana Purchase. As this purchase had not been properly conducted with them, as far as they were concerned, a huge portion of America was still under their Sovereign rule—or under the rule of the empress, whose status derived from her having been born with her placenta arranged on her head like a crown. After actually convincing a United Nations body to investigate their claim to be a Native American tribe, a claim that was rejected, the Washitaw, in true SovCit style, had simply displayed the number the investigation had been assigned as sufficient proof of their legal existence. Unlikely as it may seem, this had, in turn, impressed groups of white-supremacist Sovereign Citizens. Eager to establish their own sovereignty outside the governance of the United States, they had come to the self-declared empress to pay tribute, join the tribe, and, once under the empress's authority, charge hefty fees to members of their own groups for Washitaw license plates, passports, vehicle registrations, birth certificates, and sundry other documents. The empress—a former mayor of Richwood, Louisiana, who, in that past life, had worn a hard hat in office to protect herself from Klan assaults—had become a wealthy woman on the strength of all the tribute.

All this American weirdness was on my mind when I first read Ryan Bundy's legal declarations during the long, mad meltdown that was the summer of 2016. The Sovereign Washitaw had just been in the national news. During the weeks of unrest in Baton Rouge, Louisiana, following the circulation of disturbing video of the police shooting death of a local African American man named Alton Sterling, a member of the tribe, Gavin Long, had ambushed and killed three Baton Rouge officers before being shot and killed himself.

Other Sovereign Citizens had gotten in shootouts with police in recent years, sometimes in situations escalating from roadside stops (Sovereigns often don't have driver's licenses, or register their vehicles). But usually it didn't come to that. Mostly, in their wide and ever-morphing range of practices, the main goal of SovCits seemed to be the production of ungodly amounts of documents and bizarre or just plain silly legal arguments. The result is that very often Sovereign Citizens or those who dabble in their legal techniques sometimes win their lesser cases on sheer persistence and judicial fatigue. One Bundyite, new to Sovereign methods, told me, jubilantly, of his recent success in getting out of a Portland parking ticket; he'd argued that his car, not he, had incurred the violation The exasperated judge had apparently dismissed the case.

To Break a Bundy

Now Ryan Bundy had come with his own reams of paper, prepared to win his own Sovereign victory. However ludicrous and futile it might all look to the uninitiated, those closer to the Malheur crew remained buoyantly confident that their curious brew of stubborn naivety and ebullient nullification would triumph in the end. Ryan's wife, Angie, for one, stood firmly by her husband. Angie—who looks like she was born in denim and cowboy boots, destined to chew gum all her life and say interesting things out the side of her mouth—told an interviewer for the *Guardian* that she thought it was the government that was engaged in a foolish exercise. "I'm not so sure you can break a Bundy," she mused.

When it came to her husband, Angie Bundy might have been speaking literally. The world had tried to break Ryan early on. It's his face that I'm talking about. Most of half of it is paralyzed. It makes all his expressions half expressions, turning his visage at times into a flesh mask. This, I guess, is what a face is, but when you are talking to Ryan, you have the opportunity to learn it all over again. That his bloodhound voice emerges out of that half-frozen face only adds to the uncanniness of his presence.

The story of how he got that face goes a long way to explain Ryan's seeming unbreakability. It had all been caused by a bone chip, a piece of his skull wandering in the meat of his brain when, at age seven, he'd been run over by the family car while harvesting melons on the ranch. The car hadn't just run over him; it had stopped there a while, the tire spinning on his little head. After everyone realized what had happened and his father had pulled the LTD towncar down off his skull, little Ryan was still conscious. He remembers the whole thing, he says, the tire churning on his head, crushing his skull into the dirt. And then when it was over, he remembers, still conscious somehow, that he tried to get up. And he did. He got up. He stood all the way up before falling back—on his knees—to the ground, bleeding from every orifice in his face.

CHAPTER NINETEEN

The Wrong-Turn Clan

RYAN'S SOVEREIGN MOTIONS SEEMED totally whacked-out to me, but as a writer I also found them a blast, with their militant cadences, their total refusal of any earthly dominion; read aloud, they became a sort of paranoid conceptual poetry. Being a writer in court was a pleasure as well. My experience of the Boisterous Sea that fall was the most literal experience of being a public writer I'd ever had: I mean, all day I was writing—in public and by hand. I was grateful to the federal prohibition on devices in court that made recording impossible—the kind of hyper-attention I was paying to words and to my surrounds would have been lost if I'd simply been able to record everything and listen later.

The Ammonites did not feel the same way. This was yet more proof of the tyranny of the federal courts. Occupier Jason Patrick made the most forceful arguments when it came to the exclusion of all our devices. To his mind, our phones and cameras were the dominant media of our day, just as pen and paper were the media of days past. Excluding them—with the excuse that writing was allowed and that court transcripts were a public record—was an anachronism and a violation. He's probably right. If we were to follow our more democratic angels, we would not tolerate this priestly preciousness. The prohibition on filming and photography is, in the end, mostly about the creation of an aura of intimidating mystery—there's no way around it. There's also no way around the fact that it works. And I loved it.

I think I may have been the only one who did. At every break I watched the rush of people jockeying to be first in line to hand over their tags and get back their devices, to start tweeting and texting or typing up notes. The reporters were sending in copy. The Bundyites, so many citizen-journalist types among them, were often livestreaming to their world as they flocked to one another in the lobby, bantering, hugging, and touching; this was a very huggy bunch. But I was on my own, nobody to inform, no deadline looming, nobody to "scoop." My bemusement felt like the luxury that I suppose it was. Every day I could just wander over to the windows and look out, nine floors over the city below, at the lines of the hills, the mist straining through the dark fingers of the pines. And then I could mingle, differently awake, in the odd social life of court that bloomed there in that foyer of glass, wood, and stone.

*   *   *

One of those first days of jury selection, as I waited during a break in that ninth-floor lobby to be let back into the courtroom, Duane Ehmer came toward me grinning from ear to ear. We'd met that summer outside a preliminary hearing and had a long, animated talk. He wanted to know what I was doing here; it was good to see me, he said, but he had been sure I'd be at Standing Rock instead. The Sioux-led North Dakota protests against the Dakota Access Pipeline had galvanized the attention of a range of online and offline political communities, including that of the Patriots. Duane wished he could be there. He was thinking of asking the judge if he could be allowed to go join the protest camps, since his trial wasn't coming until well after this one. It seemed unlikely, to say the least, that a federal judge would let a defendant, charged with crimes related to a protest, leave the state to join another one, but Duane was somehow excitedly optimistic about his prospects. It was all about standing up for our water, he said, parroting some of the phrases coming out of North Dakota. It was also about standing up against the bulldozing of sacred sites, he added. I asked Duane if some of that hadn't happened at Malheur when he was there—but no, no, no, he assured me, nothing like that had gone down. It had all been very respectful.

Back in Burns that summer, Standing Rock had been the main topic of conversation among folks in the Burns-Paiute tribe. It was the first I'd learned of the protests. By September it was big news outside the social media channels of Indian Country and environmental activism—now, via the FaceWorld, it had become the big news in the ether of the Bundy Revolution as well. This was to add some more confusion and awkwardness the next day when Jarvis Kennedy showed up, along with Joe Delarosa, the newly elected tribal chairman of the Wadatika. Jeff Banta, Neil Wampler, and others approached the two, who, on leaving the courtroom at a break, had retreated, faces buried in their phones, to the far end of the foyer. The room still gleamed then with the sun of early September, and the Bundyites seemed as brightly agitated as photons, bouncing about in the glare. Having seen me sitting and talking with Joe and Jarvis, some came now to ask me about them—which is when their nervous lawyers appeared and dragged them away. In those early days, their attorneys were anxious about their clients talking to the press; soon they'd give up—nothing could restrain these people from telling their story.

"They don't know I came to see 'em hang," Jarvis said later that afternoon, when I caught up with him and Joe in a basement gastropub where they had split to eat a late lunch. The two of them were baffled that the Bundy folks didn't seem to understand why they'd come. Some thought that Joe and Jarvis were involved in Standing Rock and had come *to support* the Bundys. They shook their heads together, chuckling at a joke they'd made. It was a new name for the Bundy Rebels: the Wrong-Turn Clan, the two had decided to call them. They figured that the occupiers must have gotten lost in the fog and made a wrong turn looking for Idaho. "Why did they go to Burns? Do you know?" Joe asked me.

He also wanted to know more about who I was. We'd talked a little the night before at a rally and raffle for Standing Rock in a park in Northwest Portland, but we hadn't gotten into any depth about anything. Now, sitting across from me in the dark afternoon quiet of the restaurant, Joe interrogated me. He wanted to know what I did, what I had done, what I wrote, what I taught, where I had traveled in the past. I ended up talking about time I'd spent in Nicaragua, Guatemala, Korea, Vietnam, Bolivia. Joe nodded, as if he'd figured something out. "So you're an adventurer," he said finally, chewing the last of his food, smiling, but not too much.

All the while, Jarvis was scrolling through his phone. But now he piped up. Not one to be afraid of confrontation, he had gotten into a strange moment earlier with a band of Patriot supporters outside on the courthouse steps. Following the example of his friend Leland, he'd decided to take some photos of the group. "The Wrong-Turn Clan doesn't like it when you take their pictures," he said, grinning, as we walked out of the dim cave of the restaurant, blinking into the late-afternoon light and traffic.

* * *

It would be days before I got the rest of Jarvis's story. By then we were both back in Burns. I was glad to be back; I'd spent a few more weeks in Harney County that summer and was growing attached to the place—to the land, how it felt to move in it, through it, the distances, the wind and silence, the smells of the high desert and the forest. I'd been away only a couple of weeks, but already the season had changed; the temperatures were dropping into the thirties at night. The town was bustling—as much as Burns can bustle. It was deer-hunting season, and also the county fair was on.

On the way over, crossing the Cascades, I'd been trying to get what radio coverage I could. The news had been crazy all summer, and by September I was acting like an addict. I needed to know everything right away, every day. There was word of some big announcement out of Washington about Standing Rock. A federal appeals court judge had denied the Standing Rock tribe's request for an injunction halting the construction of the pipeline. Protesters, now numbering in the thousands, had wanted to stop the construction before it reached land held sacred by the tribe and went under Lake Oahe, a dam-created reservoir in the Missouri River—the main source of drinking water for the community. Still, the judge had appeared sympathetic to the tribe's cause, some thought. Soon, bigger news came in: the Departments of Justice, Interior, and the Army had announced that the Army Corps of Engineers would, for the moment, no longer authorize construction of the pipeline near Oahe until it could reconsider its own previous determinations. The pipeline company was formally requested to stop all construction within twenty miles of the lake.

While I was eating lunch in the cowboy town of Madras, Jarvis called me on his cell. He was pumped up—he'd heard the news about the administration, and he'd also just left a Standing Rock rally in downtown Portland, not far from the courthouse. Someone had recognized him in the crowd and badgered him to come up and say a few words, until he'd relented and agreed. Whatever his ambivalences about it (and he seemed to have many), the thrill of his new internet fame and public role was strong in his voice in that moment. It did really feel like something was happening, in his life and also out there in the encampments in North Dakota and in the momentum of the wider movement coalescing around the Standing Rock Sioux. I like lingering now in this memory—my sandwich in my fist, Jarvis's quickened voice in my ear, there in that awkward café with its baffling pastiche of styles, half hippie, half Cracker Barrel. All was glazed with a golden, late-afternoon desert sun. Jarvis's voice, too, was bright, with discovery, possibility, fresh from his own moment with the People. I had yet to hear him talk that fast, and never have since. Something was turning, yes it was. But it wasn't to turn out as we'd thought.

* * *

I met up with Jarvis the next day at the fairgrounds. The place was packed. I parked in the far end of the parking lot, where Brand and LaVoy and the rest of the "tip of the spear" had assembled to pray before heading out to take over the refuge on January 2. I wondered what direction LaVoy had pointed and proclaimed "the Rubicon." Now the building was filled with the quiet, cluttered tables and display booths of the art portion of the fair, but the main attention of the people was elsewhere, in the big grandstand where the rodeo and the horse races were under way.

I found Jarvis at one of the side stages, and we picked up his story about photographing the Wrong-Turn Clan. After he'd taken that picture, an older woman had confronted him, demanding to know who he was and why he was photographing them. And so he'd politely given his card. Since then he had been getting some curious texts, thanking him for his interest. Him taking that picture, one texter wrote, "had meant a lot." Now the voice was offering the support of a network to get him and his people out to Standing Rock. The possibility of extra technical help in the struggle, should he be interested, was also hinted at. Whoever was writing to Jarvis assured him that they had the capacity—they were from Anonymous, they'd claim in a later text—and that they were poised, ready to help, at his command. "We're your tech support," the later message proudly declared. While Jarvis dug messages out of the hundreds on his phone, we sat down under the tent of one of the fair's little side stages. Here we joined a small audience of weary fairgoers being serenaded by a cowboy, or a man dressed as one, or as old Hollywood's idea of one. He was singing standards, and also songs of his own composition, including the song he was singing now, a tune of nostalgia for the era of movie cowboys. It was about Randolph Scott, it was about his white horse, it was about asking where Scott had gone and what had happened to that world. That world, one might add, had never existed, but whatever had happened to it, the song insisted, in its melancholy, was also what had happened to the singer.

Jarvis handed me his phone. He'd finally found some of the texts.

"How'd you feel about the Bundy Trial? Hope everything's going well."

"Saw you at the courthouse. Why did you take our picture. We want to help with Standing Rock. We have a train going there and back . . . food, places to shower, places to stay."

"If things go wrong in NDakota we've got backup. We only answer to tribal council."

I handed Jarvis back his phone; it was all very confusing. "We only answer to tribal council"—what kind of fantasy was this? We looked at each other, we looked at the singer, we looked back at each other. Jarvis shrugged. I tried to analyze what the texts might all be about, but I really didn't know what to say. I sputtered, gave up, shrugged back.

* * *

There is a long-standing joke in Indian Country: What's the fastest-growing tribe in America? it went. The Wannabes, the punchline answered. For all of us non–Native Americans dreaming up a way to be at home in this land, the dreams often took a detour through fantasies of being Native, in one's secret blood or some other imagined honorary status. It seemed like most white folks (and many nonwhite folks as well) had some sort of Indian dream packed away somewhere: some dream of getting truly with the American land and going finally, wholly indigenous. There was a little Joseph Smith out there in many American hearts.

I remembered the end of an article I'd read that summer about the SovCit Washitaw. One of the group's leaders, Umar Shabazz Bey, had taken the reporter to the campus of Louisiana State—evidently built among a group of those mysterious pre-Columbian mounds. Bey had sprung up to the top of one of them and stood there, thrilled. "Do you feel it? Do you feel the energy?" he'd asked. "Look at my arms." They were covered in goose bumps, the reporter wrote. "Do you feel it?" Bey had asked again. "This is where I belong."

In the midst of all this fantasy life, folks like Jarvis were trying their best to negotiate what it means to actually be Native these days—after all the years of open violence and paper violence aimed at the permanent erasure of their very possibility. No wonder that by the end of the trial Jarvis would be ready for a break from me and my ilk—tired of reporters and Bundyites alike.

For now, though, our spirits were still high. As we talked, and the rhinestone cowboy sang, Jarvis also chatted and horsed around a bit with his nephews and the children of his girlfriend. One of these kids was amped to busting today: a county fair is a sugar bomb. He was also dressed up as a country sheriff—with a little badge, and a hat, and a toy pistol. His eyes were huge and wild behind his Coke-bottle glasses. "You're going to *jail*," he was saying, giggling, shouting, grabbing at Jarvis, whanging at him with his little hands, while Jarvis grinned down at him patiently, chortling, holding the flailing boy at an easy distance with his massive arm. Soon our conversation also turned to jail, and to justice and the court. "Pretty interesting to sit there in court and watch the proceedings," Jarvis said, his eyes on the stage, "especially when I'm not the defendant!"

We'd spent a lot of time together that summer, and I had gotten to know him a little bit on our long drives through the brittle, sun-roasted countryside. One morning, as we'd sat in his living room, facing the muted big-screen TV—a rerun of *The Fresh Prince of Bel-Air* was playing—our talk about mandatory sentencing had led us to his own experience of the criminal justice system. Back in February, when we first met, he'd told me he didn't have much sympathy for the Hammonds; they hadn't been there for him, so why should he be there for them? As a young man he'd been mandatory-sentenced himself—for seven and a half years, he said. Now, as I sat on his big, comfy couch, he told me what had happened. It had been years ago. At a party a guy had jumped him in the bathroom, "stabbed me in the head," he said. He hadn't known the girl he'd been seeing was this guy's girlfriend, or this guy thought she was, or something. Jarvis had survived this murder attempt and taken away the guy's knife. We sat in silence a while, in that living room full of feathers and power totems: poles and drums dripping with feathers. Jarvis was an artist, and one of his mediums was feathers. The silence went on. On the TV, the Fresh Prince and his family were all on some kind of game show. Will Smith was entering the stage set, looking warily at the other gleeful contestants. Finally, I got up the nerve to ask the question. "Is he still alive?" Jarvis let more silence leak in. I wasn't sure if he remembered what we were talking about, or if he was going to answer. Then he smiled a little. "Yeah, they put him back together—or else I wouldn't be here now," he drawled, and then we laughed together, still staring at the muted screen. The Fresh Prince had won something; everyone was jumping up and down.

We'd moved on quickly to other topics that August morning—like the encampments at Standing Rock. Jarvis had actually been hoping to get out there that summer, but it had proved hard to wrangle. He'd been struck by the importance the movement in North Dakota was putting on the difference between "protester" and "protector." It was a distinction he liked to make: "We're not protesters, we're protectors." This had taken us back around to the Bundyites. "How can they say they were for the land and talk about mining?" he'd asked me, bewildered. ("Get the miner back to mining" had been part of the Ammonite liturgy.) "They picked a spot they hadn't done their research on. We didn't give up nothing," he'd added. "It's always going to be ours."

* * *

At the fair we sat talking in that tent for a while longer, through a few shows. The sun was strong, and the benches were shaded and cool. Now a rodeo comedian had taken the stage. Her target audience seemed to maybe be kids, which wasn't stopping her from telling risqué double-entendre jokes, and generally exuding irony and weariness with the scene and maybe with the whole human endeavor. It was September now; she'd probably been doing the same thing at different fairs almost every day since late June. "I've learned that to be successful in showbiz, kids, you just have to learn to pretend to enjoy things you don't," she quipped at one point. "Take it from me . . ."

Soon she'd wrangled and roped up a volunteer adult from the audience, yanking him up onto the stage. Then she had him skipping rope, and, now, she said, iron in hand—where did that come from?—she was going to brand him! Ha ha, the crowd laughed, briefly, nervously. The man was hanging his head now; he looked like maybe he regretted his decision to volunteer as much as our impresario seemed to regret her entire life. "This dude needs to say the safety word," Jarvis grumbled to me, out of the side of his mouth. This cowpoke S&M routine and all the semi-dirty jokes were starting to bother him—"there are kids here," he said. But this was the climax of the performance; show done, off she went, on enormous stilts, happy face stapled on, staggering above and through the sea of people gathered at the various food stalls at the grandstand entrance. I watched her disappear, a ghost from another century's entertainments, her circus-barker voice soon swallowed in the generalized rumble and din. It was late, tilting toward evening, and now Jarvis and I parted. I headed out east and south again, around Steens, bound for California. Night slipped down from the top of the sky, darker than dark—and yet so bright, wet with all that light falling from the layers of undead stars.

CHAPTER TWENTY

Adverse Possession

WHEN I FINALLY GOT BACK TO PORTLAND, Ammon Bundy was on the second day of his testimony. But when I entered the courtroom that morning, he wasn't on the witness stand—he was up on-screen. "My dear friends," his enlarged bearded face was saying. It was that same video: there he was in his cowboy hat and flannel, at the desk with the glowing Apple icon on the laptop before him. That same open-faced expression, the brow raised in concern, never falling. The judge and the lawyers were working out just how much the defense would be allowed to show of this video, if any at all. Judge Brown was questioning the need—didn't much of it just repeat the previous day's testimony in which Ammon had described how he'd come to be involved in the Hammond case? Marcus Mumford allowed that some of the content of the video was the same, but it wasn't *really* the same. Having Ammon explain something in the witness box and seeing him explain it in the intimate format of the social media video were qualitatively different experiences. The space of court, because of "modesty," Mumford claimed, was unnatural. It didn't allow one to express things one would express in other circumstances. The video, on the other hand, was "an expression of his *state of mind*," Mumford pressed. He objected to his client "being limited to what he says on the stand."

Given the nature of the conspiracy charge, which was a crime of intention, the judge was allowing the defense much leeway to present what was called "state of mind" evidence—testimony and exhibits that demonstrated what the defendants' actions meant to them. This had brought us to Mumford's fascinating argument: that Ammon could be seen and understood more as he truly was in a video address made for the internet than he could while present in the flesh, a mere dozen feet from the jurors. In the end, the judge compromised and let Mumford show the video's last six minutes. Most of it was redundant, she said—"cumulative" in the language of the court—"with the exception of Mr. Bundy's articulation of divine expression."

*　*　*

As novel as the issues involved in it were, Judge Anna Brown and Marcus Mumford had come fairly quickly to this compromise. There was much haggling like this about evidence and witnesses, and it wasn't always going so smoothly or so fast. The chaos of the defense had been trying the judge's patience; most mornings of the defense's case seemed to be like this. You never really knew who was going to testify the next day, or what evidence they were going to display. An experienced defense attorney like Matthew Schindler was stunned by it—he'd never seen anything like this in twenty years of trying cases in federal court. "I went to our joint exhibition file the night before the trial," he told me. "There was one set of exhibits staged, and they were just mine." As the defense case progressed, Schindler found himself often going to bed at night having no idea what he was going to do in court the next day. He didn't even know who was going to be on the stand. "It was an exercise in group improvisation," he said. After a while it began to seem like that improvisatory defense strategy—or non-strategy—actively mirrored the occupation itself. Who was in charge, what were they doing today, what would they do tomorrow? "Freedom 'n' stuff" is the answer Jason Patrick had offered one night from the refuge, when the livestream had asked for the next day's plan. Some days freedom 'n' stuff seemed to be the defense's plan as well.

On those days, absent longer testimony from one of the defendants, witness after witness paraded through, reiterating the same points: that these guys were likable; that they only wanted to preach Freedom and the Constitution and justice for the Hammonds; that they had believed in their hearts and minds that what they were doing was legal and just; that they weren't threatening anybody; and that whole families—families with kids— were going out there to visit, that's how safe it was. One of the parents, called up to the stand for only a little longer than it took to swear her in, spoke of an article her boy had written about the occupation for the newspaper, the

Desert Rat, of the rural elementary school in Fields (population 6). There was a seeming obsession among the defendants and defense attorneys with presenting testimony and evidence of how much the occupiers had cleaned the place up. They were especially offended by evidence the feds had presented about what a mess the place had been in February when the Final Four had surrendered. But it wasn't just that. Improving the place was a big part of the argument the defense was making about what had really been going on at the refuge. The whole occupation, according to Ammon, had been a kind of legal game, an exercise in what was called, captivatingly, "adverse possession."

*   *   *

Now the jury was coming in, and Ammon was up in the witness box. He had been wearing his prisoner scrubs every day for weeks—a decision born in that argument over his courtroom attire the first day of jury selection. Ammon had refused to speak with the court about his choice. Instead, he'd let Morgan Philpot, his other attorney, read his statement on the matter: "Mr. Bundy desires to appear as he is, a political prisoner not free to dress as if presumed innocent. He would prefer to drop the facade." In the space of the courtroom, I finally understood the full effect Ammon was achieving with his garb. This was a subtle but powerful bit of Bundy Revolution theater. Its main acts were these moments—the arrivals and departures of the jury. When this happened, Ammon, like the rest of us, would stand, but elevated above us all, up in the witness box. Each time he rose, Ammon stood with his arms behind his back, as if shackled. As the jurors entered through that door in the back of the court chamber, or as they climbed down out of the jury box and vanished again into their deliberation room, Ammon would proudly face them, making what eye contact he could. He looked lashed to something up there, like he was already being punished, like he was on the scaffold and we, jury included, were all witnesses to his final ordeal. This, of course, was the point. He'd been in prison since January; he *was* being punished. At the same time, it also made the witness box look like the prow of a ship, with him as its captain—or maybe what it really looked like was a pulpit, with him up there, the prisoner-prophet, with his holy texts, including the Book of Doctrine and Covenants, and that same pocket Constitution. He brought these with him to the stand every day.

Ammon Bundy, newly defiant political prisoner, hadn't known much about the criminal justice system before 2016. He admitted he'd been naive, assumed people were in jail simply because they deserved to be there. Now that he himself was in prison, and talking with fellow prisoners every day, his opinions were changing fast. But when he came to the story of the Hammonds, the naiveté of his outrage still showed. He hadn't been able to believe it, that Dwight and Steven could get *resentenced* and sent away *again*, for a clearly excessive length of time, even though the judge had disapproved of it and sentenced them to less. And then the fact that all his petitions about the Hammonds had just been ignored. *Ignored!* He was getting emotional up there. His drawl, as it did sometimes when he was upset, was rounding the bend into what had to be called a whine. Really, I suppose he hadn't actually known how things worked. After eight and a half months in prison, he told Mumford and the jury, he was beginning to understand. But back then he'd been shocked. Something had needed to be done—God was demanding it, guiding him to demand it. And the plan that began to be revealed to him had taken the form of this little-known legal ploy called adverse possession.

There had been a number of other ideas for direct action about the Hammond case, Ammon told the jurors, making an effort to gaze directly at them as he answered his lawyer's questions. They'd considered doing some unpermitted burns on federal land, as an act of civil disobedience. Or pooling resources and buying cows and running them on the Hammonds' grazing allotments, which the family had been barred from in the wake of all their legal trouble. It seemed to me that both these actions made a lot more organic sense as protests: they targeted the BLM and activated the more mainstream rural western argument that local folks had real knowledge about how to use and take care of their public lands. But in the end, Ammon had settled on the refuge and an occupation, with a goal of staking an adverse-possession claim, he said, so as to get the whole issue of federal land ownership into the courts.

Adverse possession was a legal maneuver straight out of the Sovereign Citizen canon. (If you look it up, you'll come upon many cases, especially in Florida, of SovCits trying to use the tactic to take over unoccupied houses and commercial real estate, particularly in the years after the housing crash of 2008.) What you were doing, in applying the method, was staking a claim on someone's unused land, "quieting title" while you "perfected" the property. When adverse possession worked, it was usually applied on abandoned real estate, where the adverse possessor established residency or use, improved the place, posted notices of what they were up to, and waited—all as part of "quieting" any other claims. If, after a certain number of years, nobody objected and "trespassed" you, then you could actually claim the property as yours. It's all what's known colloquially as "squatter's rights." Everything that Ammon was describing was actually legit—except that he'd been proposing to do it to an operational Federal Wildlife Refuge. Given this, he'd assumed, he told Mumford and the jury, that they'd be trespassed fairly quickly and that then the case would run its course and he'd get a chance to challenge the federal government's title. All the new signs they'd made at the refuge, the renaming of it as the Harney County Resource Center, the highlighting of the improvements they were making to the place, the press conferences—this was all part of this adverse-possession claim, as Ammon now framed it. During the occupation there had been very little public talk about this idea, but now it was all about adverse possession. It just hadn't worked out as he'd intended. The trespass charges he'd anticipated had never come, and now here he was, accused of something far grander: conspiracy to intimidate.

*   *   *

The federal government loves conspiracy charges. The criminalization of collective intent is an invaluable tool for prosecutors when dealing with organized crime. But in this case, the U.S. attorney's office had also settled on the charge of conspiring to impede federal officials because there simply weren't other felony charges available to them. Trespassing was a mere misdemeanor. There had been no one on the refuge when the Bundyites took it over; no one had been kidnapped or assaulted or even threatened on the refuge. It wasn't even really illegal to have firearms; hunting was allowed there, and Oregon is an open-carry state. The conspiracy charge brought advantages and disadvantages to the government. They didn't have to prove that anyone had actually been threatened or intimidated, just that this had been the intention of a group of people, a criminal one. On the other hand, this meant that the crime itself was more vaporous, a crime of collective mind. Because of that, the occupiers' thoughts and feelings—their states of mind—mattered tremendously, while what fear and anger the folks in Harney County may have felt did not. It sounds unfair, but it makes sense. You can't prosecute people just because other people are afraid of them; you have to show that defendants have intended to produce fear for a specific criminal purpose. Ammon, of course, saw no criminal purpose, only this elaborate adverse-possession protest scheme to get his cause into the courts and save the People and the Constitution.

All this meant that Ammon now had to deal with the most intimidating aspect of his group's actions: the use of firearms. If it hadn't been for the presence of so many guns, and the apocalyptic bravado of some of the statements coming out of the occupied compound, Ammon would not have been where he was today; few of us would have ever heard of him. Guns had been at the heart of the case the bland and efficient team of federal prosecutors had just presented against Ammon and friends. They'd showed a startling video of occupiers engaged in military-style training and shooting practice and rested their case with a dramatic in-courtroom display of recovered weapons along with boxes and boxes of ammo. But all those guns and all that ammo, Ammon now insisted, had never been there to intimidate or to initiate violence in any way. They had been there merely to support the First Amendment rights of the protesters who had chosen to join him in occupying the refuge. Without the Second Amendment supporting the first, Ammon asserted, you couldn't fully use your First Amendment rights, not these days. Without the Second Amendment, when you did a direct-action protest like they were doing, the police just zip-tied you up and took you away and nobody listened. What was the point in that?

He seemed shocked to have discovered this, that this was how protest was managed by law enforcement. He had been a good Mormon all his life, and good Mormons don't challenge law and order, so maybe he'd really had no idea. And it *was* really flabbergasting when you considered it afresh. How could it be that only certain, highly regulated, permitted forms of protest were deemed legal expressions of free speech? What was the point in protest if any forms of it disapproved by authorities, and the corporate powers that held such sway over their priorities, ended with everyone quickly zip-tied and stuffed in vans? How was an officially permitted march even a protest at all? Without the hard stand, Ammon said, "we're going to go to a rally and feel good about it." Was that all it was about—protesters feeling good about themselves? It was a hard question, and a basic one activists continually have to ask themselves, though few reach the answer Ammon had.

The Bundy Revolution had come into being in a spontaneous mass reaction to these questions, provoked by a display, at Bunkerville, of America's increasingly militarized policing methods—largely as applied to the body of the man now on the stand. It had all begun in the circulation of images of cops in tactical gear tasing Ammon, as well as tossing his aunt to the ground, and arresting his brother David for filming police activity. It was these images that had gone viral in the Patriot ether and helped bring all the Necessary Bodies and all the guns to Bunkerville. Of course, there had been many such images available for a long time, of body-armored cops applying brute force to protesters—but not so many of this happening to iconic conservative white protesters like these cowboys and their kin.

Along with these more sensational images, a much quieter group of images had helped stir outrage and recruit supporters to the Bundy cause: photos of the two "First Amendment Areas" that federal law enforcement had set up near the Bunkerville allotment. The pens, made of temporary safety-orange plastic fencing, had been intended as designated spaces for pro-Bundy protesters to assemble and express their objections to the roundup of Cliven's ornery cows. In the photos, they were empty; they were likely always empty. These made for stark, absurd images of the bureaucratic magic of police power—small, fenced-in areas of free speech in the wide-open space of the desert. (The rest of the desert, one had to assume from the logic of the intervention, was now a First Amendment–Free Area.) Against the background of this Sovereign Federal Geography, the Freest Place on Earth had been born.

Ammon's position on the First and Second Amendments wasn't a new one. On the left, in the 1960s and '70s, militant groups had debated the issues extensively—some had decided that armed protest was sometimes the only kind that made sense. The more knowledgeable of the Malheur occupiers liked to compare what they had done with past actions by groups such as the Black Panthers. They loved those famous images of armed Panthers in the California statehouse, carrying long guns in a 1967 protest against a proposed anti-open-carry law. The Panthers had emerged in the mid-1960s to protect the black population of Oakland from brutal and criminally corrupt racist policing. In May 1967, a white lawmaker had proposed a bill explicitly intended to limit the Panther's rights to openly carry arms—it would be passed and signed into law enthusiastically by the future NRA hero California governor Ronald Reagan. The Panthers had taken guns to their state capitol that spring to voice their dissent to the pending legislation. Five of the group's leaders were arrested after the fact and charged with felony conspiracy. (In the end, they pleaded guilty to a misdemeanor charge of disrupting a legislative session.) Neil Wampler and others also brought up the Native American occupations of Alcatraz and Wounded Knee as precedents. Guns had not played a big role at Alcatraz, but the latter action had been a fully armed takeover of a village on the Sioux Pine Ridge Reservation in South Dakota—the site of the horrific 1890 massacre of Sioux and Cheyenne Ghost Dance practitioners. It had turned into a full-blown siege, and a media circus, with Natives, led by the pan-tribal American Indian Movement (AIM), encircled by federal forces for months. In the Malheur trial, the defense hoped to replicate the legal success of Russell Means and other AIM leaders: around 90 percent of Wounded Knee trials had ended in dismissals or acquittals. Even if the government's legal assault on AIM had bankrupted it financially and helped bring on its unraveling, the Native movement had had real success in turning the tables and doing what the Ammonites dreamed of: putting the federal government on trial.

But even given these relatively recent precedents of important armed protests, had Malheur really been a protest? Hadn't there been more to it than that? Hadn't Ammon and friends basically tried to take over the county—with all their demands and threats to the sheriff, and then with their provisional "body politic," the Committee of Safety? It seemed to me they had at least started down that road; but then again, that's not what anyone was being charged with here in Portland. David Ward was not a federal employee, and the charges were about conspiring to impede federal employees. Nothing in the charges had anything to do with the occupiers' invasion of the political space of Harney County, how they'd openly—and probably largely legally—challenged the political order of a place most of them had never heard of just a few weeks before they arrived there. Neither did the charges have anything to do—beyond the defendants' individual and collective states of mind—with their ill-considered plans to "unwind" our federal public land.

In court the issue of the occupation had been narrowed all the way down to this: had it been an exercise in free speech supported by the right to bear arms, or was it intimidation, violence, and lawlessness? This framing made it harder to just blithely accept either side's arguments. Allowing the government to use conspiracy charges to define which protests were criminal and which weren't could set truly frightful precedents, ones which would be used. At the same time, there just had to be something wrong in some way, something somehow unlawful about what Ammon and his dear friends had done with their guns in Harney County. Around and around it went. I wondered how Ammon's emotional appeal to big constitutional issues was playing in the buzzing brains of the jurors. Were Ammon's arguments gaining any traction as he sought to counter the prosecution's gun-based case? If they were, it was going to make the decision a very difficult one. No one could tell what the jurors were thinking; you could read anything you wanted into their blank faces, their shifting in their seats. By now we were deep into the afternoon, and it was time for another break. Everyone rose again in silence; again Ammon stood, up above us all, arms behind his back as if bound, proudly facing the representatives of the People, as they filed past and out that secret door where none of us could follow.

*   *   *

The next morning Ammon was back on the stand. Aside from adverse possession, the other message Mumford was trying to drive home was that the occupation had been a peaceful enterprise. He showed the jury more videos, including one of an improvised church service. Here was a whole room full of occupiers linked in what looked like a rugby scrum, kneeling with arms and shoulders interlocked, so that the room they were in seemed filled with the living flesh of one single organism: the peaceful community in prayer. At times it became downright cloying. Ammon already had holy scripture and a Constitution up there with him on the stand. Now he invoked apple pie, telling the jury how he'd enjoyed making pies the previous fall with apples from his orchard in Emmett and delivering them in person to his new neighbors.

Eventually, though, it all got darker, as Mumford led his client into Devine Canyon and the story of his arrest. Ammon had been napping in the back of occupier Mark McConnell's Jeep, when the Law and its caravan of dark vans had rolled on out of the pines. The prosecution had been obliged to reveal that McConnell was actually an FBI informer who had helped coordinate the takedown; at the time, of course, Ammon hadn't known. Awake, and then out of the car, and then down on the highway, he found himself with rifles pointing at him from all sides. "I had red dots all over me," he said. If he had moved, he wouldn't have lived, he thought.

"They were up in the trees—up all around. They began yelling at us." As he was taken into custody, he attempted to talk with the agents, to find out what it was he was being taken in for. "I began inquiring, and they did not know." Then he corrected himself. "I don't know that they did not know. They did not answer." Once it got dark, they'd moved him off the pavement and into a van with the other arrested occupiers, which drove down into the basin and out west along Route 26 to a rest area, where each was put in a separate vehicle and driven in a high-speed caravan though the sage and over the snowy Cascades to Portland and the Multnomah County jail, where he'd been ever since.

Mumford was building Ammon's testimony toward its conclusion. "Did you feel like you were risking your life?" he asked.

"At some point there's a risk that had to be taken," Ammon answered.

There was a lot of back-and-forth now, a lot of starts and stops. Mumford was stuttering more powerfully than ever, trying to ask Ammon questions about being labeled a terrorist—but the objections were coming fast and they were being sustained. Ammon got something in about how, in the years after Bundy Ranch, he'd been strip-searched in a back room every time he flew. He must have flown forty times, he said, and it had happened every time.

Then we were waiting for Marcus Mumford to ask his final question. His stuttering had gotten very intense, which it often seemed to do with extreme emotion. He was totally stuck on a syllable, head jerking back, face reddening, his stocky, fistlike body pulsing. But only watery, choking, clicky sounds were coming out of his throat. Briefly, he seemed to give up. "No more questions," he finally got out, but then immediately recanted. Wait, he did have one. Again he fought hard through the stutter. "Is it still wor-wor-wor-wor-worth it?"

The prosecution objected immediately—before Ammon could answer—and the objection was sustained. But in the meantime, Mumford had gotten his speech back. "Was it worth it?" he asked now, in a fluent, raspy whisper.

"Absolutely," Ammon replied.

*   *   *

You could feel the excitement in the room as chief prosecutor Ethan Knight began, seated at a table alone, directly across from Ammon. Imagine for yourself an efficient federal prosecutor, and there's a good chance you may picture someone like Ethan Knight. He wears Brooks Brothers suits; he's balding, stiff postured, and well-controlled in all movements of his extremities. His voice sounds like the officious white-man voice that hip-hop artists like to splice into their songs for comic effect. A former supervisor once said of Knight that he spoke "almost like he's yelling at someone who is deaf." He made a strong contrast with his chief opponent, the rumpled, gesticulating, stuttering Mumford—and also with Judge Brown, with her ironic wisecracks, informal asides, and skeptical demeanor.

We all hunkered down for what was sure to be a long afternoon of combative questioning—how was Knight going to approach Bundy? Would he break through his aw-shucks, apple-pie demeanor? So much of what Ammon had said on the stand, despite all his disavowals, did seem to offer angles for arguing that there had been a conspiracy of some kind. For one, that meeting at Ye Olde Castle had sounded like a conspiratorial gathering to me. At the same time, Ammon's "sunlight is the best disinfectant" approach—he loved this quote and used it often—seemed like it would make a "gotcha" style of questioning more difficult. What kinds of lies and inconsistencies could they catch him in when he was laying it all out there? Also, how to impeach kitsch, like that apple-pie routine—how to impeach faith? Knight worked fast, firing off questions in a voice as hard as his stare. He tried to tangle Ammon up in some of the contradictions of the whole adverse-possession claim, beginning with the absurdity that Ammon had said on the stand that he'd never even been to the refuge until January 2, when he and his friends took it over.

"You had to use GPS to get there even though you planned to control it until 2036?" Knight asked him. The twenty-year estimate was based on how adverse possession works in Oregon. "My question is you went to a location you've never been to before for that purpose?"

"You're assuming I'm acknowledging it's a federal property," Ammon answered. "We were there disputing it was a federal property."

"So you're saying the property you went to was not, in your belief, a federal property?" Knight countered.

"No," Ammon replied.

"Yet you were trying to adversely possess it . . . isn't that correct?" Knight questioned.

"Yes," said Ammon.

Knight took a detour now into an issue that Ammon had been pilloried for on liberal-leaning websites during the occupation—that his fleet-repair business had taken out a $530,000 loan from the federal Small Business

Administration, despite all Ammon's anti-federal rhetoric. And then he abruptly ended the cross-examination. Seemingly banking on everyone's fatigue with the hours and hours of Ammon, and perhaps satisfied with all the potentially self-incriminating statements Ammon had made voluntarily on the stand, Knight announced that he had no further questions. Ammon had testified for three days; the prosecution had examined him for fifteen minutes.

*   *   *

As if the day hadn't been intense enough, there was another witness waiting: Jeanette Finicum, LaVoy's grieving widow. Judge Brown warned the attorneys that no one was allowed to ask her about her husband's death; she had a wrongful-death suit pending. Also now the FBI was looking into something that had come up in the police investigation conducted by the Deschutes County sheriff. The shooting had been justified, the investigators had declared, but there was an irregularity. Footage revealed that unreported shots had been fired at Finicum's truck in the snowbank before he'd been killed, but the casings were nowhere to be found. Other footage showed FBI agents looking around on the ground for something. Agents on the scene had denied firing those shots, but now it seemed like no one believed them. Soon one of them would be charged in the case, for lying and covering up. One of the bullets, or part of one, was believed by many to be in the courtroom this day, carried in the living flesh of sovereign ryan c. of the bundy society, who had been unbreakable in his refusal to allow its removal.

Jeanette Finicum was often in tears that afternoon, regardless of the fact that no one asked her directly about her husband's death. It didn't matter—all the questions were still about him, and about his final days, and the decisions that had taken him there. Much about the life of the absent rancher was now entered into the record. When she'd met him, he'd been a single dad, working for Raindance Services for the Navajo reservation, doing therapeutic foster care, the same work she and her husband had done on their ranch, hosting troubled and traumatized teenage boys. She told the room about LaVoy's boyhood—he'd grown up on the Navajo reservation, where his father worked on a road crew. He'd done his Mormon missionary work on the Lakota reservation in South Dakota; his time on the refuge had carried him back to the purposeful days of his mission.

Afterward Matt Schindler took Jeanette Finicum's testimony as evidence of how much the defense had been able to push back against the usually constrictive environment of federal court. At moments during Finicum's testimony, he couldn't believe what was happening. He'd watched Tiffany Harris promise the judge that they'd only be going into a few questions about Jeanette's time on the refuge, and now we were getting the dead man's life story, with his widow crying on the stand—and the judge herself offering Jeanette tissues. Sure, no one asked her about her husband's death, but no one needed to, the whole testimony was about memories of a man now dead. Memories of him sleeping in a parking lot on a flying visit back from the refuge while she watched over him. Memories of how the couple had first thought David Fry—when the young Ohioan had befriended LaVoy on the internet—was one of their old foster kids playing a joke on them. Once it had started, the memories, the tears, it was pretty easy to understand how the prosecution might feel mostly disempowered to object. It wasn't just the prosecution that the defense's chaotic strategy (or lack thereof) had gotten to; watching the judge permit all this moving testimony from LaVoy's widow, it sure looked like they'd gotten to Judge Brown as well. "We ran her over too," Schindler said.

NecroNation

After all the emotion of the day's testimony, I also felt run over. When it was finally done, I was glad to get outside. The air felt heavy. It was a dark afternoon, but the sky was bright and fluffy compared with the mood that had descended in the courtroom. I was sitting on one of the fat bullet-shaped barriers that separate the big sidewalk and the courthouse steps from the street, writing down the words *adverse possession*, and then underlining them over and over. I guess I was feeling adversely possessed. I looked up and saw Matthew Deatherage walking by. He was carrying a bright yellow, red, and blue flag, wild with figures and lines—what nation or cause it represented, I couldn't then recognize. When I greeted him, he stopped in his tracks and glared at me, as much as Matthew can glare—he isn't exactly the glaring kind. He wanted to know if I was happy, happy about what had happened. What did he mean? I wondered.

I'd met him that summer at the same hearing where I'd met Duane Ehmer as well as Matthew's cousin, John Lamb, a recently ex-Amish carpenter from Montana who was in the process of becoming one of the main figures of the movement. Matthew himself had never been Amish. What he was right now was mad at me. Quickly I realized the cause—and took off my cap. He had mistaken me for Kierán Suckling, the environmentalist and long-term Bundy foe who had led counterprotests at the refuge. I watched the realization of the error unfold in his face; revisiting the death of LaVoy had set him off, it seemed. Maybe I needed a new hat.

Soon we were chatting amicably again, traveling through Matthew's favorite topics, like marijuana and its effectiveness when it came to chronic pain. He was afflicted with serious joint pain, and I wondered if discomfort or medication was responsible for his affect; he had an expressionless way of being very present and very far away at once. Most of the time his face was as blank and open as a clean, polished plate—it was the face of someone continually processing; but it was also a kind of face I associate with pain. We talked some more about drug law and prison populations, and then suddenly he was talking about Donald Trump.

It was the first time anyone in his crew had brought up Trump with me. Matthew positively despised the man. Even as a libertarian, he was certain Trump would be much worse than Hillary; the man was repulsive—he was *a rapist*, he said. Then he recounted a story that I had not yet heard, about how Ivana Trump, in their contentious divorce proceedings, had alleged that her husband had raped her in a rage after some kind of hair-implant surgery gone wrong. (Ivana had later changed her account of the event, stating that she hadn't meant rape in a "literal or criminal" sense.) The Donald was everything Matthew was against; he was gross and he wasn't for freedom. It was hard on Matthew that lots of folks in the Patriot world were so excited about the candidacy, but he felt sure that more than half of the movement was not for Trump at all. Many were only anti-Hillary, he thought.

And then he asserted something that really unnerved me. What he told me was this: Donald Trump was a disaster, but we should get ready, because there was no way he wasn't going to win. No, he responded to each of my objections. I was wrong. It was totally terrible but Donald Trump was absolutely going to win. According to Matthew, there was simply no way he could lose.

*   *   *

I had felt a twinge of something similar in the summer when I'd read the entirety of the Republican candidate's apocalyptic convention speech. I had pulled into the parking lot of my local grocery store and, before going in, had compulsively opened up the news on my phone. The Republican convention was on in Cleveland, and probably I was hoping for a report of some kind of meltdown, the *big one* that would finally bring the Trump nightmare to an end.

I started reading Trump's speech, which he'd just given—the text had been provided to the press. I had meant to skim it, but once I started reading, I couldn't stop. I read it all the way through right there in the parking lot. The policy messages and the spirit behind them were mostly entirely toxic to my mind, but the tone it captured was so skillfully constructed—a masterful distillation of the right-wing version of that intangible thing: a country's mood. *The mood of the country*—we'd hear this and similar phrases a lot that summer and fall, even more than in most election years. It's confusing: how can a fictional thing like a nation have feelings? And yet what is a country but multiple currents of Sovereign Feelings, intertwining, churning, turning this way and that, a great flood, which those fighting for power attempt to sound, channel, and name? Trump's adviser Stephen Miller, or whoever else had written this speech, had a real handle on the American feelings now traversing all our platforms. What was worse was that the author of these words had a strong sense of how to link this inchoate mood maximally to ugliness, fear, mourning, grievance, fractiousness, and vengeance. It was an angry, tribal, funereal speech, the speech of a country so hungry for a victor's meaning and purpose that it was prepared to die, and to take as much of the world as it could with it. How could the technocratic efficiency of Hillary Clinton win out against this? I sat in my car for a long time afterward—too aghast, too full of dread to enter the alienated space of the store and circulate, among all the glistening aisles, to the piped-in tunes of lost love and longing.

* * *

Matthew was pulled away from me now, into an improbably chipper bipartisan photo-op. A group of anti-Bundy protesters were on the steps today. After some back-and-forth, the two opposing crews of environmentalists and Patriots seemed to have come to some kind of agree-to-disagree détente. Now they were taking group pictures. Some of Matthew's friends were calling him to join. His colorful Tibetan flag added to the improvised pageantry of it. They took two tableaux vivants. In one, the two groups of foes all held up signs against the "Bundy Land Grab." In the other, they all,

Bundyites and tree-huggers alike, opened copies of those ubiquitous pocket Constitutions and then pretended, each one, to be absorbed in silent reading together.

I lingered a while, watching the cheery opponents perform for their cameras and for one another, before starting the journey back to my motel across the river. As amused—as touched, even—as I felt about this rare show of American antagonists enjoying one another's company, after Matthew's prognosis I was feeling rather gloomy, adversely possessed even. By what, I wasn't sure exactly. *Adverse Possession*—I turned the phrase over and over in my head and on my tongue. There it was again, in front of me, underlined on my pad. Ammon and friends had a real knack for suggesting metaphors, even when they hadn't meant to. Weren't we all Adversely Possessed? Isn't that what being in a nation was—bound and haunted in our laws, words, feelings, and ceremonies, by the urges and dreams of the dead, victors and vanquished alike? And wasn't that also what the platforms of the internet worked to do? Despite all their promises of a new tech-enabled democracy, didn't they mostly work by keeping us glued to one another so that our lives could be monetized, privatized by new corporate behemoths? Wasn't it old, undead feelings that kept us clumped on those platforms? Ugly ones like the resentments and terrors embodied in Donald Trump, who, Matthew had assured me, would be our next president?

Before I rounded the corner to head to the light rail, I stopped to take another photo of those words of Thomas Jefferson engraved into the dark stone alongside the courthouse steps. The Boisterous Sea of Liberty was pitching hard these days; Jefferson was coming to mind a lot. In the early days of the country, the undue authority of the dead over the living was one of the aspects of nationhood that had worried him the most. He had gone so far as to propose, in a remarkable letter to his friend James Madison, himself still relatively fresh from the business of constitution making, "that no society can make a perpetual constitution, or even a perpetual law." A nation needed to be reinvented with each successive generation, or else the dead would establish an unconscionable tyranny over the living, a tyranny, he pointed out to Madison, one would not tolerate to such an extreme in other legal circumstances. Every constitution and law should really expire with its natural authority, after nineteen years—nineteen years being what Jefferson had calculated with his usual nerdiness, using population mortality data, as the real length of a generation in its majority. "Every constitution then, & every law, naturally expires at the end of 19 years. If it be enforced longer, it is an act of force, & not of right," he'd concluded. "The earth belongs in usufruct to the living," he told Madison. "The dead," he continued, "have neither powers nor rights over it."

Adverse Possession—yes, that was it. We were under the Law of the Dead and had been for more than two hundred years. Trump even looked kind of dead, like an animated corpse, tarted up with whatever made his flesh so orange. That's why I felt so tired and dispirited; the dead were drinking up all my life, all of our lives. We existed to *feed* them. As much as I was enjoying the majesty of court, I was also tired of the monumental, deathly pretension of it; I was even more tired of seeing the Constitution fetish of the Patriots wagged about, with its wax-face Washington on the cover—his empty, undead eyes.

This was all fanciful hyperbole, the kind to jot in a notebook on a slow-moving train. What I was really, though, was tuckered out. I looked up from my notes at the silent strangers on the train and at the rainy streets outside. If my brain could have had a face of its own, its expression would have been like young Matthew's, frozen in the act of taking it all in. As I rode back through the dark city to my motel, it was especially Jeanette Finicum's feelings that began to return to me—and through her the feelings of her dead husband. LaVoy Finicum, property rights radical, militant for the Dead Man's Law of the Constitution. Maybe it was also LaVoy who was adversely possessing me tonight, now that he'd joined the heap of souls, the vast pantheon of the American dead. Alive, he'd loved it out there on the land of the Arizona Strip, with his dog, and the wind, and his fat and sassy cows. Why'd he have to go and die for some dead men's ideas? "Property," of all things.

I put my pad away. Paused at an intersection, I watched more strangers in the lit-up storefront of an exercise studio, frantically moving their bodies to music I couldn't hear. Soon I was back at my room. I did what one does in such circumstances—or at least what I do when I find myself having feelings in a motel. I turned on the TV and prepared to zone out. But that didn't work. The final scene of the film *The Revenant* was on; Leonardo DiCaprio was dying, or maybe he doesn't die—it's unclear. His character, Hugh Glass, trapper and frontiersman, was bleeding a lot, panting desperately in the snow, while hallucinating a specter of his dead wife, a beautiful Pawnee woman murdered years earlier by Glass's countrymen. She whispered to him in his vision. Then the screen went black and the credits began to roll. I shut off the TV and the lights, pulled the blankets up, and lay in the dark. It was pouring outside now. I listened to the rain bucketing down, drooling on everything, flowing in dark sheets across the empty intersections, illuminated by the traffic lights blinking out the rules, flashing guidance to no one at all.

CHAPTER TWENTY-ONE

Medenbach v. Marshall

OVER THE HOLIDAY WEEKEND THAT FOLLOWED Ammon's three days on the stand, the presidential election took another wild turn, an ugly one—but one that improved the long-term outlook for the nation, as far as I was concerned. The infamous pussy-grabbing tape was released. Trump, already such an image of aged-male obscenity that he seemed mythological, had been caught on camera and audio boasting to a sycophantic male entertainment reporter about how, as a celebrity, he enjoyed the privilege of just taking what he wanted from women—you could "grab them by the pussy." When you were a star, they just let you, he said. Clearly, the Trump moment was over. Matthew Deatherage was wrong: the man would never be president. Now feeling less panicked by America, I headed back to court—for what turned out to be yet another lesson in adverse possession. This time it came from Ken Medenbach, who took the stand and regaled the court for three hours with the story of how he'd become the Sovereign Weirdo we saw before us.

Medenbach's adventures in adverse possession had begun back in 1988, when he'd bought five acres—for seven hundred dollars—near Crescent, Oregon. He'd built cabins and dragged a mobile home out there. Then, after a long stretch, Klamath County had appeared one day and red-tagged his buildings. He'd had no building permits. He lived two miles from the nearest neighbor; it hadn't occurred to him to get any. "They started fining me and taking me to court," Medenbach said. He couldn't afford the fines and permits, which were more than he'd paid for the land. He self-represented in the dispute, and this seems to be the point when he started getting seriously into reading the law on his own. After refusing to show up when he was denied trial by jury, he was hit with contempt; now he owed the court more than ten thousand dollars. But then he won his right to trial by judge and somehow in the end he didn't have to pay anything. It was confusing; there was some kind of obscure provision involved that got him out of it all, something to do with some kind of Oregon homesteading law, his co-counsel Matt Schindler told me. Whatever it was, now Ken was hooked.

It was also around that time, the early '90s, that he joined the Central Oregon Militia; the first years of the Clinton administration were a heyday for militias, before the Oklahoma City bombing put a damper on the whole thing. It was the militia that had first showed him the map of all the federally owned land in the western states. Evidently, still revved up from his fight over his own property, he'd decided it was time to take action on this bigger issue as well. There was federal land right next to his own plot, so he dragged a cabin onto it, "dolled it up a bit," he said, and then sent the BLM notice that he was claiming the land for the State of Oregon.

In this act of two decades past, the Ken Medenbach we had before us had been born, his personal Rubicon crossed. His letter to the BLM invoked the enclave clause and adverse possession—the same key principles that Ammon and all his friends had brought back to life here in crazy 2016. "They sent me a notice telling me to stop cutting trees and get off the land," Ken said. "I just waited, hoping they'd take some action; they sent me notices. I called them. I said I wanted to resolve it. They said they wanted to resolve it too—I told them I didn't want them sending any SWAT teams in." He was served with a removal notice and got summoned to federal district court in Eugene. He'd tried to walk out of that courtroom because of what he called the judge's bias against him, a bias the judge, to Ken's mind, held by virtue of being part of the cabal called the Oregon State Bar Association. Somehow the court audience (how was unclear) had persuaded Ken, at the time, to go back and talk to the judge. He lost this case, like he'd lose all his public land cases to come, but it hadn't deterred him, and sometime after that he'd done it all over again, this time in Washington State. He'd gone up there to give a militia presentation on adverse possession, but when he'd realized that nobody up there was really going to do anything, he did it himself, this time on land under the administration of "the alleged Forest Service." It was a criminal matter, but it was like a ticket, Ken said—though he ended up in jail anyway because of his refusal to recognize federal jurisdiction.

*　*　*

There was such compulsion in all this, *historical compulsion*. With his sovereign, neo-homesteader performances, Medenbach seemed to be trying, over and over, to reopen the long-closed American frontier, or to reawaken it in fantasy anyway, there in the shadowlands it cast across the secret body of the Law. All of it seemed to be about the undead fantasy of the fresh start in the wilderness, and its powerful role in a certain lingering vision of American society and democracy. This was the society and democracy Thomas Jefferson had praised and that the late nineteenth-century American historian Frederick Turner had famously eulogized—a sparse, individualist society, characterized by defiantly democratic politics and also (to Jefferson's chagrin) charismatic religion. This society, to Turner's mind, made a sociopolitical world stripped of the weight of the conventions and institutions of the European past.

"For a moment, at the frontier, bonds of custom are broken and unrestraint is triumphant," Turner wrote in an influential paper, "The Significance of the Frontier in American History," delivered at the 1893 Columbian Exposition in Chicago. "There is not tabula rasa. The stubborn American environment is there with its imperious summons to accept its conditions; the inherited ways of doing things are also there; and yet, in spite of environment, and in spite of custom, each frontier did indeed furnish a new field of opportunity, a gate of escape from the bondage of the past; and freshness, and confidence, and scorn of older society, impatience of its restraints and its ideas, and indifference to its lessons, have accompanied the frontier." But this was all coming to an end now, he'd said, closing what might still be the single most cited paper ever presented by an American historian: "And now, four centuries from the discovery of America, at the end of a hundred years of life under the Constitution, the frontier has gone, and with its going has closed the first period of American history."

More than one hundred years later, Ken Medenbach and his friends, the Bundy family, weren't buying that Turner's frontier America—arguably a phantasm in the first place—was forever gone. I remembered there being vague talk of homesteading during the occupation, though how that would have really worked on such thickly delineated land—every blade of grass adjudicated, as rancher and county commissioner Dan Nichols had put it—was never explained. Dreams of homesteaders and cowboys were all part of a generalized nostalgia for the wide-open frontier, all its hardships and deadly conflicts and genocidal practices smeared over in a patina of glory. The Bundy plan of unwinding, tracking down "rightful owners," and of turning land over to the states wasn't really any more likely to solve the West's rural problems than a return to nineteenth-century homesteading. But I'd begun to suspect that feasibility didn't really matter here. The strength of the Bundy Revolution lay in what it was able to do by selectively mining the past and our founding documents to extract raw material for the creation of Sovereign Feelings in the bodies and lives of its adherents in the present. Ammon did the same with land-law terms like *adverse possession*, taking arcane concepts, foreign to most, and turning them into the movement's liturgy. Now people who'd never ranched the West could be heard, wherever the Bundy Revolution gathered, routinely rattling off phrases like *water rights, preemptive rights, beneficial use*, and *grazing rights* in the same tone of reverent certainty with which the Constitution and Article I, Section 8, Clause 17 were invoked. Sometimes the land seemed to exist just so that the legal concepts could be extracted from it and made into populist political theology, and a phantasmic territory of feeling in which the Bundy faithful could continually assemble.

*   *   *

The forging of a community and its imaginary space is an important element of activist life, perhaps more prominent on the left, but also strongly present on the right. The Patriots were making the world they wanted alongside their friends in their community of action. In the case of the Bundy Revolution, there was also a kind of conservative populist geography to it: a vision of how the world is mapped, and how the feeling of constitutive power and popular sovereignty—or Freedom, as it is understood in Bundyland—emerges through the claiming of territory. It was a settler's geography. Ammon's Beautiful Pattern was one example, and Kenny's log-cabin theater was another. It all reminded me a bit of what had been going on that summer and fall with the imaginary southern border wall that Donald Trump had been promising to build at his campaign rallies. It seemed to me that the main purpose of Trump's wall wasn't *really* the wall. The point, rather, was a bunch of people chanting, "Build the wall," and in that act becoming, themselves, the wall. As ugly as they looked and sounded, those people in those arenas clearly were feeling great—and terribly real—as, together in the moment, they imagined *their* place, *their* boundaries, *their* border. I didn't doubt their desire for an actual wall, nor the real human and ecological damages—and potential horrors—that such a wall would be part of if it were built. It's just that the chant didn't seem to me to have all that much to do with the people or the terrain of the U.S.-Mexico border. What the Trumpites were engaged in at their rallies was a mass reactionary rite of Sovereign Magic Mapmaking, a ritual intervention in a rapidly shifting world geography whose changes had far outpaced most of our understandings. Kenny was up to something similar but also very different in his geographical interventions. If the people in the Trumpite-filled arenas were imagining themselves as an idealized, vast, militarily powerful, and racially exclusive twentieth-century nation-state, Medenbach's theater was all nineteenth century, about the freedom, and the bare-bones society of the white-settler frontier that Turner had eulogized more than a century earlier.

All those generations of trappers, land-hungry pioneers, desperate immigrants, loners, miners, fanatics, sociopaths, and saints, all these ragged and improbable souls, the necessary—whitewashed—bodies of Manifest Destiny—seemed resurrected in Ken Medenbach and his sovereign log-cabin theater. Adverse Possession was his own first-time-as-tragedy, second-time-as-farce reenactment of the American dream, just as Malheur had been for the Patriots, whether they saw it that way or not. Matt Schindler told me that after Kenny's testimony, an excited reporter had exclaimed to him that his client "was the OG of all this stuff!" I suppose he was: Chainsaw Ken, a lonely voice in the Oregon wilderness, prophesying, without knowing, the coming of the Bundy Revolution. Of course he hadn't ever been doing it *all alone*—sagebrush rebel, sovereign citizen, and militia currents had all mingled in him—but he was still a very singular figure. I wondered what would have happened, or what would have never happened, if way back in the '80s, Klamath County had just left him alone and not hauled him into court over his unpermitted buildings out in the woods. Maybe in his old age he would have stuck to grumbling to his Facebook friends about how America was to be punished for its godlessness. But those building inspectors had come for him—and now he was here, and glad of it. "I've been waiting for twenty-one years to get where I am right now," he told the room. All this was being typed into the federal record, where it would live as long as the nation, as long as *information*. This was his moment of glory. "I am where I want to be," he said.

The Creator and the Creation

Medenbach was happy to be in court for another reason; now he had a chance to tell lawyers and judges what he thought about the Law. This included his chance to tell federal prosecutor Craig Gabriel, during cross-examination, that the ruling of the federal judge in one of his cabin cases, as to the constitutionality of the use of adverse possession on federal land, was "just his opinion." "He doesn't have the power to interpret the Constitution," Kenny further informed the assistant U.S. attorney.

Getting to say stuff like that was all worth going to jail for someone like him. Ken told me so himself, out in the lobby, later that week, still pumped up from his big afternoon on the stand. He and Schindler had gotten the rough copy of the transcript of his testimony—getting to read it over was another dream come true. He wouldn't mind being convicted for being a patriot now, he said. "It beats the hell out of going to jail for drunk driving!" he told me, "And I know, because I've done that too!"

He then pulled out a pen and began writing down court decisions for me to look up, in support of his contentions about the limits of judicial power. The internet, he told me, had made this all a lot easier. How else would he have been able to read all this stuff, to learn so much on his own, isolated out there on the east side of the mountains.

Outside the courthouse, right after Medenbach's time on the stand, I got a further lesson in some of Kenny's principles from Brand Thornton. Brand was as jazzed up by Kenny's testimony as Kenny was, maybe even more so, if that were possible. But it wasn't about adverse possession, or public land, or any of that stuff; it was what he had said about the Constitution, what he'd said to Gabriel about the exclusive right of the judiciary to interpret it that had thrilled Brand. Ken had attacked, on the stand, the most foundational ruling of the early Supreme Court, the decision *Marbury v. Madison*, in which the high court had established the principal of judicial review that most of us, I'd guess, assume is actually part of the text of the Constitution—as part of the separation of powers and the famous checks and balances. It's one of the answers the English-as-a-second-language learners I'd taught back in Brooklyn years ago would practice in our citizenship-test prep sessions—"Q: What are the duties of the Supreme Court? A: To interpret and explain the laws." No, said Kenny and Brand, that role was everyone's, especially when it came to the highest law of the land. Understanding their Constitution was the role, the duty *of the People*. The federal judiciary had usurped it more than two hundred years ago. In Brand's amped-up language, it all sounded like a constitutionalist's version of populist Evangelical Protestantism—no priests between the people and *their* text.

"Ken Medenbach brought something up that is really awesome," he told a small group of folks clumped around him, as John Lamb, the ex-Amish new media man of the Bundy flock, livestreamed. "He says the Supreme Court does not have the right to interpret the Constitution. He's a hundred percent correct. Think about it like this, just so you can wrap your brain around it," Brand went on, slipping into the preacher mode that came so easily to him. "It is patently false that the creator does not understand the creation. The creator was the people that created the Constitution of the United States. It is the creation. And the word *interpret*, the proper usage of the word *interpret*, is to interpret from one language into another. The Constitution was written in its time for an eighth-grade education. For those people—the feds—to assume, falsely, that the people do not understand what is in the Constitution is the height of arrogance . . . and Ken Medenbach got that point across, very, very well."

Ken, Brand, and their friends were so often just plain wrong about history and the law and the Constitution that it was a surprise to realize how sometimes, on certain fairly complex points, they could be at least partly right. With the notion that the People were the creators of the Constitution, Brand had taken the word-magic of the preamble so literally he had strayed into pure theology. But as wrong as they all could be about their secular scripture, as wrong as they were to believe it had been created wholly to empower, rather than restrain "the People," they weren't totally wrong about what had happened back in 1803, in the case of *Marbury v. Madison*. It was in this decision that the Supreme Court had given itself the power of judicial review, and thus formally inserted a kind of judicial supremacy into the U.S. system of government. If you didn't accept that move, then, to your mind, Ken Medenbach could be absolutely right. As Brand praised Kenny's legal acumen, he was standing right in front of the engraved words of one of the principal characters in that early controversy, one who had, on this point, largely agreed with them both—though he certainly would have phrased it all quite differently.

*   *   *

Thomas Jefferson distrusted and disliked his cousin John Marshall, who had become chief justice of the Supreme Court in 1800. To Jefferson's eyes, Marshall, through his opinions and the rulings of his court, acted as a die-hard Federalist and judicial partisan, dedicated on the one hand to increasing federal power over the states and on the other to augmenting the powers of the judiciary in relation to the other branches of the federal government. This latter point Jefferson found especially vexing: the judiciary was the one unelected branch. When it established its supremacy over the two elected branches, the legislative and the executive, it was also establishing its supremacy over the People.

The power of Marshall's court had been established early on in Jefferson's first presidential administration. After Jefferson's victory over his erstwhile (and future) friend John Adams in the election of 1800, one of the ugliest elections the nation has ever seen, the departing Federalists, who'd also lost control of Congress in the election, passed the Judicial Act of 1801. This law created sixteen new federal circuit court judgeships and forty-two justices of the peace. The Adams administration filled the positions with loyal Federalists—appointing the fifty-eight judges on March 2, 1801. The Senate confirmed them the next day, which was the day before Jefferson took office. One of these so-called midnight judges was William Marbury of Georgetown. After being sworn in, Jefferson discovered on the desk of his yet-to-arrive secretary of state a number of appointment letters for some of these judges, Marbury's among them. These hadn't yet been delivered and Jefferson was determined not to deliver them. Once in office, James Madison, Jefferson's new secretary of state, was the agent of the executive branch who officially refused to hand over the remaining appointments. Marbury, a die-hard Federalist, sought redress from the Supreme Court, asking that Madison be forced to give over the letter.

Politically, Marshall's court faced a considerable challenge. Everyone knew that if the court ordered the Jefferson administration to hand over the appointment, that Jefferson and Madison would refuse and that that would be that. The court had no enforcement powers and the affair would have left it in a very weak position. The remedy that the Marshall court devised was a breathtaking and highly convoluted power move, even for a Supreme Court decision. In the pages of the ruling, Marbury both regained and then instantly lost his appointment, while Marshall expanded the jurisdiction of the court and firmly established the judiciary as arbiter of the constitutionality of the laws of Congress, as well as the actions of the executive. The court declared Marbury had a right to his commission. However, the Marshall-written decision went on to say, the Judiciary Act of 1789, which contained a provision giving the Supreme Court original instead of appellate jurisdiction over so-called writs of mandamus—court orders compelling actions—was itself in violation of Article III of the Constitution. This meant that Marbury was mistaken in bringing his grievance to the court; the court did not have the right to compel Madison to deliver the appointment. Now came the truly important part of the decision. In determining the earlier law to be unconstitutional, the court established its supremacy in such matters, voiding the portion of that earlier Judiciary Act that had given it the authority to act first in Marbury's case. It was a huge step. Nowhere in the actual Constitution is the right or obligation of judicial review directly stated—but the court felt that it was definitively implied. Thomas Jefferson had been appalled by the implications of the decision. He'd stayed appalled to his dying days.

He was especially troubled by the notion that judges might somehow be special beings, capable of lifting themselves above the fray of partisanship. "To consider the judges as the ultimate arbiters of all constitutional questions [is] a very dangerous doctrine indeed, and one which would place us under the despotism of an oligarchy," he wrote to William Jarvis. "Our judges are as honest as other men and not more so. They have with others the same passions for party, for power, and the privilege of their corps. Their maxim is *boni judicis est ampliare jurisdictionem* [good justice is broad jurisdiction], and their power the more dangerous as they are in office for life and not responsible, as the other functionaries are, to the elective control."

Whether Jefferson's judgment here was ultimately wise no longer matters much on a practical level. The court has exercised this power for more than two hundred years; it was already a long-done deal by the time he penned this last complaint in 1820. Jefferson seems, to my mind, to have been at least partly wrong—what kind of functioning high court could be denied the right of determining the legality of laws and of enforcing those determinations? In his opposition, his old ambivalences about the Constitution—and constitution making in general—seemed to show through; with the move of Marshall's court, lifetime-appointed judges would have more explicit power to bind the present and future generations to their own aging desires, as well as to the words and urges of the dead encoded in the nation's charter. It all meant more ghostly restraint upon the vitality of the Boisterous Sea. Which is also how Marshall understood it; he just saw that as a good thing. "The principles, therefore, so established are deemed fundamental. And as the authority from which they proceed, is supreme, and can seldom act, they are designed to be permanent," he wrote in *Marbury v. Madison*.

Permanence is exactly what Jefferson had feared about constitutions in general—it's related to another problem with judicial appointments with which we are very familiar in our own time: they give presidents the power, because of the inevitable partisanship of judges that Jefferson correctly diagnosed, to exert immense influence long after the departure of their administrations, even from beyond the grave. This would prove exceedingly true in the case of John Marshall himself, whose Federalist court would continue to exert tremendous partisan power well beyond the death of the man who'd appointed him, as well as the slow death and dissolution of the Federalist Party itself.

As I contemplate a contemporary Supreme Court seemingly ideologically dedicated to extending corporate rights and power, this is where Jefferson's objections feel most prescient to me. While it is true that in the abstract Marshall's stance can seem admirable, placing the court in the position of rock-solid arbiter of what the Constitution says, and thus providing a stabilizing gravitational force, this holds only if people accept and respect the court; that is, if the court doesn't seem too partisan. The intervening years have shown us that Supreme Court justices are often very much like how Jefferson imagined they would be: partisans with immense power and lifetime appointments. It's not an easy issue. Elected federal judges seem like a nightmare—would we want our highest court judges measuring their world-shaping decisions in the light of the next primary? I think not. Some have proposed making the Supreme Court and perhaps other federal judge terms shorter—Jefferson's nineteen years might be a fair number.

All this considered, it was no wonder that in their political theology, Brand and Kenny and friends had found a sovereign route, albeit mostly in fantasy, around the whole dilemma. Who was supreme? The people, not the judges. If the Constitution belonged to the people, why did the people need the Supreme Court to tell them what it said? Regardless of the delusional nature of many of the principle beliefs of their constitutionalist credo and the reactionary blather of a fair chunk of their political platform, here in the abstract terrain of the law, the Bundyites were an illuminating bit of ordnance, continually going off. Their insistence exposed accepted customs, rules, and precedents of that system for what they often were: things a few people had decided at some point, powers a class of people had given themselves. The federal justice system didn't have to be exactly the way it was. Maybe it would be better—much better even—if it were not.

CHAPTER TWENTY-TWO

The Day of Atonement

THE SOVEREIGNS OF MALHEUR were in exceptionally high spirits. Ken Medenbach had them all wound up. It was taking me a long time to talk to the person I was waiting around to speak with: John Lamb, the new, informal media guy of the Bundyites. As always, John was running around on the courthouse steps filming everyone, broadcasting them live to the wider community of watching Patriots. It was hard to interview someone so busy interviewing everyone else; it was also hard to stay out of his footage. Before the day was over, I'd be up on YouTube, in the background of John's reposted livestream video report. There I was chatting with Matthew Deatherage about his time on the stand. He'd told the court that day how Malheur had been the only community he'd ever known, but it was the prosecution's revelation of his online petition to impeach the judge that had his friends excited. Now John swooped in to interview Matthew, and I clumsily backed out of the frame.

I looked enough like these people—scruffy, middle-aged, flanneled. Did it make me seem like some kind of infiltrator, I wondered? Or did it seem that I was one of them to those on the other side? Jarvis had already been grumbling about journalists, even those from obviously liberal outlets; sometimes he thought they were Bundy supporters too, he told me. I suppose all of us white reporters were suspect at some point, with our undisguised fascination for the Ammonite weirdos. Finally, to my relief, John's livestreaming was done. We made plans to meet right back here the next morning—it was a free day, and there would be no court session. It was Yom Kippur, the Day of Atonement.

* * *

283

John and I met up at what he and his friends were calling Patriots' Corner, a group of benches in the park across from the courthouse and the county jail. After he'd done his morning work of setting up the movement's signs on jury nullification and the evils of the Bureau of Land Management, we went around the corner behind the courthouse, down closer to the river, to the same café that had been providing box lunches for the jurors. It was a typical Portland establishment; even here, stuffed into the base of an institutional building, it had all the markers of the place—the informality, the ingredients that really came from nearby farms. John seemed to know everyone in the joint. The cashier asked how the case was going, and so I found myself waiting while John Lamb gave yet another Bundy trial update. Finally, we made it into the outdoor dining area; it wasn't raining today, and sometimes a little sun was even breaking through. We partook together of the bounty of the Willamette Valley, that rich land that had caused so much nineteenth-century tumult, mass migration, and wholesale murder. It was this lush valley, which Portland sat at the top of, that had attracted so many pioneers west across the Oregon Trail, including so many who'd met ugly deaths of starvation, disease, and thirst. Many had died on detours through the lands of Malheur, following mistaken shortcuts. It was one of the foundational stories of Harney County; there were still places you could go to see the ruts their wagon wheels had left in the alkaline dust.

* * *

How to explain John Lamb? When I'd met him in August, he'd given me his email but warned me he was new to all that computer stuff. Not anymore. Now he had two smartphones and was in a state of constant connectivity with hundreds, even thousands of people—he was the hub of that connectivity. When he'd started doing his livestreams, he told me, he'd been lucky to get one hundred viewers; now sometimes he was getting twenty thousand. One morning, at the break, when we came out of a court session, he showed me that in the few hours we'd been sequestered in the chamber, he'd already received almost three hundred texts.

It was all doubly strange because John *is Amish*. Or was Amish until very recently, when his small Montana community had dissolved. He still had the big Amish beard and a thick midwestern drawl, filled with moments of odd usage and syntax that seemed to be the cultural residue of German in his English. But he drove now and generally lived a life no longer simple and plain. Far from it. In Portland, he shuttled around the Patriot faithful every day in his minivan and organized protests and meals, all while keeping the larger community up-to-date via livestream and text on what was happening in court.

John made a curious figure—inside and outside the movement—and he knew it. He hadn't participated in either the Nevada or Oregon standoffs, and he was a pacifist. Even though he drove and livestreamed now, he hadn't abandoned his faith; talk of God and love peppered his speech, and he was still a devout believer in the Amish practice of nonresistance. "It's church doctrine," he said. "We don't fight, we don't go in the military, we don't pick up arms." In a movement so associated with the Second Amendment and with the militia, did people find him odd? Most people accepted his nonresistance stance, he said, though some told him they could never do it themselves. He'd had some conflict with militia types though. "Some militia guys have called me a stupid farmer," he said, chuckling through his big farmer's beard. The militia dudes had been frustrated because he'd refused their offers of help; they'd been "begging us to invite them to protect us," John said. This had seemed like a terrible idea—the whole long-guns and tactical-gear show. The problem with their thinking, John told me, was that it was too much about power. Power was the real problem: you had to accept that you had none. "I'm not to trying to overthrow the government. I don't have no power," he said, laughing again. Even the lack of a mustache in John's beard was part of the old Amish critique of power. Amish men shaved their mustaches because of nonresistance. A mustache was a symbol of authority— associated with European military men back in the day.

How had this guy ended up as the new face of the Bundy Revolution? What was it, I asked, in his life history that had led him to support the Bundys and the Malheur Occupiers—authors of an *armed takeover*? What could be less Amish? He'd been suspicious of the occupation at first, he said, but he had known Jake Ryan, one of the youngest of the occupiers charged by the government, since Jake was a boy, and so he'd become convinced that these all just had to be good people. Besides, growing up Amish, when and where he did, in Indiana in the '60s and '70s, had instilled in him a deep fear of government authority at a very early age. There had been an especially frightening period in his early youth when his parents had believed the State of Indiana was going to take him and his siblings away as part of a long struggle between the state and its Amish population over compulsory schooling. "My dad hid us out," he recalled. He'd been terrified. "I grew up scared to death of law enforcement," he said, "paranoid of any law enforcement because of it—like they are going to come and take us."

Nowadays, John mostly chafed at smaller things—like being told it was against the law for him to sell or give away raw milk to his friends and neighbors. He'd had some trouble with state regulatory agencies over a side scrap-metal business he ran, and he sympathized with the struggles of some "English" neighbors (John still called non-Amish "English" sometimes, grinning whenever he did) to keep their economic access to federal lands. He was also proud that he and his family still didn't have social security numbers or birth certificates, and openly enjoyed how I marveled at the fact. Many marveled at such facts about John—so now he had a book of his own planned, he told me; the title would be *The Last Free Man*.

To my mind, it still didn't add up. It was the Supreme Court that had resolved the compulsory-schooling issue in Indiana in favor of the Amish, and *against* the states—and here he was in a constitutionalist group so very fundamentalist that it denied the right of the Supreme Court to interpret the Constitution at all. But over time and across different experiences, maybe that kind of specificity gets lost. However John's various run-ins with government authority converged, it seemed more to me that something in him was itching for a new kind of involvement in the world, and this had been his way in. While almost none of the Patriots had ever lived the vanishing cowboy life of the family of heroes at the center of the movement, John had actually lived a rural, traditional life, way outside the American mainstream—up till very recently. His Amish community in Montana had basically dissipated, he explained. He laughed as he described how in their last years, they'd taken to driving, but stashed their cars out of each other's sight. After that deeply community-oriented traditional life had dissolved, it seemed that he'd found new meaning, new community—and a key role—in a contemporary, highly charged conservative political life.

Even if it still wasn't entirely clear what had drawn John into the Bundy struggle, it was easy to see why Ammon and Ryan and the other occupiers had come to put so much faith in John Lamb. What better face for the movement, for the story they wanted to tell now? Here was a gentle, endlessly amiable, religious *pacifist*. Beyond this public relations aspect, John was also just an incredibly organized person. Here he was at the center of an undisciplined, horizontal movement full of folks in need of a little life coaching. He still marveled at their chaos. "I feel bad," he said, "like I'm being real bossy,

but sometimes I just have to say it . . . 'OK! How about we all do laundry?' . . .
And then everybody says, 'Oh, OK. Good idea!' "

His Portland routine reached beyond the Bundy Revolution. He'd gotten
involved in the life of this place: starting with the Multnomah County
Detention Center. He'd noticed while visiting Ryan and Ammon and the
other occupiers that there were long-term prisoners being held on federal
charges in this county facility who got no visitors. So he'd started visiting
them too, just so they had somebody to talk to. Maybe they'd done bad
things, but they still deserved some contact. Outside the jail, he was very
troubled by how many homeless people there were. He had not been prepared
for this. I heard this from other rural Bundy Revolution folks as well—their
shock at the number of the unhoused, living in tents under seemingly every
overpass, in squares of grass and dirt between highway ramps, and along
whatever hidden infrastructural conduits and bike paths from which they
hadn't been shuffled along. For my part, I had grown too quickly accustomed to it. It hadn't been long since I'd left L.A. for good. There the ever-
rising housing costs associated with the ongoing tech-boom and all the
global capital flowing into the built environment had made tent cities a
basic fact of life. I suspect I had also accepted it all, during my time in L.A.,
out of a kind of recognition, dread, and denial. I was a poet struggling in
those days to get by as an underpaid, precariously employed college instructor,
and so I was always a class reduction and a few months away from being
terribly close to some very hard decisions. There hadn't been a lot of elbow
room in my '94 Corolla.

The lives of the unhoused seemed even harder here in Portland now that
the rains were coming in. The news was full of political infighting over
different ideas of how to tackle the issue, which had ambushed the city. In
the face of all that, John's naive shock that a place this prosperous could
have this many unhoused felt refreshing—it *was* shocking; it was totally
unacceptable. So much in our American lives is. He said he'd started going
out and bringing food to folks whenever he could. I had no way of knowing
how often he was really doing this, but it was easy to believe John. I liked
him; everybody liked him—the Bundyites, reporters, federal marshals, neigh-
borhood businesspeople. No matter how much I disagreed with most of the
main objects of John's newly adopted movement, he still made being an
American feel like an interesting proposition. I think it was because he
himself had just decided, despite having lived here all his life, to become

one. Few get the chance to just choose such a thing, but John had, and now he was inventing what it meant in his own terms as he went along.

Our Tempestuous Day

As if on cue, our American day was beginning to get more interesting all around us. We didn't notice at first. John was telling me the story of his gradual alienation from his church, a tale that even involved a reality-television show appearance. He'd been sued in an "English" court by a relative of his wife, Rebekah, over the construction of a St. Louis hotel. (Amish are famous builders, and John's family's main business these days is the construction of half-barns for their English neighbors across Montana.) According to John, included in the suit's demands were two mules—for John's alleged failure to pay a proper Amish dowry for Rebekah. The novelty of an Amish lawsuit had caught the attention of someone at the *Judge Joe Brown* program, and so John and Rebekah had found themselves in L.A., which John had been unable to differentiate in his mind at the time from Las Vegas. He'd thought they were basically the same thing. In restaurants they were an object of fascination; many folks assumed they were Orthodox Jews. The absurdity of John's TV adventure had us both in stitches, which is maybe why we didn't catch on at first that, around us, downtown Portland seemed to be going on some kind of militarized alert.

There were helicopters circling low overhead. We watched as cops in riot gear—full body armor, with shields and tear-gas guns—ran up the streets away from the river toward the courthouse and Portland City Hall. I began to feel alarmed, but not John. He described the wild scene to his bewildered mother when she called him on one of his two cell phones from her simple and plain community somewhere in Arkansas. "First I thought they were for me!" he told his mom, about the helicopter noise overhead. "But they've got bigger fish to fry!" He was enjoying his time in the city, he told her—a whole month with pavement underfoot! He'd also been spending a lot of time in jail, he added teasingly, raising his laughing eyebrows at me while he listened to her response.

He was thrilled to be in the same public spaces that were being so forcefully contested every week by Black Lives Matter activists: that, John said, was likely what was going on today. He was right. While we wouldn't learn the details until later, one of the fall's biggest battles between activists and city hall was developing around us as we spoke. The outgoing mayor of Portland had convened a closed-to-the-public session of the city council in a separate chamber to rush through the approval of a new—and strongly opposed—police contract without any more public comment or disruption. The protesters, led by the insurgent local Black Lives Matter group Don't Shoot Portland, were doing all they could to remain at city hall, and the heavily armored cops we saw had been called in to remove them.

It didn't make "good optics," as they say these days. Video published later showed visibly angry cops shoving, pushing, tromping on, and pepper-spraying civilians as they forced them out of city hall—all while the council was approving these same cops' generous new contract. The deal included, among other provisions, one that would allow officers to retire, collect their pensions, and still be rehired back by the department for up to six years. Another item had aroused the ire of protesters: under the new contract, officers would be able review body camera footage before writing up incident reports.

The Don't Shoot demonstrators would lose this particular fight, but they'd been having and would continue to have plenty of success as well—provoking audits of the police and drawing attention to black life and black struggle in this overwhelmingly white city. While many of the group's important street protests were about the high-profile shootings of young black men, the audits and investigations that Don't Shoot and other Portland organizations had helped to instigate had discovered statistical disparities that were stunning even to those used to these sorts of numbers. The activists zoomed in on the figures regarding routine harassment and data collection. African Americans in Portland were cited at astonishingly higher rates for minor offenses of the kind that all urban residents regularly commit in their daily lives. Black Portland residents were charged for *spitting in public* at twenty-seven times the rate of white Portland residents. African Americans were charged with "failing to cross the street at a right angle" at a rate fifteen times higher than that of whites. Jaywalking was a little lower; blacks were charged at a rate eight and a half times higher. Something was clearly going on, and Don't Shoot Portland founder Teressa Raiford and her fellow activists knew what it was: police routinely went to great lengths to get the data of black residents into their system.

Data on traffic stops, from a separate audit, further supported the group's contentions.

*   *   *

Depressing facts like these confirmed undeniable truths about who mattered and how in Portland, but the work Teressa Raiford and her friends were doing was inspirational and auspicious. Here were people contesting the reality-defining authority of the police and allied bureaucracies. Here were people standing up with all the vitality of their fragile bodies against the armored and increasingly automatic will of powers grown comfortably insulated from vigorous public oversight and participation. These were among the few things that could make me feel proudly American. I know some find the bursts of public disorder that unpermitted protest engenders to be threatening—but didn't both the Bundyites and the Don't Shoot Portland protesters have a point when they asserted that this was what being an American was all about? Isn't this what the country was for? If it wasn't, what exactly was it about? Was there anything else besides faith in self-governance that bound us? Everyone was simply demanding the right to live in a world more of their own making. There had even been some real conversations between Don't Shoot Portland leaders and some of the Bundyites this fall. They hadn't gone anywhere meaningful in the end, but they'd happened out there in the shared spaces of the Boisterous Sea.

Soon enough, the weight of history and events would intervene, but for the moment, briefly, I was almost feeling patriotic. What I was feeling was Jeffersonian. This kind of American rhapsody I was indulging in always seems to lead back to the words of the inspiring and disappointing "sage of Monticello." Jefferson is the "founder" to whom proponents of a more disruptive liberty most often turn for their quotes. "The boisterous sea of liberty is never without a wave" is one of his greatest hits. Deployed arguably to cynical perfection on the face of the federal courthouse, it had become for me, at the same time, the name of this place, the literal public squares, the blocks of tree-lined parks under the prison and the court. It also named the tumult and feeling of this day: the helicopters, the clatter of armored cops, the upside-down flags of the Ammonites, the cry of Brand Thornton's shofar, and the distant voices of the Don't Shoot Portland protesters raised in shouted slogans—as now, ejected from *their* city hall, they spilled out into the streets, *their streets*, to continue to express their dissent with their bodies. They would go on now to turn the downtown rush hour into chaos, blocking trains and traffic into nightfall.

Freedom and a Dagger

The quote on the courthouse is part of a trio of famous Jeffersonisms on Liberty and the necessity of turbulence and even rebellion for its preservation. The earlier two are probably better known. "A little rebellion now and then is a good thing," he had famously written from Paris to his friend James Madison. Madison had written to Jefferson, troubled about the uprisings in Massachusetts that he and his friends were already using to help drum up urgency for their upcoming Constitutional Convention. This letter included some of Jefferson's most famous thoughts on the nature of human government and society. From Paris in 1787, Jefferson performed himself at his most optimistic about human nature and the future of democratic republics.

> Societies exist under three forms sufficiently distinguishable. 1. Without government, as among our Indians. 2. Under governments wherein the will of every one has a just influence, as is the case in England in a slight degree, and in our states in a great one. 3. Under governments of force: as is the case in all other monarchies and in most of the other republics . . . It is a problem, not clear in my mind, that the 1st. condition is not the best. But I believe it to be inconsistent with any great degree of population. The second state has a great deal of good in it. The mass of mankind under that enjoys a precious degree of liberty and happiness. It has its evils too: the principal of which is the turbulence to which it is subject. Even this evil is productive of good. It prevents the degeneracy of government, and nourishes a general attention to the public affairs. I hold it that a little rebellion now and then is a good thing, and as necessary in the political world as storms in the physical . . . An observation of this truth should render honest republican governors so mild in their punishment of rebellions, as not to discourage them too much. It is a medicine necessary for the sound health of government.

As the trial wore on, I could see what Jefferson meant about turbulence. I had seen the tumult and fear Ammon Bundy and friends had brought to Harney County; there the necessity of their eventual removal or departure had seemed obvious. And yet I had no desire to see federal power grow more comfortable with deciding what protest activity was unlawful conspiracy to intimidate. The effects of such legal practice, were it to spread, would be chilling on the vital dissent of the kind happening this very afternoon at Portland City Hall. As 2016 wore on, and took some more unforeseen turns, the idea that direct-action dissent could be prosecuted as conspiracy was to become only more ominous.

Jefferson's quote about liking a little rebellion now and then is usually accompanied by another about Shays' Rebellion in Massachusetts, this one from another letter from Paris, after Jefferson had had a chance to digest what that uprising had been used to justify in the draft of the Constitution that had emerged from behind the locked doors and shuttered windows of the secret convention of 1787. He found that his earlier concerns had been warranted; the insurrection had been used as pretext to a constitutional crackdown on Liberty, even if most of the actual rebels had gotten off lightly. He was especially troubled by the enormous amount of power given in the new charter to the national executive, whom he saw as a kind of elected king. He blamed this error on the climate of fear following the Massachusetts revolt: "Our Convention has been too much impressed by the insurrection of Massachusetts: and in the spur of the moment they are setting up a kite to keep the hen-yard in order. I hope in God this article [meaning Article II, on executive power] will be rectified before the new constitution is accepted."

Jefferson's doubts about the enormous power given to the presidency still feel relevant today, especially among those of us longing for a less autocratic executive branch and a more robustly functional—and representative—legislative one. More proper, Jefferson thought, would have been for the men of the convention to have accepted the Massachusetts uprising as a natural and necessary event in a society dedicated to the fostering of liberty:

> We have had 13 states independent 11 years. There has been one rebellion. That comes to one rebellion in a century & a half for each state. What country before ever existed a century & a half without a rebellion? & what country can preserve its liberties if their rulers are not warned from time to time that their people preserve the spirit of resistance? Let them take arms. The remedy

is to set them right as to facts, pardon & pacify them. What signify a few lives lost in a century or two? The tree of liberty must be refreshed from time to time with the blood of patriots & tyrants. It is its natural manure.

* * *

The last of Jefferson's three famous quotes on the necessity of turbulence, from much later in his life, was the one about the boisterous sea. Together they made a T-shirt–ready sequence of slogans, a liturgy of liberty: a little rebellion was good, the tree of liberty was watered with blood, may the bois- terous sea forever churn. But that's where it got complicated. I knew the origins of the first two quotes, but I didn't remember the context of the last. Maybe I'd never known it. I'd been hearing the line all my life, but what had he actually meant by it? Why had he written it, and to whom? On the Day of Atonement, caught up in the Boisterous Sea of downtown Portland, the answer, when I found time to look it up on my phone, proved sobering.

The last quote had a very different history from the earlier two. It was not written from an optimistic middle-aged Jefferson in France to American friends in America, but from an old and increasingly embittered Jefferson writing in America to a French friend in France. The phrase itself, from an 1820 letter to his old friend the Marquis de Lafayette, emerges from an outright lie. "With us," he says of America, "things are going on well." In 1820, this was not true, and everyone knew it. The issue of the expansion, or not, of slavery into Missouri was embroiling the nation in a level of strife not seen since the struggles between Jefferson's Democratic-Republicans and Hamilton's and Adams's Federalists—over, among other things, support for Lafayette's France and the French Revolution. Jefferson seems to know that he can't really hide the fact, and his famous phrase follows immedi- ately, qualifying the untruth of the paragraph's opening pleasantry.

> With us things are going on well. The boisterous sea of liberty indeed is never without a wave, and that from Missouri is now rolling towards us: but we shall ride over it as we have over all others. It is not a moral question, but one merely of power. Its object is to raise a geographical principle for the choice of a presi- dent, and the noise will be kept up till that is effected. All know that permitting the slaves of the South to spread into the West will not add one being to that unfortunate condition, that it will increase

the happiness of those existing, and by spreading them over a larger surface, will dilute the evil everywhere and facilitate the means of getting finally rid of it, an event more anxiously wished by those on whom it presses than by the noisy pretenders to exclusive humanity. In the meantime it is a ladder for rivals climbing to power.

Dispiriting words from Mr. All-Men-Are-Created-Equal. There were hardly any *moral* questions of equal weight, in Jefferson's America, to that of slavery's spread or eradication; but like a grumpy old reactionary, he dismisses that moral claim as mere political noise, more jockeying for position among the ambitious. The metaphor of the boisterous sea had not been invoked as a celebration of the kind of intoxicating tumult that had gripped me on the Day of Atonement on the streets of Portland, but as part of a specious argument meant to assure his antislavery French comrade (and perhaps himself) that somehow spreading slavery to the western states was actually the *best* way to—eventually, gradually, someday, some *other* day—bring it to an end.

Those familiar with Jefferson's writings will not be surprised by this; his reasoning on the subject of slavery is full of the contortions and hypocrisies of the complicated, self-absorbed, and deeply morally compromised man he seems to have been. Strongly against slavery *in principle* (especially for how he saw it as a moral corrupter of white people), he always hedged when it came to its actual elimination. In his maritime metaphor, his main concern comes down to his own personal boat, that it not be unduly rocked in his final days—not even by the cause of human freedom. Jefferson was, after all, wholly dependent on the comforts and wealth slavery personally afforded him; in their defense he'd even go as far as endorsing ugly racist theories about the innate inferiorities of African blood. He was also terrifically fearful of what would happen to him and his fellow white slaveholders if freedom were bestowed—too abruptly, in his lifetime—on those they had brutally deprived of liberty for their own profit, ease, and pleasure.

It was in his long, famous twilight correspondence with John Adams—his once friend, then bitter political enemy, and then friend again—that Jefferson revealed more openly what lay behind his boisterous sea rhetoric on the Missouri issue. In a telling letter written a few months after his letter to Lafayette, Jefferson writes: "The real question, as seen in the states afflicted with this unfortunate population, is, Are our slaves to be presented with freedom and a dagger?" He goes on to give some familiar arguments—that slaves aren't ready for freedom, etc. More importantly, he revealed what he really meant about it all being a question of power. It *was* about power: the federal government's power to end the injustice on which his life and the culture and history of his beloved Virginia were founded—as distasteful as he found this injustice to be, and as eloquently as he may, at times, have expressed that distaste. It was also about another power that he feared: popular power, the power of the People if the People were no longer understood to be exclusively white.

*   *   *

I shouldn't have been surprised. I knew about Jefferson; his racist hypocrisies have been a subject of public debate my whole life. Still, somehow, I was stunned—startled into clarity. History is full of such vertiginous revelations, sudden images, phrases, bare facts that strike like silent lightning—illuminating all over again the world you'd been standing in, disclosing new figures and depths of view that you had never quite seen or let yourself see, but that had been there, nonetheless, right in front of you the whole time. It seemed that 2016 was a year full of such lightning strikes for many of us (the more naive—or the whiter of us, some would add). So much that was happening in the American surround felt not just electrified, but also like it had happened in some form before, or was the resumption of an unfinished, needful argument—usually because it was.

Now the federal courthouse's co-optive use of Jefferson's words seemed much more in line with the purpose of the man's original utterance—to dismiss political turmoil as so much noise. Now the Boisterous Sea seemed also a figure of what Don't Shoot Portland leader Teressa Raiford was describing when she spoke of the left-right conflicts that were to consume Portland—and these same streets and parks—in the coming years: "White people fighting white people for white power," she'd say. On the other hand, maybe it was possible that at some level it didn't matter what Jefferson had meant by the boisterous sea in his letter; maybe his words could still be differently true when fully repurposed by others. This was the hope in Barack Obama's Hope and Change, or the more revolutionary dream behind Martin Luther King's invocations of Freedom: the faith that, despite the fact that the most stirring of American phrases have so often been deployed as ideological smoke, despite the moral failures of the persons who'd said them and written them, that beyond the limited intentions of their authors, the more radical words of the American scriptures could still come to mean what they seemed, on their own, to want to say. Whether or not the words could come true, it seemed to me, would determine how much longer the fiction of America would remain a plausible, livable, useful place. I could see only two other options, neither of which looked remotely useful or livable to me. One was a reactionary, back-to-the-future Trumpism of some sort to which many of the Bundyites seemed easily susceptible. The other was an increasingly unlikely mass acceptance of the status quo: that beyond a common allegiance to the Dollar and the Pentagon, "We" were little more than a bunch of people who hated each other.

The Promised Land

I was likely the only person downtown that afternoon contending with the contorted legacies of Jeffersonian rhapsody and hypocrisy. Everyone else was too busy being their own version of the Boisterous Sea to care. John Lamb was certainly busy. Our conversation was interrupted often—by the roar of the helicopters, the rattle and tromp of body-armored cops, and, more than anything, by the ringing of one of John's two phones. Patriot supporters needed logistical help, as did his own family—because Rebekah was on her way from Montana, and she was bringing a bunch of their eleven kids. (John had delivered most of them. Rebekah had delivered far more children herself; she was a midwife and had presided over the births of hundreds of her neighbors' children.) This was to be Rebekah's first time driving a long distance, and it would also be the first time she had driven in a city; she was a little nervous about it. No longer simple and plain, the family had bought an old public-transport vehicle, a half-size city bus, the kind you see in rural communities or transporting residents from nursing homes. It was the only vehicle big enough to carry them all. Rebekah also liked taking it grocery shopping; she could use its wheelchair ramp to push her shopping cart right up inside.

Our interview done, we walked together, as the clouds and mist began to roll in, to where a few of John's friends had been assembled all day. Their Patriots' Corner had been set up in the shadow of the towering county jail, which doubled as a federal holding facility. It was Yom Kippur, and so it seemed appropriate that periodically Brand would pick up the shofar and the horn-blast would vibrate in the leaves of the ginkgoes above the gathering downtown traffic. Somewhere up there Ammon and Ryan could hear,

Brand assured me. Cops clomped by again, headed in the opposite direction; distant voices raised a shout, and now I felt a tug at my sleeve. Two elderly Chinese women who'd been picking fallen ginkgo berries off the lawn in the park since morning now wanted to borrow my height advantage again. We'd been interacting in improvised sign language off and on since I'd arrived in the park earlier in the day. Now they needed me again, to shake down more of the berries still stubbornly clinging to their branches. I tried to free as many as I could for them, while the women laughed and, as far as I could tell, mock-scolded me for my undeniably poor efforts. It had begun to drizzle a little. Visible through the leaves, beneath the ashy clouds overhead, the police helicopters droned on.

I was still in an expansive, democratic mood, and this little scene only added to it: these women, their laughter, their public harvest of the fallen fruits of the polis, my awkward attempts at assistance. Brand blew another blast on the shofar; the women came closer, fascinated it seemed, pointing at it, talking between themselves. I was taking notes on the whole tableau when I felt another tug on my sleeve. The women had a question, it seemed, their faces bright with that sort of excitement—they were pointing at the shofar, which Brand had placed now on a bench. What was it, I guessed they were asking. "Yes," I said. Not knowing what to say, since they couldn't understand me at all. "Sho-far," I said, pronouncing the thing, nodding my head. "It's a horn," I added moronically. But I'd misunderstood, and now they explained, improvising some charades. They pointed at me, pointed at the shofar, mimed me picking it up, walked to the nearest ginkgo, and mimed me reaching up and whacking at those higher-up berries—the ones I'd failed to reach before. Now they were pointing at Brand. Ah, they wanted me to ask him. They were huddling at me now, beaming the question at me with bright eyes and open faces. So I did it; I went over, tapped Brand on the shoulder, pointed out the expectant pair, explained their request. "No!" Brand said, flabbergasted, furrowing his brow, his usually buoyant demeanor vanishing. "It is not for that!" he scolded me and the women and then turned away. I shrugged at my new friends, trying, and failing, to contain my laughter at this American scene—their determination to get the last of those berries, Brand's offended petulance. It occurred to me that it was more than likely these women had no idea who any of us were—why we were here, why there were so many cops and helicopters about. They probably had no idea what was going on at all. Did they care? Would they have cared if they'd known? They were on another mission, a big and important one, judging by the girth of the sack of berries they'd collected. This also seemed marvelous to me, another layer of public life, a whole other world right here in the midst of the noisy scrum of Liberty. Belatedly, I began to wonder what they were going to make with all those berries. I made to ask; using my face, lips, and hands in the crude sign language we'd deployed earlier. I tried to mime tea-making, food-eating, grinding, mashing, chewing. They gazed back at me with what seemed a vague indifference—and then they, too, turned away. I guessed that I'd failed them—twice. I guessed that they were done with me now. This delighted me too. I was an American poet, exposed again in my uselessness.

* * *

My Day of Atonement tour of downtown Portland still had one more stop. Matthew Deatherage had just arrived in the cluster of Bundyites at Patriots' Corner, and now we took a stroll together around the parks of downtown. He walked very slowly; I wondered if he was in pain. We spoke again of his transformative experience of community on the refuge, and how his own alienated experience of unneighborly American neighbors had impeded, to his mind, access to anything like what he'd felt for the very first time out at Malheur. As Matthew and I perambulated, sometimes raising our voices to hear each other over the helicopter din, we passed the various monuments that adorned the walks under the trees in the two parks—Lownsdale and Chapman Squares—that are framed by the city hall, jail, federal building, and federal courthouse. Most prominent was a huge sculptural fountain of an elk. I remembered seeing images of Occupy Portland protesters astride it back in 2011, when these same parks had been occupied by that tent-city rebellion against the financial elite. There was also an exemplar of a main-stay of public park sculpture in America: a monument to veterans of the mostly forgotten Spanish-American War, when the United States, founded in a colonial revolt, had taken on new colonies by force in the Caribbean and Pacific. A verdigrised foot soldier was posed atop a high pedestal, his eyes wary, his carbine thrust forward, ready to charge or hold his ground. Next we came to a statue I somehow hadn't noticed before in all my time downtown. Seriously overwrought, even for a public monument, this one looked like a 3-D model of a vintage movie poster—an image advertising a western, something about heroic pioneers. As we passed it, absorbed in conversation, out of the corner of my eye I caught some of the words of the inscription in the base. These too were from the sage of Monticello; Thomas Jefferson was everywhere today.

The human figures that rose from the sculpture's Jeffersonian base were a trio of Caucasians, a family, in bronze. The tallest, a bearded man, really looked an awful lot like the Charlton Heston of *The Ten Commandments*. His left arm was around his pioneer bride, who was pressed lovingly to him, as he gestured sweepingly, animatedly, upward with his right arm at some unseen, splendid promontory toward which her eyes followed. The couple's boy-child looked rigid and serious, even with his mother's hands on his shoulder and in his hair. I knew these white folks were hearty pioneers because they were standing in front of a wagon wheel. There is no wagon in the sculpture, but the wheel does the trick. Leaning on that wheel is a single flint-lock rifle. Completing this scene, behind the trio and above the trees, rose the concrete and steel of the Multnomah County jail. Goddamn, I guffawed to myself. Ain't that America: armed, sentimental white people dreaming of the frontier while a big prison creeps up from behind. And good old Thomas Jefferson himself providing the inscription, this time in full presidential mode, from one of his addresses to those he was in the habit of calling "my children"—the Native Peoples of America. In this case the text was from a presidential address to the Osage people of the country that later became the states of Kansas and Missouri. But you wouldn't know this from the monument. "It is so long since our forefathers came from beyond the great water, that we have lost the memory of it, and seem to have grown out of this land, as you have done," says faceless, undead Jefferson. "We are all now of one family, born in the same land, and bound to live as brothers. The Great Spirit has given you strength, and has given us strength, not that we may hurt one another, but to do each other all the good in our power."

If Ammon was being guided by the Holy Ghost, the story he'd set in motion was guiding me, over and over, to figures like this one, where something about American Being seemed, in a flash, laid bare. Here Jefferson's sovereign pronouncement actually declared *historical amnesia* a national and racial condition. But that wasn't all; in doing so, it laid white claims to the American continent on that very condition of forgetfulness. These movie-poster pioneers, these sovereign homesteaders, these original adverse possessors weren't rising, as the quotation suggested, out of the American soil. They sprung directly from Jefferson's words, words that were, in turn, being whispered to No One. This land claim was addressed to phantoms; the Osage are completely erased from the production. There is no suggestion of their existence anywhere in the sculpture, and besides, their homeland was nearly two thousand miles away.

I was alone now. My conversation with Matthew finished, I'd left him back at the benches with Brand Thornton and John Lamb and the rest of Jefferson's living amnesiacs. Jason Patrick was also there now, as were Angie and Lisa Bundy and some people I didn't recognize. I stopped to look back at them all after I'd parted—they made quite a figure themselves. Brand blowing his shofar, the others clustered about him with their banners and flags. Seemingly totally unnoticed by them, the old women were also still there, gathering up the very last of the ginkgo berries of the park. The indifference appeared wholly mutual. Now I turned away from that living American tableau and returned to gaze on *The Promised Land*—because that's what the wagon wheel sculpture, erected in 1993, was actually called. It really was hideous—a historically *and* morally stupid chunk of sentimental schlock. I shudder to imagine the hysteria that would ensue should anyone ever propose to take it down. Above me the helicopters still moved in and out of the mist. There was a blast of sirens, and from somewhere to the west of me, I thought I could hear voices, shouted slogans, it seemed— mingling with the robotic, amplified voice of the law.

CHAPTER TWENTY-THREE

The Day of Judgment

Sagebrush Melancholy

IT WASN'T OVER YET. Not the trial, not 2016 either; both were headed for some more sharp turns. In Portland over the next few days, the parade of defense witnesses went on. Some of these were a poignant reminder of all the feeling, especially male feeling, involved in the saga. Now we found ourselves, most of us for the first time, in the presence of an actual member of the Hammond family whose troubles had started this whole thing. The defense had called Rusty Hammond to the stand. Rusty was Dwight and Susie's son and Steven's brother. The man stomped into the courtroom like he'd emerged directly from the sagebrush. He certainly seemed like he wished he were back there. He was a barrel-bodied bear of a man, with an enormous bear-size skull. Up on the stand, when asked if he'd swear to tell the whole truth, etc., he grumbled in reply, "If you'll let me." And then he glared about—was it sadly or angrily?—at everyone. He'd been brought in to answer one question really, to verify something Ammon had said. Hammond had just arrived on the stand and now already he was done. He stomped back out of the courtroom and vanished.

If Hammond reminded me of a bear, Duane Schrock's face seemed chiseled out of stone, a kind of stone that was also a feeling. What was it about life on the sagebrush steppe that grew men of this size and with this kind of melancholy, this kind of anger? Could it really just be "federal oppression"? I supposed I was seeing them under exceptionally fraught circumstances; maybe they were lighthearted sorts once returned to the range and the comfort of their own homes. I supposed it was possible, but it seemed very hard to imagine, especially with Schrock, who projected a silent, hardened sorrow of a class I've rarely witnessed in a fellow human person.

Schrock had been ranching eight years in Harney County, which made him a newcomer in that place, where people in the ranching community often pointedly counted back the generations into the nineteenth century and the days of Pete French. He'd been one of the principal members of Ammon and Ryan's Committee of Safety, elected the evening of the Beautiful Pattern speech. Schrock was also one of the committee officers who'd stayed on board with the cause, even after Ammon and friends had taken the refuge, a move that had outraged some of his colleagues.

This trial was grueling, and Marcus Mumford's stuttering seemed to grow worse with emotion and fatigue. Sometimes Schrock seemed not to understand if he was supposed to say something in response to the lawyer; he just sat up there blinking, his big, sad, stone face tracking Mumford with what looked like mild bewilderment, a bewilderment that turned at times to amusement, as Mumford struggled onward with himself, hurling his being against that catch in his throat, and the constrictive objections of the prosecution and the judge. Still, together they managed to get a certain narrative flowing—yet another version of Ammon Bundy, Selfless Constitutional Scholar of the People. Along the way, Schrock revealed some things I'd never heard. The most shocking was what he said about the Committee of Safety—that it had been preparing to take over administration of the public lands of the county once Ammon and the crew had left. "Setting up a Revolutionary Government!" I noted on my yellow pad. Why were they telling the jury this? I wondered. It sounded a bit like a conspiracy, an old-fashioned, overthrowing-the-government kind of conspiracy, in a trial where not all that much actually had.

Finished, Schrock stepped down from the stand. On his way out of the courtroom he managed to briefly evade the guidance of the marshals. Slowly he passed up the interior aisle near where Ammon sat. On the table in front of Bundy he deposited his big white cowboy hat, which he'd carried with him into the room and up to the witness box. The marshals noticed belatedly, grabbed the hat, and chased him down to return it before he left the courtroom. There had been a note in it; "I love you," it had read.

The Overflow Room

The whole social circumstance of the trial kept getting at once stranger and more comfortable. Most striking was the feeling that this was something we were all doing together, despite the fact that what we were involved in was a conflict, a conflict now heading toward its climax. The process, the ritual, all the weeks and hours in those rooms, they did their work to grind down antagonisms and make us all a singularity. Every now and then it could produce moments of giddy camaraderie that erased, if briefly, all the pathos and conflict. One came on my last day at the trial. I'd moved up to the overflow room, frankly glad to be out of the main courtroom after the emotion of Shawna Cox's testimony the day before. (She'd played her video, the one she'd shot from inside LaVoy's truck at Devine Canyon, and so we'd all watched those horrible moments together, in rigid silence, while Shawna sobbed, quietly, alone on the stand.) There were fewer of us up here now in the auxiliary room, some having gone home for the day. We the Spectators spread casually around the chamber. Some lounged in the comfy juror seats. The rest of us were down in the pit on the chairs that had been set up on the cleared courtroom floor in front of the gigantic screen. All of us were watching the lawyers and defendants mill about up there on the live feed—it was some kind of short break—and then suddenly something strange happened with the camera. We were all looking at ourselves—We the People of the Overflow Room—but we couldn't understand it. Maybe it was because the courtrooms were identical, but it took us quite a while to get it. You could feel the confusion, the cognitive strain, building in the room among all of us—the reporters, the curiosity seekers, the Ammonites and Ammon-nots. The first person to get it seemed to be Brand Thornton, sitting alone in the front row, looking up at a huge image of himself. You could feel the moment when he recognized what was happening because his arm jerked up and he gave himself the finger—and it was then that we all instantly understood. Many guffawed or burst into trills of loud, open laughter, which brought in a marshal, who scolded and hushed us through our subsiding giggles and snorts, back into mutters and whispers and then sleepy late-in-the-day silence as the image of the downstairs courtroom returned and we returned to watching it: the lawyers murmuring with each other on the floor, the judge sitting alone in silence up at the bench.

It took me a year to finally consider the bigger weirdness behind this moment: the fact that this extra courtroom was available to us at all, that it had been available for weeks and weeks—that this trial was able to take up two of the courtrooms in federal court for basically two months without any evident scheduling trouble. Looking back, it occurs to me that I rarely saw anyone in that enormous building who wasn't involved in this trial or who didn't work for the justice system. Federal courtrooms and courthouses, for all their artfully crafted majesty, are very often quite empty. The truth is, because of pressured plea deals—and the resultant vanishment of the jury from our public life—when compared with the number of indictments and convictions the federal system generates, there are really hardly any jury trials at all.

* * *

This trial was winding down. It felt, on the surface of the proceedings, like the defense was simply running out of things to say. But beneath the surface, something big was happening. In between witnesses, in the conversations between the attorneys, in the back-and-forth emails between the defense and the prosecution, something was brewing, an issue that would explode into the very last minutes of the trial: the issue of who all the occupiers actually were. More specifically the issue was this: how many of the occupiers, at any given moment, had been working in some capacity for the FBI. The government had admitted to the involvement of fifteen confidential informants, including at least nine who had been on the refuge. We knew of two. One was Mark McConnell, the occupation's Judas figure—the Arizona militiaman who'd driven Ammon to his arrest. The other was Terri Linnell, a Patriot activist known on the refuge as "Mama Bear," who'd repented her government collaboration and testified earlier for the defense. But there were so many others—who were they? In discovery, the defendants had received a list of informants, with minor details about them, but with all the names redacted. The defense was pushing at this, led by Neil's attorney, Lisa Maxfield, and Shawna Cox's co-counsel, Tiffany Harris. It was all relevant, as the judge concurred, because one can't conspire with a government agent, and this was a conspiracy trial. By Friday it was agreed that the prosecution would turn over an unredacted list of informants to the judge, who would determine if any of the names needed to be revealed. Meanwhile, Maxfield and Harris were involved in some serious sleuthing, detective work that had begun after a conversation with Matthew Deatherage about a strange man who'd appeared on the refuge in its final days, a dude with a weird European accent who'd led that firearms-training session in the video that the prosecution had shown as one of its key exhibits. It had seemed an especially damning piece of evidence: in it, occupiers poured round after round of semiautomatic gunfire out into the marshlands of the refuge, while appearing to prepare for a federal assault. Maxfield and Harris thought this guy, John Killman, sounded an awful lot like one of the redacted informants; it would turn out that they were right.

*   *   *

The week ended with a long discussion of jury instructions. The jury itself was gone, sent home for the day. Now it was just the lawyers, the defendants, and the judge. They were preparing the text the judge would deliver to the jurors before they began their deliberations, instructing them on the meaning of the charges as well as other procedural issues. They were talking a lot now about language, including minute points of grammar and usage. The judge invoked her early schooling and what the Sisters of the Holy Names had taught her about the proper use of *regardless* and *whether*. Debated for a long time was the use of an *or*. Shawna Cox raised another language concern about the word *elect*. She didn't like this word at all, *elect*. No, it wasn't right. Jury decisions needed to be consensus agreements; *elect* did not imply this. She was right, I thought. After a careful discussion, *select* was the word they hit upon together. Change *elect* to *select*. For a long time, we sat watching while the judge typed notes into her laptop. In the silence we could hear the tippy-tap of her fingers on the plastic keys.

Through the whole conversation about language, the most important word had remained *conspiracy*. What constituted a conspiracy—as opposed to a random gathering of like-minded persons? How did one join a conspiracy? As I listened, I recalled David Fry's hours on the stand earlier that day—he'd been the last of the defendants to testify, and his would be the last long piece of testimony of the trial. As the lawyers and the judge and the pro se defendants continued on about things like the need for a demonstrable "specific intent to join the conspiracy," I pictured Fry arriving late one night in early January, as he'd described today in the witness box. He'd never understood much at all about where he was or the public land issues involved. His time on the stand had made that clear—documenting largely things like his social isolation on the refuge. His lawyer had played some of his Malheur videos, including one of David alone querying a ground squirrel. "Hello, buddy! What are you?" he asked in a high-pitched, cutie-animal voice, while following it around. They didn't have this kind of squirrel in Ohio. Was *this* a conspiracy? He and the squirrel?

This was, of course, the kind of question Fry and his lawyer, Per Olson, wanted the jurors to be asking themselves. At the same time, David had been there; he'd driven more than two thousand miles to join this little rebellion. And if there were a *conspiracy*, if the jury were to decide that this word was the name of the armed community at the refuge, there was a definite moment that Fry, like the others, had chosen to enter into its body. He'd detailed it on the stand. After a Walmart stop in Winnemucca, a name he still hadn't learned to pronounce, he had driven up the back way around Steens and arrived at the gate. It was eleven at night. The truck blocking the entrance was pulled back, and he was asked to follow another truck into the head-quarters. He remembered following its red taillights down into the dark.

*   *   *

I was ready to go. After all these days in court I'd been fragmented into pieces of attention. I didn't remember who I was anymore. I wanted to be home, and to be alone, out in the desert, away from all these American voices. At the same time, I also felt that I would somehow miss this space—the courtroom and all these people I mostly hardly knew. I made more notes about the room as the day's session came to an end, but they were just the same details I'd noted so many times before—the soft polished wood, the carpets, etc. I listened to the rustle of bodies and voices, packing up, heading for the doors, and then I imagined the room alone all weekend, just here, this space, living its own time, without any of them, without any of us. Only much later did it occur to me that this is likely how it very often was here. This quiet sanctum, built for gathering the attention of the People to the lofty work of justice, was likely quite regularly empty. Weekdays *and* week-ends, it sat alone with itself.

On the steps I ran into Neil Wampler. Despite his crew's constant vilifica-tion of the judge, he was willing to admit that it sounded as if Anna Brown's jury instructions were going to be quite a boon to him and his friends. The more specifically that *conspiracy* was defined, the less this sounded like one, regardless of what you thought of their actions. He was in a joking mood, and he imagined proposing an arbitrated solution to the judge: the occu-piers would agree to go back to the refuge and fight the invasive carp that were destroying the lake, one of the biggest issues confronting the Fish and Wildlife staff at Malheur. We all laughed at the image. Then it began to pour. A huge storm was coming in, rain that even worried Portlanders. It was too heavy to make it to my train stop. I called a cab, and even in the few steps from the courthouse overhang to the inside of the car, I was completely drenched.

That Famous Thing

At home, I tried to recover from the scrum, gathering myself back to myself. I spent a few days just going for walks out in the trans-human conspiracy of the desert. Here they all were: the alien plants, spread out and clumped, shooting up tentacles, raspy with pods. Here were the globular assemblages of the rocks, the rattle and cry of birds and coyotes and the sudden flash of jackrabbits—springing from stillness to warp speed and then onward to vanishment. And here was that light, that desert light, touching everything, enforcing an almost unbearable presence, a presence outside all the sovereign claims of the human. But even on my walks alone, out in all that wind and light, the world of the trial had a great pull on my thoughts, sucking me away, out of the wide-open desert and back into the rain and the mist and the windowless courtroom of Portland. Also, the trial wasn't the only thing troubling me, dragging me from the desert moment. It was all mixed together now with the acceleration of the final weeks of the presidential election.

Just days earlier, that contest had seemed essentially finished; it had seemed so clear that Donald Trump had definitively done himself in with his ugly boasts of a predatory sex life. But somehow he was still hanging on and it was making me very uncomfortable—anxious and afraid of what was awaiting us, but also uncomfortable in my own being. It was making me feel awfully, uncomfortably white.

I hadn't thought of Donald Trump for years, until his presidential campaign, but now here he was, on my brain every day, an archetype of "that famous thing—the white man," as the poet Charles Olson had put it, in an earlier moment of our ongoing American racial crisis. Trump had dedicated his life to becoming a thingified cartoon of himself. He was as much a brand as a person; all his stiff movements and his repetitive phrasing added to the impression that he was a sort of pull-string doll. The thinginess that attends all commodities was an impression he actively cultivated in all his live performances. His objectness allowed the white feelings of his fervid supporters to be more easily objectified in him—in the bulky aura of his fame. He seemed like he could hardly move his body, just his hands and neck and mouth, as if all the turbulent, frantic, fearful white American being of his fans was bloating him, engorging him. It was horrible to watch: all those people screaming with pleasure as Trump told them how much they loved him.

This was not a mirror that I enjoyed looking into. I didn't enjoy looking into it because I felt like I understood it: these people were afraid. Their very being felt in jeopardy. Many of their economic lives were increasingly precarious, but their losses hadn't been exclusively material. The primary sites of meaning in most human lives, family and community, had been crumbling for decades now in many American places—both were being further undone presently by the epidemic of opioid addiction. Important in all this were also other kinds of feeling, social feeling, our national feelings about what an ethical person was, what gender and race meant, what justice meant, and what America itself was for. All these had been up for negotiation in recent years in ways that took a lot of emotional work to feel one's way through. Lots of my fellow white folks weren't up to it, it seemed, not yet—or they weren't capable of it, hadn't been given the necessary tools by life or their upbringings or their crumbling communities. Most folks had grown up with almost no understanding of American history—and that was a real disability. The thing was, even if you did commit to doing that work, to feeling and thinking your way through this period of Great American Reckonings, the reward would never be getting to feel completely good or whole. The good feeling of being "a good person" wasn't really available anymore, not to white folks, not in the same ways. America does not prepare people for this, for feeling bad—though it ensures that plenty of them do. It's a nation built instead on Jefferson's amnesia, and on expansive sentiment and action. Trump was offering all of that.

He was offering the biggest, most-winning feelings ever. He offered Sovereign Feelings, in a political world where feeling increasingly ruled. And if I gazed into all this, I saw the ugliest feelings in myself, my middle-age white-man feelings, my own feelings of "left-behindness." I saw those years of repressed fear that I'd end up homeless in Los Angeles. Those fears hadn't gone away when I'd moved to the desert. I'd just run off to where, for the moment, someone like me could afford to live. But that could change in an instant, any instant. When I saw all those Trumpites chanting on my screen, I saw my own poorly repressed paranoia about what "not mattering" would mean for my biological existence and my social and economic being. I did not want to look at that at all. So I kept heading out into the desert, to where there were no mirrors, not for human things like me. But that wasn't really true: anything can be a mirror.

*   *   *

Once again, I was headed out into it. I'd just parked my car near a path into a favorite hike of mine in Joshua Tree National Park, one that led down to an informal monument in a valley filled with desert willows and the creaturely trees from which the park takes its name. The monument was really just a pile of rocks that had been carved on by a miner in the 1920s—an off-and-on psychotic Swedish immigrant named John Samuelson. He'd ended up in the desert, the story went, because he'd turned up in Boston with amnesia and been told by a doctor that the desert air would do his memory good. So he'd headed west, working first with another local miner, before staking his own claim. In his free time he devoted himself to his master-piece. Behind the cabin he'd built for himself was a lump of rocks, granite slabs, many with flat faces, already like the faces of tombstones. He'd applied himself with a chisel and hammer to setting down his thoughts for eternity. They are desert thoughts, in prophet voice, complaints about the corruption of the world and exhortations, often misspelled—English was not his first language—to pay more attention to the earth in front of you. He hadn't lasted long in the desert, not out of a lack of hardiness or desire: the government had reviewed his mining claim and pulled it because he wasn't a citizen.

Losing his claim had been a disaster in the life of Samuelson. He was already unhinged. His time in the desert had allowed him to recover his memory, he'd said, but his recovered memories sounded an awful lot like psychotic delusion. At their center was a fantasy of having been shipwrecked off the coast of Africa, where he'd been captured and made to be the long-time consort of a "pygmy princess," before somehow washing up again, brain erased, on the streets of Boston. Dispossessed of his mining claim, the mad Swede then drifted farther west to Los Angeles County, where his life had turned into another kind of American story. He shot two men in a psychotic drunken episode in a roadhouse. The court noticed his insanity;

he was remanded to a mental hospital, from which he escaped to spend the last of his days cutting down old-growth trees in a logging camp in Washington's soggy Olympic Peninsula, dreaming, in letters back to a Mojave miner friend, of returning to the desert that he'd never see again.

Unable, in my desert walks, to escape any of my own thoughts or the thoughts of the nation, I'd felt like it was a good time to pay old John Samuelson a visit again, check out his peculiar strand of white madness, out there in the big lovely he'd called home for a few years, with its host of Joshua trees, arms lifted—in contorted praise of what? Of what water there was. Of life. "Nature. Is. God. The. Key. To. Life. Is. Contact." is how Samuelson himself had tried to describe it, his halting words chiseled into desert stone.

There was a shiny, well-cared-for Harley parked at the little turnout out near the connector trail that led down to Samuelson's world. I'd been careful not to come too close to it, but there wasn't a lot of room, and so I'd gotten out of my car and run back to make sure that I hadn't gotten too close; bikers can be sensitive snowflakes when it comes to their bikes. And that's when I heard a voice out in the desert, an angry voice screaming—screaming at me. Here now came a big white dude with long, streaming white hair and a beard, dressed all in motorcycle black, running toward me through the scrub. "You touch that bike," he was yelling, "I will put a bullet in your skull!"

I'm not a gun-toting kind of guy, so I don't know why I wasn't afraid of him. Maybe it was all the gun talk in the courtroom. It all just seemed too preposterous to believe—he was going to shoot me for looking at his bike? For trying to make sure I didn't hurt it? Well, if he wanted to, let him, I thought. *Whatever*. Again, I don't know exactly why. Maybe the Trump business had me feeling a little suicidal? Mostly I think I was just beginning the process of getting old; tired of all my own feelings and the feelings of the nation. It was the worst part about 2016—the feelings. "And the worst thing about getting older / Is recognizing the lie inherent in every emotion" was how a contemporary poet, Rod Smith, had put it in a recent book. He was right; every feeling was also a kind of lie—people and their nations were made of so many of them. In a good mood the weirdness of it could be enlivening—as I'd felt in the Boisterous Sea of Portland. In a very good mood I could even believe that the old American lies could be recuperated, that freedom could still come true. But when that wore off, it was all just stupid. Let this fucker shoot me if he wants. Goddamn it. Why not?

"Really, you are going to kill me?" I asked him. "What for?" It turned out he was sure I was eyeing his bike to steal it. And he told me so; he just knew I was trying to take it. "I was just parking my car, man," I told him. "Nobody parks here!" he thundered. At that I had to laugh and I did. It was a parking area. Well, actually, I did. I came here quite a bit, I said. This informal trailhead led to a number of trails, all favorites of mine; I probably came here every week. The guy was right up on me now, a tall, lanky guy, Jeff Banta–like, but considerably hairier, like me I guess, but with a big still-lit joint in his hand. I watched his face process what I was saying, and then I watched it melt. "Aw, man," he said. "I'm sorry. I'm so ashamed. I don't know what got into me—I wasn't going to shoot you anyway." He didn't even have his gun, he told me; it was packed away in his saddlebags. "You want some?" he said, offering me the joint.

It seemed clear to me what had gotten into him. He explained he'd been sitting up in a pile of rocks—the national park is famously full of them, great curvaceous assemblies of monzogranites—smoking a jay and enjoying himself and the view. Then he'd seen me pull up, with clear intent to steal his bike and leave him stranded in the middle of nowhere, hundreds of miles from home. He was on a cross-country solo tour, been going all summer and into the fall, all over the country, was back in the West now, headed for home soon, up in Northern Cali. We chatted, friends now somehow, two middle-aged, dusty white dudes out in the desert. He told me about his trip and all he'd seen, people he'd met along the way—I hoped under better circumstances—and then I said I needed to get on with my hike, and he apologized for keeping me, and again, for threatening to kill me. "Aw, man," he said again. "I feel so ashamed." I told him not to worry. He looked so forlorn about it though, and lonely about it—the man smelled a bit of loneliness, just as much as he smelled of that fragrant reefer—so I ended up giving him a little hug before heading off. I guess I should've felt mad, or scared, but the whole thing seemed exciting and funny now—and it had totally improved my mood. It was also already a part of the story, this story, a part of this book I hadn't even begun yet. As I walked away into the desert, I was already practicing how I was going to tell the tale to my own beloved when I got home that evening, and how afterward I would tell it here, on this page, to you.

And that's when I saw the tortoise. I'd crested a little rise and dropped down into a little canyon, turning up the path that would lead me down to Samuelson's monument. This is when I got what was really the day's biggest desert surprise—more surprising to me even than a big, stoned, paranoid white dude who wanted to ventilate my skull. It was a desert tortoise. For real, right there. Right in front of me. I had seen tortoises before out here—I loved seeing them; they were like a living portal to another kind of experience of time. But one usually saw them only in spring when they came out to munch the desert green-up—what was this big feller doing out here in late October? And why did I assume a tortoise was a feller? I decided, right then, to gender her *she*—what was she here for? Regardless, I got no answer from the tortoise. I could see her watching me; not seeing me, but seeing me. Tortoises have very poor eyesight. I knew I was just a moving shadow to her; she reacted only when I moved, retracting her head a little, otherwise I was invisible. I didn't want to scare her, because I knew that a scared tortoise can pee out a significant amount of moisture—even if their piss was dry—crystalline, a kind of dust. I remembered being told that, but was this really true? Could that be possible? I didn't want to find out either way. No need to scare the crystal piss out of anyone. So I stood there in silence, watching her not seeing me, gazing with wonder on her ancient head. She was big, so she was old, older than me probably. That long, leathery neck; the dark, unseeing eyes; and the big clumpy feet—like a kid's drawing of an elephant's foot.

This fantastic creature—its species-mates, to be precise—had been the inadvertent cause of all this trouble with the Bundy family. Efforts to protect them had spawned this grand, tragical, farcical tale that had dragged me all over the West. All because of you, buddy, I said. They had to clear you out so that Vegas could keep growing, so that rich people's money could turn into buildings, so that it could then turn back into even more money. But we'd begun to feel guilty about that, so they'd needed to clear a little place just for you, which turned out to be the homeland of ornery old Cliven. Jeez—and Cliven kinda looked a bit like a tortoise himself, it now occurred to me, now that I was looking so close-up at a real one. It was all making me feel very sensitive. I guess someone had just threatened to kill me. I guess I'd been scared, but I was more worried about the tortoise. Whatever she'd been doing, I was getting in the way, so I backed off slowly, trying to move without moving, imagining myself as the world's stillest but also vanishing shadow. I got back on the path and headed out over the rocks and into the open desert.

Secrets and Judgments

And then, a few days later, it happened. I knew exactly what it was before I even heard the words. I got a text from a friend. Three words and I knew what had just gone down. "What the fuck?" the text said, nothing more. I scrambled to my computer and googled, and there it was. Not guilty, not guilty, not guilty . . . on it went. All of them had been acquitted. There was footage from those familiar steps of the courthouse. Lots of hugs and shouting and running around. Here was video footage of an exultant Neil Wampler telling a reporter how all this commitment had changed his life, encouraging his fellow Americans to consider taking it up themselves, while indulging in a little stink-eye for the camera as he addressed the feds and the cops, who, he pointed out, had done the only killing in this saga. The texts kept coming in—mostly shock and outrage from my own social world. In that sphere I had become the one who was supposed to explain it, but how could I explain it in a text message, except to say that I had felt this coming in those last days I'd been in court and in the news filtering down from the trial since.

It had been building to this; looking back, that was easy to see. The trial had been weird and loose. The stranger it had gotten, the more it had become about protest and freedom, which was considerably to the advantage of the defense. After I'd left, the case had had perhaps its most dramatic moments. The first came when Neil's attorney, Lisa Maxfield, had summoned to the stand the final, reluctant witness for the defense, FBI informant John Killman. Unsurprisingly, John Killman turned out not to be his real name.

*   *   *

His real name was Fabio Minoggio and he was Swiss, a Swiss special forces veteran who now lived in Las Vegas, which is where Lisa Maxfield's private eye had tracked him down and presented him with a subpoena. In Portland, in interviews with Maxfield and Harris, and then finally on the stand, under oath, the whole story came tumbling out. Minoggio, who was now just finishing the process of becoming a tribal cop in Arizona with the Hualapai tribe, had been following the occupation closely that winter and had wanted to check it out for himself. So he'd called the FBI and volunteered—I guess you can do that. The FBI had given him money for a ballistic vest and to fix his truck so he could get there—that, he said, was all the payment he'd received. He'd gone to Oregon because of his "keen sense of history," he said; he didn't want to miss "a moment in history." As for the cause of the occupiers, he told attorneys Harris and Maxfield when they interviewed him, "My heart is with Ammon, but he is badly advised." Minoggio had also gone because of his "love of gun safety."

His trainings up at the refuge were about gun safety, he claimed. "When I saw how they shot—and how they manipulate the muzzles at each other, I nearly fainted," he reported to Maxfield's investigator. "Gun safety" evidently included teaching newcomers like Jeff Banta hand-to-hand combat and the way to remove someone from a vehicle you've stopped at a roadblock. With the revelation of Minoggio's presence on the refuge and the fact that he, while working for the FBI, had supervised the shooting range depicted in the video that had been perhaps the prosecution's single most dramatic piece of evidence, the defense rested its case. But the drama hadn't ended there.

The closing arguments and the rebuttal had gone off smoothly enough. The defense alleged there'd been no conspiracy, merely a protest. Where was the evidence of intimidation? Matt Schindler asked pointedly. All these weeks, all these witnesses, and no federal officers on the stand talking about being intimidated or threatened. The prosecution argued, shrewdly it had seemed to me, that the occupiers' avowed plan of adverse possession was tantamount to a confession to conspiring to impede: how could you adversely possess something with guns without being involved in planning to keep away the employees who normally worked there? After the arguments were done, the jury had taken up the case, and after weeks of watching the wild trial unfold from the comfort of the jury box, provided some last-minute hijinks of its own.

The deliberations had been going on for days when the jury sent Judge Brown a note. All the defendants and lawyers were summoned to the courtroom—the jury still sequestered in their sanctum—for the reading of this message. There were two notes actually, one from the jury's chosen representative and another from Juror 4. It was the note from Juror 4 that turned everything upside down.

"CAN A JUROR, A FORMER EMPLOYEE OF THE BUREAU OF LAND MANAGEMENT, WHO OPENS THEIR REMARKS IN DELIBERATIONS BY STATING, 'I AM VERY BIASED . . .' BE CONSIDERED AN IMPARTIAL JUDGE IN THIS CASE?" the all-caps note said. The other note, from the jury's representative, had asked what would happen if the jury returned verdicts on three of the defendants but declared itself deadlocked on the other four. It is common for jurors to send notes like this second one, pertaining to jury instructions and the like, but this first note was new ground even for the veterans in the room, including the judge. She took a break, went upstairs to another courtroom, and sentenced a man who had pleaded guilty in the case: Booda Cavalier, Ammon's bodyguard. Cavalier had been in jail in Portland since he'd been taken into custody with Ammon and the others that afternoon in the pines. The judge sentenced him to time served and returned to the courtroom, and the conundrum facing them all.

The situation was fragile. Mere questioning of jurors on the issue could risk mistrial. Federal jury rules made it imperative that no one from outside their inner sanctuary enter the deliberations to influence the jury in any way. The judge confirmed whom Juror 4 had been talking about and then finally decided to take on the delicate task of questioning that juror, Juror 11, separately in her chambers. A court reporter, one of the prosecutors, and two of the defense lawyers came along to witness.

David Fry's attorney, Per Olsen, urged the judge to ask more about whether or not the juror, a man from rural eastern Oregon, had actually made the statement alleged in the note, but the judge had felt that was pressing too far into the internal dynamic of the jury's deliberations. She asked him only about what he had been asked in voir dire back in September, if he recalled what he had said then, and if anything had happened between now and then which he felt might impair his ability to act as an impartial juror. "No," the man said. "No," the court reporter read from her notes, back to the other lawyers and defendants gathered in the courtroom, once the judge and her party of witnesses had returned.

It didn't help the situation. "It's possible this alleged bias may be associated with lack of unanimity on certain charges," the judge observed. She also noted the big, unspoken question in the room; no one knew in what direction this man's alleged bias ran. It had gotten late, the jurors had been sent home for the day, and it was decided to take the issue up again the next morning.

* * *

I had been hearing about all this from the Oregon media—and also from Neil Wampler. The way the woodworker artfully turned his sentences as he spoke had drawn me to him, and we'd struck up a rapport at the trial, chatting in the interstices about history and literature. In his emails from Portland,

Neil was certain he knew which way things were headed; clearly this juror was the one standing in the way of acquittal. It seemed possible to me, but I had nothing to judge his optimism on, except his own certainty and desire—which is what had gotten him into this mess in the first place. Regardless, he was confident and, like Ken Meddenbach, seemed indifferent to the possibility of prison anyway. He ended one of his emails to me quoting T. E. Lawrence:

> "All men dream, but not equally. Those who dream by night in the dusty recesses of their minds, wake in the day to find it mere vanity. But the dreamers of the day are dangerous men, for they act on their dreams, to make them possible. . . . . . . this I have done."

* * *

The next morning the problem had not gotten less thorny. Mumford had filed a motion to dismiss Juror 11, and the judge said she tended to agree that the problem had not been adequately dealt with. She handed out copies of a decision from the Ninth District that she'd dug up on the topic. It was about a case in which a juror had been dismissed because the other jurors had accused him of disagreeing with the law—a nullifier. She was inclined to dismiss Juror 11, but she was not willing to do it unilaterally. If both sides did not agree, she'd have to begin questioning the jurors one by one, which ran a high risk of a mistrial. To avoid that, there would have to be consensus on the dismissal. The defense had already moved in favor, so now Juror 11's immediate fate was up to the prosecution; after a fifteen-minute break, head prosecutor Ethan Knight agreed. It was probably the biggest single decision of the trial.

Some of what had happened in the sanctum spilled out later. This hadn't been a case of jury nullification. After the verdicts finally came, ejected Juror 11 talked to the press from his home in Baker City, Oregon. His name was Curt Nickens, and he'd worked summers for the BLM when he was in college; he'd served on fire crews and been a range tech. It was common for folks out in eastern Oregon to have worked for either the BLM or the Forest Service. These were two of the most reliable employers, outside the state prison system, which is where juror Nickens had worked as a guard for the last twenty years. He was back on the job within a day of his dismissal from the jury, which he credited entirely to the Machiavellian maneuvers of Juror 4, the man who'd sent the secret note about him. He claimed the note had placed true statements and facts in misleading context. Nickens said that he had spoken of feeling biased—but it was as a prison guard, and not as a BLM worker. He claimed he had expressed bias toward one defendant, Jeff Banta, whose tough-guy attitude toward marshals had upset him. (After watching Banta's behavior in court one day, he said, he'd had to go pace in a hallway to calm down.) But he still felt his bias was immaterial; with everyone else, Nickens had agreed that Banta should be *acquitted*. Whatever his personal animus toward the man, he felt there was no evidence Banta had been part of a conspiracy. Regardless, once he'd been removed, it didn't matter if Nickens's version of events was the true one. "Well played Juror number 4," he posted to Facebook when it was all over.

For the moment, all this was yet to be revealed. The judge literally picked the replacement juror out of a hat—from the names of one of the eight standby jurors who'd sat through the trial but not participated in deliberations. The jury had to start all over again now, Anna Brown explained. They'd have to consider carefully all the evidence anew. They were now a new body, a new collective mind, and they would have to arrive at what consensus they could find all over again.

Given this, it seemed like things would take a while, at least another day or two—but no, the very next day word came from the secret chamber: the jury was ready. From nearby coffee shops and law offices, defendants, attorneys, reporters, and spectators rushed back to the courtroom. The jurors entered, the verdicts were passed to the judge. One by one, the defendants stood, facing the jury as Anna Brown read out the judgments. First was Ammon. He rose and faced the twelve strangers—the sibyls, as Neil had been calling them in his emails. Curiously, today Ammon was not wearing his jail scrubs; he was in his street clothes again as he faced the silent representatives of the People. This was the moment. "Not guilty," read the judge. The room was a collective gasp as one by one each of the others stood. Not guilty, not guilty, not guilty. Everyone had been acquitted. It was over, but in the front of the room something else was already happening. Marcus Mumford, in collaboration with the eager U.S. Marshal Service, was about to provide one last moment of high drama.

Upon the announcement of the verdicts, Mumford had immediately moved that his client, in the absence of specific writs from Nevada for his continued detention, be released. It wasn't a strong legal argument—but Mumford was making it with all his heart, which meant he was making a show of himself as always, and he and the judge were getting into it yet again, which is when the marshals closed in on him. Ignoring the judge's orders that they back off, already they were on top of him, wrestling him to the ground. Then he was being tased—right here in the courtroom. Over Mumford's screams, the judge ordered the chamber cleared; soon everyone found themselves in the foyer, bewildered, shocked, and, if you were a Bundyite, elated. Was this really how it had ended: acquittals across the board and Marcus Mumford on the courtroom floor, tased and screaming? Yes, it was.

*   *   *

Out in the matrix the reactions were near-instant; in my spheres, they were mostly horror and shock. *How could these guys get off? White privilege strikes again*, etc., went the chorus. I knew I might have felt the same way if I hadn't been there, but being at the trial had changed the terms for me—it had become a different battle in a different terrain. In Harney County, the Ammonite seizure of old Wadatika land had seemed like a neo-settler reenactment of national crimes, performed with clueless audacity and live ammunition. Then there was the fact that, as outsiders, they'd made their revolutionary stand in the name of militant localism in a place none of them really understood. No wonder many folks—especially given our investments in punishment, amped up across the automated public life of our screens—wanted these people locked up for a long time. But the trial hadn't been about their revolutionary intentions, nor their ignorance or offensiveness—it had been about dissent versus conspiracy and given this, that the Bundyites had won was probably not a bad thing.

That it didn't feel like a good thing to everyone was something I understood. It hadn't helped that that very day some big news had come in from Standing Rock. In North Dakota, body-armored cops had come in armored vehicles (reportedly both BearCats and MRAPs), and used pepper spray, tasers, concussion grenades, and nonlethal rounds in the arrest of 141 protesters. They'd cleared an encampment blocking the Dakota Access Pipeline, despite the earlier decisions of federal agencies to review whether or not the pipeline would be allowed to go forward. The whole history of the continent since 1492 was Adverse Possession as far as the protesters at Standing Rock were concerned, and now there they were, getting gassed and hammered, on the day of triumph for the Adverse Possessors of the Bundy Revolution. The contrast was harsh and instant, ready-made for Twitter. It didn't earn the Patriots any slack that many of them had supported the

Dakota protests. In the moment, the message to many on the left seemed clear: the law set white people free when they committed armed acts of aggression and beat up Natives when they tried to protest peacefully.

Really, everybody was too worked up for there to be much of a conversation. The whole nation was gathered up in the general acceleration pouring us all toward Election Day, less than two weeks off. Someone I knew from the publishing world of New York wrote to me, panicked by the verdict: Did I think this meant that Trump was going to win? No, no, I didn't, I said. I didn't think that at all. I wrote back about how I saw the case, and forwarded a YouTube video of Matt Schindler talking on the courthouse steps about the role state-of-mind evidence and the nuances of conspiracy charges had played in the verdicts. Yes, the timing was disturbing, but really the trial had been too complex, and too particular, to read as an electoral indicator. This seemed mostly like magical thinking to me, spiced with an elite New Yorker's fears of the white rural working class. Still, the question unsettled me. Could it really also mean that somehow? Maybe this was how tides turned.

Then I got a text from Jarvis. "I'm done talking with everybody," he wrote. "You're a cool dude," he said, to console me, I suppose. "Good luck on your book," he added. We'd be in touch often over the coming months, but never with the same regularity as before. I can't imagine he or anyone in Harney County had seen this coming. Really, nobody who hadn't sat in court every day during the defense testimony could have predicted it. Up until the end, and all the shenanigans with Fabio and the jurors, I'd still assumed they'd be convicted; John Lamb had told me he'd assumed the same. I imagined Jarvis in his big chair in his living room, tapping away in the light of his phone screen. Other people from Burns came back to me too. I remembered the expressions of anxiety and anger that had overtaken their faces as they'd recalled for me some of the more harrowing and infuriating moments of the occupation. I put down my phone, got up, and went outside. There was wind, and there were stars. I imagined the sky one thousand miles north in the basin. I imagined the colder darkness of the basin night, as it turned toward winter, toward the deeper cool of November. In a few days it would be exactly one year since Ammon's night of holy googling had spurred him out the door and over the Stinkingwater Mountains to the Hammond Ranch. I imagined the land now, under those stars that had led Jeff Banta and the rest of the Final Four to gasp with ecstasy and bewilderment that first night around their fire.

My mind traveled, south from the refuge, up into Steens. I saw the gorges, and I heard the roar of the water, touched the huge chunks of basalt, smoothed into paws by the millennial passage of the stream. I had lain on one of those rocks under the chiming aspens on a long, bright afternoon just a couple of months earlier. There wouldn't be nearly as much water now, but it would still be roaring, down off the gorges into the sage and juniper, out through the willow-lined channels, past the land of the Hammonds. Maybe at the ranch that surly bear of a man, Rusty Hammond, now exulted. Maybe. I couldn't imagine that man would ever really *exult*—so I imagined him heavily asleep instead, breathing unconsciously in the dark while the heavens whirled above the roof. I went back inside and I typed up a starlit basin rhapsody, pouring all my torn feeling about the verdict into a lyrical celebration of that place I'd come to love. When I stopped typing, I searched the actual weather. In the Harney Basin it had been overcast all day and evening. There would be no stars there now; the cloud cover was thick. It was raining a little. It looked as though it had been drizzling all day.

CHAPTER TWENTY-FOUR

Reconstitutions

Dead in America

I WAS ALONE WHEN IT HAPPENED. I had been at work, teaching at the art school I've taught at for more than a decade. It's not a place where the possibility of Donald Trump's victory had been taken seriously, except perhaps in quickly repressed spasms of dread of the sort I'd been suffering. But that evening, as the tallies began coming in from the East Coast, the results from Florida hadn't looked right. A panicked colleague stopped me in the hall to tell me it was over, the numbers were clear, we were doomed. He'd closely watched the returns come in from every presidential election for decades, and he knew those counties in Florida; the future was written in the numbers he was pulling up on his screen. I didn't believe him; I didn't want to believe him, and so I didn't. Besides, if this were happening, which I was certain it wasn't, I didn't want to be at work. I left my colleague inconsolably pacing the hall, saying something about people getting rounded up, old dissenters like him. Clearly this was all hyperbole, clearly he was panicking, cracking a little. It had been a mad year, so I excused him for it, silently, in my head, as I fled his company. I got in my car and started home. I had almost three hours of driving ahead of me. By the time I'd crossed over the mountains and hit the open desert, I'd learned that I'd been wrong. It really was happening. Out there under the Mojave stars my radio strained to pick up the news. Shocked voices gurgled in and out through the static, but their message was perfectly clear. My colleague had been right; the gloomy prognostication of Matthew Deatherage had come true. The next morning when

I woke up, I felt something I had never felt in all my days. For the first time in my life I wanted to own a gun. No, I didn't just want *a gun*; I wanted *a lot of guns*.

My next thoughts were practical. Where would I keep all the assault rifles I now wanted, needed, for what was coming—this new American future, this resurgence of all the worst impulses, unfettered, of the American past? I'd probably need to bury my arsenal somewhere, to keep it safe. Would I need a backhoe to dig a proper hole? Would I just wrap the guns in a tarp, or did I need some kind of metal chest? Would I be pouring concrete? About that backhoe—how could I borrow or rent one, but secretly, or without anyone knowing my purpose? As the images developed—myself rooting in the desert dirt to bury my new weapons cache—it startled me back into humor, and sanity, maybe. Was it sanity, or was that just complacence? Were they the same thing? When were they not?

All this led to another alarming thought: How could the election of a person as innocuous as Barack Obama have provoked similar reactions in so many panicked white folks across America eight years ago? That the election of the country's first black president had occasioned an extended mass version of the same level of existential panic I had just been briefly experiencing—well, that went a long way to explaining, all over again, in miniature and from the inside of the feeling, how crazy the last eight years had been. A craziness 2016 had condensed and recapitulated.

Not that this intimation was very helpful. If that is how millions of people had felt, looking at the first African American in the White House, if this had helped make them willing to vote for "The Donald," then maybe we were just finally, terminally fucked. (Forgive the obscenity, but *doomed* is too sweet, too soft, too round and pleasing a word.) Maybe this America thing, this Freedom thing, this aspirational nation, this futureland built on the faith that America's best words might yet still come true, maybe this phantasm had just dissolved for the very, very last time. It was probably all just Jeffersonian nonsense anyway. Maybe America just wasn't something that was ever *really* going to work out. Probably that should have been clear to everyone a long time ago.

Mostly this was a feeling. I was having a lot of feelings, but they all fit inside this one big, horrible, historical feeling. Now I was feeling Adversely Possessed for real. And the president-elect looked like he was too. Trump seemed entirely crammed with ugly, historical feelings, stuffed-up with a rabid self-regard made mostly of anger and paranoia—feelings that weren't only his, or even really his, but were rather the big feelings of the worst of our history. It made him look, to me, like a monster conjured up by that history. *We* were *made* of that bad history—other things too, but also always that—and he was it, condensed. He was like a god of fear, and under his star, our vaunted diversity was reduced to the diversity of our inherited terrors.

Now I was ranting. I could tell—I was saying "we" a lot. But it didn't stop me. I've been ranting on and off ever since. In the car, walking in the desert, doing the dishes, cooking dinner, lying on the couch. Sometimes, in the early days after the election and then the inauguration, I'd wake up seemingly mid-rant, already reaching for my phone to see what had happened in Washington that morning while the California desert was still dark. Yes, there were moments of hope, and laughter, always hope and laughter, thank god, but then the baseline feeling came back: fucked, fucked, terminally fucked. In the last minute, when what was most needed was to make a grand turn, a turn en masse, to face the horrors of our history and the enormous ecological consequence of that history, this fictive political entity I was calling "we" had somehow *chosen* the electrified corpse of Manifest Destiny. This is real, this is where we are, this is what we are made of. No—no passing the buck—this is what *I'm* made of. "It's good to be dead in America," I began saying to myself, a mantra borrowed from a poem of Peter Gizzi's. I said it a lot in those months, maybe every day in late 2016 and on through 2017. I was still saying it when I arrived back in Portland for the second Malheur trial.

*   *   *

I was glad to be back in the Boisterous Sea, back in the American story, instead of just watching. A lot had happened right here in Portland since I'd been gone, beginning before the election, in the days right after the not-guilty verdicts of the first trial. Jubilant Bundyites had gone on celebrating for a few days in the parks under the towers of the courthouse and the prison. They'd carried on into the weekend, when some other protesters came by and dampened their spirits—with fire.

These protesters were from the same group, Don't Shoot Portland, that had been pushed out of city hall on the Day of Atonement in the protest melee that had filled the court district with armored cops. Teressa Raiford, the group's leader, and her friends had all been feeling a gap between the kind of justice the occupiers had been able to get and their own comparatively brutal treatment in Portland over the last month. When the group came past the courthouse in a loose unpermitted mass, more like a flock than a march really, the Ammonites were having a cookout; they also had a big collection of full-size American flags they were passing around. Teressa told one of her fellow protesters to get one of them—it was time for a little counter theater. "Well, burn that motherfucker!" she said when her comrade returned. "We're activists. We have to do it," she recalled prodding her reluctant friends. She explained to me why later that winter. "We had to say, symbolically, that, look, there's an inequity, you celebrating your victory here at the same time as our brothers and sisters in Standing Rock were getting sprayed with rubber bullets, the same time we're getting beat up and pepper-sprayed for protesting in city hall. It was a symbolic gesture with our community around the world."

Somebody had found a lighter, and the flag burst instantly into flames. "This was perfect," Teressa recalled. "It burned *so fast*." She'd burned other flags in her day, but something was wrong with this one—or right, if what it was for was for burning. "Made-in-China flag!" she said, laughing. "Last flag took me five lighters!" A tearful woman from the Bundy crew—the person they'd gotten the flag from—now confronted them. "Give me back my property!" she was saying. "Why would you burn *my* property?"

The situation grew truly tense, ugly for a moment. In video footage you can see a man at the Bundy Revolution cookout, a middle-age white dude in a wheelchair, whom I'd never seen during the trial and have never seen since, yelling at the protesters. "Black Lives are thieves!" he was shouting. Don't Shoot activists were yelling back about burning crosses and "your friends in the KKK!" But then, just as quickly as the tensions had escalated, it was all defused. A Don't Shoot protester had grabbed the bullhorn and his voice rose up above all the others; he was shouting that there was no excuse for these two sides not to get along, that both "were fighting the same fight, on different playing grounds, different battlefields." The problem was the "rich motherfuckers just janked up some more cash." Applause and laughter burst out on both sides; there were even hugs as the protest moved along, herded up the street by the Portland cops who'd been nosing their cars into the Don't Shoot crowd the whole time.

The call to *"get a-fuck along!"*—as the young man with the bullhorn had put it—had worked that afternoon, briefly, in the moment on the streets of the Boisterous Sea, but in the days immediately ahead, something much bigger was coming, and no single person was going be able to grab center stage and calm everyone down. The panic that would grip much of the nation postelection would seem strongest in Portland. Mass protests, led by a newly emergent local group, the Portland Resistance (headed up by one of the leaders of Don't Shoot Portland, Gregory McKelvey), turned into what the police had labeled riots, with seemingly nightly confrontations between more radical, masked protesters and police. These provided news feeds with images and video of smashed windows and tear gas and hundreds of arrests. Other footage showed riot-geared police shooting tear gas canisters and tossing flash-bang grenades into milling, chanting crowds that had taken to the streets and refused to disperse. In the long months that followed, the Bundyites and the Don't Shoot protesters started to seem like figures from another era. In those same parks under the jail and the federal courthouse, new, more amped-up camps of angry American bodies, tattooed Trumpites and masked antifascist anarchists, would clash. Now there would be no drive to get along: these different crews seemed intent only on screaming at each other, provoking and abusing and beating on each other whenever they could land a blow through the running lines of armored cops struggling to enforce a fluid, moving borderline between them. These gatherings wouldn't look like protests anymore; they'd look like rehearsals for something more like civil war.

$$* \quad * \quad *$$

Unlike so many in Portland and in the rest of America, Teressa Raiford was not panicking in 2017. She was playing a longer game, and the battles over Trump didn't interest her so much: "White people fighting white people for white power," she told me, that's what it all looked like to her. "Their 'our power' doesn't include me . . . They aren't fighting for us. 'We need to just do it now'—that's part of the narcissism of white supremacy—the liberator, you know, the top dog—*the voice* is in their heads and it's *right*," she explained. "Everybody thinking they're *the answer*, I don't think anybody's the answer—not individually. You need to engage with a dynamic." Engaging dynamics was the constant work of her movement, and her life—and that's all there was really. That work, that engagement—the secret abundance of it all seemed reflected in Teressa's quiet and dynamic face, in how her visage called upon and then sloughed off any description I sought to give it. She had melancholy glee; she had warm severity. The full tonality of her commitment made me very glad to be around her that winter.

Her family had been here for five generations—the magic Oregon number I had heard so often—or longer than anyone could guess, if you traveled back along some of the Native American strands in her ancestry. In Portland, her family's story traversed local twentieth-century history. Her great-grandfather had been part of the first black auxiliary police, and her grandmother had lived in Vanport, the community along the Columbia River that had sprung up to house workers during World War II and had been wiped out conveniently in a disastrous flood when the war was over. More recently, her family had also been at the center of one of the uglier later twentieth-century moments between the black community and Portland cops. One night in 1981, Portland police officers had laid dead opossums at the door of her grandfather's restaurant. The cops had surplus opossum corpses on hand because of a game they'd been playing among themselves—a competition to see which officers could kill more opossums. There were rules and a scoreboard, evidently. Forgotten by many now is the racism long attached to North America's marsupials, but at the time there was no ambiguity in the message the tittering cops were leaving on the doorstep of Teressa's grandfather's soul-food restaurant, an important social site in the community. An angry protest had resulted in the firing of the officers, which had resulted in counterprotests from the police union, which had won their reinstatement. The incident, like most of the history of Oregon, like most history of most places in America, was largely forgotten by the white majority of the city by the time the twenty-first century came around. Portland had been famously populated with newcomers from the 1990s on, as young white folks had established its reputation as a bohemian, progressive-lifestyle paradise.

The history of Oregon included an especially troubled relationship to the document in the pockets of the Bundyites. According to the official narrative, the state had somehow "forgotten" to ratify the Fourteenth Amendment to the U.S. Constitution and hadn't gotten around to it until 1973. There was a lot of embarrassment, shame, and silence around what was framed as a simple error of omission—unsurprisingly, there was more to the story. The truth was that Oregon had actually not forgotten to ratify the Fourteenth Amendment. In fact, it had ratified the amendment. But shortly afterward, anti–Fourteenth Amendment Democrats had regained the legislative majority. Despite the fact that the amendment had already been passed on the national level and become part of the Constitution, in a fit of racist pique, Oregon legislators went ahead in their symbolic but resoundingly meaningful vote and rescinded the state's earlier ratification. And so things had stood until 1972, when a man from North Portland named William McCoy was elected to the Oregon State Legislature as its first African American member.

As McCoy would have known well, at stake in that de-ratification had been the desire at the time, widely expressed, of a majority of Oregon's tiny white population to set itself up as a kind of white utopia, something that had been encoded a decade earlier, with overwhelming public support, into the state's founding document, the Oregon Constitution. In the 1850s, white Oregonians, newly settled in the territory, had come to that magic moment that Ammon had performed on stage for his prospective Committee of Safety: the crossing over from territorial status to the status of statehood. This was the ritual instant in Ammon's Beautiful Pattern that produced nothing less than Freedom itself. In the Oregon territory, in the 1850s, however, as Oregonians debated the issue of statehood and then moved on to the framing of their own constitution, issues of race and *unfreedom* were foremost on everyone's minds.

While some Southern transplants advocated for entering the union as a slave state, the state was mostly antislavery. Many of Oregon's early pioneers were non-slaveholding whites from Southern states and midwestern border regions. These settlers often hated both slavery *and* the idea of living among free persons of African descent; these sentiments were encoded into Oregon's foundational document. While voters overwhelmingly rejected slavery— voting 7,727–2,645 against it—the vote in favor of excluding free blacks and "mulattooes" from the newly created free state was even more one-sided, by a margin of 8,640–1,081. The tiny white populace seemed to agree with the sentiments of their chief justice George Williams, who had urged that the new constitution "consecrate Oregon to the use of the white man." In the end, Oregon was to be the only state ever to be admitted to the union with a black exclusion clause in its founding charter.

Even before statehood had been on the immediate horizon, excluding non-whites had been a priority in the territory. In the 1840s, Oregon had banned slavery, but also banned settlement by persons of African descent; flogging, at one point, was the official punishment for any black person caught attempting residence in the territory. Oregon's territorial delegate to the U.S. Congress explained the necessity of such exclusions, in terms of frontier military strategy. The real danger of a black population lay, he argued, in what it could give in an antiwhite alliance with the Indians:

> The negroes associate with the Indians and intermarry, and, if
> their free ingress is encouraged or allowed, there would a relation-
> ship spring up between them and the different tribes, and a mixed
> race would ensue inimical to the whites; and the Indians being led
> on by the negro who is better acquainted with the customs, language,
> and manners of the whites, than the Indian, these savages would
> become much more formidable than they otherwise would, and
> long and bloody wars would be the fruits of the commingling of
> the races.

I'd call this quote remarkable, but in American history, it isn't. Still, it
opens quite a window onto the psychic terror at the interior of settler life.
Here was yet another kind of Adverse Possession. Black folks, to the white
minds of Oregon—or at least to their spokesperson—had been natural
spies lurking in the houses of their enslavers, just waiting to get out to the
frontier to pass on crucial, cultural intelligence to the "savages." At all costs,
this unholy conspiracy had to be nipped in the bud, before a new, formidable superrace could be formed: black Indians, with freedom, intimate
reconnaissance, and a whole bunch of daggers. Reading these words aloud,
you can feel it—the terror rising from the chest, constricting the throats of
dead white bodies now long vanished, dissolved in earth and time. The
bodies might be gone, but in America today the fear is still around.

Teressa cracked up when I read her the quote from Samuel Thurston,
Oregon's territorial representative—she'd never heard this one before.
"Ha! Wow. That's me. The Black Savage. It's true. He was right. That guy
was right. But hey, stop killing people and we will stop protecting people."
The terror that rises off that long-dead man's words was the core of the
whole issue for Teressa—it was that fear that still posed mortal danger to
people who looked like her. The officer who'd shot Tamir Rice in Cleveland
had been afraid of the twelve-year-old, he said; the officer who'd shot
Michael Brown in Ferguson, Missouri, had also cited fear in his defense—
Brown was "like a demon," he claimed. Closer to home, the Portland officer
who'd shot seventeen-year-old Quanice Hayes in the head, one week before
the second Malheur trial began, had explained under questioning that
though the young man had been unarmed, kneeling on the ground, and in
the process of surrendering, his fatal shooting of the teen—after seeing
Hayes reach for his waistband—had been "absolutely a conscious decision
on my part to defend myself." (A replica gun was found near Hayes after

his death, though officers at no time had seen Hayes with the realistic-looking toy weapon.)

To Teressa's mind, it was fear, not the police, that she and her friends were confronting in their street protests. Unlike the Bundyites, who spoke often of taking stands—or in the settler idiom of claiming, using, and defending—hers was a fugitive vision of people in movement as they repurposed the spaces of the city. Teressa proudly showed me video footage of a recent Don't Shoot protest. It was full of people gathering and flowing through the streets, *their streets*, pursued, slowly, by the police and an armored sound truck. The sound truck was really a voice truck, a Voice of the Law truck. Over and over the Voice—of a flesh-and-blood officer, well trained to simulate bodilessness—repeatedly declared true what was patently untrue: that this street full of flocking human bodies was *open to vehicular traffic*.

To Teressa, it was this flocking that was the goal—not standoffs with the cops. "It's a continual engagement with a dynamic," she explained. "I think it's street art at this point." What she and her friends were developing was a different idea of safety. "All white people have to say is that they are afraid in order to kill us; we have normalized violence in the name of safety." Real safety, to Teressa, was something else. "Safety is an acknowledgment of each other. Protest makes us work that out in a fire. The transgressions, the arguments—they have to happen. It's all a part of our growth. All of that is necessary for us to get to know each other. We are building safety. We don't have to be afraid of each other; we can live together."

"Thanks, but No Tanks"

Jason Patrick agreed with Teressa Raiford when it came to fear in America. The most prominent of the occupiers facing trial this time around, Jason had come to the Bundy Revolution through anti-police-militarization activism and libertarian citizen journalism. He'd protested against the nationwide arming-up of local police forces with military-grade equipment—everything from tanklike armored personnel carriers to rocket launchers to bayonets purchased with government grants or donated directly from the Department of Defense. Images of the use of tanklike vehicles and snipers by Ferguson police after the shooting of unarmed teen Michael Brown had provoked congressional hearings. Finally, the mainstream of the country had looked at the statistics and the budget lines. The numbers were staggering. Billions and billions of dollars had been spent in recent years outfitting local police forces like armies and training military-style rapid-response teams. Fear, to Jason's mind, is what had allowed it to happen—fear and good old complacency. "Americans are superficial—they just are. It's frustrating," he told me. Superficiality and the power of fear had allowed the passage of crime bill after crime bill. Always, it seemed, framed in military terms: the war on crime, the war on drugs, the war on terror. Now we had more prisoners than anyone in the world, and even small towns had fully militarized SWAT teams with little to do but train and wait for the first opportunity to kick down some doors and storm American homes. It was not meant to be this way, Jason thought; being an American meant standing up to this and saying no.

Jason Patrick always introduced himself simply as "an American" when asked by the press for his group affiliation. I asked him what that meant to him. "It's taking a hold of the Constitution and it's realizing that it's a contract we handle that allows the government to exist; it's the rules they are supposed to follow to exist," he told me. To Jason's mind, popular sovereignty had by no means been given over to the government in the act of creating it, of constituting it. "The power absolutely remains there. The government does not exist without our consent," he said. That the founding charter was a contract, to his mind, established certain serious responsibilities—for the people as well as for the government. "If it's a contract, who enforces it? You have rights but only if you claim, use, and defend them. And I claim them, I use them. I show up to be the press."

Jason had been showing up for a while now. Like many of the more libertarian-leaning Bundyites, he'd been inspired by presidential candidate Ron Paul. It was to Paul he credited the initial exhortation to "be the media." (Disappointed by the strikingly poor percentage of media coverage—given the actual polling numbers—devoted to Paul's campaign for the Republican nomination, many of his followers had taken to the internet in 2012, where his positive blog coverage had considerably surpassed other Republican candidates.) Like Jason, the activist focus of many libertarians in the second decade of the century had been often trained on the militarization of police. The large, vocal libertarian community of Keene, New Hampshire, had mobilized forcefully against that town's acquisition, with federal money, of a BearCat armored vehicle. One of the rationales put forward for the purchase of this chunk of serious military hardware—that the local pumpkin festival could be a target for terrorism—had earned the town its share of

ridicule and helped garner the anti-BearCat protestors some national attention. When a municipality in his rural Georgia county had gotten its own
BearCat, Jason had helped lead protests against it. The slogan of the New
Hampshire protestors—"Thanks, but no Tanks"—had been his slogan as
well. This activity seemed to him to have resulted in his being targeted by
local law enforcement. "Suddenly," he said, "they all knew my name." The
extra police attention did not deter him in his activism. He traveled near and
far following stories. There was no shortage of abominations.

He'd been one of a small group of activists who'd flocked to the rural
township of Cornelia, Georgia, in the Allegheny foothills, in the wake of yet
another American tale of a no-knock warrant gone wrong. An overeager
small-town SWAT team had stormed the home of a family of Laotian immigrants with a warrant they'd obtained when a confidential informant had
bought a small amount of meth from a relative of the family's who didn't
live at the house but had met the informant nearby. On the basis of the buy,
local law enforcement had deployed its tactical assault team. Kicking the
door in without knocking, they'd stormed the place, assault rifles at the
ready. Right before bursting in, they tossed a flash-bang grenade through
the window. It had landed in the crib of nineteen-month-old Bounkham
Phonesavanh—called Baby Bou Bou by the family—scorching him all over
his body and tearing open his little face. Somehow Baby Bou Bou survived;
he's been through fifteen surgeries since. In the days after the event, Jason
visited the house in Cornelia, talked to the family, and confirmed for himself
and his online network of friends that this wasn't any kind of drug house.
He knew, as many Americans were now coming to learn through stories
like the tale of Baby Bou Bou, just how common such raids had become in
America, often based on warrants obtained through mistaken, outdated, or
incomplete information. Such raids often resulted in no arrests, the location
of no contraband or only minuscule amounts of drugs, costly lawsuits,
serious injuries, and even deaths. The ready availability of SWAT teams had
also provoked one of the more alarming popular cultural mutations of recent
years: the online video gamer subcultural practice of "swatting," where
gamers call in fake live-shooter scenarios at the addresses of their rivals,
resulting in overeager, sometimes lethal SWAT responses. To Jason, none
of this was acceptable; something had to be done.

In April 2014, he'd been at a worksite—he's a roofer by trade—when
messages came through on his phone about Bundy Ranch. "I think I saw the
video of Ammon Bundy getting tased about two hours after it happened . . .

I was on a roof in Georgia." He read more about Ammon on the internet right there on that roof. "This guy's the real deal," he thought, and off he'd gone, the very next day. He'd meant to take a detour on his way out to investigate another police shooting he'd been troubled by, the killing of an unarmed and homeless mentally ill man named James Boyd, shot while camping on public land at the edges of Albuquerque, New Mexico. Instead, he got swept up in the Bundy Revolution. Over the next year it had led him to the Sugar Pine mine standoff in southwestern Oregon and then to Burns, where he'd been one of the earliest Bundy supporters to arrive in town. He'd spoken at the very end of Ammon and Ryan's Committee of Safety meeting, where he told his roof story and promised the crowd that many more folks like him would come in support of the People should they choose to stand. He'd then been one of the first to enter and occupy the refuge on January 2. And now here he was, the principal defendant in the second Malheur conspiracy trial.

Jason's tale made him sound a bit like a missionary, which is what he was, I suppose—preaching America to the Americans. He is engaging, sharp, and funny, with a pleasant Irish sort of face; when bearded, as he was then, he did look a little like the actor who'd given him his Malheur nickname, "Clooney"—absent the Hollywood physique. During the occupation he'd been a notable voice for moderation and against fear, the intoxicating effects of which were all around him. To Jason, Malheur had not been a standoff but an assembly. He had seen the occupation as something more like a peasant rebellion of old; they were the farmers out there with pitchforks and torches, asking for their grievances to be redressed. He thought the federal government could be properly restrained *before* something like civil war or revolution happened. "We can push this thing back into a box," he told me. But what that required was a greater awakening to what was going on, and to what it meant to accept the full responsibility of being an American—a constitutor, not an object of government. "We exist *without* them," he said, "without the identifications—that's a magic trick."

*   *   *

For the Patriots it always came back to the preamble of the Constitution. *We the People . . . in order to form a more perfect union.* It was our government, we came before it, and we existed beyond it; it was an appendage of us, and not vice versa. But was there really such a "we"? Did this entity—this original community, the People of the Preamble—even exist? Had it ever?

A tour through the words of the actual delegates to the Convention of 1787 makes it hard to understand the first phrase of the preamble as anything other than a cynical formality. As historian Woody Holton, who has written extensively about the debates of the Constitution, told me frankly: "The preamble starts with a bullshit phrase, 'We the People'—'don't worry, you aren't going to lose your popular sovereignty.' But the rest of the preamble consists of very honest statements about how the federal government is going to exert power over the people." That is what it did, and has done. "Domestic tranquility doesn't mean me sitting by the fireside with my family and my cat," Woody explained. It meant having the power to squash uprisings like Shays' Rebellion. It meant, 230 years later, having the power to squash the Bundy Revolution as well.

This has created a historical conundrum over the decades and centuries since ratification—for both the right and the left, Holton pointed out. Many critics of power have discovered, when they've looked into things, that it is an anti-Federalist position that is closer to their hearts—but with that comes a very difficult choice: "Do you get the cachet of being just like George Washington, or do you see your actual fathers were the people that Washington was trying to put down?" The Bundyites had chosen, by and large, the first option. Few of them even spoke about Thomas Jefferson, much less the more radical anti-Federalists, like Herman Husband, whose positions on government were often closer to their own. Ammon even called himself a Federalist. Jason and Neil wouldn't go that far: Jason stated flatly that he was not a Federalist; Neil suggested that there was some confusion in the ranks on that subject—but they both still had that Constitution in their pockets. There they stood, in that contradiction. They dwelt in the No Place you found yourself in if you tried to reconcile the idea of a total popular sovereignty retained in "We the People" with the reality of the federal government that the phrase had been adroitly deployed to create, and to which "the People" were subject.

Bending Toward Utopia

No Place is a translation of Utopia, and Utopia is another thing that Jason Patrick liked to talk about. "We're never going to get to Utopia, but we have to bend toward it. I don't believe in the utopian idea as a destination we're going to get to—but you need it as a balance. Mine is based on the Bible:

love your God, love your neighbor as yourself." The spirit of Christian neighborliness was something he loved about the Patriot movement: "We care about each other. Black Lives Matter movement too—they care about each other." It was that mutual care that he wanted to communicate to his fellow Patriots in the fall of 2016, when he'd hoped to bring the two movements together during the first Malheur trial. His efforts hadn't gone so well. He'd spoken with Teressa and other Don't Shoot leaders about possible collaboration. "I knew the plight [Teressa] was talking about. She was a little skeptical of me, and I wouldn't blame her." Besides, she'd told him, they simply had too many people on their side who wouldn't look kindly on such an alliance. Jason admitted that he had the same problem on his side— "because we're people," he said. Again it came back to fear. "People love their fear," he told me. "They like to take it out, pet it, stroke it. They love it," he said, "because it is theirs."

Jason wished he'd been there that day when Don't Shoot Portland had marched past the courthouse and the Bundyite celebratory barbecue. Teressa and her friends had done a die-in in front of the courthouse—and the Patriots had just watched. If only he'd been there, Jason rued. "I would have joined them, I would have said, 'Come on, let's lie down in the street with them. They're sad about their guy, we're sad about our guy.'" I pictured it for a moment: as an image it bent toward Utopia. All of them, all the bodies, all necessary, all play-dying in the street together—and then rising up again, and walking. It was an image of a ceremonial Reconstitution, the kind that still has never happened in America, with the erasure of Reconstruction and so much of the rest of our history. I suspect the idea of We the People is always only that: an idea, an image. But if it were ever to be meaningfully more, beyond fleeting moments of direct action and brief assertions of popular will, it would have to look like that somehow. Everyone dying together, rising together. One by one. A miracle: the great American die-in and resurrection.

But that's not what happened. Instead Teressa and friends got a flag and burned it and then there was all the shouting about "give me back my property" and all the name-calling. Fear had won the day, as far as Jason was concerned, even if there'd been the little moment of reconciliation at the end. He was glum about it. "I don't think we bridged a lot of divides. I think there were people who understood and they did OK, and there were people who didn't and they weren't OK."

Teressa Raiford had another take on what kept her and Jason apart, despite their shared convictions on policing. She appreciated Jason's support for her principles, but there was still a basic problem underneath it all. It was a problem all American believers had to contend with, in one way or another: that the difficult historical and psychological inheritances we all carry within us often get in the way of the best of our ideas. "His views are who he thinks *he is*," she said. "He can't let go of that."

"The Carp Lady"

It didn't seem that Jason's trial was going so well. Occupier Blaine Cooper had testified against him and the trial's other three defendants, Duane Ehmer, Jake Ryan, and a young man from Washington State named Darryl Thorn. I had arrived in Portland just in time for the prosecution's rebuttal case and the closing arguments of both sides. First came the rebuttal. Earlier in the trial, Ammon, shipped up from prison in the Nevada desert, had testified for the defense. During cross-examination, the prosecution had been careful to get Ammon to state on the stand that refuge employees had been free to come work during the occupation. It seemed like a simple-enough assertion—one the occupiers had continually made. But uttered in this context, Ammon's statement allowed the prosecution leeway to impeach it. Which is why Linda Beck was now up in the witness box.

Beck was the refuge's fish biologist. Because of Ammon, she was doing something she hadn't been allowed to do this fall—she was talking about her fear. Beck had been especially afraid during the occupation, she said, because she'd been one of the only refuge employees the occupiers had ever mentioned by name. Ammon and his brother Ryan had been interviewed by a Reuters reporter in her office, which Ammon had chosen as his personal work station. In the article, the brothers had brought her up as the person they had displaced. "The Carp Lady," they'd also called her. While she was welcome to come collect her things, the brothers didn't want her to go back to doing her job. "She's part of what's destroying America," Ryan had said. The article had been accompanied by photos of Ammon and Ryan and others in the office; some long guns had been plainly visible, including one held by Ryan. The emotions brought on by these memories had been difficult for Beck to contain. On her way out of the courtroom, she was still struggling to hold back tears.

I felt terrible for Linda Beck; it was also hard to imagine that her feelings weren't going to have a very strong impact on the jury. Think of her situation: she was a fish biologist, just trying to save the lake from the damn carp, which devoured everything and muddied up the water, causing trouble for every kind of species. Because of the carp, there was little for the birds to eat out on the lake; because of the carp, water temperatures were rising and rare trout habitat was being destroyed. And this is what she'd gotten for her trouble? The hatred that the Bundys at times seemed to feel for government employees, especially the ones doing anything involving resource protection, offered compelling evidence of how bitter their family's struggle seemed to have turned them. At other moments both could exude religious beatitude as they spoke of a peaceful vision of a mostly ungoverned human coexistence: a utopia, not unlike Jason's, where no one told anyone else what to do. But somewhere early on in their lives they'd decided that gentle folks like Linda Beck were their enemies—bureaucratic foes of Liberty and the People. When these feelings surged up in them, it could make the brothers appear thoroughly fanatical. Whatever your vision of freedom, unless you were a carp, Linda Beck and her efforts to save Malheur Lake were really not what was standing in your way.

By day's end, all the attorneys had finished their closing arguments—all compelling in their ways, all predictable at this point. Now it was in the hands of a new batch of jurors. When this jury returned from its sanctum, we'd know which version of this story would be called true. Only we wouldn't: no matter what happened, it would not be final. Not in this case, and everybody knew it. No matter what, this jury was going to leave things unresolved. Already seven of the Malheur defendants had been acquitted, including Ammon and his brother. Already more than that had pleaded guilty, including Ryan Payne and Jon Ritzheimer. No verdict was going to change how anyone arrayed on the various sides of the issue felt about what the true story was, or much else, for that matter. We'd be left to ourselves with no answers and no resolutions.

What Americans Do

Now we would wait. The lawyers in their nearby offices, and the rest of us in the coffee shops and the soggy parks of the Boisterous Sea. Mostly it was Bundyites I'd be chatting with over the coming days; there were far fewer reporters at this trial. And except for a brief appearance by Jarvis and Joe during closing arguments, there had been hardly any anti-Bundyites present at all. On his short visit to the proceedings, Jarvis had gotten into a little verbal dustup with Jason Patrick, when Jason had attempted to apologize for any offense he had caused Jarvis with the occupation. Hoping that an apology like this was something he could accomplish in the lobby of the courthouse might seem like further evidence of what Teressa had seen as Jason's fundamental error: thinking he was the things he believed. Jason, on the other hand, felt he was just trying to learn where Jarvis was coming from. "I wanted to understand what he thought more. I was trying to understand him," Jason told me. Shifting his grammar to address Jarvis directly in his imagination, he continued, "I do understand the level of disrespect I saw from people that you didn't approve of. I didn't approve of it either. But do you really want the federal government to provide these protections or can we find a common ground?" There had been no chance to ask such questions. Jason's reach out had not gone well. Jarvis's angry rejection had happened in front of a reporter, and soon the confrontation was detailed on the web. Jarvis, for his part, earlier that day, had proudly shown me a shot of his latest painting: a striking image of a gaunt, dead cavalryman on horseback riddled with arrows. After a quick lunch in the courthouse cafeteria with me and Joe and our friend Sue, he'd headed back over the mountains, satisfied with Linda Beck's rebuttal testimony and Ethan Knight's revamped final arguments.

That all quickly seemed long ago. Across the empty days now we waited for the jury to return. I chatted often with Brand Thornton—he was a guy who knew how to pass dead time. He regaled me with long tales of hunting down bighorn across Nevada mountains and of his experiences of divine truth, how it had traveled down his body like a drop of spiritual liquid when, as a young man, he'd first been able to receive the veracity of Joseph Smith's message. The rain slid down the plate glass of the coffee shop as Brand's friends scrolled down the screens of their phones. I suppose they'd already heard all his stories.

Eventually even Brand ran out of adventures; there was always more dead time, hours of it. I caught up on work, took strolls by myself in the rain—often stopping to visit the sculptural pioneer family of *The Promised Land*. They were still there, rising out of Jefferson's foundational invocations of white American forgetting. They looked a little bit fleshier now under the relentless rain, water drooling over their cold metal faces. In the wet, it almost seemed like something living was trapped there in all that bronze. I took to visiting them each afternoon when I got sick of my screen and the piped-in alterna-pop of café world. Now I began to notice something else about these American amnesiacs, another function of their unmoored forget-fulness: they really looked like they could be anywhere at all. And yet when I began relocating them in my bored imagination—like a crew of patriotic garden gnomes—I could only ever see them in shopping mall parking lots. I guess it made a kind of sense. The parking lot might be the ultimate expression of American amnesia: the earth leveled, history buried, the land-scape features reduced to a minimum. The same was true of shopping mall and big box store buildings. Sometimes in a Walmart or a Target I could easily become confused about what town from my life was going to be there when I finally exited. It all created comfort and amnesia, comfort *as* amnesia. I imagined leaving a store, any store, anywhere. I imagined the doors sliding open—and there I saw them again, my bronze pioneers. Father gesturing heroically across the frontage road at the Applebee's or the Pay Day Loans. Mother and son, blandly adoring, following his dead-eyed gaze.

* * *

Neil Wampler had a more-inspired notion of what it might mean to be an American today. One rainy afternoon, my friend Sue convinced him to play hooky from the waiting game and head back to her and her partner, Richard's, house to do a formal interview for the film they were making on the occupa-tion. Once at their house, Neil was soon bracketed from out of the gray, wet world and lit up in the glow of the lamps.

"That's not what Americans do, shrug your shoulders and go home," Neil was saying. He was talking about the Japanese internment camps in his beloved California. Every time I came and went from Burns, I drove past one of those camps, Manzanar—now a museum—on the desert floor, under the otherworldly ridgeline of the eastern Sierras. This was something people like him should have been there to stand against in the 1940s, something the federal government shouldn't have been *allowed* to do. The People shouldn't have let them. That's just not what Americans do, Neil insisted.

History suggested otherwise. Still, my ears perked up at this definition of American being. Taken at its letter, here being American wasn't about Being at all—it was about practice and action. It reduced Americanness to a kind of extreme ethical aspiration—something to bend toward, a generalized willingness and readiness to act, to stand up and say no when called upon by circumstance. Could a nation be an aspirational practice—a promise and a debt to one another, in the last, most dire instance, to show up and care? It was tremendously appealing in a monkish way, though I had a sinking feeling that the coming months under Donald J. Trump were going to put Neil's formula to the test. Even if Americans learned to see themselves this way, who was *really* willing to show up for whom? And when? And how often?

Now Richard had another, more personal question for Neil. He asked if he wanted to address the issue that had publicly hung over him since the story had hit the media late in the occupation: the tale of how he'd killed his father. Neil was ready. "I murdered my father in a drunken rage," he said to the camera. "I won't describe the circumstances, because it sounds like I am trying to excuse my actions, and I take all responsibility for what I did . . . My dad wasn't the best dad," he added, and then cut himself off. That, too, sounded to him like an excuse. There wasn't a day, he said, that he didn't think about what he'd done. "The weight of it comes back to me all the time." He wasn't a religious man, he said, but in the Bundy cause, he felt he had given himself over to God so that He might use him as He wished. He supposed in doing so he was "looking for redemption . . . I'm putting myself out there in God's hands to dispose of me as He will. I let the higher power—I leave it up to Him. I'm available, I'm willing," he added. "Perhaps the day will come when I realize the atonement is accomplished."

Interview finished, Sue drove us back downtown, through sheets of dark rain. We three sat together in the coffee shop, waiting, still waiting for the signal from the court. Sue had brought the catalog of an art show she wanted to show us both—sculptural work made of intricately shaped wood, crazy forms, dream figures. Neil was fascinated by it, turning the pages, squinting in closer, admiring the lines and the craft. And then the word came—somebody texted somebody who told somebody who told Neil—that the jury was done for the day. We'd start waiting again tomorrow.

"Na-na Na-na Boo-boo"

The last day of that long rainy week, miraculously, the sun returned. People in the city were going nuts. They always do in the rainy Northwest when the sky opens up for the first time in months. It's involuntary. Voices were louder, people's gaits were more erratic; they were looking up, shouting, hailing each other with rediscovered enthusiasm for human contact. You never knew when one of these besotted Portlanders was going to leap out into your path—they were all zigzaggy today—but I made it, carefully threading my way through all that solar-powered exuberance to the courthouse.

The Bundyites were filling the square and spilling into the streets, everybody out in the sun. Duane Ehmer had parked his truck alongside the park in front of the court. He had a forge mounted on the flatbed and the thing was fired up—it was roaring. He was heating up metal, whanging on it with hammers, banging out shapes. A little smithery to pass the time while he awaited his judgment. When I approached, he was putting the finishing touches on a Celtic-looking cross. I'd see one of these crosses of Duane's again soon, adorning a makeshift solitary confinement cell at a protest in the Nevada desert. While he did this, he was also instructing Jake Ryan on the basics of blacksmithing. Young Jake was heating some metal up to red hot. He'd been super antsy all week, trying to get his older comrades to go bowling with him, to do *something*, anything besides sitting and waiting in the café scrolling through their Facebook feeds. The anxiety was eating him alive. Now he was hammering away, banging out a horseshoe, and positively gleaming about it, grinning from ear to ear.

Neil was here too. As we chatted and watched the blacksmiths at work, he was approached by two heavily tattooed guys looking to bum smokes and a light—they'd just gotten out of jail, they said, nodding back at the county facility across the park. I watched Neil go into revolutionary mode, prison-recruitment style. As he handed them cigarettes and lit them, he pointed out the crude tattoo of LaVoy's brand on the webbing between his thumb and forefinger. Do you know what this is? he asked the men. With some prodding, they finally recognized it. "Right on!" one of them said, and pulled open his shirt; he was covered with tattoos, but dead center, over the hollow of his throat, was the sign of Anarchy—he tapped it for Neil with his forefinger. Puffing on their first post-jail smokes, the two now went on their way, out into the streets, toward whatever their new day of freedom and sunlight might bring them. It did seem like a damn nice day to get out of jail; I guess any day is a good day for that.

Like everyone else, I'd had a feeling today would be it. Near noon, I was sitting in a café, chomping on a bagel, looking out at the miraculously sunlit park and the courthouse beyond it. Suddenly I saw Neil in the distance. He looked strange. Finally I figured out why—he was running. He was running up the courthouse steps. Then I saw it happening everywhere. There was motion throughout the park, bodies flowing all in that one direction. No one had to tell me now that the jury was ready. When I heard Brand blowing one last blast on the shofar, I was already clomping up the courthouse steps, opening the front door.

Inside, we all waited. Neither the judge nor the jury had arrived yet. The vibe was one I hadn't felt before in this room. The Ammonites were jazzed up with expectation of another victory. The deliberations had taken days and that, their lawyers were saying, was a very good sign. A gurgly and resonant bird cry kept rising up. It took me a long time to figure out who it was coming from—it was Jason Patrick. He was doing turkey calls. Turkey hunting season had just begun back in Georgia, he said. Matt Schindler, Ken Medenbach's co-counsel from the previous trial, was here somehow too, adding to the jocularity. "Who's getting tased?" he shouted. Jason and Duane both pointed immediately at Jason's lawyer, Andrew Kohlmetz, and grinned back. One of the defendants, Darryl Thorn, didn't seem so sure about the whole thing though; he was praying loudly.

Finally the judge and jury arrived, pressing the room into silence. And then it was happening. The jury had reached unanimous decisions on all counts; these were now passed to Judge Anna Brown to read. After admonishing us against the display of any kind of emotion—there were to be no repeats of October's tumult—Judge Brown asked Jason Patrick to rise and face the jury. On the charge of conspiracy, the jury had found the defendant Jason Patrick guilty; on the firearms charge that accompanied it, not guilty. Now Duane rose. He was found not guilty on the conspiracy charge, but guilty of damaging property, for digging that ditch in the parking lot the panicked day after LaVoy's death. Jake Ryan, who stood next, received the same two verdicts. Last up was Darryl Thorn, among the least involved—if maybe more publicly bellicose—of the occupiers to be charged with anything. Just before the trial he'd been offered a chance to plead out to misdemeanor trespassing, but he'd refused. He'd cited LaVoy about taking a stand. Now he, too, was found guilty—of conspiracy *and* of the firearms charge. And with that, it was done.

Sentencing was scheduled for May. Almost immediately the room began to empty out. I passed Neil, still seated in a pew; he looked devastated, jaw open, leaning back into the wood. Out in the ninth-floor foyer, sunlight was pouring through the windows; it was still a gorgeous day. I didn't know what to do with myself. I had never watched a verdict be pronounced in person before. I'd seen it often in movies, but that hadn't prepared me for what it was like to be in a room when it actually happened—everyone struggling to restrain their faces and bodies as the words arrived, and the meanings sank in, and emotion surged. As I headed up to the glass to look out at the city, I heard a desperate voice, weeping and murmuring beneath me. I looked down and there was Darryl Thorn, on his knees, one hand on a leather-bound Bible, feverishly praying. I stepped away, found the elevator, and headed down and out.

Out on the steps, where the Bundyites had celebrated so wildly back in October, reporters were clustering around Matthew Schindler, who was always so good at explaining these things. Why Matt was even there that day was a whole other story about the justice system—one nobody had covered. Schindler was there representing an African American client named Douglas Lyons Jr., a man who had done time in the past. The feds were trying to send him back to prison for a firearms violation. This was despite the fact that Mr. Lyons was a demonstrably rehabilitated individual, Matt argued. He'd been working steadily, raised a family, all despite growing up in an environment of shocking violence. A year earlier, an unloaded gun had been found by police in his home; there had been a warrant, though the circumstances that had produced the warrant were murky. Lyons's first attorney had accepted a plea deal—*a ten-year sentence*—but when Matt took over the case, he found that important discovery evidence had been with-held. The end result of Schindler's intervention had been that Mr. Lyons had walked free today. He'd been lucky. That is not how it usually went in federal court, Matt said. Now he stood before the crowd of reporters eager to tap his knowledge of the Bundy case for which he'd been a spectator today. One asked if it was *just* that these men were convicted while the leaders had been acquitted, of conspiracy no less? Matt pushed back at the question—a question about justice on the steps of a federal courthouse.

"I've been a criminal defense lawyer far too long to think about justice as an abstract concept," he responded. "We live in a world and in a society where incarceration is one of our core values." With the exception of the Lyons case that morning, he struggled to think of there ever having been an example of real justice being accomplished in this building:

What happened in this trial was the government overreacting—
well, first underreacting and then dramatically overreacting—to a

protest. And when you start and try to criminalize all those activities using the same kind of allegations that you use for drug trafficking or for fraud, it's not going to work. And that's the issue here. So is it fair to Darryl Thorn that he's convicted and Ammon Bundy is not? I don't know—Ammon Bundy's been in jail this entire time. So, you know, fairness in the context of the criminal justice system is difficult to sort of track. This result is the kind of result that inheres in the jury system. Sometimes you win for showing up. And that isn't necessarily justice; that's just the nature of a competitive, adversarial enterprise. You know, I respect the employees, the people who work for the federal government; I think they are doing a good job, they're doing what they can do. But this doesn't make their lives any easier or any better, or change really anything.

"What I can tell you is this," he concluded, in response to another question about fairness. "I wish that you guys were at every trial that we did in federal court. I wish that this system in general had the transparency that this level of attention forces upon it—because ninety-nine percent of the time, the room is empty and no one cares."

* * *

The impact of the verdicts was sinking in among the Bundyites. Neil was still stunned, trying to figure out what they meant. It had seemed like a split victory for both sides, with Duane and Jake avoiding conspiracy convictions, but now folks remembered that the charges for damaging federal property potentially carried stiffer sentences. Unlike his comrades, Jason Patrick seemed entirely unimpressed by his conviction. As he emerged from the courthouse, he was singing an improvised child's taunt—"Na-na na-na boo-boo, I'm a convicted felon"—and smiling from ear to ear. The night before, I'd had a long visit with Teressa Raiford; I told Jason now how she had asked if I thought he'd been serious about his endorsement of her write-in campaign for sheriff that fall. "Hell yeah," he answered. "Teressa's awesome. She's exposing the stuff that needs to be exposed!" Then he was gone, already crossing the street toward his friends at Patriots' Corner, singing his silly song.

PART III

Afterworlds

CHAPTER TWENTY-FIVE

The Republic of Birds

A FEW WEEKS LATER I WENT OUT and I occupied the refuge myself. I was alone when it happened. No, that wasn't true. I was in a crowd, I was never alone. It was occupied when I got there, though there wasn't a human soul around.

I had been beginning to get a feel for Harney County, now having spent a couple of months there spread out over various visits—longer already than any of the occupiers, a strange fact, meaning mostly that they hadn't spent much time there at all. Neither had I, really. Which is what I was learning right now. I hadn't been here yet in spring, and I don't think you can begin to understand the place if you haven't. It was totally transformed, unrecognizable in places. It had been crackly dry the last time I was here, in the fall; now there was so much water—there were lakes, actual lakes, where before had been hayfields, and these were all full of birds. The birds. How had I forgotten about the birds? I probably prefer birds to people. How have I written most of an entire book about people taking over a bird refuge and forgotten to talk about birds?

There was no forgetting them now, or vanishing them in metaphor. There were too many of them, far too many. In spring in the Harney Basin, humans are openly, terrifically outnumbered. The birds are simply everywhere you look—everywhere you put your ears as well. The soundscape is the phatic web of their coexistence: honks, clicks, rubbery gurgles, shrieks, quacks, and trills of song, along with what we used to mean when we spoke of twitters and tweets. We humans are always outnumbered—just try counting up the ants—but it usually takes great imaginative work to remind ourselves, we're so big and self-involved, so fully immersed in our people worlds. In March, in the land of Malheur, momentarily the evidence of our minority was openly present and undeniable. All you had to do was be there to feel it.

*   *   *

It took me forever to get out to the refuge that day. I was writing too much, stopping every quarter mile or less just to freak out about what I was seeing, about how changed this world was—this place I thought I had known:

> What kind of desert is this? What breed of ducks are these? Another lake that this fall was a field, a dry hayfield, full of bales, haystacks everywhere. I step from the car and the ducks leap up together in an oddly twittery song, into the air I mean—that's where they go. I didn't know ducks could make such sounds—and then they swing off and land again a little farther off—must be hundreds of them, right here. A few others in another impromptu lake-pond, just to the south, black-headed male with coppery belly, white breast, a swooped long beak made for digging. All day I've been passing ducks, ass in air, beaks in the muck, bright orange feet. The sky to the west now full of light and noise. Big white snow geese—no these are Ross geese—lit up now in amber-gold, the heartbreak light of March. They are swimming in that light. All the geese, in the air, bright, clamorous bodies against a background of charcoal-colored cloud. Heavy heavy cloud, dark as black mold, thick with rain, whips of rain coming off it now. Now they are flying past the smokestack, the biggest human-made thing around here—towering over the ruins of the old lumber mill, all of it now gilded up in sun.

Finally I made it. I figured the refuge headquarters would still be closed, but I headed out Sodhouse Lane anyway. The headquarters compound had been shut for more than a year, and word was that it wouldn't be open for this year's fast-approaching bird festival either. But the rest of the refuge was open, as it always was, the actual land of it. I figured I'd poke around, see what bird action was happening down there. But then I encountered another miracle: I got to the headquarters, and the gate was open; all the signs barring entry that had been up since early 2016 were gone. There was nothing at all about it being closed to the public. Nothing but the usual closed-at-sunset notices. And there was nobody around to ask what was up—no guards, no other vehicles; it was just me and the compound.

I was a little hesitant to walk right in—having just sat through parts of two separate trials of individuals whose legal ordeals had begun the moment they'd done the same. I moved along the edges of the compound, peering through the trees, looking at those buildings that had become characters themselves in a drama broadcast worldwide. I went back up the slope to the fire tower, gazed up at its height. It really was tall. I didn't dare try to pull down its ladder and climb it, but just from up here on the rise I could see in all directions, which meant I could see both sun and rain moving in patchworks over the steppe and the buttes. To the north, I saw something that made me jump. There was Malheur Lake, and it was huge; I'd hardly ever been able to make it out in the distance before, but now it covered the whole northeast corner of my view.

I'd texted my friends Sue and Richard. They were very nearby, shepherding historian Patty Limerick and her partner, Houston, around the basin, visiting ranches. They'd be here in a second, they said, and then they were, and then we were walking right onto the compound. It was freaky how well I knew the place, though I'd never been here. I'd studied so many photos, aerial views, maps, drone footage. Here were all the old Conservation Corps buildings as I knew them from images. I touched their stone surfaces, circled them, looking at the red-painted doorways, familiar from so many photos and videos. We all wandered around, a little dazed to be there. Sue recounted tales of the occupation—she'd made many visits when it was taking place. We were standing in the little gazebo now, where the grazing-rights ceremony had been held, Sue recounting the day, while I recalled footage she'd shown me earlier. An image came back: LaVoy, eyes closed, listening to the voices of the Sharp Family Singers. He'd be dead in three days, and that family torn apart within a few months, but for a moment there they'd been united in a kind of blissful community—the children, riding their own voices; LaVoy, drinking those voices in.

My companions had to split, and I was left alone with the refuge. Now in the absence of human voices, I could really hear how many other voices there were here, bird voices. The place wasn't empty at all. The bare cottonwoods of the refuge were full of red-wing blackbirds—all of them yammering at one another—in a rubbery *cheet cheet*. The wind was softer now; no longer howling up in the sky. A raven flew overhead, carrying a huge ball of white fluff in its beak, the heavy whoosh of its wings audible. A bronze stream of light busted through the clouds, flashed out across the pond and then farther, lighting up the sage and the grasses, and there, at the edges, the escarpments, the far buttes. Another cacophony of white geese entered, passing before the dark clouds, lit up in the band of sun.

I wandered through the grasses out to the pond. Today this was the territory of the swallows. They were mostly silent; their community was one of shapes, constellations in motion. Sometimes one of them would fly straight at my face. They were so intent-looking when they did this, with their little masked faces, their blue caps. Charging at me, tiny bulls, but so nimble—at the last moment they'd swerve and buzz me, or yank up and wheel away. I admired the tightly banked turns they pulled as they zipped out over the pond. They'd hang for a moment out at the edge of their arcs, before looping back, gathering speed as they zoomed out over the reeds and the grasses. There were so many of them up there in the air, doing their late-afternoon dance in the gathering hour. They must have been feeding, yes, but also they were dancing, because they are a dance, an engagement with the dynamic that they are when they're together—their phatic web, their connectivity, their society. Even in silence they are a *gregarious* species. It looked like Liberty to me, in flight, each touching at the passage of each in the air. Could people ever look free like this, seen like this, from outside?

Besides myself, human persons weren't entirely absent from the compound; their absences were present. Someone had raised the flag, which sputtered and clapped in the wind—asserting dominion over what? Over more human absence, I guess. Here was also the human gone-ness of the Ammonites. The wind, the birds, the flag, the noise of my own feet on the paths—all of it gave body, faintly, to my imaginings of their human blather, the effervescence of them, the puffed-up rattle of people trying to matter, giving shape to their imaginary worlds.

I found the doorway, I was sure of it, where LaVoy had shot his last video address about the Wadatika. Here was the one where he'd squatted in the sun and pleaded with the tribe—"we are not your enemies!" And here was where he'd leaned back against the wall the next day, told "America" that he and the crew were going to "stay the course." He'd be dead in a few hours, but for the moment, he'd been alive, leaning the living weight of himself against this wall, right there. Exactly here. I pulled my hand away and made myself not touch.

Democracy Calls for Hypocrisy

Historian Patty Limerick is what they call a character, which made her fit right into the Malheur story. She's a tremendously successful academic with an ironic wit and what seems like an open yearning to be something other than just an academic—maybe a stand-up comedian. Patty's use of humor is sneakily layered—she uses it to weave pleasing complexity and irony into situations that might otherwise simply be fraught, because they are fraught. She was uniquely suited to the impossible task presented to her this evening: being an outside expert addressing a roomful of Harney County residents about a conflict they'd lived and she hadn't.

She began with a joke about a marriage counselor giving the same exact answer to two aggrieved spouses: *I think you are absolutely right.* This suggested what she saw as a kind of credo for the historian, something that she hoped to offer to the room—maybe it would be of use to us as well: "Never let yourself settle into one viewpoint." In our current political land-scape, these seemed like radical words.

Conflict was not a catastrophe. Disagreement was a great thing, she said. It saved us from what she called, her face recoiling at the thought, as if she'd taken a slug of milk gone sour, the "cloying and very dreadful experience of everyone being delighted with each other." I laughed, the whole room laughed. She had just described Bundyite Rural Electrification, and its limits. I thought of my swallows out at the refuge. I wondered if they experienced one another's proximity as joy. What if they hadn't been dancing? What if they were squabbling? What if squabbling was also dancing?

Patty's real topic tonight, what she seemed most to be trying to get at anyway, very casually, was the troubled historical and contemporary rela-tionship between conservation and democracy. Conservation, with its aris-tocratic origins, she reminded us, had not had the most democratic of births. It was still up in the air how compatible the two really were. But it sure was an interesting dilemma! Public land, and all the issues surrounding it—this is a great experiment, Patty said, to see if conservation can coexist with democracy. Can it be compatible with people making their own choices and decisions? "We don't know how the experiment will come out," she said, but we were, all of us, involved in it. At issue were two conflicting modes that she thought could be intertwined: the faith in local control and local wisdom, and the faith in centralized expertise.

It was more complex than that even. Because as an experiment in the limits of democracy, public land became the ground and occasion of something even more fundamental. "Public lands," she said, "give us a chance to have a conversation about our common inheritance." Here she was talking about the spiritual and cultural value of the commons and, through all her irony, or because of it, what she was saying was becoming quite moving. "The fighting over an inheritance can be very bad," she acknowledged, "but let's use this as an occasion to figure out who we are to each other." But how could we do this—someone from the audience was asking—how could we talk to "people who enjoy camping on their differences?"

"I think hypocrisy is undervalued," Patty responded, to howls of enjoyment from the room—especially the many teenagers present tonight, who were making delighted eyes at one another, clearly overjoyed to hear a well-respected adult puncture an adult-world piety. It wasn't going to work to wait to be "one hundred percent ready to hear each other," Patty said. That just wasn't going to happen. "So just pretend. *Misrepresent* yourself. Democracy calls for hypocrisy."

A Common Vocabulary

Brenda Smith was there that night, and she was also tickled by Patty's ironic suggestion. It sounded about right to her. She had never been one for conflict, which maybe had something to do with how she'd ended up doing what she did for a living: facilitating the collaboratives of Harney County's High Desert Partnership. "That might be a reasonable way to go through life!" she said, laughing, when I asked later that week about Patty's bon mot on hypocrisy. "It's something I struggle with. I get more information if I don't come out and say what I'm thinking, particularly when people are being *my way or the highway*. I don't feel like I'm being disingenuous," she added. "My interest is in understanding where folks are coming from."

More seriously, and more directly to the point for Brenda, was one of Patty's less ironic maxims from that night: *Don't ever let yourself settle into one viewpoint.* It wasn't Brenda's job to have a single viewpoint or opinion; it was her work to help the stakeholders in public land issues in the county get to the table, as they had been doing for quite some time under the aegis of the High Desert Partnership. And with remarkable success. The stakeholder groups of the partnership had been practicing local, consensus-based democracy in coordination with federal agencies for more than a decade: major land-management decisions were now being made collaboratively in the county, through the collective agreement of ranchers, loggers, farmers, environmentalists, local government officials, tribal officials, federal agencies, and other local residents. And it was the common inheritance of public land that had allowed these groups and individuals, often bitter opponents in years past, to find out, as Patty had suggested, what they were to one another. "If you have private land, you don't have to have that conversation," Brenda mused. "What she said gave me a different perspective about the discussions—a good feeling that it could help us figure out what we are."

The story of the High Desert Partnership wasn't the sort of political story one hears often or ever in America today—and it really was public land that was making it possible. A quiet transformation in how federal power operated in local contexts had begun in the West, and Harney County was at the forefront. This is what Georgia Marshall, whose husband, Gary, was one of the founders of the partnership, had been so angry about that night at the first town hall meeting after the takeover. This was why she'd been so insistent that this was not the time, that Harney County was not the place for Ammon's reactionary rebellion. Since the bad years of the 1990s, things had been changing in the West, and her community had helped pioneer the methods.

How had this happened? The first answer was that the High Desert Partnership had been born of the politics of exhaustion. Years of litigation had created a definitive stalemate when it came to land management in the West. Lawsuit after lawsuit had resulted in no clear victory for anyone. This led to realizations like the one Jack Southworth, a fifth-generation rancher from the Bear Valley, up in the mountains north of Burns, described to me. "I had no power," Jack said. "The only thing I had was my patience." Jack's small community of Seneca, which his great-grandfather had helped found, was dying. There wasn't enough work left in the national forest to sustain it; soon there wouldn't be enough kids to keep the school open. All around he could also see signs that the forests were growing unhealthier by the year. These weren't the sort of things he had the power to fix on his own, but he had patience, a patience born in dedication to this place that he loved. "I didn't have the influence for legislation, I didn't have the money for litigation. All that was open to me was collaboration." Once other take-no-prisoners modes of political and legal action had been exhausted, other stakeholders, even those with influence and budgets, had come to

see it the same way. In Harney County the new mode of collaboration had
emerged out of the Malheur National Wildlife Refuge. Its current director,
Chad Karges, along with a few local ranchers, had assembled the region's
first collaborative of stakeholders in order to draft the refuge's fifteen-
year comprehensive conservation plan. From this group the High Desert
Partnership had been born. After the hard years of the '90s, when conflict
between the Hammond family and the refuge had boiled over, Karges was
bringing a new approach. No longer would Fish and Wildlife simply craft
its plan of operation unilaterally according to its own vision of its mission
and priorities. The '90s had been rough across the West, and constant
lawsuits in all directions had made it difficult, nearly impossible, for
federal agencies, already chronically understaffed and underfunded, to get
anything done. Meanwhile, desperate region-wide problems, like fire in
the dry pine forests of the whole Intermountain West, and smaller-scale
local problems, like the invasive carp population in the waters of the
refuge, were only getting worse.

The group that built the refuge conservation plan had brought together
usually contentious antagonists: environmentalists, ranchers, local government officials (county and tribal), federal land managers, and other local
stakeholders, and forged the fifteen-year plan *by consensus*. Everyone had
agreed on it. There was no voting in the collaboratives of the High Desert
Partnership, only conversation—hours and hours, months and months,
years and years of it. What it required more than anything was the patience
Jack talked of. The results spoke for themselves. The refuge had instituted
its plan and *nobody had sued anybody* to stop its being put into action. It was
the first such community-developed conservation plan ever instituted in the
nation. In the contentious West, that seemed like a miracle.

Consensus meant that no one who joined a collaborative felt outvoted
and irrelevant; no decision was made until everyone agreed what it was that
was to be done. Jack Southworth had become the facilitator of the High
Desert Partnership's Forest Restoration Collaborative, which worked on the
forest health of the southern reach of the Malheur National Forest, where he
lived. I attended a session in the summer of 2017 and saw how it worked.
The group went around the room until everyone had spoken on a given
issue—and responded to each other's thoughts. It took forever—patience
was indeed necessary—but it also meant that people were intently listening
to each other, and that was what was most important, Jack said. In other

kinds of meetings, people didn't hear each other; everyone was too anxious about whether or not they'd get to say their thing, anxious about trying to find their space to speak. If everyone knows their time is coming, they can relax, listen, and learn from one another. "You gain knowledge and the whole room accepts you," Jack said. "The main thing we've learned is that there aren't any experts. We let the room find the answer."

Collaboration and consensus also required a different approach when it came to the issues under discussion. As environmentalist Esther Lev of the Wetlands Conservancy explained, it meant that you didn't begin with a single divisive hot-button question. Esther had been part of the original refuge conservation-plan group that had become the Harney Basin Wetlands Initiative, which she'd also been a member of from its beginnings. These groups had started out, she said, "looking for the places where there was commonality rather than differences—if we had begun with the issue of 'should there be cows on the refuge or not,' it would have been a different story. It was facilitated to look for commonalities." Seemingly against all odds, fifteen years later, liberal environmentalists, conservative ranchers, and federal land managers were still finding commonalities and acting on them together. Right in the middle of Ammon's occupation, when he and his friends had proposed to liberate the people and lands of Harney County from an unresponsive, aloof, and oppressive federal government, the HDP's Wetlands Initiative had received a grant of six million dollars—a huge amount of money for a place like Harney County—to implement collaborative projects the group had agreed on and designed together.

As I interviewed partnership participants in the spring and summer of 2017, one thing that struck me was the role of the landscape itself in the political life these people had been able to develop. The forest and the wetlands—with their complex, dynamic ecosystems—stood apart from the desires and ideological bent of any one stakeholder. As the groups continued to meet and ask questions about the public land they were engaging with, they often found that none of them knew the answers. They would have to ask the land itself—through scientific study. What, they started by asking, is really going on out there? The answers were often surprising—and these answers led to new questions. All the while, the participants were developing what Esther Lev called "a common vocabulary" to be able discuss what they had learned and what problems their knowledge posed for them in terms of action.

A Surface Expression

One point of consensus for the group was the importance of flood irrigation. Research had revealed just how important the old-school Harney County
style of flood irrigation had become to bird populations. But now the old
ranching practice, a source of much pride in the county, had come under
threat. It was flood irrigation that was responsible for the miraculous transformation of the northern part of the basin I witnessed during the week of
Patty's lecture in Burns. Since the nineteenth century, Harney County
ranchers had been diverting water from spring-swollen streams to turn their
fields into temporary lakes. From these fields would grow the native grasses
that they'd harvest in summer to feed their cows all through the cold winter.
These hayfields reproduced many of the conditions of the natural flood
meadows that had existed before white settlement, often produced in that
time by the ceaseless work of beavers. New studies were showing that
dozens of species of birds were relying on the flood-irrigated meadows of
Harney County farmers, for the forage they needed to reproduce each spring.
All those geese and ducks, tails up, rooting in the muck in the flooded
meadows, the dinosaur-esque sandhill cranes I'd seen hopping and clicking
at one another as they picked their way across stubbly fields—all these
depended on the Harney Basin for their life cycle. As out of the way as this
place was for humans, it was a cosmopolitan hub for the transcontinental
birdlife of the Pacific Flyway. The numbers of birds that passed through
were staggering; up to one-half of all the Ross geese in the world came
through the region every year.

Local ecological problems—like the carp in Malheur Lake—were making
the traditional flood-irrigated meadows of the Harney Basin ranchers more
important than ever. And yet, partly due to public policy, ranchers were
beginning to abandon the practice. Chris Colson, a biologist with Ducks
Unlimited and a member of the High Desert Partnership's wetlands collaborative, explained: "What we found in the last fifteen years . . . in these
staging areas . . . they [the birds] are feeding like mad. As we continued
peeling that onion, these livestock operations were converting from flood
irrigation to sprinkler." Flood irrigation had been getting a bad name in
recent years, its patent inefficiency in certain ecosystems, especially in times
of drought, had led to policies in which farmers were being subsidized to
put in pivot wells tapping directly into aquifers. This despite the fact that
flood irrigation was not necessarily a problem in wetland—as opposed to

dry land—ecosystems. In Harney County, flood irrigation, in the wetlands where it was possible, was better than pivot irrigation for stream flow and wildlife habitat. It also seemed to be considerably better for the water table. "The flood irrigation was a surrogate," Chris said, "that was mimicking the flood-plain function—most notably in terms of aquifer recharge." It meant that the flooded fields were crucial for wetlands health. "They [wetlands] are only as wet as the aquifer is full: wetlands are a surface expression of a full aquifer."

Just when the group was discovering the full range of benefits of flood irrigation in the basin, more and more farmers were drilling pivot wells directly into the aquifer and irrigating fields with pivot sprinklers, often growing non-native grasses, like alfalfa, which some were even exporting as far afield as China. This was akin to sucking up precious water from a very dry zone, storing it in bales, and shipping it out of the ecosystem—just one of the thousands of absurdities of our supposedly efficient globalized economy. In Harney County the negative results had recently been confirmed. By 2015, a moratorium on all new agricultural wells in the county had been declared; some older wells were starting to run dry. The future problems water issues like this could potentially bring to the area would be far greater and more divisive than anything Ammon and friends had done. Still, Chris remained optimistic. The conditions in Harney County were perfect for the kind of collaboration that the partnership fostered. "Flood irrigation is a win-win," Chris explained. "Everybody benefits if you can get the system under balance. We'll have our wetland resource for wildlife, more forage for ranchers, more water for farmers on the periphery. Harney County is a nice discrete area: it's all within them to fix it—they will receive all the benefits." It wasn't always like this, Chris explained. Some systems weren't as self-contained as the basin was, and sometimes more dire ecological scenarios triggered regulatory responses, making such collaboration nearly impossible.

Looking forward, flood irrigation also provided wetland advocates a way to deal with the issues of climate change in a zone full of climate change skeptics. The way he saw it, with what climate change seemed certain to bring to this dry part of North America, it was imperative to entangle the wetlands and birdlife conservation issues further with the human ones. "The concern in the Harney Basin is that if you don't make conservation of all natural resources part of the plans, agriculture is always going to win. So getting intimately intertwined with ag resources now is key," he told me. "If there's a groundwater problem, they are going to take care of municipal and ag needs before waterfowl." Thus it had become essential, he added, to get in and identify "all the interdependence of waterfowl, ag, and municipal on each other . . . the interdependence of all water uses." The group had had success in this. "That interdependence is recognized. The groundwater pumping moratorium has helped. They might not be willing to acknowledge climate change, but they are willing to acknowledge drought."

*   *   *

That the rural West was an entanglement of the wild and the human was no secret to the ranchers in the partnership, who'd lived that entanglement all their lives. One of the more intangible rewards that ranchers got out of these conversations was an acknowledgment that not everything they did had been uniformly bad for the land they loved—and that they really knew quite a bit about the place they'd worked all their lives. Of course they did; all their lives were lived in constant connection with the land and the dynamic system of weather and water that produced and sustained life in the basin: the life of the birds, the fish, the plants, their cows, and themselves. "You are creating life," Dan Nichols told me, when I asked what was special about the ranching life for him. It meant you were out there, all the time, in the middle of life as it happened. "You have the opportunity to see things that people just don't see in the realm of wildlife and nature." But the misunderstandings of outsiders about the blurriness of human/nature distinctions had long bothered him. He'd had an inn on his family's ranch for some years, and every day he'd fielded questions from guests, often dealing with their misperceptions about the "naturalness" of what it was they were looking at. "'A trout creek! . . . Oh, what a beautiful place . . . You are so lucky to live here . . . What beautiful natural meadows.' 'Natural' my ass! And by the way, there's been cattle on this place a hundred-plus years. That was the door for me to walk through and kind of get them intrigued enough to talk a bit—with some."

"The ranchers have a deep connection to the land," Esther Lev said. They spoke of wondrous things, like watching the sun rise over the same butte every day for twenty years. The other members had their attachments to the place as well. "Everybody has a spiritual and visceral connection to that landscape—their poetry or music is different, the way they come to it, but they do," she told me. "We love that place," she added. "Now that's scary: now we have another connection. You don't make time [during the meetings] for honoring that shared connection really, but it is really there in the background—the unspoken woven background of the work we do is that connection."

That connection, as Esther explained, was not a connection to a static thing—it was to a place, but that place was an endless flux. It changed constantly. If there was one word folks used in talking about the basin, it was *dynamic* or *dynamism*. "That system is so dynamic," Gary Ivey, a former biologist on the refuge, told me. "Two hundred surface acres to forty-five thousand surface acres, it will flood across the boundaries." Or, as Esther said, you could just go up on a rise, any rise, "turn in a three-hundred-and-sixty-degree arc, and the weather is different in *every* direction. To me it tells you how dynamic that landscape is . . . how those landscapes *play* the weather . . . It's the dynamic of the place . . . If I wanted to study weather, that's where I would."

I had only been coming to the basin for a couple of years, but when she said this, I knew exactly what she was talking about. In my limited experience, she wasn't exaggerating at all. Weather could change massively, maybe not in a minute, but definitely in twenty, sometimes in five or ten. While watching the birdlife in someone's flood-irrigated meadow that spring, I'd marveled as the temperature dropped and rose again by at least twenty degrees—three times over thirty minutes. It was sunny, blindingly so, warm even, and then it was dark and the wind was howling, and then it was spitting tiny, pointy-feeling drops of rain, and then it was snowing a little, and then it was hailing a little, and then it was sunny again, and still, the redwing blackbirds were *cheet-cheet*ing at themselves and everything else while cranes went clicking their way through the muck and stubble of an unsubmerged field, and the ducks and geese rummaged on in the flooded meadow.

* * *

Following what they'd learned from the basin, the wetlands collaborative had found a new—small but nimble—kind of political life. That life seemed to me like a kind of surface expression of the place itself. I'm not trying to suggest that they "got in touch with the earth" and thus found some kind of peace or harmony. This was still politics; it wasn't religion. "It is not necessarily a big kumbaya group hug," Chris Colson cautioned me. "Everybody needs to be able say what they need to say." There was no long-term danger here of what Patty had called the "cloying and very dreadful experience of everyone being delighted with each other." In fact, the social pleasures seemed to be of a different sort—the ones that came from getting to know the minds of those who thought and felt differently than you did. Esther described it as part of the focus on inquiry the group had discovered early on: "The inquiry is also into one another, getting to know one another, 'what do you think about this place?'" After all these years, she said, she can now often guess what the other folks in the group are thinking on a topic. "'I assume that's what you are thinking,' I say to Dan, for example, about an issue, and ninety percent of the time now I'm right. But what's really interesting is that other ten percent when he's like, 'No, not at all—why would you think I'd think that?'"

Instead of a group hug or a political bubble, they had found a politics that was informed by what the landscape was telling them. They were responding to it as well as to one another, and this seemed to make all the difference. We were a long way here from the worldview and theological language of the Bundy family, from Ryan Bundy's talk of his citizenship in heaven and of our total God-bestowed dominion over the land and the creatures and the plants for the brief duration of our earthly sojourn. Here were people, from very different perspectives, sharing their different entanglements with this place as they inquired together into what was going on in the basin's ecology—and into what was going on in each other. In the basin, nature and human society passed back and forth into each other: each flooded over the boundaries. To imagine some kind of absolute human sovereignty here was as impossible as to imagine that this place, with its invasive carp, its irrigated flood meadows, its cows and hay farmers and birders and federal wildlife managers, its centuries of human fire-use, and the millennia of manipulation and use by the Wadatika and their ancestors, was wholly natural—if *natural* meant somehow entirely outside human influence. It made sense that a new political form that had emerged in this place should reflect that basic entangled condition.

After all my time with the Patriots in the Boisterous Sea, I couldn't help but notice an additional irony in all this. The Bundyites insisted on a vision of American history and government in which sovereignty remained in the hands of the citizenry, a vision in which government was an appendage of We the People. Weren't these collaboratives of the High Desert Partnership a fleeting expression of this basic American fantasy of the people's sovereignty? Hadn't Chad Karges, the current refuge director, gotten the whole collaborative thing rolling by essentially offering up what federal sovereignty he managed as a tool to be operated collaboratively by a body of the People? Wasn't this a circumstance in which the federal government was now acting as an immediate appendage of popular will and power? This was the closest I had ever seen to anything like this happening in America, certainly anything involving federal power. It seemed as if the Holy Ghost had incited Ammon to restore what he saw as the proper functioning of the federal government—a functioning it had rarely ever had, and was not really intended to have—in a place where, in Ammon's own idealized terms, it had already been working that way for years.

CHAPTER TWENTY-SIX

Camp Liberty

PAHRUMP HAS THE HALF-ASSED feel of many Nevada towns; it staggers about this way and that, before petering off into incoherency and the silence of the desert, which is where the Bundyites had hunkered down. The Patriots had picked an impressive stage for their next action. True, what they'd dubbed "Camp Liberty" was sandwiched between a private prison and the town dump—but it was perched on the slope that rose up out of the basin where Pahrump sprawled about, doing its best to feign municipality. I could see seventy miles in multiple directions from where I now stood. To the east, still snowcapped, was Charleston Peak, the highest of the Spring Mountains. There were lots of bighorn sheep up there, and plenty of room to get totally lost, or so Brand Thornton told me. To the west was the Nopah Range, separating us from the alien mud-hill landscape of the Shoshone Valley, just over the state line in California. To the northwest, farther off, were the jagged and darkly striated Funeral Mountains, rising above the plunge to Death Valley. Adding to the drama of the views was the drama in the air. It was spring, and in spring the Mojave fills up with wind; it roared now in the flags, tents, and tarps, and in our shirts and ears.

Now the Patriots were within a few hours of my own desert home, and I'd come to check out their new scene. It had been a thrilling drive that morning up through the geologic time and space of the Mojave, greened-up extra now from a winter of heavy rain. I arrived just in time to join in one of the main rites of Camp Liberty life. Their "Jericho March" was performed daily at two P.M., when whoever was around headed out to stumble up and down through washes and over the scrabbly desert, as they circled the entire complex of the Nevada Southern Detention Facility.

That prison was why we were all here. More precisely, we were here because of who was inside. Since Malheur, Ammon Bundy had taken to his new role of political prisoner, which meant, in the eyes of his jailers, he was not a very good prisoner at all. In short, Ammon had been getting himself in a lot of trouble. Most recently, a punishment he'd received had approached what sounded, one had to admit, an awful lot like torture, even if it was evidently legal in the United States of America. A few weeks earlier, as Ammon told it, he'd been dragged into a shower stall and left for thirteen hours with his hands cuffed tightly behind his back, a technique that impedes circulation while causing constant pain. A brief argument with a guard about a shirt he had left hanging on his bunk bed had escalated. The conflict seemed possibly related to ongoing tensions over Ammon's pronounced acts of passive refusal regarding the use of strip searches in the prison. Ammon had been threatened with twenty-four hours in this excruciating position, he said, but after the complaints of other inmates he'd finally been uncuffed, stripped, as always, searched, and probed, yet again, in his most private parts, and tossed naked into solitary confinement—"the hole"—where he'd been spending a great deal of time in recent months. A guard later tossed him his sacred Latter-day Saint undergarment. From the cell, he had managed to get a call out to activist Kelli Stewart, who, along with John Lamb, had emerged as one of the main public faces of the Patriot movement during the Malheur trials. Stewart, drawn to the cause by the death of LaVoy, had become an impassioned advocate in the peaceful mode Ammon and others seemed to favor post-occupation. She was not a militia member; she was a politicized Oregon homemaker, galvanized into commitment by what she saw as the murderous abuses committed by her government. What she heard on the phone the night Ammon called—a call she broadcast live over the internet—seemed to only confirm her in her purpose. She promised him she would be there by the weekend, and she kept her promise. Soon a Bundyite compound had emerged in the Mojave Desert, just outside the walls of the detention center. This one was notably free of strutting militia types and of firearms of any kind. The focus now was on the theater of protest.

Core Civics

It was a long way through the desert around this prison. Here and there a lonely Joshua tree rose up, its arms frozen to our human eyes, caught in the midst of the spiky Shiva dance of its growth. The prison was always on our right, a vague clump of structures of the sort that seem designed to defy description, or even perception. I tried anyway: "Earthwork walls," I wrote in my pad, "some flat beige buildings—lots of fences, lots of wire." In the distance was a large metal sun structure for the prisoners; we could see orange shirts hurling themselves around a court in a game of basketball. This time was chosen for the march each day because the prisoners were always out in the yard after lunch—unless, like Ammon Bundy, they were locked in solitary. The CoreCivic corporation was not known to be sparing in its use of the hole—and had been recently called out in a U.S. Department of Justice report for its improper use of solitary to house new inmates for extended periods due to shortages of bed space.

Everywhere the Bundyites went they seemed to stumble into metaphor. What American pictures they made, often without seeming to fully intend it. Out in Malheur, they'd made a Facebook figure of Manifest Destiny in their neo-settler reenactment. Now here they were, on their Jericho March, circumnavigating a prison operated by a private for-profit entity that had had the wicked temerity (or inadvertent honesty) to call itself CoreCivic. Incarceration *and* profit—when it came down to it, weren't those two of our truest core civic values at this point? The Patriots, with their flocking energies, were just drawing a big circle around it, over and over every day—We the People bound to the privatized, secret carceral heart of the nation.

CoreCivic hadn't been the company's original name; the Corrections Corporation of America (CCA, as many still called it) had very recently undergone a big rebranding. A certain amount of poor publicity goes with the territory when you lock people up for profit, what with stories of prisoner abuse, poor working conditions, and eyebrow-raising donations to candidates who supported tougher sentencing laws. CCA had seemed to have had an especially bad run—including a news story about its employees participating in a surprise high school locker search in Arizona. But bigger trends in American attitudes to law and order were presenting a far grander threat to the company's business model. CCA had noted with alarm in its 2014 annual report the adverse effects changes in parole and sentencing guidelines could have on their business. Possible alterations in drug laws and immigration policy were also troubling to the corrections giant. "Any changes with respect to drugs and controlled substances or illegal immigration could affect the number of persons arrested, convicted, and sentenced, thereby potentially reducing demand for correctional facilities to house them," as the report had bluntly put it. Even more troubling for the company and its shareholders, the Justice Department had announced, in 2016, after its OIG report, that it would discontinue the use of private prisons. The Department of Homeland Security had been considering a similar move. Unsurprisingly, the stock price of CCA had been severely affected, so much so that shareholders had rebelled and sued. But now the company had a new logo and this cynical new name, which made it sound like a Soros-funded democracy initiative. And with the change of presidential administrations, the DOJ decision had been reversed. Share values were back up, just in time for a new boom in immigrant detention.

All this meant that much of what the Bundyites were saying at Camp Liberty was making total sense to me. I'd been impressed with their spirit during the trials in Portland, when the Bundy Revolution had thrown itself, like so many wrenches, into the gears of our troubling justice system. I'd been impressed with their challenge to the federal government's right to define what was protest and what was not. The thoughts of more sophisticated Ammonites, like Jason, about police militarization were ones I mostly agreed with. But Jason's ideas weren't at the center of the movement, which had remained focused on some terribly shortsighted ideas about public land and fantastical notions about what the Constitution actually said and intended. This was different. Now the Bundyites were actually advocating things that I agreed with. Instead of signs blaming the EPA or the Bureau of Land Management for our national woes and loss of liberty, the Patriots were waving STOP HUMAN TRAFFICKING signs at the prison buses and at the guards coming to and from work. I couldn't agree more: this was human trafficking; that's what a private prison *is*. Now, oddly, it was Bundyites pumping me with the same stats I already knew from editorials, the Black Lives Matter movement, leftist anti-incarceration friends, and works like Michelle Alexander's *The New Jim Crow*: we incarcerated more people than China, and at a shockingly higher rate; we spent $182 billion on prisons every year; in 2017 CoreCivic's revenue would top $1.7 billion.

Soon Ammon would take it further, delivering another Dear Friends speech, this one by telephone from solitary confinement. He'd thank his comrades outside for all the attention they had brought to his and his family's situation, but this message, he said, was for those who had no such supporters.

> My words today are for the forgotten. For those who have had to live with this unjust system—this wicked system—without hope for any chance of correction; for those who are innocent, and for those who know they have done wrong but are not being allowed a chance to make it right. For those who stole a dollar and are being punished like a bank robber. My voice is for the many wives, husbands, children, and loved ones who have had their loved ones ripped from them and their lives turned upside down. Those who have experienced the wrath of this system and know that it is anything but just. These words are for you. I know your pain; my family and friends know your pain. We see it now and must consider things we have not considered before.

He'd go on to advocate for what would essentially be the abolition of the entire prison system as we know it, and its replacement with a system of restitution and rehabilitation. Some of his old friends had already picked up the new message and distilled it into the Patriot idiom. As we marched, a large, red-shirted, animated fellow was shouting slogans through the megaphone. He seemed like a Nevada Bundyite for sure, a Vegas one; they had a different tone about them—jollier, louder.

"You are all heroes . . . victims of a corrupt system!" he shouted at those distant, faceless orange figures. "You have not been forgotten!"

"What do we want? Freedom!"

"When do we want it? YESTERDAAYYYYYYY!"

Occasionally megaphone dude paused, and Brand would hit the shofar, and the horn blast would rise up above the wind, its long notes drifting out over the prison and the desert before vanishing.

On we trudged. Now the megaphone guy was making short speeches about assorted unconstitutionalities and imploring the guards to quit their jobs. Then there was some stuff about CoreCivic donations to the Clinton Foundation. I guess the Clinton Foundation thing still mattered to these folks even though election season was over, and CoreCivic was considerably more generous to politicians on the right.

Near me another Nevada Bundyite, bearded and wiry, struggled with the great flagpole he bore, its base sheathed in a holster at his hip. It was more of a mast than a flagpole. At least twenty feet above us flapped two flags: On top was an upside-down American flag, a favorite gesture of the Bundy crew. Beneath this distress signal was an American Revolution–era pine tree flag. On its white field was a single conifer, a liberty tree, and beneath it ran the old words AN APPEAL TO HEAVEN. Above us the flags clapped loud as sails, as their standard bearer was blown back and forth across the desert. At especially rough moments, it seemed that he just might be sucked right up into the sky.

Along the way I had struck up a conversation with a chatty young fellow who seemed out of place—from his clothes to his East Coast college accent to his still-only-basic familiarity with the Bundy story. I found myself filling him in on details of the events in Oregon. Dustin was a libertarian, and a mathematician, or at least that's what his degree was in; but mostly he was a gambler, a card player, a real pro. He'd been set up in Vegas playing cards, as he usually did at least once a year, when the internet had drawn his attention to the Camp Liberty protest. So now, as I circled the prison, and Flagpole Man blew back and forth past us, I got to learn all about what it meant to be a professional gambler in America today.

Dustin was a math guy. He was explaining what that meant and how he had learned to deal with what was apparently the Achilles' heel of math guys: all the talented psych-oriented gamblers out there. He'd had to learn to insert randomized emotional fluctuations into his own game—to disrupt all those patterns of feeling that flowed through it, invisible to him, behind his every cognition. That's how the psych guys got you: they knew how to suss out the patterns in your choices, patterns you didn't even know you had. There was really nothing you could do about those patterns, they were part of who you were, but if you added more chance elements, cluttered things up with randomized decisions that weren't really yours, maybe you could become more difficult to read.

As we'd talked, the wind gradually tore the clouds away and revealed the gas-flame blue of the Mojave, the Great Unsheltering Sky. Soon the whole valley seemed to be shaking—a bowl full of quivering light. The creosote bushes were talking, whistling in the wind, their smell blowing off them like it does when it rains, though it was totally dry today, the humidity easily under 10 percent. It was just the wind doing this to them—gathering up that signature desert scent, a smoky patchouli-like smell, and shooting it everywhere. If you've experienced rain in the Mojave, you'll know the smell. I say "patchouli-like," but there's really nothing else like it. Sometimes when walking I grab a few of the tiny oily leaves off the ganglia-like limbs of a creosote—big bushes, they look like fright wigs. I like to rub the leaves into a pulp between my fingers till they give off a hint of that rain smell that now somehow the wind was culling from them all of its own.

Dustin and I were walking closely together, but we still had to shout because of that wind. I was interested, and Dustin was enjoying my interest. Gambling, he continued, was, to his mind, one of the only ways to make an honest living in America, in this corrupt economy, at least according to his libertarian principles. I wasn't so sure gambling was outside that economy, but he could have found worse things to do with his talents, that was for sure. Young Dustin's ethical claims got him talking about the federal government. He, like Ammon, held that it was government that was mostly responsible for all our predicaments. I pushed back. Look right there, I said, pointing. It's a *for-profit prison.* Isn't *that* the root of the problem, *corporations* taking over the public sphere? The privatization of *everything?* Look at the results. That wasn't the right way to think, Dustin told me. He couldn't blame greed. That, to his mind, was like blaming the snowflake for the avalanche. You can guess who had caused the avalanche in this metaphor. Government was mainly or wholly to blame, because it had created this world and the distorted policies and unfree markets that gave companies opportunities to do these unethical things. Given the chance, they just did them; it was just natural, Dustin assured me. And there we were, back at the leftist/libertarian divide. We'd also finally arrived back at windblown Camp Liberty; a chair and a milk crate flew past us, clattering into the road, as other Bundyites came running past to retrieve them.

*   *   *

Back in the camp, a friend of Neil's, an Oath Keeper militia member and retired corrections officer named Rocky Hall, got out her notebook to show me the list of all the major funds that invested heavily in CoreCivic. Vanguard looked to be the biggest. My adopted home state of California's employee pension fund was high up there too. It turned out all fall, when Neil and the gang had been on trial, Rocky had been in North Dakota, out at the protests at Standing Rock. Now the Standing Rock stories came tumbling out of her. "It broke my heart," she said. "I thought *it* was *happening.* We had the attention of the world."

In the end, it was Rocky's long-term involvement with the Bundy struggle that had caused her maybe the most pain at Standing Rock. She'd been kicked out of Sacred Stone Camp after being there for five weeks. She said she was told it was because of her Bundy associations, that her having been at Bundy Ranch meant she was a white supremacist. This, too, had been heartbreaking. She identified as being of Choctaw descent, which was a big part of why she'd gone to North Dakota in the first place.

Seeing what happened after her departure from North Dakota had also been heartrending for Rocky. It had been terrible to watch the camps get demolished. So many donations had gone into all those tepees, and all the other stuff. She just hoped the workers at the landfill had gotten something from it. She began lamenting how hard it was to get donations for the Bundy cause in comparison. I said something about how Standing Rock sure had captured imaginations and energies. "You know what it all was?" Rocky asked, leaving a good dramatic pause, through which the desert wind poured. "White guilt," she said, answering her own question, nodding her head. "Just white guilt—and where did it go? It broke my heart."

People flowed in and out from under the big tarp at the center of the camp. A number of young mothers were here—they were talking of the wonders of raw milk and of the links they saw between vaccines and autism (vaccine fears were strong in this circle). I met a brightly intense young Mormon woman from the suburbs of Salt Lake City. She was a bit of a political pariah, she said, as a libertarian in her stolid Republican world; Mitt and Anne Romney were in her ward. She explained to me how the issue of the Bundys was handled in a suburban Latter-day Saint milieu like hers: "Nobody even says their names." To her mind, though, Ammon was in touch with the earlier energies of the church. "Ammon's someone who understands that Joseph Smith went to jail many times," she told me. The religion had been born in persecution. The Saints had been murdered and hounded out of Missouri and then Illinois. "We can't forget that," she said.

The Compliance Room

I wandered about in the camp. By the main road I came upon the stage set for the other regular performance the Bundyites had been livestreaming into the social ether. A handwritten sign on the structure identified it. CCA COMPLIANCE ROOM TIME OUT, it read. (CoreCivic's name change was still in process; the new logo hadn't even gone up on all its own facilities yet.) Basically the thing was a plywood box, with a gate of white rods, built to the size specifications Ammon had given of the shower stall in which he'd been left, handcuffed, for thirteen hours. All around its sides someone had stuck little American flags on sticks; these, miraculously, were still attached despite the wind, though they flapped like mad, giving the Compliance Room an oddly animate, cartoony presence. On the back wall of the chamber hung a metal Celtic cross, the handiwork of Duane Ehmer. It looked exactly like the one I'd watched him pound out at the forge on his flatbed truck in front of Portland's federal courthouse on the morning he was convicted.

In front of the box stood a camera tripod. Today no one was inside, performing for the Facebook Live audience; it was far too windy, even for this crew. Over the past couple of weeks many campers and visitors had done their time in the box. The idea—which was credited to Pacific Patriot Network leader B. J. Soper, who'd come down from Oregon early in the protest—was for the Patriots to take turns suffering as Ammon had.

To make the most of this devotional exercise, they were to do it on the livestream, reporting on the experience, on what was happening to their bodies in real time, as they tried to imagine what their hero had gone through. Participants regularly took care to point out just how much more Ammon and his family had been through, how this pain ceremony was only an exercise in beginning to make his greater pain imaginable. *Imagine* was a word they often used. Imagine! Thirteen hours of this!

I knew what it was because earlier in the week I'd watched Neil take his turn in the box. He'd put on a real show. It had all started mellow enough. John Lamb was behind the camera, chatting and answering questions as they popped up on his screen from the real-time audience. Someone named Michael promised to pledge five hundred dollars to the Bundy defense fund in support of Neil's performance if Neil, the old woodworker, would sign his hammer for him. Neil, freshly fettered, hands firmly cuffed behind his back, turned to the camera and flashed a big grin: "I will do it, Michael," he replied as he stepped into the box.

These pledges were a big part of the performance—it was a telethon essentially, a live-torture telethon, to collect funds for Ammon's legal defense. And it was pain they were selling in exchange for this financial support. A lot of the on-screen and off-screen chatter was about the medical details of that pain they were learning together: arm stiffness, swelling, joint pain, general discomfort, restlessness. The Patriots shared and compared what they had learned about what it felt like to be cuffed-up like that in such a space, what they had observed, empirically with their own flesh and also in the flesh of others. Folks on the livestream were also texting in with their two cents. "Yes, Debra," John responded to one now—a viewer who had noticed Neil's wedding ring—"we should take the rings off of people before they go in; that's probably why they do it somewhat in jail, take all the jewelry off, because your hands do swell."

Neil Wampler was a model fake prisoner. During his time in the box, he gave one of the great performances of the story of Malheur, starting with a little history of the Patriots' impulse to identify and express solidarity with the Bundy family and Ammon in particular. "You know, up in the Oregon trial, for a while there, Ammon wore jail scrubs in the courtroom," he recalled. He explained how he and John and others had then donned the same garb. This compliance-room performance was another exercise in identification with the Bundys. "Any way we can express solidarity with these noble men, we have to—it is imperative that we do it," Neil explained. "I am very hopeful that Ammon will see me putting myself in the same position that he has been in."

Neil continued on about the nobility of the family, how qualified they were for pretrial release—which seemed like a pipe dream that May, but was something a judge would eventually order, if not for another seven months, after a series of wild revelations about the case. "Our own Constitution specifies that excessive bail shall not be required," Neil reminded the screen before shifting into a whole other mode of discourse: poetry, a song, memorized, a dystopian set of rhymed lyrics about a society in total meltdown, about police violence and riots in the streets. His friends giggled nervously, stunned, unsure of what it was that he was doing. "Trouble Every Day" was the name of this ditty; on he went, rhyming up all that trouble, the failure of the New Deal dream of a Great Society ending in class war and a great American conflagration. He ended exultantly, managing to be cheerful and ominous at once, his eyes making contact with each viewer through the screen.

John Lamb clearly never had never seen anything like this in his entire Amish life; you can hear the giddiness in his voice as he whoops and congratulates Neil on his performance. Neil grinned sheepishly and backed into the corner of his cell, as John and a few other Patriots clapped. It occurred to me, watching these two unlikely friends, how many stories there were in this story. Neil, the Bay Area hippie and reformed killer, drunk for much of his early adulthood—and John Lamb, Amish most of his days, whose own kids, he told me, had grown up never even knowing who the president was until very recently. Now here they were laughing together, live on Facebook, out in the Mojave Desert, outside the walls of a private for-profit prison.

I had never heard the song Neil recited. I had to look it up. It's one of Frank Zappa's, from 1966—a rollicking, distorted, and jangly garage rock number, allegedly written a year earlier in the Echo Park apartment of a meth dealer, known, at least to Zappa, as "Wild Bill the Mannequin-Fucker," and then recorded with his band, the Mothers of Invention. The song was Zappa's response to watching the Watts Riots on TV in L.A. in 1965—the same riots that young Cliven Bundy had witnessed in person in L.A., reminiscences of which had prompted his infamous racist comments about slavery and "the Negro's" federally enforced unfreedom. Hard as it was to imagine Cliven Bundy being in L.A. at all, let alone witnessing the riots, it might be even stranger imagining Frank Zappa, Wild Bill the Mannequin-Fucker, and Cliven Bundy all existing in the same dimension, much less the same city at the same time, even before adding in the thousands of uprisen people of Watts. It was hard to imagine, but they had all been there, just like John and Neil and all the rest of us were somehow part of the same country in 2017, whether or not we could handle it.

*   *   *

The grand finale of the Compliance Room came the next week, when the encampment's two logistical leaders, Kelli and John, gave a tandem performance. In the meantime, the Compliance Room had reproduced; now there were two shower-stall cages, side by side. Both had been gussied up since my visit, painted the classic institutional color—battleship gray. John and Kelli declared that they weren't getting out of the cuffs or their boxes until they'd raised ten thousand dollars for Ammon's legal team, or until they, too, reached the thirteen hours that Ammon had been forced to suffer. They began at ten P.M.

It was another windy desert night. The two, dressed in full prison scrubs, were cuffed and lit up by solar-powered lamps that had been charging all day for the occasion. They were both livestreaming simultaneously, on their separate channels. Extra battery packs were hooked up to everything; they were prepared to go on past dawn and into the new day. Their tech guy tonight was Gavin Seim, the same Gavin Seim who, on his own livestream, had helped shepherd David Fry and the other members of the Final Four out of Camp Finicum in the final, terrifying moments of the occupation.

It starts off jocular, John joking around about spiders and scorpions. Then Kelli explains how everything they are doing out here tonight, cuffed in their makeshift shower-stalls, is an attempt to re-create Ammon's experience on the inside. The desert wind rises around them, turning into another noise, an unexpected human one: the whoosh of traffic. It's the shift change at the prison, Gavin explains. John and Kelli peer out at the road, at the departing and arriving guards; some, they report to their feeds, have stopped and turned around to peer back at them, illuminated in their little cages out in the desert night.

Soon the pain is growing in them; over the hours it just gets worse and worse. Both are pacing back and forth constantly, leaning in contorted positions, resting their heads on the walls, trying to find that elusive pose of momentary relief and comfort while keeping their eyes on their screens, so they can respond to messages from the watchers on their separate livestreams. Over and over, as new viewers hop on to their feeds, they tell the story of private prisons, of modern human trafficking, and of Ammon's torture, and how they are trying to experience it themselves, all while interspersing pitches and pleas for donations.

Along the way they also tell the story of Ammon and their movement's very recent break with Richard Mack. "Sheriff Mack came and visited him yesterday," Kelli says, "and asked him to have us leave, that we weren't doing any good. And Ammon's response was, 'Well, it brought you here, didn't it?'" She's outraged. How could a constitutional sheriff fail to support them? she wonders aloud. They are peaceful protesters on private land that they actually have permission to camp on. Mack hadn't even stopped to talk with the community, which upset John, who speaks up next. He had called the former Arizona sheriff weeks ago, he says, to try to get him to investigate what was going on with Ammon, but now he'd come and not even stopped to talk with them, to hear their side. It was an important turn for the Patriots. Now Richard Mack was out: he'd betrayed them; more importantly, he'd betrayed Ammon. In his own public statements, Mack would basically side with the prison's version of events. Sure, Ammon had been confined in handcuffs for thirteen hours pretty much as he'd described, but if Ammon had complied with guard requests, his cuffs would have been removed. Or that's how Mack had understood the incident. Given that the man was still called *Sheriff* after all these years, his judgments didn't seem all that surprising. Ammon would put it to me more bluntly when I spoke with him about it months later: "I learned that he [Sheriff Mack] wasn't for freedom," he told me. "He was for law enforcement."

* * *

By the fourth hour John couldn't stay still at all, and he could no longer keep up the banter with Kelli or with his livestream. It was painful just to watch him, twisting this way and that, turning and pacing, his usually bright face and eyes now heavy, visibly wincing and sagging with the pain. He was breathing hard now too, whooshing like the wind. This was childbirth breathing. He'd delivered a lot of kids, most of his own children, and he'd seen what that pain was like. He figured the breathing that his wife, Rebekah, used in birth might help him now. It came whistling out of him, as he twisted and turned in the box, leaning here and there, but finding no rest. It was past three o'clock, and both John and Kelli were delirious, their voices raspy and quiet. "I don't like handcuffs, that's for sure," Kelli said, almost in a whisper. "No, me neither," John echoed. He admitted he wasn't going to make it much longer, but he wanted to push into the next hour, and he asked Gavin to cue up the recording of the phone call Ammon had made after enduring the trial that they were seeking to emulate. He thought it might help him carry on just a little further. Now Ammon's voice, also thick and weird with pain, was being broadcast into the desert night as he recounted, step by step, the whole ordeal.

> They drug me down and they took me and threw me in a shower . . . It's probably about a three-by-three-block brick shower. It's got a metal door . . . They did take my leg irons off, but my leg irons had cut around my ankle on both my legs, so they were bleeding . . . I'm handcuffed behind my back—they got my arms turned out, so it's a really bad positioning. So with that little room I couldn't just curl up. I couldn't get any comfortable . . . It was hurting my shoulders . . . They were tight, my hands were starting to swell up and cutting circulation off my hands . . . I was in there for thirteen hours . . . and they were telling me that I was going to be in there for seventy-two hours.

As Ammon told his story, the desert had gone silent again; the wind had vanished. John shifted and twisted in his cell. He often turned his back to the camera now, and for long stretches all one could see of the bulk of him was his back—POLITICAL PRISONER written in faded marker across his blue prison-scrub shirt. Ammon's voice was having involuntary effects on him and he didn't want the livestream to see the tears. Finally the recording ended. John was coming out. Uncuffed, he sat in a chair while his friends marveled at what had just happened to his body. Especially his hands. He got up and displayed them to the camera. And his arms, he could not lift his arms at all. What did they feel like? "Just getting my feeling back in my arms," he said, and then corrected himself. "I *had* feeling—it was just the wrong kind of feeling."

Kelli seconded John from her cage, describing the pain she was feeling and also a strange heat. "It affects everything—my neck, my back, my hips hurt." But none of this stopped her from teasing her friend. "You still lost to a girl," she said, and the two laughed hoarsely.

*　*　*

Now the livestream stage in this theater of pain belonged solely to Kelli Stewart—for the next five hours into the dawn and the full heat of the desert day. Often she is alone, asleep—or trying to be—in a disheveled clump of shadows on the floor of her cell. Wind and then crickets, wind and then crickets, accompany her. The hours pass and then the light is coming and she's sitting up again and talking. She bows her head in the shade of whatever Gavin Seim has dragged between her and the sun. Her voice is weak with the pain, but she's still got a lot to say.

> This is torture and it needs to stop—and it's not going to stop until We the People stand together like Martin Luther King did, and Rosa Parks, and all of our Founding Fathers who came together and said, *Not on my watch*. We need to reinstate civil rights . . . This prison is the new cotton field. This prison is the new cotton field. This is where the slaves are. Black, White, Hispanic, Mexican . . . uh . . . Muslim. This is where they are being held as slaves. Sixty-five thousand a year this facility makes . . . Sixty-five thousand a year *per person* they make to hold these people and deny them bail and to feed them crap and to lock them in boxes. Are you OK with that, America? Are you OK with that? Or will you come out and stand by me? Will you come out and stand for these prisoners—all of these prisoners—will you let them know they're not alone?

She's not done yet. Much of what she's said has echoed things Ammon has also said, but then she takes it further, into territory that Ammon himself wouldn't enter, at least not publicly, for another year or more. Kelli's take on the immigration policies of the new administration seemed as likely to lose donations from much of the Patriot fan base as to win them.

> Please come and stand by us in Nevada: Southern Detention Center, CCA, CoreCivic private prison. But they're all over the country. You can find them all over the country. CCA, after Trump was elected in, their stocks *skyrocketed* because of what was about to happen with all the people that were going to be incarcerated for being illegal aliens. And how many of you Americans cheered them on? And don't you realize that Ammon Bundy could be Mexican? Don't you realize that as you cheer that Mexican on for being arrested because he's an illegal alien, or whatever nationality he is, don't you realize that that's exactly what they did to Ammon Bundy, and there's good men just like Ammon Bundy of different nationalities that are being filled in these prisons? And you think it's to keep us safe? You think we're going to drain the swamp? You think we're going to empty our country of illegals? They're arresting 'em to make money on them is what they're doing—and you are cheering them on!

She's regained the power in her voice, openly shouting, but then she stops, cuts herself off, checks the donation numbers—"we're at seven thousand," she says quietly, and then picks up mid-rant and carries on: "You're cheering them on as they fill their human warehouses, and they traffic human beings, you're cheering them on, because of the color of their skin— and you don't even realize you are being played! . . . It was the best day of their life when Trump was elected in; it should have been the worst day of their life. We should have been tearing down the walls of the private prisons, saying we're going to reinstate the Constitution!" Worked up, she turns her face to the wall and sighs and goes silent again.

Government Solutions

Kelli Stewart was right: CoreCivic stock had jumped around fourteen dollars per share, up to eighteen dollars. *Skyrocket* was not an exaggeration; it was, if anything, an understatement. By mid-2017 the shares were at twenty-seven dollars. The stock had plummeted in the last year of the Obama administration, when that Department of Justice report on failures and abuses at private prisons had provoked a new policy—the phasing out of the use of private facilities for prisoners in the federal system. This hadn't included immigration detainees, the numbers of whom had risen under Obama, and who were often housed in private facilities, many run by CCA and its main rival, GEO Group. Still, this policy had been enough to seriously rattle investor confidence. Now that had been more than fully restored. A bonanza was anticipated. If you're looking for a new source of moral outrage today, look up the recommendations to investors on why prisons are a good investment bet. And then maybe look to see if your own retirement funds (if you are lucky enough to have such a thing) are invested in CoreCivic or GEO Group; there's a very good chance they are.

"We are a diversified government solutions company with the scale and experience needed to solve tough government challenges in flexible, cost-effective ways." This is how CoreCivic defines its mission. The company also recently reclassified itself: it is now a real estate investment trust, a move that earned it tremendous tax advantages, including an additional 25 percent or so in tax breaks with the new 2017 Republican tax plan. *Diversified Government Solutions.* In the coming years these words wouldn't seem less euphemistic, as CoreCivic, along with its principal competitor, GEO Group, reaped the rewards of the refugee detention policies of President Donald Trump, whose inauguration both had contributed to heavily. The phrase, much like CoreCivic's shiny new name, also says something tremendously revealing about our historical moment, about our current American crisis, and about the story of Malheur.

It also made me think again, longingly, of the High Desert Partnership. As our *government solutions diversify,* as the push to privatize everything continues, as public life is further privatized, in new ways and to new effects we still don't understand—especially on the privately owned public platforms of social media—what will remain in the public sphere? Will there be such a thing? This—to me—was one of the central questions of the occupation. Maybe it was the main one. Ammon, to my mind, had offered one of the worst possible answers when it came to public land: it seemed like some kind of neo-homesteader privatization, cloaked in rhetoric about local governance. Ammon himself would describe to me the occupiers' plan of unwinding land transactions as an effort to "basically privatize the refuge like it used to be." But here in Pahrump he was learning with his own body what privatization could be like when what was privatized included the sovereign punishment power of the State. In the absolute final instance, such sovereign power is what debates about privatization are all about.

CoreCivic and the High Desert Partnership are both diversified government solutions, diffused figures of sovereign power, particularly the sovereignty of the federal government. While the High Desert Partnership performs a community-based diffusion of federal power in its consensus-based collaboratives, CoreCivic provides a very different (and dystopian) model of how dispersed federal sovereignty can operate—via privatization—in American life. Here, a key federal power—the power to inflict and manage punishment—had been auctioned off to the corporation with the best bid and the best lobbyists. Placed in the private hands of a corporate person, federal sovereignty was further from the hands of the people than the Founding Fathers could ever have dreamed. Despite their urge to keep governance at a distance from popular control, here we may have found an instance where we can say with certainty that this is something the aristocratic founders would not have wanted. How could anybody want private prisons? What comes after them? How about privately owned police forces? Some cash-strapped rural communities had already sold off their ambulance services and fire departments, often with disappointing results. Could the cops be next? In fact, such private police forces already existed—the French Quarter Task Force in New Orleans was one example. How about the military itself? Oh, right, that had already begun with the infamous Blackwater, whose founder, Erik Prince, and his sister Betsy DeVos—herself eager to privatize education—were now tightly connected to the Trump administration.

Similar questions of privatized social goods hovered over the medium John and Kelli were using for their theater. Did social media allow for a new horizontality in politics? Did it make for a more sovereign We the People, a peaceful militia armed with phones, as people like Ammon and Jason Patrick imagined? Or was it really a tool to transform the totality of human coexistence—or at least the shadowlands it cast as data—into the private property of the superrich? All while destroying the credibility of more detailed journalistic investigations into the operations of power that yielded us the dirt on entities like CoreCivic.

Which of these worlds is coming for us now? One full of High Desert Partnerships or of CoreCivics? A world of social media platforms locked down and patrolled by security states and corporate overlords, or a new buoyant democracy, full of real public participation? Or will it be some Frankensteined combination of both—as our present seems to uneasily contain. Jason Patrick told me he thought that Facebook hadn't decided yet if it was the worst or the best thing ever. It seemed a fair-enough diagnosis. The same thing might be said about the platform we call the United States of America.

*　*　*

All the possibilities had mingled together, democratic and dystopian, in John and Kelli's marathon. Now it was coming to an end. Gavin had decided that Kelli had suffered enough, dug up some of his own cash, and began proposing matching funds to the livestream audience. He took the telethon to a new level now—and it worked. The donations started coming in a frenzy, over Kelli's delirious objections—she felt this was cheating somehow, but no, said Gavin, this is how they do it; they do it like this for a reason. She was slumped on the floor of her cell, grinning, still in pain, and wiped out from her ten hours in cuffs, but gleaming, somehow, with evident happiness. John was back now, and he and Gavin were sitting on a bench in front of her cell, while Gavin slapped matching cash down dramatically for the entertainment of the morning viewers. "If you guys are ever in jail," Kelli said, her voice raspy with fatigue, "you want these two guys on each side of you."

CHAPTER TWENTY-SEVEN

Totality

JARVIS TOLD US ABOUT a lake up in the pines, beautiful, quiet, ringed in some old growth. He'd been going there to cool off after his days clearing the meadows, struggling with the high thistles that had overtaken the tribe's land in the John Day Valley. The Wadatika were hosting a campout up here for the 2017 total solar eclipse, and I'd come up with K, my beloved, to partake of the phenomena. Jarvis was right about the lake; it was a lovely spot, beautiful *timber*, as he said, his years working for the Forest Service showing through. But it wasn't quiet today, not at all. The mountains had been turned into what seemed like a massive commercial for Subaru—something we were very conscious of, driving one ourselves. Everywhere we looked, it seemed there was a Subaru posed for ad copy, with a white, outdoorsy family unit setting up camp nearby. Down in the valley meadows and up on the steep slopes, interspersed throughout the pines, orange, turquoise, yellow, and lime-green tents sprouted in all directions.

It's a little embarrassing to admit, but I had come to the eclipse in our Subaru looking for the end of this book. Intuition told me that I might find it here, where the tale, for me, returned to its beginning. For me, the story of Malheur had begun long before the occupation, with my interest in another western tale—one that had begun with a total solar eclipse. This was the story of Wovoka, Paiute Shaman, and the most famous of the Native American prophets of the nineteenth-century Intermountain West.

* * *

It was January 1, 1889, and the prophet-to-be was gravely ill. He was lying on the dirt floor of his wickiup as the whole world went dark in the daytime. It was in the middle of this darkness that he was given his vision: images of a returning, refreshed earth, and the reunion of the living and the dead. From this vision, Wovoka crafted a faith and a rite—the five-night dance in which participants entered into entranced, dream-communion with their departed. Keeping the dance, Wovoka said, would help bring on the coming world, when the dead would return permanently in the flesh along with all the animals that had vanished from the land with the coming of whites. Also returning would be the earth itself—made new. The earth was old—that was Wovoka's message. According to Porcupine, a Cheyenne pilgrim who'd traveled all the way to Nevada to meet the prophet himself, Wovoka had said, recalling his initial vision, "My father told me the earth was getting old and worn out and the people bad." "This Earth too old, grass too old, trees too old, our lives too old" is how one English-speaking Arapaho practitioner described it. "Then all be new again." Wovoka had seen that the creator "would do away with heaven and make the earth large enough to contain us all." To other visitors he'd dictated a letter. "Jesus is now upon the earth. He appears like a cloud. The dead are all alive again. I do not know when they will be here."

Wovoka's vision borrowed from earlier visions, like those of Smohalla, the prophet of the Dreamer sect, who'd also foretold the return of a redeemed earth, while warning the faithful against holding property or working for money like white men. Wovoka's teachings didn't bother with such prohibitions. It was too late; white dominion over the West was now complete. (Going by the name Jack Wilson, Wovoka himself was a ranch hand.) Instead, his vision erased that white world in compelling, collective fantasy.

As the dance developed and spread, becoming a pantribal religion, it created new threads of communication and solidarity between far-flung Native groups. Some adherents said that this movement of the new earth would slide from west to east, displacing Europeans back in the direction from which they had come. Cheyenne, Arapaho, Kiowa, and other groups described how the new earth would slide over the old, like the right hand over the left. As the new earth arrived, dancers would be lifted upward and deposited onto the new land with the help of the sacred feathers they wore in their hair. Then they would fall into a trance for four days and awaken on the new earth, alongside their old relatives, and all the buffalo, and everything that had been lost.

*   *   *

The path of the returning, redeemed earth in Ghost Dance theology happened to coincide with "the path of totality," the transcontinental route of the solar eclipse that I'd come back to Oregon to see. The occluded sun's route would also follow, quite precisely, the line that Jon Ritzheimer had traced on the map of the United States in his "Great Unfuck" video, back in the preamble days of the occupation. The event would start in Oregon and sweep east across the state into Idaho, then farther south and east through Wyoming, Nebraska, Missouri, and Kentucky, passing finally through Tennessee and South Carolina before heading out into the Atlantic. All across the country, along this narrow band, the moon would slide across the sun, casting the shadow of totality from horizon to horizon—before moving on, as the spinning Earth also moved on.

A nation is an abstraction, pinned to the earth. That pinning action creates a territory, a geography, which is to say the mix of earth and human fantasy that we call "world." A country is an imaginary place made of real lives and real stuff—dirt, rock, water, animals, plants—but mostly it's made of human persons who mingle with all this, consuming and transforming it. Despite Thomas Jefferson's objections, a nation is also the main modern secular form in which the living and the dead continually meet. The Ghost Dance was another modern form, a religious one, and what Wovoka had made into a dance was also a geography, a vision of a kind of nation—a different America. It fostered political unities between disparate groups and demographic resilience in tribes that had been decimated to the point of near extinction. The Dance made an impossible nation, but a useful one. No one could really live in the Ghost Dance, but I don't know how much longer we'll be able to live here in this country either.

*　*　*

I don't know what exactly I was looking for at the eclipse of 2017. What would make for a true end to this book? Maybe some conversations about living in a time of crisis, about living in a time that feels like an end, conversations about climate change and our political situation, about our dishonest relationship to the dead, to historical events and persons, about all our American reckonings with history, race, and the earth—all while waiting around for the sun to vanish. It sounds overwrought when I put it that way, but that's probably what I wanted, why I was here. K was interested in such things, but that's not why she was here. She was here with me because there was going to be a total solar eclipse and that was going to be amazing. I had actually lost sight of that. At the last minute, made nervous by alarmist traffic reports and media-amplified fears of fire, I'd balked at coming; she'd had to convince me it was worth driving the additional miles north from Burns. Now it all hit me—*the moon* was going to cover up *the sun*! What would that be like? I had no idea.

Totality would last for a couple minutes, the more informed were telling us, but the shadow of the moon would be passing over the sun for a couple of hours. Other campers had shown up while we were off on our excursion through the Subaru National Forest, but we were still a small group here in the meadow at the Wadatika campout. We wandered over to watch the evening's eclipse-eve entertainment. The tribe had hired a comedian, a performer very much of our American time. He told jokes, funny ones, about race and sex and masturbation and about being fat, mixed in with jokes about being a contemporary Native and all the attendant mix-ups and absurdities that involved. There was one about an online dating site, about our comedian going to meet a woman who'd posted about all her mouthwatering traditional skills—butchering deer, preparing trad food, and the like, as well as her trad garb. Excited, he goes to the first date—and it's his auntie. Another joke ended with our portly urban antihero trying to sneak up with Native stealth on an elk by hiding his bulk behind a tree—in a clear-cut.

Later than night, a crew of youths showed up, relatives of the Wadatika from the Duck Valley reservation down at the Nevada-Oregon border. Among them was a young cousin of Jarvis's, whom he'd never met before—he was very excited about this. These newcomers were also long-distance runners in training. The Paiute had been famous—like many desert-dwelling, originally non-equestrian peoples—for what had seemed to whites their superhuman long-distance running abilities. Early white settlers told stories of Northern Paiute running alongside their horses or wagons, attempting amiable conversation for a few miles, unfazed by their exertions or the language barrier, before parting and heading off into the desert, never losing pace, never seeming out of breath or tired. These kids planned to run from here to the refuge after the eclipse, a journey of around 110 miles. They figured it would take about twenty-four hours, through John Day and Bear Valley and down into the basin. Full of youthful energy, their preparations consisted of singing and drumming late into the night under the Milky Way.

Totality

It started slowly, the moon biting into the sun; we watched it through our eclipse glasses. The sun and the dark nibble of the moon in the corner, growing and growing. From time to time we'd take off our glasses and look around at the rest of the world—it was there that the uncanniness really started. After a while, the light becomes a light you've never seen before. It gets coppery, but it's not like any other coppery light you've seen. It makes you want to look at everything—it makes you an earthling hungry for the sights of earth. At least that's what it did to me. I went off wandering. I wanted to move around and look at everything at once—the leaves, the bark, the grass, the buttes, my hands. Everything looked exactly like what it was, and yet, at the same time, somehow totally changed.

I wandered over to the other long meadow on the tribe's property. This meadow was almost empty. Way at the far end of the valley a couple of RVs were parked in the grass under the cottonwoods. In the middle of the valley was a lone human figure, standing beside a flatbed truck, looking up at the sun through his eclipse glasses. On the truck's bed was a whole sound system, and it was blasting music, mournful chanting and drumming— tribal music, fluid drumming and song. It flowed over the whole scene. This valley was a bowl really, a dish of golden grass under a huge golden butte. Chunks of craggled basalt thrust through the earth here and there; a line of junipers marched along the crest of the ridge. I was staring up at them when I noticed that the guy with the truck was calling to me. "Hey, bro!" he said. "You got time to BS?" And so before I had time to think about it, suddenly there I was, in the middle of a total solar eclipse, talking about Wovoka and the ends and rebirths of worlds.

My interlocutor had a blue bandanna wrapped around his closely shorn head, a sleeveless white shirt baring long, muscled arms, and a cheerful, inquisitive face, the kind that searches you out in conversation, requiring that you be totally present. This guy really wanted to talk. What did I think about all this? he asked, gesturing with his long arms at the sky and also at the earth gripped in the spell of eclipse light. He knew the Native perspectives—how some say you shouldn't look on such a thing. Some folks here had already headed into the tribe's huge teepee over in the other meadow, he told me. They would not emerge till it was over. But what he wanted to know was what the eclipse meant—culturally—to me, the white guy suddenly on the scene. I didn't know what to say except that it freaked me out in a way I liked. I guessed what I was feeling was a kind of delight. And then he was asking me if I'd heard of a guy called Wovoka. Well, yes, I said. In fact I had. We talked about the prophet's eclipse vision of renewal, and then I told him about my book, and soon we were talking about Wadatika history, and then the occupation. He had some stories for me, he said.

I realized then that I knew who he was; I'd been trying to talk to this man for months and then had given up. He was Leland Dick; he'd been one of the instigators of the watchpost vigil that Jarvis and friends had kept over the reservation during the occupation. "Go up there and turn on the lights for the people," he said his mother had told him.

When talking with folks in the tribe about the occupation, Leland had mostly been a curious absence. More precisely, it had been his name that was missing. The stories of Leland were many, but the tellers, guarded, generally wouldn't say his name aloud to me: in the tales he was just a guy from the tribe, someone who was upset about the occupation and the militia in town. He was a young man, or a friend, or a cousin whom folks were concerned about; they'd been worried about what he might do. He'd especially raised people's fears of open conflict when he'd gotten in a brief standoff of his own with a clump of militiamen in the local McDonald's. Now Leland was telling me his story of that day.

"I whistled, you know, like you whistle at a deer. And all these armed militia guys, there were twelve of 'em, their heads just snapped around, and they looked at me. And I took their picture with my phone, and they all got up. There were like twelve of 'em and they surrounded me." He hadn't been afraid, Leland said. Instead he'd challenged them about their firearms. "'Why you all got guns? What you all afraid of?' And they say, you know, 'This is America.' And I say, 'Sure, I been places where you gotta carry just to go to the store for a Pepsi' . . . I'd heard that one of 'em had said he was ready to die. 'OK,' I said, 'let's go. Me too, I'm ready. I'm Paiute.'"

No one in the county had really confronted the militia guys like this, much less anyone as ready for action as Leland, and certainly not anyone as animated as Leland was by the history of this place. (It had all been Paiute land, Leland reiterated. And they'd never given it up, their treaty hadn't been ratified. "The wars with us were some of the only wars the U.S. Army qualified as a war.") I could see how Leland had made people worry. But in the end, the showdown had been averted; an older tribal member had guided him out of it. On the way home, the cops had pulled over the car he was in; he wasn't the driver, and when they'd asked him for his ID, Leland had refused to give it or his name. "You've got a Paiute Ghost Warrior here," was all he'd told them. And that had gone out over all the police radios.

Above us, the moon kept on eating the sun. K joined us now, and Leland told us more about himself. He'd traveled the world, played basketball professionally in China; having been all over, he hadn't been afraid of those militia guys. He'd been at Standing Rock too, been there for weeks during that fall following the occupation, and gotten in some very hairy situations. (It was important to know when it was time to back down, he said—something else he'd learned growing up.) The Native protesters were unarmed as always—"except for our war drums!" he qualified, laughing. "Going out without war drums is like going to a gunfight without your guns." "There's some things worth dying for," he added, "like the land. We can't sell this land here." He gestured at the meadow and the creek behind it. "This water is just going to get more valuable." At the same time he wondered about how long our current systems of value would hold out. "Do you think the money system will collapse soon?" he asked. "Me, I don't care. I'm Paiute, I'm ready. I can go up and hunt my elk, chill up in the mountains with the bros. I never cared about money. I've never believed it. You want me to go somewhere and fight for your oil? I don't think so." Somehow, the way Leland talked, none of this had been anything like a rant; he was just enjoying himself, beaming the whole time, gesturing broadly and laughing brightly as the world grew dark.

*   *   *

It was all really bending toward totality now. I went to wander around with K and stare at it some more; Leland stayed at the truck with the drum music still flowing from the speakers, coating everything with sound and meaning, singing the event forward. I'd thought the light was nuts before, but this—this was officially insane. We staggered about in the bronze-blue world, under the darkening hills. Every leaf, every rock, was at once the same and somehow absolutely altered. The hillsides and the butte rims were like shapes in a haunted painting—a landscape at dusk, but dusk in another world, a new country on a planet that was still somehow ours.

And then it was time. We were looking up through our glasses, K and I; there was just a sliver of sun left, and then there was nothing. It was all black. I took my glasses off. The sun was totally covered by the moon, ringed in the pale, cold light of the corona. The temperature had dropped, it seemed instantly, something like thirty degrees. It had been a hot, dry summer morning when this started; now cold enveloped us, as if it were rising from the earth. I could hear one bird, only one. The rest had gone silent. It was like night now, like a moonlit night, only duller—a dark glow on the land.

I don't know if those two minutes were long or if they were short; it was like a kiss, is what I thought. I was an eager earthling in the weird dark. And then it passed and the moon began sliding off. The weird copper light came back, gradually yellowing toward the sun of midday. We wandered back over to Leland at his truck. What did you think? I asked; it was my turn now. "Imagine if you didn't know that was coming," he said. He'd heard the people used to go nuts in the old days, that they'd start shooting arrows in the crazy midday dark. "Some things," he said, "you aren't supposed to see. I was wondering if this was something I was supposed to see."

We talked more about Wovoka's vision. Leland thought the path of totality could be the path of a new beginning. "Natives say that the eclipse brings destruction, but now maybe this brings healing, a reversal. So much has been happening," he said. "It makes you wonder—all those statues coming down." Out in the meadow, the heat of the day was beginning to touch us again. "It makes you glad for the sun," Leland said, "that it came back. You never know—I'm just glad it came back!" We all bowed together, laughing, to our star.

The path of totality slid on away from us, the moon continuously gliding in front of the sun farther and farther southeast, across the whole continent, the whole country—yes, it was a sea-to-shining-sea American event, well beyond the Subaru National Forest. All across the nation, people in this narrow band were experiencing earthlinghood made wholly, briefly strange. They were even experiencing it together. Totality passed nowhere near D.C., but still a good portion of the sun was occluded there. Something of the event could be viewed, so the president, making an unusual effort toward national unity, stepped onto a balcony with his scowling bride and their bewildered-looking little boy. Was anyone surprised when he did what we'd all been reminding our loved ones not to do? He looked up and stared straight into the sun.

CHAPTER TWENTY-EIGHT

Shadowlands

FROM THE TOP FLOOR OF THE LLOYD D. GEORGE Federal Courthouse in Las Vegas, you can see directly into the shadowlands. It's an effect often available in Vegas, a bloom of human growth pinned in by desert peaks and alluvial fans. You get up high enough and you are looking out past all that. It's like looking into a different kind of time, geologic time maybe, a time in which this improbable city has not yet been or is already long gone. You could also just be looking into the very recent historical past. There was hardly anything here in terms of human structures one hundred years ago. Only at the midpoint of the twentieth century had the population crept above twenty thousand. I loved standing in that window outside the court-room, watching the cloud shadows play across the alluvial fans and the stolid peaks of the Sheep Range, marbled with the soft colors of their mineral striations. From up on the top floor it hardly seemed that there was a city—or a nation—down there at all.

It was winter now, which meant more fast-running clouds dragging dark shapes over the earth—more shadows for the shadowlands; more swaths of mountain illuminated fleetingly in the quiet, whitened light of year's end. I had just come out of the courtroom behind me, where the tale of the Bundy Revolution had taken one of its most dramatic turns yet.

It was becoming clearer to me how much I and others had misunder-stood aspects of the Bundy story. The family had not helped things, and neither had their allies, with all the terrible ideas about public land, the fanatical bravado, the jacked-up macho attitudes, and all the guns. With his infamous ramblings on slavery and freedom, Cliven had also made himself a deserving target for the kind of ritualized shunning that helps other white people distance themselves from the entrenched realities of American racism. It had all done much to help to advance a generally accepted narrative of the Nevada standoff—a story of crazed, deplorable white gun nuts pointing long arms at federal officials so that some old backward freeloading rancher could keep ranching on public land. "Welfare Queen!" the internet had cried. ("Welfare Queen in a Cowboy Hat" is how one CNN host had put it.) This story mirrored the one that the U.S. attorney's office had been telling in court. But now that legal story line was crumbling, undermined largely by the way the government had been telling it. In the end, what the prosecution had left out of their story would destroy it, at least for the purposes of sustaining a trial. The end had begun today.

I'd been hearing whispers through the Bundyite ether for months. Way back in October, Brand Thornton had asserted that this case would be thrown out before it ever reached a jury. These sorts of claims often came coated with talk of divine providence, imprecations against the judge for her satanic hatred for the Constitution, and so on—which had made it all pretty easy to discard. I'd thought Brand and others had been dreaming. But just now I had watched Judge Gloria Navarro of the United States District Court for Nevada, a Barack Obama appointee, declare a mistrial in the federal case against Cliven, Ammon, and Ryan Bundy, and their friend Ryan Payne.

Judges have a kind of baseline world weariness to their manner; Judge Navarro seemed especially world-weary today. She appeared to have passed beyond a standard judicial exasperation into a new land of existential fatigue. Given the ruling she was reading to us, and the reasons for it, it was easy to understand why. The prosecution, over the preceding weeks, had mocked the Bundys' continual efforts to track down evidence they suspected had been withheld. Prosecutors had used words and phrases like *fantastical* and *fishing expedition* to deride the defense's inquiries. This bluster hadn't helped; in the end the prosecution had been forced to hand over more than 3,300 pages of discovery evidence, most of which should have been given to the defense before the trial started.

Judge Navarro's ruling, delivered in a quiet, careful voice, was relentlessly thorough. More important than the act of withholding, the judge was saying now, was the nature of the withheld evidence: most of the limited batches of material being considered today was potentially exculpatory. It could have allowed the defense to make better opening arguments, to choose jurors differently, and to impeach prosecution witnesses more effectively. What also became apparent, as the judge detailed specific items, is that some of this hidden evidence undermined the indictment itself—and, with it, the prosecution's entire narrative, right at its foundations. What we were talking about here mostly were Brady violations, after the 1963 Supreme Court decision in *Brady v. Maryland*, in which the court had ruled that the prosecution must not withhold potentially exculpatory or mitigating evidence, and is essentially responsible if law enforcement does so as well.

The prosecution's story line had stated, more or less, that the Bundys and Payne, the "most culpable" defendants, had lied about feeling threatened by an aggressive militarized federal presence involved in the roundup of the family's herd. They had done so in order to criminally recruit an army of militiamen, who had then illegally obstructed and threatened federal officials. When the family talked about surveillance, snipers, and provocations, they were essentially lying—these were deliberate misrepresentations, or so went the federal case. Now—as the judge detailed documentation of surveillance, of law enforcement officers with long guns in what could easily be understood as sniper roles (they were, in fact, described by law enforcement as such)—it looked like the federal government had willfully withheld substantial evidence that suggested the Bundys had been, at least partly, telling the truth.

The government had also been made to produce four separate threat assessments that had not been shared earlier, none of which characterized the Bundys as a threat. A federal internal affairs report also stated that no documented evidence of damage to tortoise habitat had been found on Bundy grazing lands, potentially undermining the reasons for restricting the Bundys' use of their federal grazing areas in the first place. The judge now reminded the room that the government had insisted "that this report was 'an urban legend' and 'a shiny object'" meant to distract the court. "The report does exist," she added pointedly. She declared a mistrial; her final decision on whether to dismiss the indictment would be announced on January 8.

Slowly the jury filed in. Nowhere near all-white, this was a Vegas jury, not an Oregon one. That familiar silence—heavy and austere—overtook the room as we all rose together, watching them enter and scan *our faces*. Today the usual dynamic was reversed. Now it was the jurors who were trying to read us, and we who were the ones in the know. Still, they looked wholly unsurprised when the judge apologized, thanked them, and dismissed them. In the end, they had spent far more time waiting to hear testimony than hearing any; they must have known something was up. The Bundys would claim that afterward a few jurors had approached Ryan, asking to take him up on his invitation to visit the family's ranch. He'd made the suggestion in his opening argument, when he'd rhapsodized about rural life and what it meant to him and his kin. "I'll take you to our ranch; you can see all the beauty of the land, the fresh air, sunsets and sunrises, the brush," he'd offered back in October. "You're on a horse in front of the cattle—*place yourself there*—feel the freedom." Ryan told me later that the speech had been entirely improvised. He'd gone blank as he stepped up to the podium that day—but then the Holy Ghost had rushed in, guided him to the right words, and he'd talked for well over an hour.

"Anytime We Are Willing"

As you can guess, it is an uncanny thing to come face-to-face with someone whose face and mode of speaking you've studied as long as I'd studied Ammon Bundy. I'd watched so many hours of him on video, and then watched him in court in Oregon for hours on end as well. He was so familiar, and yet not at all. The effect someone has when they are right in front of you, when the totality of their presence is engaged with yours, is always different. And Ammon's talents are all about presence. His political skill is in how much he involves listeners in his own speech, how attentive he stays to his speech as it takes place in you. I think it's a fair guess that more often than not people are listening to Ammon rather than the other way around, but the way Ammon talks, the way his ideas take possession of him, and the delight you can see in his own eyes and face as he chases down the thing he's going to say, all make you feel like you are having the thoughts as well. It adds to the general feeling of inspiration that surrounds him, and his brother as well—something Ammon and Ryan understand with a psychology that is entirely theological. It is the Spirit of God, the Holy Ghost, third person of the trinity of the Mormon Godhead, who guides speakers like Ammon and Ryan to the things they discover they have to say.

"Our detractors say, 'Oh, you guys are just too emotional,'" Ryan told me. "Well, anytime you are in tune with the Holy Ghost, you will have tender feelings. *That is truth*—tears of joy."

Tears of joy? Truth? These are compelling things. It also helped that Ammon and Ryan were often making fairly inventive, easy-to-understand utopian figures for inspiring stuff: elucidations of great political and theological forms, big ones like *the People*, theoretical *and* emotional spaces ample enough for all their listeners to dwell inside. It was an especially capacious version of *We the People* that Ammon was telling me about now— one as big as the internet itself.

We were outside, standing in the bare, elevated plaza that stretched out from the fortified entrance of the towering L-shaped courthouse. Earlier, Ammon and his brother and Ryan Payne, along with Jeanette Finicum and Angie Bundy, had emerged into the waiting swarm of reporters and supporters. With arms linked, smiling silently, stepping slowly, measuredly, they'd crossed the plaza toward the rest of us while the digital cameras clicked all around them. It was like a line dance—and a curtain call. These people had a feel for spectacle, you had to hand it to 'em: I had been waiting for them to actually take a bow.

That had been about an hour ago; now the other reporters were mostly gone, and the circle that had gathered around us on the empty plaza was made mostly of Bundy family and friends—Shawna, Neil, Angie, Ryan, and others. All were listening, rapt, as Ammon improvised his response to a question I'd asked about social media and the intensity of the community that had sprung up around him and his family.

"I'll kinda answer that in a little bit of maybe an odd way," he began. "The Second Amendment says—"

I started laughing. I couldn't help it. He was going to bring in the Second Amendment here too? "But I'm gonna tie the two together," Ammon said, grinning at my skepticism. "The militia is, by law, every able-bodied man . . . it would include women now . . . My point is . . . that power is distributed between every person in this country, every able-bodied person . . . and they could unite quickly, they could defend liberty. Well, that's the way media has become. Every person has a cell phone; every person has now become a reporter; every person has an audience."

"You see that as the militia?" I asked.

"Well, absolutely," Ammon replied. "It's the same concept. It's the distribution of power among the people. What we see the federal government trying to do—and many others—they're trying to consolidate power into one body and then it can be controlled, manipulated, abused. Social media has made it so it's distributed amongst everybody. And that is why it's necessary for the security of a free state."

I knew he was reading my face and could tell that I was impressed with the grandiosity of this figure he'd just conjured on the spot. The internet was the people, the people were the media, the media was the militia—and so the militia, in turn, was the internet, where power was finally distributed through everyone. It was strange to hear Ammon sounding like a Silicon Valley anarcho-capitalist, strange to hear him painting a techno-utopia not so unlike that of a Mark Zuckerberg. It was strange, but it wasn't. It was in line with the rest of his thinking, with the social utopia his understanding of his faith bent toward: everyone together under the divine Constitution, protected and protecting one another from overweening federal power. His new cell phone militia, consisting of pretty much every adult, was an image of popular regulation of government so pervasive it almost seemed like total self-governance—and self-governance was what Ammon Bundy seemed to love talking about more than anything else.

*   *   *

About a month later, after it was all over, he'd tell me more about it on the phone. He was home now, up in Idaho in that house with the orchard that he and Lisa had been guided to by the Spirit of God back in 2015. I could hear his youngest son brightly babbling in the background, and it sounded like Ammon was doing the dishes as he talked. He'd been home for a week, getting to know that youngest son, who'd been only a year old when Ammon had first been arrested. I asked him again about the spirit of the community at the refuge and about the supposed leaderlessness of the occupation.

As seemed to be his nature when confronted with a big question, Ammon immediately got theological. "Man should be free to choose for himself what direction we will take," he said. "I believe God does not ever infringe on our agency. If God came down and straightened everybody out, there would be no agency." He'd experienced firsthand what self-governing community could be like because, to his mind, that's what was happening at the refuge. "Each person had the agency to be there, they could leave at any point, and that was what was amazing—they were still there! It wasn't me leading them. I was walking right beside them." If he wanted to go this way and others wanted to go with him, they could join him, and their line could swing that way, or not, he told me. As a model of society, or collective action, it sounded like a line dance, a little like the line dance he and Ryan and the rest had made while exiting the courthouse.

Maybe everyone's utopia is some kind of dance, a dispensation of bodies and souls arranged in constellations of freedom and bliss. Maybe that's what heaven is—a dance we'll never dance. Not with these un-glorified bodies, not with these twisted-up minds; not with all our competing desires and urges, the ecological and historical traumas and challenges that make up the realities of our earthly existences and our actual, always political, lives. But we can still imagine heavenly dances with our words, erasing the thorny realities of all our differences. Ammon was very talented with these kinds of words, not just at saying them, but at making them into stories and actual physical places for him and his friends to be. The freest place they'd made for themselves during the occupation had terrified, offended, and enraged many others, often with very good reason, but it had been a place of incommensurable value for Ammon and his community. Out at the refuge, he said, there'd been "a spirit of unity." One that was "based on mutual respect." "We can have that anytime we are willing to live that way," he added. "If the people are willing to work together . . . that's one of the things that we can have."

All You Can Eat

January 8 came around fast, and now I was back up in that same window at the top of the courthouse, looking out again at the shadowlands. Neil Wampler was here with me. The plaza below us was empty, but up here the lobby was packed. I'd arrived early, but not early enough. There was no over-flow room for the trials in Vegas. The huge courtroom had been big enough up until today, but now some of us would miss out, Neil and me among them. We stood by the window and talked. I had asked Neil about the internet, about what Ammon had said back in December. His thoughts moved to some of the more non-utopian aspects of the technology. There had been a lot of internet squabbles in the movement, he said. Of late, he'd been taken aback at how much feeling passes around on the web. He got reflective about it: so much had changed in media in his lifetime. He remembered watching the Pabst Blue Ribbon ads with his dad, back when the ads were still live. The two of them would watch to catch the moments when the beer wasn't poured exactly right and the foam spilled over the edges. He stopped for a second to marvel at something: the strangeness of it—they are all gone now, he told me. His family, he meant. His father, mother, and brothers. Neil was the only one left. We continued on chatting quietly about the past—moving onto the tumult of the sixties, the personal shock he'd felt at the Kennedy assassination, "the godawful, colossal folly of Vietnam," as he put it. "*We had to destroy it to save it,*" he cited, laughing, shaking his head.

Neil seemed to be enjoying himself here at the window reflecting on the past, but I knew he'd have rather been inside hearing what Gloria Navarro was saying. In that room behind us, Neil's movement was receiving its greatest vindication yet. Judge Navarro declared that she had found the government's arguments "disingenuous." The conduct here was so flagrant, she said, that the court was left no option but to apply the strongest remedy at its disposal—mistrial with prejudice—which meant a dismissal of the indictment. The alternative—a new trial—would have substantially benefited the government, which had been able to gain knowledge of the defense's strategy.

The kind of illegal prosecutorial and police behavior the judge was calling out today happens all the time. We learn of it only in special circumstances, often when convictions are overturned, usually because of discovery violations like the ones in this trial. Add the notorious and widespread police practice of "testilying," and the picture just gets uglier. The effects of all this have been corrosive. Story after story of wrongful conviction, evidence suppression, and other forms of prosecutorial and police misconduct, often in very serious, sometimes capital cases, have eroded Americans' trust in police and the justice system. By 2018, the chickens had come home to roost. Now we had a president with arguably clear contempt for the idea that he was not above the law. In 2017 and on into 2018, Donald Trump was finding that belittling the practices of the federal criminal justice edifice seemed to only strengthen his popularity with his political base. In response to Trump's anti–"deep state" rhetoric, we were now regularly subjected to pious editorials warning us of the chaos we would face *if* our trust in the justice system were somehow to be undermined. Where, I wondered, had these people been?

*   *   *

A ripple went through the crowd milling about near the entrance to the courtroom. The doors had swung open and I watched as the news passed from body to body for a long time before I could actually make out what anyone was saying. Reporters were running out of the courtroom, grabbing their devices from the marshals. Faces were turning to faces. The strangest thing was how long it took for a shout to actually go up. The news was a rustle first, a game of telephone, but then finally the first shout came, and then the roar, and more bodies pouring from the courtroom, and then mini-scrums of Bundyites whooping it up. Then the praying began. I'd gone around the corner to sit on the floor and write. From here, through the glass, I could see them and also see the mountains—whips of rain were falling from dark clouds. I imagined the drops hitting the cold sand, and the sizzle sound rain makes out in the desert. Soon everyone was hustled along into the elevators by the marshals, and then we were all out in that plaza again, waiting for the big moment when Cliven Bundy himself would be released.

In December, Ammon and Ryan and the others had been able to slowly approach the bubble of supporters and media in their curtain-call line—but here there was only the bubble. It swallowed Cliven Bundy immediately. As soon as he emerged into the lobby—out of his prison clothes and now dressed in his usual formal western wear—the crowd was on him. Cliven's voice was hoarse today—he kind of croaks and warbles at best—so hardly anyone could hear what he was trying to say. More whoops went up, while the cameras kept clicking away. He could barely inch his way into the plaza. It was like he was magnetized and all the other bodies were so many little iron filings, stuck to him, fanning out from him, as inch by inch he tried to push out from the building. It must have looked insane from up on the top floor, I thought—these human shapes, all this *behavior*. I was tempted to go through security again just to get back up there to watch it.

* * *

The next day I woke to torrential rain. I'd planned to head out to Bundy Ranch; John Lamb had invited me to go along. His entire family was here now; they'd all been at the ruling yesterday, as well as afterward at the group's victory celebration in a chain sports bar out in suburban Henderson. Rebekah and the girls were still looking Amish in their home-made dresses; the boys, scrawny-beanpole versions of their father, looked like farm kids from another century. I'd enjoyed watching them mill about on the plaza and in the bar, with its million TVs and standardized decor, and I had been looking forward to this field trip with the whole Lamb family. But with this rain, it wasn't going to happen, John said. Instead there would be a press conference in Vegas with Cliven in the early afternoon.

When the rain let up a tiny bit, I headed out to get some coffee and breakfast. Even in Vegas, at that hour in that rain, there was no one out but the mentally ill. Many of these folks were openly howling today. It was a bad day to be without a home, wandering the streets in the company of your internal tormenters. To make it worse, the rain seemed to be drawing forward the scent of piss on concrete instead of washing it away. Soon it was pouring even harder. I sheltered under an awning directly across the street from the Vegas abomination known as the Heart Attack Grill. A big glowing red sign promised that patrons weighing over 350 pounds would eat for free. Look it up, if you don't believe me. "Great concept!" says one admiring review.

I stood there, stunned, watching this neon provocation to suicidal indulgence. The dark morning was refusing to brighten. Around me, the indistinguishable masses of concrete and neon—each advertising more avenues to excess: booze, gambling, sex, food—were vomiting out torrents of roof scuzz from long metal tubes stuck into their flanks. These were painted red, making them look like prolapsed rectums. It was all gross. Sometimes I'm really ready to revolt, and this was one of those days: look at this place, look at our world. I remembered a video clip I'd seen of Jon Ritzheimer, alone in his vehicle bemoaning how the Founding Fathers hadn't wanted this world of ours. Sure, he'd meant something else, but it had stuck in my head because Ritzheimer was right. They didn't want this. Jon was right to be aggrieved. They—the elitist Founding Fathers—hadn't wanted people like him, or most of the rest of us for that matter. But the phrase rang even truer applied to our world, when our world looked like the world I was looking at. *Place yourself here.* Had anybody wanted this? Nobody *really* wanted this, but we got it anyway. And just like the Heart Attack Grill, it was going to kill us. If climate change didn't finish us off first, we'd find a way to do it ourselves. In the end I surrendered: this rain was not letting up. I sprinted from my awning through the torrent back to my casino hotel, to wait out the hours till Cliven's presser.

A Beautiful Day

One day out of prison and Cliven Bundy was already headed down to rebuke the sheriff. The man had not stood up for the people, and Cliven was going to give him hell for it, that and whatever else he thought to pull out of his constitutionalist hat. I was on my way to hear him, if I could ever get out of this casino hotel. On my way to my car, I found myself trapped in a little atrium, waiting for an elevator up into the parking garage. I was wound up with coffee and ideas, and I guess I wasn't standing very still. The elevator was taking its time. I've always been a fidgeter, but I'd never found myself in an atrium as sensitive as this one. Every movement of my body was triggering automated responses from the building. As soon as I'd lose myself in thought, evidently some part of me would move—I'd pace or turn, or sway my arm, or reach up and scratch at my animal skull—and that would provoke a sensor somewhere. An automatic door would slide open—bringing in either the stale smell of cigarette smoke and the undead glitter and clack of a gaming room, or the cold scent of the rain, thick with petroleum, along with the zombie soundtrack that the casino blasted at the streets of downtown 24/7. This had played at full volume all night, to my horror, though I'd finally managed to sleep. It seemed to be some kind of gaming industry imperative, a psy-ops tactic deployed so that we'd know for sure that this place *absolutely did not sleep.* "The Wanderer" was playing now to the empty, sodden street. It was at least the fifth time I'd heard it since checking in. I kept trying to hold still, but the elevator was taking forever. Soon my resolve would give way to more thoughts and I'd flail about and set off another sensor and another door. Around and around I went. Finally it was the elevator door that opened, and I was removed from this automated spasm into the drooling, concrete maw of the garage.

When I arrived at the massive Metropolitan Police Headquarters, the rain had gone biblical. I ran into Neil near one of the many entrances to this edifice of the Law, and we sheltered from the rain under an awning. Neil had been asking me the day before about what it was like writing books; he said he imagined it must be something like the experience of being lost in a woodworking project. He wondered if writing felt like that too—seeing a problem from all the angles and working it out, drawing the connections, the shape of it, "so that the prose has a pungency." I asked him now to tell me more about what it felt like to him to be in the moment of creation. "It's like a Labrador in water!" he said, motioning with his hands, so they became frantic dog paws, figures of a moving mind. The thought of it made his eyes light up; he loved spending all day working out a design problem in his head. People would hire him to do a simple cabinet job in a kitchen—"maybe a hack job was what it was supposed to be—but not by the time I was done with it!" He wondered again if there was a parallel to my experience. I told him about being trapped in the automated atrium, unable to stop moving because I'd been working out scenes in my head, and how strange it was sometimes to walk into a moment as it was unfolding and realize where it belonged in the book, like the thing was writing itself as events. With him and woodworking, he mused, it was "probably genetically programmed—all my family worked in three-dimensional-object making." His mother had been an architect, his father an industrial pattern maker, creating the molds that molten metal or plastic is poured into to create fire hydrants and the like. One of his brothers had been a furniture designer, the other a master carpenter, and he a woodworker, cabinet- and furniture maker. Now he was the only one left.

By then we'd been told Cliven wouldn't be coming—he was still caught up in a meeting with his lawyer—but he'd be speaking later to supporters and reporters in his lawyer's office. Neil and I made our way very slowly across the parking lot, Neil slipping and sliding in his ratty, treadless moccasins. I think he may have had no other pair of shoes with him; he was still wearing the same raincoat they had given him in prison in Oregon. His skinniness and slipping about alarmed me; he looked awfully frail. I covered us both with the fraying sun shield I had brought along as a makeshift umbrella. Finally we reached my car, and we sat for a bit with time to kill. He was rhapsodizing now about the Winchester Mystery House, the bonkers mansion of the heir to the rifle fortune, a real woodworking dreamscape and a favorite site of his. The widow had developed some idea, Neil told me, that as long as the house was being added to, she'd keep living, and so it grew in all directions, a Victorian labyrinth, a swarm of rooms, all of the finest handcrafted woodwork. With all Neil's talk of fine design, we couldn't help noting what ugliness we were now directly looking out on. Ugliness of the kind we're all familiar with in America. Across from the sheriff's department were a series of box stores and, behind them, the elevated freeway. What is it, I asked Neil, that makes what we are looking at so ugly?

He pointed out the decorative arch built into the side of one of the box stores—not an arch, really, but a design suggestion, an angular memory

of arches. "Look at that arch right there," he was saying. "It's perfectly functional. They just picked it out of a manual. I'd have done something with
an ellipse; half of an ellipse is nicer. Curved shapes have a dynamism and
a power to them, a tension, like when you draw back a long bow. Or you can
do a hack job, throw a bunch of elements together." That's what we were
looking at right in front of us, and all over the city, in places like Henderson,
and in mall-scapes all over the country—a bunch of elements thrown
together. There was hardly any design in that at all, not in the way Neil
meant it.

"The colonial makers were masters at that stuff—the dynamics, the
tension," he added. They were his ideal artisans. It all came to an end really
with the industrial revolution. And that was the tradeoff: because these
pieces of handmade furniture were tremendously expensive, many could
never afford them; with manufacturing, well, then people could. But something wonderful was lost. He quoted Wallace Nutting, famed photographer,
furniture maker, and leading instigator of the colonial-revival style: " 'Not all
the old was good, but all the new is bad!' " Neil said, chuckling.

We were driving now, we'd turned down Charleston Boulevard, the other
main drag of Vegas—not the glitzy one, but the raggedy strip mall one. Brett
Whipple's law office was an entirely missable one-story building across the
boulevard from a headshop and stoner-wear boutique called Gear and
Clothing in Las Vegas. Two rattled-looking dudes were up on Whipple's roof
in the rain trying to patch a leak. Neil and I stood under the building's lip,
watching pages of rain slide across the poorly draining streets while Neil
smoked. It reminded him of something he'd watched on the internet the
night before—images of huge sheets of ice, moving like animate beings
across a lake somewhere—in Minnesota, he thought it was. They were
gliding right up out of the water, as if with wills of their own, up against the
houses along the shore, crushing them.

When Cliven was finally ready, we joined the rest of the crowd in Whipple's
waiting area. On the office wall, there was a cross section of a tree, cut and
polished into a map of Nevada—the sort of crafty art-piece you'd expect to
see in an old western hotel next to a hundred other curios like it, though
here it was alone and framed behind glass. Cliven was standing alongside it
as he began to address his adoring supporters.

It was a beautiful day, Cliven told us, to laughter. No, it's always a beautiful day for a rancher when it rains, he explained. And the ranching life is
what he wanted to talk about today—beginning with a celebration of its

product. His family had cooked him up "the nicest tender steak you ever seen," he told the delighted room. He marveled at its perfection. "You know, I'm sort of a little bit toothless, but I was able to just sort of chew on that and enjoy it, and I really did enjoy it, some good Bundy beef!" It was all about good food, Cliven wanted us to know—his whole struggle:

> That's really something that I'd like everybody in the world to enjoy—is some good food. And that's what I do, is I harvest Southwest desert, Nevada, the brush and the bushes and the grass. And I harvest that with my cattle, and my cattle convert that feed into an edible commodity—something that's good to eat, good for human beings to eat . . . Everybody in the world ought to be able to have a plate of good food every day, let's put it that way. And, you know, that's really how I feel about what I fight for. I fight for the freedom for a man to be able to *produce* and to *thrive* and to *be happy*, and I think that the only way that can be done is through freedom. One of the main things that we have in this country that a lot of countries don't have is we have the *United States Constitution*. It's a blueprint for this type of life that I just talked about here. It's a blueprint where We the People are the government.

I still couldn't understand how this crowd could read the Constitution closely and come to Cliven's conclusion about the People. I wondered how many really did read it, and how many just trusted it said what the Bundys said it did. Now Cliven was telling us that the federal government was for only a few basic things: defense against foreign powers; delivering the mail; and for doing other important things like standardizing weights and measures. "You know we want a pound to be a pound in Nevada the same as it is in New York. Them things the federal government can do—but don't you ever let them come and act like they own the land within the state of Nevada or Arizona or New Mexico."

"Amen! Amen!" someone shouted.

In the middle of his talk, Cliven went on a curious detour about the desert tortoise. The main idea seemed to be that there was no way for the creature to be an entity that the federal government, under the Constitution, could in any way govern or regulate or protect. In Cliven's political ontology, the tortoise had no legal being. This was because "the critter," to Cliven's eye, didn't qualify as a *commercial good*. Not only that, but as a wild animal it wasn't part of any kind of interstate commerce. "If you had a tortoise that was in a pet shop in Las Vegas and, say, he was imported from Mexico . . . well, that tortoise would qualify to come under the Endangered Species Act of the federal government." Otherwise, the federal government had no right to regulate anything about it. It was a fairly incoherent argument, even by Cliven's standards, but it was also very revealing. Here was a worldview in which the existence of animals became truly legible in a legal sense only when they were owned by people.

A different owned animal played a curious role in another of Cliven's pedantic digressions today—this one on beneficial use, maybe the single most important concept in the whole Bundy ethos. In the family's dogma, beneficial use was at the center of the origin myth of Bundy Ranch itself—the story of how wild land was turned into private property. The most important actor in the story, as Cliven improvised it today, was a horse.

He was talking specifically about his grazing rights and his water rights. The land, he insisted, why, that belonged to We the People; but the water, the brush—that was his by right. "Them rights were all created through *beneficial use*," he explained. "Back there, when the pioneers first came in here, the first ones that used that water—when he unbuckled his team—horses' team—off his wagon, he was thirsty and he took the horse up in the creek or the spring or whatever and give the horse a drink of water. When that horse very first sipped the very first drop of water he drunk out of that spring, guess what he was doing? Creating beneficial use!"

Beneficial use created property, and property was exchangeable, and thus the grass and water of that public land had become Cliven's—and that was that. Here I was, at the ur-ground of the whole Bundy thing; face-to-face with Papa Bundy's political theology, the one on which his boys had built their own, more eloquent rhetoric. Basically this was Cliven's version of his son Ammon's Beautiful Pattern. This is what Ryan Bundy called "teaching truth": the sovereign citizen and his thirsty pony turning land into property, just like that. You could go from there straight to prosperity and happiness and freedom, as long as you had the gumption to continually "claim, use, and defend" all your rights, as the movement's refrain went. Notably absent in this creation story were cities, governments, corporations, Native people, wild animals, exigencies of the globalized marketplace, weather—in other words, almost everything. Just a man, his horse, the land, and freedom.

Curious that in the story it was the horse who had done the magic deed: one piece of property had created another with its thirst, adding another layer of legal complexity. The family loved these little stories of legal magic, turning land into political abstraction. Their followers loved this stuff too; it was part of the theological pedantry of the whole thing—and the empowering fantasy of it. But what a curious dogma to have caught on with a room full of people who were clearly not ranchers and were never going to be.

It occurred to me watching Cliven—here in his lawyer's unremarkable office, off one of the uglier streets of this ugly town—that I don't think the Bundy family would have gotten very far on their dogma alone. Their constitutionalist ideas were pretty abstract, but what made the Bundy mix gel was the fact of their actual lives. They were flesh-and-blood emissaries from a time and place that was largely gone, but remained, in the lives of the Bundys themselves, at least partly, demonstrably real. They were actual cowboys and that gave substance to a dream of a world that did not look at all like the world Neil and I had been looking at earlier—or like the shabbier excrescences of money we were gazing at now looking south on Charleston Boulevard.

Cliven had been pulled into the back office for more conversations with his lawyer, and slowly the faithful were departing. Neil and I were standing under the eaves again while he smoked, looking out at those crappy strip malls, liquor stores, and pawnshops. It was a world that looked to me as if it had fallen off the back of a truck. Rain still poured in massive sheets down the poorly drained boulevard. Again we marveled at the ugliness. I asked him what he thought when he looked at all this, in light of the handcrafted world he'd been celebrating before. He pondered it for a moment and then asked me if I remembered the sequence in *It's a Wonderful Life* when we saw what the town would have become without George. I laughed. That's what it was like to him, he said, what Vegas and Henderson and a lot of America looked like to him. He was right: these were Pottervilles, all across America, Pottervilles all.

What an antidote to Potterville lives the Bundys offered, even if they were really only offering it as fantasy and a current of political feeling. How much more appealing—that ranching life out in the brush along the Virgin River, with the mountains and the sky. "Place yourself there," Ryan had said. I got it. That's exactly what I wanted. I wanted to be out there—I wanted to be out there now. To be standing out in it, drinking in the scent of the creosote and the other brush, all the smells released by the rain, listening to the cold sizzle it made in the sand, feeling that spongy feel the desert has under my feet when it's wet. Maybe take off my shoes and feel it with my toes.

The deep irony was that the only lasting access to his anti-Potterville that Cliven seemed able to offer We the People was through the story of property—of legal magic and capitalist dominion. A story where a tortoise only had measurable reality as a commodity, a legally defined commercial object shipped across state lines. A story where a person's freedom didn't go much further than the property they were able to claim, until the bank took it away. In the end, the freedom Cliven offered was not the freedom of people, but of things—his freedom was just another version of the form of governance we call "the economy." This was the real problem with the whole Bundy thing, I thought. The very same dominion of commodities, money, and property—including the repressed traumatic legacies of slavery and conquest—were what had built the Pottervilles of America in the first place. It was the priorities of the developers and the bankers and the other powers of this particular Potterville, Vegas, that had come for the Bundys in the nineties and provoked this whole drama. There would be no escaping Potterville by doubling down on its guiding principles and immutable laws. This seemed the saddest thing of all about the Bundy Revolution. Cliven was offering something kind of beautiful, a rural, community-oriented life, lived on and from and with the land, but he only knew how to offer it in the very terms that were its death. Agriculture in America had been consolidating and automating as much as any other field for decades. Small organic farming had become a difficult but sometimes feasible life in recent years for those so inclined—but not so much in the dry Intermountain West. No matter how much they loved the story he was telling, most of these folks that had listened to him today in his lawyer's office had about as much chance of becoming Cliven as I had of becoming a tortoise. They had a leg up on me, with Cliven being a human being and all—but really both were just acts of pure imaginative identification. I mentally threw my lot in with liberty *and* the tortoise, with everyone's liberty, critters and plants included.

I kept my thoughts in my head; I wanted to be alone with them and with the desert. Besides, this shindig was done. I walked Neil to his friend's car, said goodbye to John and Brand, and hit the highway southwest to California. When I reached the Mojave National Preserve, the rain was slacking off and the sun had begun to break through, just in time to go down. I pulled over at a turnout and wandered into the public land, among the brush and the

Joshua trees. The ground was still wet underfoot, crinkly and slushy at once. The air was sweetly musky with the life of the plants. The Joshua trees were black with rain. Fingers of mist moved through the peaks of the Providence Mountains. Now this little world went blue and purple in the dusk. I got back in the car. The night came down fast. At bends in the road, my headlights isolated limbs of the Joshuas so that they looked like spiny, undulating, underwater creatures. *This was all underwater once; it could all happen again. Maybe anything could happen—even the future.* I was dictating these words into the recording function on my phone, but who was I talking to? Live, tonight, from the bottom of the sea.

A Note on Sources

Shadowlands draws on a wide range of nonfiction genres, a fact that is reflected in the sources used in its writing. Key sources by category are highlighted in the non-exhaustive set of notes that follows.

In-Person Reportage and Viewed Video Documentation

Beginning in early 2016 I spent hundreds of hours in conversation with the people who appear in this book, and with others who do not but who had some expertise related to the events and histories coalesced on these pages. Many of my initial in-person conversations were followed up with lengthy phone interviews. I am grateful to all who spent so much of their valuable time giving me their takes on this multifaceted American tale.

I also attended both Malheur trials. Much that appears in the second section of this book comes from my notes from these days in court, and from the afternoons I spent outside court, mingling with the folks of the Bundy Revolution and others—curious, opposed, indifferent, and agnostic—in the parks, in cafés, and on the courthouse steps of the Boisterous Sea.

Also indispensable in the writing of this book was the massive online video record of the events of Malheur and its aftermath. The occupation, as well as the trials and protest events that followed it, were documented to such a degree that, as I have speculated in the book, the hours of video filmed by participants, journalists, documentary filmmakers, friends and foes of the occupiers, law enforcement, and the otherwise curious might easily surpass the hours taken up by the events themselves. Much of this video record was streamed, posted, and reposted to social media platforms, including YouTube. These videos included documentation of some of the main events of the occupation and video documents, such as Ammon Bundy's "Dear Friends" video, that were themselves among the central events—and piece of evidence—in the saga of Malheur. Documentarians Sue Arbuthnot and Richard Wilhelm graciously allowed me to preview essential raw footage from their film *Refuge*. David Byars's documentary *No Man's Land* was helpful, particularly for its nuanced attention to the role of occupier Jason Patrick. The indefatigable—and intriguingly artful—video compilation work of the Valley Forge Network was a key source of material for anyone going deep into the story of Malheur. Another important source for the book is video footage shot by the *Oregonian* of the occupiers' informational meeting and recruiting session at the hot springs in Crane and of the fence-cutting action out on the refuge, and *Vice*'s multi-camera footage of Dave Ward and Ammon Bundy's meeting out on that frozen tarmac in early January 2016.

LANDSCAPE, ECOLOGY, AND ECOLOGICAL AND AGRICULTURAL HISTORY

Landscapes have been among the principal characters of *Shadowlands*. My impressions of Harney County and the Mojave Desert are based on many long walks, drives, and camping excursions. I owe what deeper understanding I've been able to gather of the ecologies and land politics of Harney County and the Great Basin to conversations with Charlotte Roderique, Brenda Smith, Dan Nichols, Gary Ivey, Esther Lev, Chris Colson, Jack Southworth, Sue Arbuthnot, Richard Wilhelm, Steve Grasty, Jarvis Kennedy, Diane Teeman, Leisl Carr Childers, and the members of the High Desert Partnership's Forest Rehabilitation Cooperative, as well as online video interviews with Refuge director Chad Karges and fish biologist Linda Beck.

Further knowledge of the ecology and ecological history of Harney County was gathered from two wonderful books by environmental historian Nancy Langston. Her book on the ecological history of the Harney Basin and the lands of the refuge—*Where Land & Water Meet: A Western Landscape Transformed*—helped me develop my understanding of what I was looking at on my sojourns into the riparian wetlands, sagebrush steppe, and juniper scrublands of the refuge and the Blitzen Valley as well as on the slopes and in the gorges of Steens Mountain. Her book on the Malheur National Forest, *Forest Dreams, Forest Nightmares: The Paradox of Old Growth in the*

Inland West, enhanced my engagement with the public lands of the forest, central to the life of so many in Harney County.

Peter K. Simpson's venerable history on the early years of the cattle industry in the region—*The Community of Cattlemen: A Social History of the Cattle Industry in Southeastern Oregon, 1869–1912*—offered crucial facts, perspective, and analysis of the epoch of the Cattle Barons in Harney County. Leisl Carr Childers's compelling work on the history of public land in the Nevada lands of the Great Basin—*The Size of the Risk: Histories of Multiple Use in the Great Basin*—provided valuable background information for the saga of the Bundy family and the history of desert public lands ranching and conservation.

Years ago, Mary Hunter Austin's masterpiece, *The Land of Little Rain*, opened the door to the landscapes of the Great Basin and the Mojave Desert, and thus to this book. Edward Abbey's *Desert Solitaire* woke me further to the shapes, ecologies, legends, dreams, and brutal facts of the arid west. Marc Reisner's classic work on western aridity and water use, *Cadillac Desert: The American West and Its Disappearing Water*, set me down many fruitful paths. *Sacred Cows at the Public Trough*, Denzel and Mary Ferguson's jeremiad on the negative effects of ranching on public lands, elucidated the intensity of the older conflict between the Hammonds and the refuge, without which Ammon Bundy may never have visited the lands of the Harney Basin.

American History

Shadowlands travels much in American history, from Native American history and the history of the West to the history of the Constitution and the Revolutionary period. The reading across all these histories that the project demanded of me has been one of the great pleasures of making this book. Here I offer a non-exhaustive selection of key sources that provided details, concepts, and/or important background for the book and may be of interest to readers for further explorations of their own.

Paiute History, Smohalla and the Dreamer Sect, Native History of the Great Basin, Native American Politics and Activism

Sarah Winnemucca's *Life Among the Piutes: Their Wrongs and Claims* provides essential, acutely delivered, first-person experience to anyone attempting to write about the history of the Northern Paiute and the Malheur Reservation. Sally Zanjani's biography of Winnemucca provides even more detail of the life and times of this most remarkable of Americans. Other sources on the history of the Northern Paiute include James Mooney's work on Wovoka, the prophet of the Ghost Dance, whom Mooney personally visited in the late nineteenth century. Mooney's *The Ghost-Dance Religion and the Sioux Outbreak of 1890* remains an indispensable source on Messianic Native American religious practices of the nineteenth century, including the practices of the pan-tribal Dreamer sect of the Wanapum prophet Smohalla. Also important for my understanding of Ghost Dance practice was Russell Thornton's *We Shall Live Again: The 1870 and 1890 Ghost Dance Movements as Demographic Revitalization*. Thornton compellingly presents the Ghost Dance as what it truly seems to have been—not primarily a tragic death ritual, as it is so often understood to be in Non-Native versions of the history of the West, but rather as a widely successful pan-tribal cultural movement of demographic revitalization—one whose impact can be felt to this day.

Like a Hurricane: The Indian Movement from Alcatraz to Wounded Knee by Paul Chaat Smith and Robert Allen Warrior gives a compelling, in-depth account of Native activism; its thorough documentation of the occupations of Alcatraz and Wounded Knee were of special import in the writing of this book. Paul Chaat Smith's *Everything You Know about Indians is Wrong* likewise illuminated and textured key issues in Native history, politics, and aesthetics, as did the work of Gerald Vizenor, especially the essays contained in his influential work *Manifest Manners: Narratives on Postindian Survivance*. Ned Blackhawk's *Violence over the Land* is crucial reading for anyone interested in the history of the Great Basin, and especially of the experience of Native peoples of that region in the periods leading up to and including the violent era of conquest documented in person by Sarah Winnemucca. Frederick Hoxie's book *This Indian Country: American Indian Activists and the Place They Made* offers an excellent overview of the history of Native activism and the different struggles for Native Sovereignty dating back to the colonial era.

In conversation Diane Teeman provided hours of invaluable insight into the history and traditional practices of the Wadatika. Also of import for *Shadowlands* was her essay "Cultural Resource Management and the Protection of Valued Tribal Spaces: A View from the Western United States," included in *Handbook of Landscape Archaeology*, edited by Bruno David and Julian Thomas. Additional historical background on the Burns-Paiute came from the late Minerva Soucie's essay "The End of a Way of Life: The Burns Paiute Indian Tribe," collected in *The First Oregonians* (published by the Oregon Council for the Humanities, eds. Carolyn M. Buan and Richard Lewis), as well as the tribe's own official history, "The History of the Wadatika Band of the Northern Paiute."

The Patriot Era

One of the many fascinating facets of the Malheur saga is the insistence with which it returned all who were involved, in fantasy and fact, to the foundation of the nation. In addition to primary sources, including James Madison's notes on the Constitutional Convention, *The Federalist Papers*, and the letters of Madison, Thomas Jefferson, John Adams, George Washington, and other founding figures, the following scholarly books were valuable companions in the writing of the book, providing background and, in some cases, material directly discussed in the text. Foremost among these was Woody Holton's *Unruly Americans and the Origins of the Constitution*, a masterful tour of the unrest and the economic, social, and political issues attending the writing and ratification of the Constitution. Likewise vital were the books of William Hogeland on the era of the Revolution, the first years of the Republic, and the role of finance and class conflict in many of the principal struggles of the founding era. Titles include *Founding Finance: How Debt, Speculation, Foreclosures, Protests, and Crackdowns Made Us a Nation*; *The Whiskey Rebellion: George Washington, Alexander Hamilton, and the Frontier Rebels Who Challenged America's Newfound Sovereignty*; *Declaration: The Nine Tumultuous Weeks When America Became Independent, May 1–July 4, 1776*; and *Autumn of the Black Snake: The Creation of the U.S. Army and the Invasion that Opened the West*. The acclaimed work of Gordon S. Wood provided essential background on the politics and society of the revolutionary era (*The Radicalism of the American Revolution*) and guidance through the life and thought of Thomas Jefferson and John Adams (*Friends Divided*). Gary B. Nash's tour of the radical cultural, political, and religious underpinnings of the Patriot era in *The Unknown American Revolution: The Unruly Birth of Democracy and the Struggle to Create America* provided similarly crucial context, as did Carol Berkin's *A Sovereign People: The Crises of the 1790s and the Birth of American Nationalism*. Further details on the lives and politics of popular rebels of the early years of American independence were gleaned from three important essays collected in *Revolutionary Founders:*

Rebels, Radicals and Reformers in the Making of the Nation, edited by Alfred F. Young, Gary B. Nash, and Ray Raphael: Gregory Nobles's "Satan, Smith, Shattuck and Shays: The People's Leaders in the Massachusetts Regulation of 1786," Wythe Holt's "The New Jerusalem: Herman Husband's Egalitarian Alternative to the United States Constitution," and "William Findley, David Bradford, and the Pennsylvania Regulation of 1794" by Terry Bouton.

Additional History of the West, History of Joseph Smith and the Latter-Day Saints

There would have been no Malheur occupation without the legacy of Joseph Smith. One could spend several lifetimes researching the ongoing effects of the dispensation Smith unfurled. Malheur is but one tiny episode. Beyond the primary sources of the Latter-day Saints—the Book of Mormon, The Doctrine and Covenants, The Pearl of Great Price, The History of Joseph Smith, letters of Smith, and the source texts of the White Horse Prophecy (itself not accepted as church doctrine)—the following books were of great importance for *Shadowlands'* discussions of the historical, theological, and cultural underpinnings of the occupation. Fawn Brodie's masterful biography of Joseph Smith, *No Man Knows My History*, has to be one of the most compelling historical biographies of an American figure yet written. The depth of research and the writerly feel for the scope and dynamism of Smith's vision were inspirational to me in the making of *Shadowlands*. *Mormonism Unveiled; Or the Life and Confession of John D. Lee* provided an in-depth first-person experience of the rise of the faith in the nineteenth century from one of Smith's most steadfast followers. *On the Ragged Edge: The Life and Times of Dudley Leavitt*, by the Latter-day Saint historian and Bunkerville native Juanita Brooks, offered fascinating details of the lives of the Bundy ancestors—including Leavitt himself, Cliven's maternal great-grandfather—who first settled the Virgin River Valley. Wallace Stegner's justly famous *Mormon Country* lent the perspective of a gentile observer, critic, and admirer of Mormon ways and history. To Stegner I owe the insight of just how intensely parallel the Mormon dispensation runs to the profane dispensations of Manifest Destiny—and also to the intimations of the possible intensities of disappointment produced when such a dispensation, that promised so much utopia, seemed to yield, as Stegner puts it, not a glorious future, but a dead past. "All honor the accomplishments of a perfervid dynamism that believed exclusively in the future," Stegner writes in *Mormon Country*. "The rock the fathers planted was the future; the crop the sons harvest is the past. The Mormon Country is not yet Heaven on Earth, and it no longer expects to be." As can perhaps be guessed from this passage, Stegner's insights into the utopianism of the United Order and the community of Orderville were especially useful in the writing of parts of *Shadowlands*. Also helpful was Stegner's *The Gathering of Zion*, with its account of the traumas and travails of the Mormon Trail. The searing fiction of Brian Evenson also provided a deep interior psychic view into the darker possibilities of a contemporary Latter-day Saint relationship to prophecy and scripture. There is much of Malheur to be found in Evenson's brilliant comic short story "The Prophets" and its tale of a right-wing LDS mystic, so hell-bent on reviving the church, he's willing to go as far as reanimating the corpse of Ezra Taft Benson, prophet, church president, and right-wing hero of many associated with the Bundy Revolution.

I also am in great debt to Ammon and Ryan Bundy for the time they took to elucidate, with great clarity, their understanding of the theology of their faith, including the operations of free agency and God's governance of the world. I owe an even deeper debt to Brand Thornton for the hours he spent explaining his relationship to church dogma and history.

Beyond the insights she gave me and the people of Burns in her 2017 talk at the Harney County Chamber of Commerce, Patricia Limerick's books have prodded my thinking throughout this process. I should mention especially *Desert Passages: Encounters with the American Deserts* for her shrewd unpacking of desert writing, and *The Legacy of Conquest: The Unbroken Past of the American West*, for its deft explication of the role of the intersection of private property and feeling in the history of the West; Limerick's book *Something in the Soil: Legacies and Reckonings in the New West* may also be of interest to readers intrigued by issues of western history raised in *Shadowlands*.

Mark Twain's *Roughing It*, one of the books Limerick discusses in *Desert Passages*, added a valuable, if hyperbolized, literary first-person experience of Anglo settlement of the Great Basin. *Terrible Trail: The Meek Cutoff, 1845* by Keith Clark and Lowell Tiller is a wonderful portrait, through letters and other documents, of the catastrophe experienced by the unfortunate Oregon Trail pioneers who chose to take a shortcut through what is now Harney County. (Also recommended is Kelly Reichardt's 2011 film on this bit of Oregon pioneer lore, *Meek's Cutoff*. Destined to be understood as one of the greatest American Westerns, it was beautifully filmed in the lands of Malheur.) The journals of Peter Skene Ogden, quoted from in *Shadowlands*, were likewise essential for their sparse portrait of the first major white incursion into the region. Frederick Jackson Turner's "The Significance of the Frontier in American History" remains alive and well; despite decades of deserved critique, it goes far to explain the mythic hold that the experience of the frontier still has on American political imaginings (a topic Limerick explores in depth in *Something in the Soil*).

The archival materials I found in the Western History Room of the Harney County Library were as responsible as any one person or text or event in securing my lasting dedication to the story of the occupation as a story of the Harney Basin. Any visitor to Burns with an interest in the region should check out its collections of materials on the history of the region. Thanks to Karen Nitz, the librarian of the resource room, and to Claire, whose last name I never learned, who was so incredibly helpful to me when I was first beginning my research on what would later become this book. Warm thanks go to Elerina Aldamar and Nicole Yashuara at the Oregon Historical Society and to Keith Lachowicz at the Regional Arts and Culture Council, for their enthusiastic help in my efforts to track down the history of "The Promised Land," the piece of Portland public art (by sculptor David Manuel) discussed at some length in part II of *Shadowlands*.

The Law, Prisons, and the Jury

I'm grateful, like many, to the website JUSTIA, for its archive of court decisions, including *USA v. Dougherty*, and perhaps the biggest American court decision of them all, *Marbury v. Madison*. Michelle Alexander's *The New Jim Crow* remains a touchstone for the story of mass incarceration. Long-form reporting, some of which I'll mention below in the section on journalism, helped carry Alexander's analysis and clarion call forward, at once helping shift discussion of incarceration to such a degree that it may be the only issue of true consensus on the right and left in America today, and explaining how that shift has occurred. I'm additionally very grateful to Albert W. Dzur's *Punishment, Participatory Democracy, and the Jury* for confirming and considerably broadening my understanding of the quietly catastrophic nature of the disappearance of the jury from American public life. *Shadowlands* has few polemical goals, but one of them would be this: the return of the jury to a more central role in a revitalized American public sphere.

Cheryl Brooks's deeply researched and finely argued "Race, Politics, and Denial: Why Oregon Forgot to Ratify the Fourteenth Amendment" (originally published in the *Oregon Law Review*) was an essential source for the discussion of Oregon's troubled racial and constitutional history in chapter twenty-four. That chapter's title, "Reconstitutions," takes its name from her call for "a reconstitution of the people." Insofar as this book has arguments to make, seconding such a call is also one of its central proposals. Brooks draws on the work of important legal scholar Reva B. Siegel, whose article "Collective Memory and the Nineteenth Amendment: Reasoning about 'the Woman Question' in the Discourse of Sex Discrimination" I also found of great assistance in thinking about the peculiar relationship of Americans to their founding document. Likewise helpful in this regard was Michael Kammen's *A Machine That Would Go of Itself: The Constitution in American Culture.*

Contemporary Politics, Social Media Technology, the Contemporary American Right

In the final editing stages of *Shadowlands*, the following key works on American Conservatism confirmed my own understandings of what my days in the Bundy Revolution had taught me about the imaginative life of the contemporary right: Corey Robin's *The Reactionary Mind: Conservatism from Edmund Burke to Donald Trump*; and two works by Rick Perlstein, *Nixonland: The Rise of a President and the Fracturing of America* and *The Invisible Bridge: The Fall of Nixon and the Rise of Reagan.* In addition to a plethora of online archival sources, I am indebted to Daniel Levitas's *The Terrorist Next Door: The Militia Movement and the Radical Right*, especially for its deeply researched unpacking of the troubling life of William Gale, whose ugly ideas and violent words haunt this story.

Moving into the present, Benjamin Bratton's *The Stack: On Software and Sovereignty* stimulated my thoughts on the connections between social media platforms and the crises and panics of sovereignty explored in *Shadowlands.* Zeynep Tufecki's *Twitter and Tear Gas: The Power and Fragility of Networked Protest* is the most elucidating exploration of social media and activism that I have encountered; I recommend it strongly to interested readers and practitioners. Adam Tooze's *Crashed: How a Decade of Financial Crises Changed the World* lent insight into the nature of the collapse of 2008 that lurks in the background of this story. Wendy Brown is one of our epoch's most important political thinkers; her essay "The Desire to Be Punished," indispensable to my analysis in chapter eleven, "It's the Economy, Stupid," can be found in her book *Politics Out of History*.

Shawna Cox's *Last Rancher Standing* helped me with important fact-checking on the Bundy Ranch event. Christopher Hooks's profile in *Politico* on Michele Fiore, "The Lady Is a Trump," added depth to other coverage of the Nevada legislator's inflammatory comments. LaVoy Finicum's *Only by Blood and Suffering* is, without doubt, one of the most fascinating documents of the occupation; in addition to providing a portal into the intensity of Finicum's individualism, it is also a page turner.

BIG IDEAS

Along with Wendy Brown's notions regarding the psychic economies of punishment, the work of a few other philosophers and theorists were essential to the analytical frames *Shadowlands* brings to the tale of Malheur. I owe much of my thinking about the theology of capitalist economy and governance to Giorgio Agamben—especially to his book *The Kingdom and the Glory: For a Theological Genealogy of Economy and Government*. Agamben's *The Sacrament of Language: An Archaeology of the Oath* contributed to my thinking on oath magic. I owe an additional debt for much of my thought on messianism, history, and politics to Agamben's *The Time that Remains: A Commentary on the Letter to the Romans*, as well as to the theoretical work of Walter Benjamin, so influential for Agamben.

James Baldwin has long held a great influence over my understanding of race in America, especially of that dangerous living fiction we call "whiteness." While Baldwin's thinking was developed across decades, in many works, it was his short essay "On Being White and Other Lies" that I found myself repeatedly returning to in the course of my time with the American tale of Malheur. Additionally, the thoughts of Afro-pessimist theorist Frank B. Wilderson III contributed to my understandings of the racialized economies of being and mattering so plainly operative in the fantasy dynamics of the occupation. Lastly, my understandings of the fetishism and magical practices involved in the relationship of citizens of modern nations to the State emerges from a long engagement with the work of anthropologist Michael Taussig, especially his genre-bending book *The Magic of the State*.

Journalism Sources

The occupation was a mass media extravaganza, a circus, as we say. The coverage was constant; some of it was superficial, but much of it was not. It is impossible to single out all the talented journalists who covered Malheur, so I will confine myself here to the work that had a direct impact on *Shadowlands*. The single furthest-reaching piece on the occupation that I read was Hal Herring's "The Darkness at the Heart of Malheur," arguments from which I tarry with at length in chapter eleven. "The Darkness at the Heart of Malheur" appeared in the *High Country News* (HCN), itself an indispensable publication for coverage of public land and environmental and cultural politics of the West. HCN's excellent reporting on the Sagebrush Rebellion and the Patriot movement is familiar to all of us who've been following this tale; Tay Wiles's long-form HCN piece on the Sugar Pine mine standoff is a great place to start. Other long-form pieces on the occupation that stand out include Leah Sottile's work on David Fry. While it arrived too late to become a reference in this book, I also recommend Sottile's justly acclaimed podcast, "Bundyville," which covers the whole Bundy Revolution. Sottile's piece in *Longreads* on the tragic shooting death of Quanice Hayes in Portland provides a painstakingly nuanced take on an all-too-common occurrence and genre of news.

Sottile also provided excellent daily journalism pieces on the Nevada and Oregon trials in the *Washington Post* and elsewhere, alongside a slew of other reporters. Among these, I feel comfortable stating that none stands out quite like the tireless Maxine Bernstein, of the *Oregonian*, whose reportage on the Malheur trials ranks among the best courtroom reporting I have ever encountered. Bernstein's daily reporting helped me confirm quotes from the courtroom, and her reporting outside the courtroom tracked down the details of key moments in the drama of the trial—such as the convoluted tale behind the unmasking of John Killman. Bernstein's coverage of the Vegas trial of Ammon and company was also rewardingly thorough, delivered always with her flourish for the sharply featured moment.

Bernstein's talented colleagues at the *Oregonian* similarly provided an overwhelming amount of top-notch, nose-to-the-ground, detailed coverage of the occupation itself. In eastern Oregon, Les Zaitz has been a revered journalist for some time, and his reporting on the occupation showed why. Numerous facts and quotes in this book come from his Malheur articles as well as the work of his intrepid and thoughtful colleagues, including

Kelly House, Luke Hammill, and Fedor Zarkhin. (House's reporting on Harney County's water problems provided additional crucial information for *Shadowlands*.) Also of great help was the work of the reporting team of Oregon Public Broadcasting; Amanda Peacher, Conrad Wilson, and others captured important quotes from the actors involved in the occupation drama, and compelling audio documentation of the saga.

The work of a number of other journalists was of great help in writing this book, in terms of both direct quotes and general background story information. Sam Levin's compelling piece on the Bundy family in the *Guardian* stands out. Ted McDermott's deep-delving profile of Ryan Payne ("Freedom Fighter") in the now sadly defunct *Missoula Independent* provided some great quotes from maybe the most enigmatic of the occupiers. I also used a quote from Payne, first reported in Marnie Hanel's engaging *Vanity Fair* piece from her trip to the occupied refuge. Jonathan Allen and Jim Urquhart's Reuters article ("Pizza, Rifles and Tension: A Night Inside the Oregon Protest") and photos from the occupied refuge came to play a major role in the Prosecution's rebuttal testimony in the second Malheur trial and were cited in chapter twenty-four. Jeremy Jacobs's excellent reportage in *E&E News* provided information and quotes that helped me to flesh out the persons of Marcus Mumford and Ethan Knight. Sarah Childress, senior reporter for *Frontline*, gathered together often previously scattered elements of the Bundy saga and key quotes from participants into one compelling source in her sharply featured, detailed walk-through of the story of the Bundy family ("The Battle Over Bunkerville: The Bundys, Federal Government and the New Militia Movement"). Childress was also a co-producer of *Frontline*'s *American Patriot* documentary on the Bundy family. Jonathan Thompson's piece in HCN—"The Rise of the Sagebrush Sheriffs"—on the constitutionalist sheriffs of the west was helpful early on for background information in my research and reportage on Sovereign currents in the Bundy Revolution, as was the reporting of Ryan Lenz of the Southern Poverty Law Center (SPLC) on Richard Mack and the Constitutional Sheriffs and Peace Officers Association ("Former Arizona Sheriff Richard Mack Seeks 'Army' of Sheriffs to Resist Federal Authority"). The SPLC's collections of information on Sovereign Citizen practices also provided useful background on Sovereign practices such as "redemption." Further afield, Michael Teague's fascinating work in the *Guardian* on the Washitaw Nation ("The Washitaw Sovereign Citizens: Where the Baton Rouge Gunman Found a Home") is one of the chief sources, outside the tribe's own extensive online materials, for the discussion of this particular Sovereign Citizen group in chapters eighteen and nineteen. The quote on the suicide belt from sociologist Matt Wray is from a piece in *Live Science* by Joseph Castro.

I owe much to the assiduous reportage of journalists and the regular investigations of assorted organizations into the practices of private prisons in general, and CoreCivic (formerly CCA) in particular. Information in chapter twenty-six is gathered from and corroborated by investigative reports from the ACLU, Open Secrets, the *Nation, Mother Jones,* and the federal government itself, as well as CoreCivic's own public reports and articles from the *New York Times,* the *Hill,* the *Wall Street Journal,* the *Intercept,* the *Guardian,* PR Watch, *Reuters,* and the *Washington Post.* Reporters who've gone especially deep into the world of for-profit incarceration include Seth Freed Wessler with the *Nation* and Shane Bauer with *Mother Jones.* The most basic physical facts (that he was left handcuffed in the shower cell, etc.)—if not all the interpretations of those facts (whether they constituted torture, etc.)—of Ammon Bundy's night in the shower at Nevada Southern Detention are substantiated by investigatory documentation from the Nye County Sheriff's department as well as Richard Mack's private investigation of the incident.

Acknowledgments

The writing of books, like the act of reading itself, is a curiously solitary and social experience. No book comes into existence without the labor of countless souls. Few of us have invented what can be said to be a single wholly new word—the words were all there for us when we began. Similarly, no book can be written without the previous thought and writing of others. In the note on sources, I've given an accounting of the most specific of my literary debts when it comes to the making of *Shadowlands*. Additionally, here I want to also acknowledge the work of a few writers quoted at key moments in the book. First, the epigraph—it is taken from Octavio Paz's discussion of Walt Whitman in *El Arco y La Lira*; the translation is my own. The quote from Peter Gizzi in chapter twenty-four is from his poem "Revival" from *Some Values of Landscape and Weather* (Wesleyan University Press). The quote from Rod Smith in chapter twenty-three is from his poem "The Story of Mang Gong" from his collection *Touché* (Wave Books). The quote from Nietzsche is from *Beyond Good and Evil*, translator Walter Kaufmann. The Marx quote is from *The Eighteenth Brumaire of Louis Napoleon*. The translation is by Saul Padover. The quote on ghosts and communication technology from Franz Kafka's letter to Milena Jesenská uses the translation offered on the haunted house of the interweb by "Johann" at a.sandboxx .org—it is a personal favorite from among several excellent translations of this famous passage. Besides the authors cited in the note on sources, many others, Kafka among them, accompanied me on my journeys to Malheur— these include Charles Olson, Alice Notley, Ed Dorn, Jack Spicer, and Amiri Baraka. Next, I want to turn to some of those more directly present in my life who personally touched the making of this book.

Thanks first to Karen and Kevin McCann, my parents, who guided me into speech in the first place, and whose enthusiasm and support for this work was a constant source of encouragement. To my sister, Laura, for love and support and also for all the help tracking down obscure Malheur documents I had thought forever lost. Deep thanks is owed to Ben Ehrenreich, who told me to just drop everything and go to Malheur in the first place—and then also made the conditions of going possible before I had an opportunity to turn back. *Shadowlands* is a far better experience thanks to Ben's insightful reading and critique of early stabs at this book. Similar thanks to Ken Ehrlich for his enthusiastic interest and for his helpful suggestions about parts of an early draft. Thanks to Brian Evenson for his helpful attention to chapters from a later draft. Deep thanks also to Maggie Nelson, who provided guidance and encouragement at important stages throughout this project, and crucial criticisms of a late draft. Joshua Beckman prodded this project along in uncountable ways; it seems unlikely there would have ever been a *Shadowlands* without him. Deep gratitude to my wonderful agent Stephanie Steiker, for her guidance, her razor-sharp insights, and her tireless advocacy of this book and its often heavily overworked author. My friends Sue Arbuthnot and Richard Wilhelm, makers of the Malheur documentary *Refuge*—a film I cannot recommend strongly enough to those with any interest in the occupation drama—were inspiring guides to the worlds of Harney County, and great companions as we raced down the many paths of this mad story, often together. Gratitude to Ana Cecilia Alvarez, who applied her acuity to some much-needed last-minute help with important details. Thanks to all the Bloomsbury team for making this book come true: to Anton Mueller for having such confidence in the possibilities of the book from the beginning and all the suggestions and conversations that helped guide it to its present form; to Morgan Jones for her suggestions and help shepherding this book into wider pastures; to Jenna Dutton and all who worked on the production and design of the book for getting it into the lovely shape it finally has taken as an object in the world; and to the Bloomsbury publicity and marketing team for doing all that it took to get it into *your* hands, *Gentle Reader*. I must also express gratitude to Tom Lutz and the *Los Angeles Review of Books* for publishing the *very* long essay that birthed *Shadowlands*. Thanks also goes to my wonderful colleagues at Cal Arts for the buoying interest and support so many of them provided to this project. Thanks to Tod Goldberg and the rest of my fellow faculty at the UC Riverside Low-Residency MFA program, for pushing me—not quite kicking and screaming—down the path of prose. Thanks to everyone else who helped along the way, whether you knew you were doing it or not.

Crucially, I must express my gratitude to everyone in Harney County, the Burns-Paiute tribe, Portland, Las Vegas, the Bundy Revolution, and further afield who took the time—hours of it, often—to share their thoughts and stories. While my personal analysis of the events, histories, and ideas of this tale inevitably differs at many moments from those of some of you, and while the bad feelings engendered by the occupation are still far from dissipated (and are likely to remain so), I must say that the collective wealth of American thought, feeling, and experience I was privy to in the company of all of you has changed me in vast ways that I will be struggling for years to measure. It is my hope that something of the remarkable thing it has been to get to know each of you at least a little bit comes across in the pages of *Shadowlands*.

Lastly, there would be no book here without Kirsty Singer. I would simply not have been able to do it without her love, support, constant intellectual companionship, and incisive reads of all the many drafts of *Shadowlands*. Kirsty's poetic and scholarly work on the embodied experience of history has marked each step and nearly every page of this project. It's she who brought me back to these words of Amiri Baraka: ". . . today is the history we must learn / to desire." It is my hope that this book has briefly taken place somewhere in the movement of that imperative.

A Note on the Author

Anthony McCann is the author of the poetry collections *Thing Music, I* ♥ *Your Fate*, and *Moongarden*. He currently teaches creative writing at the California Institute of the Arts and in the Low-Residency MFA program of the University of California, Riverside. Born and raised in the Hudson Valley, McCann now lives in the Mojave Desert.